ARNOLD READERS IN HISTORY

WOMEN'S WORK

The English Experience 1650–1914

Edited by
PAMELA SHARPE
*Lecturer in Social and Economic History,
University of Bristol*

A member of the Hodder Headline Group
LONDON • NEW YORK • SYDNEY • AUCKLAND

First published in Great Britain in 1998
by Arnold, a member of the Hodder Headline Group,
338 Euston Road, London NW1 3BH

http://www.arnoldpublishers.com

Co-published in the United States of America by
Oxford University Press Inc.,
198 Madison Avenue, New York, NY10016

British Library Cataloguing in Publication Data
A catalogue entry for this book is available from the British Library

Library of Congress Cataloging-in-Publication Data
Women's work : the English experience, 1650–1914 / edited by Pamela Sharpe.
    p.   cm.—(Arnold readers in history)
Includes bibliographical references and index.
ISBN 0–340–67695–7 (hardbound).—ISBN 0–340–67696–5 (pbk.)
    1. Women—England—History.   2. Women—England—Economic
conditions.   3. Women—England—Social conditions.   4. Sex role—
England—History.   I. Sharpe, Pamela.   II. Series.
HQ 1599.E5W69   1998
305.4′0942—dc21   98–13785
CI   CIP

ISBN 0 340 67695 7 (hb)
ISBN 0 340 67696 5 (pb)

1 2 3 4 5 6 7 8 9 10

Production Editor: Rada Radojicic
Production Controller: Sarah Kett

Typeset in 10/12pt Sabon by Phoenix Photosetting, Chatham, Kent
Printed and bound in Great Britain by MPG Books Ltd, Bodmin, Cornwall

Contents

List of Figures and Tables

Figures

Tables

Preface

Both women's history, and the history of gender, are relatively new but rapidly growing research areas with a perceptible sense of dynamic potential. One measure of this is the crop of student texts that are soon to appear. While much women's history to date has looked at the case study, the micro-level analysis or the life story example, synthesis is now possible. In selecting the material for a reader that concentrates on both early modern and modern women's work, I have tried to avoid unnecessary overlap with other collections. Perhaps as a result I have chosen some fairly new pieces. My main criteria in producing a teaching aid were twofold. Firstly, based on my experience of teaching women's history to both evening-class students and to undergraduates at Essex and Bristol Universities, I chose pieces that they have found engaging and helpful. Secondly, as I have been asked many times for help by other teachers who are setting up courses in women's history, I seek to provide a fairly full bibliography for the history of English women's work within this book. Indeed, the reason for starting with my own article is not an indulgence, but because, as it was originally commissioned as an 'Essay in Bibliography and Criticism', it provides a useful list of references. The articles reproduced here also have copious footnotes. This is in part a reflection of the authors' use of a variety of primary sources (approaches from which I hope students will learn about the elements of historical research), but also because they link their topic to a broader historiography which is reflected in the secondary sources. Some additional readings are provided in the final section. One article (by de Vries) has been abridged but, in general, I have preferred to reprint articles in their entirety to preserve the coherence of the authors' arguments, even if this produces some long chapters. My own research is based on local and regional English sources and, as a result, I have chosen to focus on the English experience. However, the bibliography at the end of Reading 1 and the further reading section give pointers to the growing body of work on Scottish, Irish and Welsh women's work, as well as some indications of important secondary literature on women's work in Europe and the United States.

While the authors are often arguing against received interpretations and making the case that their sources suggest revised positions, when this book is placed in the context of other Readers in the Arnold series, the history of women's work may seem to lack the cut and thrust of some of the major historical debates. One reason for this is obviously the newness of the subject. There has not been the time for established positions to be overturned and rewritten in the light of the preoccupations of a different age. Indeed, the project of women's history as a whole might be seen as a critique of historical practice to date. Yet, as I indicate in the introduction, the history of women's work is assuredly present-minded, often taking a standpoint from present-day feminist politics and working practices. As a result perhaps consensus has tended to outweigh conflict. But, as is obvious from what follows, it would be erroneous to assume that all practitioners of women's history use feminist principles to inform their interpretations or arguments. It is also certainly not the case that the history of women's work has failed to develop as a discipline. It is now concerned more with identities and subjective constructions of work than material realities. The best work, however, remains grounded in lived experience. To some, economic history has gone out of fashion – supplanted by the trendier disciplines of cultural, social, and even the new political history. Yet the history of women's economic endeavours embraces alternative approaches and offers a challenging and creative way for students to begin to conceptualise and understand the economic past.

Acknowledgements

Thanks to all the authors whose work is reproduced in this book and for their co-operation in producing the final volume. Originally a larger Reader was planned, and I also thank the authors whose work had to be omitted from the final text. I am grateful to Christopher Wheeler for his efficiency and enthusiasm. In writing the introduction and commentaries I have developed some of my ideas gained through participation in conferences, such as the 1994 Achievement Project workshop on 'Women's Initiatives in Early Modern England' and in 1996 the Social History Conference, the European Social Science History Conference and the Berkshire Conference. I have also received support and encouragement from the interdisciplinary Bristol University Women's Research Group, the Women's History Network and the Women's Committee of the Economic History Society. Above all, I thank the students of women's history I have taught in Essex and Bristol for stimulating me to embark on this project, and to Derek Pennington for the terra firma.

The editor and publishers would like to thank the following for permission to use copyright material in this book: Pamela Sharpe, 'Continuity and change: women's history and economic history in Britain', *Economic History Review*, 48 (1995), pp. 353–69, reprinted by permission of Blackwell Publishers; Bridget Hill, 'Women's history: a study in change, continuity or standing still?' *Women's History Review*, 2 (1993), pp. 5–22, and Judith Bennett, 'Women's history: a study in continuity and change', *Women's History Review*, 2 (1993), pp. 173–84, both reprinted with the permission of Triangle Journals Ltd; a slightly amended version of K. D. M. Snell, 'Agricultural seasonal unemployment, the standard of living, and women's work, 1690–1860' from his *Annals of the Labouring Poor* (1985), pp. 15–66, reprinted by permission of Cambridge University Press; Peter Earle, 'The female labour market in London in the late seventeenth and early eighteenth centuries', *Economic History Review*, 42 (1989), pp. 328–53, reprinted by permission of Blackwell Publishers; Maxine Berg,

'What difference did women's work make to the Industrial Revolution?', *History Workshop Journal*, 35 (1993), pp. 22–44, reprinted by permission of Oxford University Press; Sara Horrell and Jane Humphries, 'Women's labour force participation and the transition to the male-breadwinner family, 1790–1865', *Economic History Review*, 48 (1995), pp. 89–117, reprinted by permission of Blackwell Publishers; a version (abridged by the author) of Jan de Vries, 'Between purchasing power and the world of goods: understanding the household economy in early modern Europe', from R. Porter and J. Brewer (eds.) *Consumption and the World of Goods* (1993), reprinted by permission of Routledge Ltd; Leonore Davidoff and Catherine Hall, 'The hidden investment': women and the enterprise', from *Family Fortunes: Men and Women of the English Middle Class 1780–1950* (1987) pp. 272–315, reprinted by permission of Routledge Ltd; Amanda Vickery, 'Golden age to separate spheres? A review of the categories and chronology of English women's history', *Historical Journal*, 36 (1993), pp. 383–414, reprinted by permission of Cambridge University Press; Joanna Bourke, 'Housewifery in working-class England 1860–1914', world copyright: The Past and Present Society, 175 Banbury Road, Oxford, England. This article is reprinted with the permission of the society and the author from *Past and Present: A Journal of Historical Studies*, no.143 (May 1994), pp.167–97.

To the best of our knowledge all copyright holders of material reproduced in this book have been traced. Any rights not acknowledged here will be noted in subsequent printings if notice is given to the publisher.

Introduction

It is often assumed that the woman worker was produced by the
Industrial Revolution, and that since that time women have taken an
increasing share in the world's work. This theory is, however, quite
unsupported by the facts.

Thus did Ivy Pinchbeck begin her classic book *Women Workers in the
Industrial Revolution 1750–1850*, first published in 1930.[1] Pinchbeck and
her precursor, Alice Clark, who in 1919 wrote a detailed account of
women's work in the seventeenth century, were pioneers in the history of
women's work.[2] They sought to dispel the myth, which is still prevalent, that
women's work in the labour market is a new phenomenon. They wrote at a
time when the first suffrage campaigns had made an impact and the
franchise had been extended to women. Women had participated in war
work and, perhaps most importantly of all, the effects of extended higher
education for women were being felt. No-one who reads the campaigner
Vera Brittain's powerful autobiographical trilogy can be left without
cognisance of this latter fact, and of her underlying conviction of the
importance of women's work.[3] Pinchbeck wrote as if in direct response to
Virginia Woolf's call in *A Room Of One's Own* (1929) for students of
Cambridge women's colleges to rewrite history – 'why should they not add
a supplement to history? – calling it, of course, by some inconspicuous name
so that women might figure there without impropriety'.[4]

This Reader does not aim to dissect current controversies in women's
history. Controversy is not absent from what may seem to many to be a
'soft' sort of social history – some of the kernel of current debate is included
in this volume, and I attempt to place this in context in the commentaries for
each of the three sections. Nevertheless there is a strong undertow of
collectivism within women's history: rather than a string of individualistic
endeavours there is a sense of a collaborative project to uncover women's
pasts. This introduction attempts to place the history of women's work in

perspective. It considers contemporary concerns about women's employment by briefly examining historical understanding of the meanings of work, and summarises the outline of women's experience of work over the period 1650–1914.

Writing history in the present

The history of women's work at the end of what Sheila Rowbotham has called 'the century of women', and at the start of a new millennium, takes its starting point from modern-day dilemmas. Are full-time work and motherhood incompatible? Indeed, in an age when masculinity is under examination, how can fatherhood and paid work be reconciled? Behind this lies an ongoing preoccupation with ideas that motherhood and housework are in the female domain. In 1997, for the first time, the new Labour government in Britain put an official value on unpaid work. Even at the lowest estimate, the value was greater than the whole of the United Kingdom manufacturing sector. Whereas men on average spent 212 minutes a day in paid work, this was almost double the 127 minutes spent by the average woman. In the home, the woman spent 295 minutes on unpaid household work and men 155 minutes.[5] In terms of participation in the labour market, the second half of the twentieth century has seen an enormous rise in women's employment. In fact, this is arguably *the* most significant social change of the last century. In 1995, women constituted 49.6 per cent of all employees in employment and, in a third of all local labour markets in the United Kingdom, women were the majority of those in work.[6] The most obvious transition since the Second World War has been the rising economic activity of married women, from 26 per cent in 1951 to 71 per cent in 1991. Their participation rate today is thus little different from that of unmarried women. If we go further back in time, the contrast over the course of the twentieth century is even more evident. While the 1911 census might be considered the first accurate recording of employment participation, it showed only 10 per cent of married women in paid work, and 35.6 per cent of women overall.[7] Much of the recent increase is in part-time work. Nevertheless the generational changes implied by these statistics are manifest and they are, as Sylvia Walby sees it, 'gender transformations'. The experience of work for women today is vastly changed from that of their mothers, and enormously different from that of their grandmothers. These disparate experiences are magnified when we turn to wages. Walby finds that the earnings differential between men and women has declined since 1970. By 1995, women earned on average 80 per cent of male earnings. Changes were also apparent in occupational segregation. There are now more women in top managerial positions than at any time in our history. As Walby states: 'These changes represent a significant restructuring of gender relations in employment.' Always bearing in mind that many women workers are still part-time, the impact of childrearing on women's work is no longer so apparent. Women are now less likely to take the career breaks which characterised their mother's working lives. (As Humphries and Horrell show in Reading 7 in this volume, rather than a break with a traditional pattern, this may be reverting to a situation similar to the common experience of women in the Industrial Revolution.)

Such enormous social change has not come without some anomalies. The transformation of women's work to a situation where Britain has one of the highest proportions of working women in Europe is combined with one of the poorest records on state-supported childcare. Catherine Hakim's research suggests that there is not only a generational divide in women's experience of work, but a polarisation of women's experience within the working age cohort: whereas some women are career-centred and pro-active in terms of work, others are home-centred and prefer and seek domesticity.[8] The implication that many women are simply not work-orientated, and even if in full-time paid work unlikely to be as committed to their jobs as men, has been very controversial. The media storm which followed Hakim's article in no less august a volume than the *British Journal of Sociology* showed the way in which she had ignited a touchpaper of political as well as social preoccupation. As the ensuing 'Call Nick Ross' programme on BBC Radio 4 made evident, men are now faced with an employment scenario which is structured to provide part-time jobs, many on short-term contracts, in traditionally female areas of work. Conversely, women are willing to work for lower wage rates and have replaced men in some of the areas of work which have usually been male-dominated. Consequently, in 1995 more men than women actually pursued sex discrimination cases in Britain. As Walby's research has shown, it is older men who are particularly vulnerable to competition from women, and as a result are moving into jobs once sex-typed 'female', such as cleaning and supermarket shelf-stacking. As a female bed-and-breakfast proprietor from Brighton said on the Nick Ross programme: 'We ain't seen nothing yet: women are adaptable, adaption is an idea which has come of age.' The flexible female labour market, of course, formed one of the linchpins of Britain's economic success in the eighteenth and nineteenth centuries (see Reading 6).

Recent media attention has focused on the effect of paid employment on motherhood – in particular how mothers' absence through full-time work might affect children's school performance. Markedly less attention is paid to British employers' expectations of their workers. The contemporary 'work ethic' dictates that work and family life still take place in separate spheres and press reports reveal some shocking details. With average working hours some of the longest in Europe, half the British male working population arrives home completely exhausted. Many fathers spend less than five minutes a week talking to their children and often return from work after the children have gone to bed.[9] And, despite the apparent stampede toward the world of paid work by women, many work situations are still characterised by authoritarian rule, top-down management and competition, rather than the more consensual, co-operative, efficient and meticulous ways of working associated with women. Change may be in the air but men still predominate in the managerial and supervisory positions, whereas women are in the lower ranks, and often in fields of employment necessitating 'feminine characteristics' such as empathy, care and general emotional investment. The social value of the work of nurturing still goes unrecognised, or is at best poorly rewarded within the labour market. These issues go beyond the limited sphere of work and into the wider compass of public debate about the family. They impact on the question of what roles and responsibilities men, women and children have in modern-day families. This is a gendered issue, for family values are still mainly seen as the province of women. The positive outcome of Hakim's work was to focus attention on the domestic sphere, since most employment surveys stop at the office door. The eleven academics who criticised Hakim argued that women are unable to make real choices because they are constrained by childcare difficulties and by social forces and institutional factors.[10] Hakim retorted that they were 'reiterating once again the feminist view of women as universal victims, denying that women are agents in their own lives, just as much as men are'.[11]

The progress women have made in the labour market has been partly the result of two waves of feminist pressure for equal opportunities. The second wave, which had its full flowering in the 1970s, was built on social science theory. These ideas drew particular weight from anthropology and argued that women's roles in society are defined by social constructions not biological realities. Social constructions are, of course, much more malleable than biological facts. The social, versus the biological, foundations of women's subordination are now again the subject of debate. Scientific evidence which suggests that sexual difference cannot be more than partially explained by social circumstances has been growing. Historians have also asserted that biological factors must be left in the account. Olwen Hufton argues in a recent *tour de force* on the history of women in early modern Europe:

> The English and American feminist movements have since the beginning of this century seen biological arguments as a way of denying women equality of opportunity and as an excuse for men not to share the traditional caring and nurturing tasks of women. In the twentieth century these arguments have much to recommend them but they remain problematic. In the early modern period, biology has to count for something. No one, for example, could plough a five-inch furrow in a condition of advanced or even early pregnancy.[12]

Another eminent historian of gender in early modern Europe has also said that her recent collection of essays marks:

> a shift on my part away from the conviction that gender is a product of cultural and linguistic practice, towards the view that sexual difference has its own physiological and psychological reality, and that recognition of this must affect the way we write history.[13]

Along with the advances recently made in the history of sexuality, the grounded material and biological realities implicit in our understanding of work will be high on the agenda of historians in years to come.

Women's work in context

Women's history developed at same time as other branches of social history sought to give more prominence to ordinary people and to investigate their lives and livelihoods 'from below'. The women's history of the 1970s developed alongside, and sometimes in partnership with, labour history. Nevertheless, until very recently the concerns of labour history have been dominated by organised labour, the male workplace, and masculine work culture, casting only a sideways glance towards women's labour.[14] In some ways, labour history declined before women's historians had become properly paid-up members of the club. With the retreat of leftist ideology came a reluctance to accept the full explanatory potential of economic determinism. Class was no longer privileged above other categories of historical analysis, and gender became more central to both analysis and the understanding of historical change. Describing and interpreting work in its past context now includes a much wider vision, emphasising cultural aspects. Drawing on social anthropology, work is viewed as a site or contested space in which the cultural and ideological impetus of societies can be examined.[15] Whereas the projects started in the 1970s considered women's role within labour markets and the material aspects of women's toil, more recent research places emphasis on the social construction of women's labour within the wider context of their lives. In the long run, these two pursuits should inform each other.

The investigation of the history of women's work proceeds from material collected by local and regional case studies. Some documents, such as poor law settlement examinations, which are used to great effect by Keith Snell in this collection, can provide a potted biography of women's employment histories. But it remains difficult to find women speaking in their own words and describing their own experiences. The best we can hope for are those records where a court clerk has taken down a woman's words verbatim as used by Peter Earle in Reading 5.[16] However, the local nature of information and time gaps in sources still defeat an overall picture. Before the nineteenth century most of our extant records are of criminals and the poor; thus they under- and misrepresent the ordinary woman's experience. More research could be carried out using collections of family papers. Informed by an economic and social history which has become increasingly sophisticated in describing the economic context and the family and household setting of much of women's labours, a pastiche of studies of certain industries and localities has emerged. For example, we have a detailed picture of the types of work women did in early modern Oxford, Salisbury and Ludlow.[17] On women's work in certain trades, such as the printing and book-producing trades, we have a reasonable amount of information through time.[18]

Early modern women's work

The English economy was distinctive within early modern Europe. England had a large proportion of landless labourers; urban areas were relatively well developed and the formation of an advanced financial system at the end of the seventeenth century both created wealth and encouraged women's participation in economic life. The local economies of late seventeenth-century England were vibrant and diverse.[19] We can envisage the changing landscape through a contemporary woman's eyes by reading the printed journals of Celia Fiennes. Fiennes travelled extensively in the 1690s and noted thriving mini-industries: silk and paper-making introduced by refugees to Canterbury, teapot-fashioning in Staffordshire, glass-blowing and cotton-knitting in Nottingham, Honiton lace and Manchester cotton. In the Cotswolds she remarked on the seasonal migration of entire families who camped in huts to grow and process woad amid fetid smells. She described the myriad productive activities taking place within households such as the making of soap, cheese and cider, Lancashire 'clap bread', and clotted cream in the West Country. As a Dissenter, Fiennes was imbued with the Protestant stress on hard work and discipline. Work, for Fiennes and her peers, had a moral dimension. She commented approvingly on the busy activity of those in East Anglia; 'the ordinary people ... knitt much and spin, some with the rock and fusoe as the French does, others at their wheeles out in the streete and lane as one passes',[20] but this contrasted with her shock at what she perceived as the sloth and lack of industry of women in the Scottish and Welsh borders. However, the overall impression given by Fiennes is that, with the exception of areas marginal to the national economy, women's efforts were increasing in both urban and rural areas (see Reading 8).

The second half of the seventeenth century was a period of population stagnation creating more work opportunities and higher wages for women.

While a rough and ready benchmark figure suggests that women's wages stood at around a third to a half of the male rate for similar work, in this period of relative labour shortage women's wages rose to around two-thirds of the male level. The women who benefited from these demographic circumstances may not have been the married women, as Alice Clark suggested, but single women and widows.[21] Evidence for the active participation of single women in seventeenth-century urban economies and 'industries in the countryside' is growing. Widows who took over their husband's trades, and perhaps operated as local creditors, were able to wield some economic power. One woman for whom a good deal of evidence can be culled from family papers is Hester Pinney (1658–1740). Hester never married but lived an active economic life as a lace trader, creditor and financial dealer.[22] She was based in London but her work involved marketing West Country lace. In terms of freedom of action, economic independence and pursuing both her work and her social life, it is notable that Hester's life story resembles a modern woman's rather than that of our great grandmothers. The demographic context is worth noting. Hester Pinney lived at the time when probably the fewest persons (in our knowable demographic history) married. It is estimated that up to 25 per cent of people of marriageable age were celibate at the end of the seventeenth century, compared with less than 3 per cent a century later.[23] These circumstances have an enormous influence on women's ability and willingness to engage in paid labour. Yet in the popular imagination there is still a belief that in the past all women married and did not work, but brought up children while men were breadwinners and worked away from the home. In the same yarn, families were somehow stable and enduring, marriages lasted for ever and single parents did not exist. Yet history tells a more complicated and more useful story.

Although single women clearly migrated into urban areas in the early modern period, there is certainly no evidence that this brought an increase in their status. Women's civic and political positions were more restricted than they had been in medieval times and court records show that single labouring women found to be out of service, and therefore free of authority, were particularly likely to raise hackles.[24] Both young men and women spent considerable years in someone else's household for a period of training by service or apprenticeship, a fact linked to the late age at marriage.[25] The household was at the centre of the economic and social world. Historians such as Tilly and Scott, and Bridget Hill, believe that the concept of a family economy is essential to understanding pre-industrial women's work.[26] Alice Clark also describes a world in which both men and women contributed to family income and the purchase of provisions. This family economy lies at the centre of the view that the pre-industrial economy provided a 'golden age' for women's work. There is an implicit assumption that women had more influence on both the family and the wider community when manufacture was household-based, and production and reproduction were integrated. Yet the evidence, albeit limited, about how power was distributed in the family does little to support a 'golden age'. In fact, there are more indications of conflictual than consensual relationships.[27]

The other basis of the 'golden age' view is the argument that, in the pre-industrial economy, women engaged in a wide variety of economic activities, ranging from craft expertise to heavy manual labour, and that as the economy became more specialised their opportunities narrowed.[28] While it is evident that a few women were engaged in trades such as goldsmithing or building, a more thorny question is the extent to which work translated into status. Today, we tend to define our identity by our occupation and often introduce ourselves to strangers by mentioning our job. In records of the past, men's occupations are frequently mentioned, but women are commonly referred to by marital status – as 'single woman', 'wife of' or 'widow'. Work provided an important and highly visible sign of male honour, both individually and collectively. As a result, some commentators suggest that women's work lacked the public esteem necessary for honourability. Much female work was perhaps too undefined and ephemeral to confer identity. Natalie Zemon Davis has explored this question in some depth for craft trades in early modern Lyon. She found that, although there were no formal apprenticeships or institutions and corporations from which a female work identity might emanate, there was a domestic work culture encompassing mistresses and female workers in textile trades. An independent female artisan could be held in esteem by her family, neighbours and clients and this is shown by the feminisation of her last name, the use of nicknames and the title of 'Dame'. The status of these women is indicated by their role as godmothers and as figures who had influence over gossip networks and the ability to disperse petty loans and gifts to kin and (especially female) neighbours. As Davis put it 'The Dames among the *menu peuple* were known for a cluster of womanly achievements, of which work skill was only one, and they were primarily rooted in their neighbourhood.'[29] In the English context, like many women of her status, Hester Pinney was referred to as 'Madam Pinney'. We can imagine that high-quality lace production and skill in embroidery conferred a sense of prestige on craftswomen. However, for women who were not artisans, we may be mistaken in assuming that a sense of work identity was entirely absent. As Garthine Walker has argued, 'it is widely accepted that women's contributions to their household economies gave them a subjective sense of social identity and self-worth, as well as neighbourhood status, all of which have a relation to honour'.[30] Contemporary literature certainly exalts the labours and merits of the good housewife and contrasts her virtues with the idle, spendthrift or mismanaging wife who did nothing to contribute to household order.

Women and industrialisation

The historiography of the 1970s and early 1980s assumed that the family economy dissolved in the eighteenth century. While 'optimists' such as Edward Shorter and Neil McKendrick thought household manufacture was superseded by wage-earning individualism,[31] 'pessimists' suggested that the family economy collapsed into a surplus of unemployed women as a distinct sexual division of labour emerged by the end of the century. Recent impressions have been much more nuanced, showing a diverse picture of women's employment. My own study of Essex shows the declining cloth trade being replaced by fashion industries producing silk, ready-made clothing, lace and straw-plait.[32] Elizabeth Sanderson's portrait of Edinburgh shows women active in their own retail businesses.[33] Most of the expanding female trades – particularly in clothing and millinery – were linked to the upturn in consumerism.[34] Modish centres, such as spa towns, provided a great deal of women's work in every kind of service trade.[35] Historians have highlighted the decline of women's work in traditional areas such as midwifery, when it became fashionable among the middling orders to employ man-midwives who were assumed to have the mastery of modern scientific techniques which were seen as superior to the traditional arts of women.[36] Recent interest in material culture has focused attention on women's role as the buyers of stylish furnishings and household durables. Eighteenth-century England was a world of fascinating ambivalence: heightened wealth and escalating consumption for some co-existed with deepening poverty for others. Such diversity was reflected in women's work. As some of the Readings in this book show, the first three-quarters of the century did offer many work opportunities for women. The high labour force participation of females is demonstrated by the analysis of listings for two villages which detail women's occupations during the 1780s and suggest a much more buoyant picture of women's opportunities than in the late Victorian era. In the lace-making village of Cardington in Bedfordshire in 1782, 82 per cent of married women in the age group 20–39 were in employment, and in all age groups 67.5 per cent of married women.[37]

There is still a need for more local studies which can give information on patterns of female participation in the eighteenth and the first half of the nineteenth centuries, and which extend our picture of the corrosive and creative effects of capitalism.[38] In particular, our view that women's employment increased during the French Wars (1793–1815) is mainly impressionistic, rather than resting on the solid foundations of local and regional research. For agriculture, Snell's view of the increasing marginalisation of female workers in the south-east (Reading 4) needs to be tested for other areas.[39] In mills and factories – the archetypal symbols of the Industrial Revolution – young women provided the greatest part of the workforce at very low wage levels.[40] At the same time, and sometimes in the same vicinity, mass production was achieved by cost-cutting, using no new methods but a proliferation of sweated labour. The nineteenth century saw much work deskilled as the sexual division of labour changed and young female machine operators replaced male artisans. The perceived dilution of skill and the resulting gender antagonism when, in the 1820s and 1830s, women started to compete with skilled labourers has been extensively studied.[41] The discussions by historians take us into the wider debates about how work comes to be viewed as skilled. The apprenticeships to trades like weaving were much longer for males than was necessary to learn the techniques of the trade, but they were used to provide a barrier to entry and to reinforce the culture of work.

Protective legislation from the 1840s restricted the hours and conditions of women's work. Reading the evidence of the Parliamentary Commissions shows the way in which the middle class and elite construed women as dependants. Exclusion from certain types of employment, such as underground work in mines, laid the theoretical basis for the 'family wage' with the man as breadwinner. This line was taken up by the emerging male trades unions which emphasised that women's employment prevented them from carrying out their 'natural' functions as wives and mothers. Thus, after 1870, when real wage levels rose to the point where it was possible for a working man to support a dependent family, the working classes followed the middle class in extolling the virtues of domesticity.[42] In some areas this was more facade than actuality. Many women still took in outwork to provide either a 'respectable' or a hidden contribution to household income.[43] Other women still worked in the labour market for very low rates of pay.[44] In demographic terms the 'low' of female employment from *c*. 1880 to 1920 coincided with early and more frequent marriage, larger family size, and children remaining within the parental home for longer.[45] Single women could still only work for 'supplementary' wage rates and the struggle for survival forced some of them into prostitution.[46]

When we place women's history into a long time frame we can see the Victorian epoch as a historical aberration – a time when incredibly powerful ideological forces laid a particular cast on gender roles and family forms. Viewed from the perspective of either the pre-industrial era or the contemporary Western world where paid work again often takes place in the home, the period 1850–1950, characterised by sex-specific occupational segregation and division into public and private spheres, stands out.[47] For the Victorian middle class the polarisation into masculine and feminine spheres affected their experiences of work (see Readings 9 and 10). Many married women, although based at home, energetically engaged in charity work and other unpaid but highly regarded pursuits.[48] Paradoxically, while a Victorian married woman might be the angel of the house and the epitome of domesticity, single women had a much more difficult struggle to live a purposeful and rewarding life. The 'surplus woman problem' of the mid-nineteenth century meant that, while some single women emigrated, others sought independent careers.[49] By the late nineteenth century, middle-class women fought to train as doctors and sought entry to other professional careers.[50]

By the 1900s it was assumed that from the start of women's working lives their place in the labour market was temporary. Wage levels reflected this and the situation applied to all classes.[51] A study undertaken in Birmingham in 1901 by Cadbury, Matheson and Shawn, entitled *Women's Work and Wages: A Phase of Life in an Industrial City*, found that the average wage of young women was only 10s a week, 4s less than was judged necessary to keep them healthy and respectable. Even middle-class jobs such as teaching, nursing and clerical work were poorly paid. Female post office clerks were envied as they had a seven- to eight-hour day, sick leave, annual holidays and pension schemes, but women sorters only got £38 a year in the 1900s and, because the civil service operated a marriage bar, sorters and clerks had to leave on marriage. The better-paid professional jobs generally excluded women. Poor pay, irregular employment and caring for large families made women reluctant to join trades unions, and their membership grew slowly before the First World War. Northern textile workers, also active in campaigning for the vote, were the largest group of organised women workers. However, many women in service trades, or in industries like fishing or agriculture, remained outside unions. In fact the most forceful female resistance, expressed in a wave of strikes in the early 1910s, began outside the 'organised' trades. Jam and pickle factory workers, bottle-washers, laundry women and Yarmouth fish-packers, who earned no more than 5s to 10s per week, struck as public concern led to investigation of sweated conditions alongside calls for a legal national minimum wage.

In 1909 the Trades Boards Act had set up fixed rates for certain trades; chain-making, box-making, lace-making and clothing. Significant regional differences remained in the extent to which women worked. In the Staffordshire Potteries and in Lancashire, for example, married women were still extensively employed. During the First World War, the scope and extent of women's work changed on a national basis.[52] From 1915 women were recruited into munitions factories. They made and filled shells and cartridges, laboured, cleaned, catered, drove vehicles and kept stores, maintained optical instruments and worked as needlewomen and carpenters, encountering objections from men that this represented a dilution of their own previous jobs and skills. Both as civilians and at the front, where women such as Vera Brittain served as nurses, women's work opportunities during the war were unprecedented and their status as workers was high. However, after the war, and also later in the twentieth century, women's experiences reflected the persistence of a domestic ideology and of a labour market structured by and for men.

Women's work and an agenda for social change

The author, Marilyn French, recently discussed the circumstances in the 1950s in which she wrote her bestseller *The Women's Room*, and how she abandoned it at one stage because it was too disturbing:

> For writing about a group demonstrated as no single story could that we were trapped, literally. It was impossible for most women to earn enough to live without a husband: we could not raise and support our families at the same time. The system encompassing us had forced us to marry, then guaranteed our confinement within marriage. All of us had problems with our husbands: once we'd had babies the equals we'd married became our bosses, because they earned money and we did not. We had no defence against this shift in power relations.[53]

Even though the number of women in the labour market has increased over the course of the twentieth century we should guard against too readily generalising about the linear progress of women. There is no single experience for the woman worker. Status, wages and work opportunities do not always run on parallel tracks. It is certainly evident that the impression of incremental growth in the number of women accessing the labour market over time vastly oversimplifies the historical evidence. Moreover, while the increasing employment of women might be seen as a hallmark of current-day modernisation, in other cultures women's work can also become a dominating issue in state policy where regimes try to maintain traditional values. The extreme Islamic group Taliban, which rose to contested rule in wartorn Afghanistan in the mid-1990s, outlawed women's work, justifying their actions by the sanctification of the Koran. Their policies have been difficult to enforce simply because the absence of men in the war years brought women into professional fields such as medicine and there are now too few trained men.[54] The reality that women's work is a political issue is less stark but equally true in the Western world. Kessler-Harris has argued (drawing on American evidence) that 'public or popular conceptions of the past can construct the future'. She believes that 'this is a moment when the voices of historians of women are needed more than ever. Some of the most significant social issues on the political agenda – family life, abortion, reproduction, and a range of issues having to do with economic equality have a special meaning for women.'[55] In current debates, such as that on the relationship between work and welfare, it is important to provide an accurate historical perspective. This is the spirit in which Pinchbeck and Clark investigated the conditions of English women workers in an industrialising nation, and it must still be our *modus operandi* today. At the turn of the twentieth century, with the spotlight on both gender issues and how work will be organised in the future, it is to be hoped that we are now in a position to place those first two authoritative contributions to the history of women's work into a broader historical context.

Notes

1 The latest is the third edition published by Virago in 1981, with an introduction by Kerry Hamilton.
2 A. Clark, *Working Life of Women in the Seventeenth Century* (London, Routledge, 1919; third edition 1992). The latest edition has an extremely useful introduction by A. L. Erickson.
3 V. Brittain, *Testament of Youth* (London, Gollancz, 1933; Virago, 1978) and her subsequent *Testament of Friendship* (London, Gollancz, 1940; Virago, 1980) and *Testament of Experience* (London, Gollancz, 1957). Specifically on work, see her *Women's Work in Modern England* (London, Noel Douglas, 1928). An earlier pioneering text was Olive Schreiner's *Women and Labour* (1911; London, Virago, 1985).
4 Quoted in J. W. Scott, 'Survey articles: women in history', *Past and Present*, 101 (1983), p. 141.
5 *The Guardian*, 7 October 1997.
6 S. Walby, *Gender Transformations* (London, Routledge, 1997), p. 1.
7 J. Lewis, *Women in England 1870–1950* (Hemel Hempstead, Harvester Wheatsheaf, 1984), p. 147. For a recent discussion see E. Garrett, 'The dawning of a new era? Women's work in England and Wales at the turn of the twentieth century', *Histoire Sociale/Social History* (1996), pp. 421–63; E. Higgs, 'Women, occupations and work in the nineteenth-century Censuses', *History Workshop Journal*, 23 (1987), pp. 59–80; B. Hill 'Women, work and the census: a problem for historians of women', *History Workshop Journal*, 35 (1993), pp. 78–94.
8 C. Hakim, 'Five feminist myths about women's employment', *British Journal of Sociology*, 46 (1995), pp. 429–55; C. Hakim, *Key Issues in Women's Work: Female Heterogeneity and the Polarisation of Women's Employment* (London, Athlone, 1996). See the debate in *The Times Higher Education Supplement*, 26 April 1996.
9 *The Guardian*, 4 February 1997: Adrienne Burgess, 'Dad's the word'.
10 J. Ginn *et al.*, 'Feminist fallacies: a reply to Hakim on women's employment', *British Journal of Sociology*, 47 (1996), pp. 167–74 and subsequent rejoinder.
11 *Times Higher Education Supplement*, 26 April 1996, p. 17.
12 O. Hufton, *The Prospect Before Her* (London, HarperCollins, 1995) p. 5.
13 L. Roper, *Oedipus and the Devil* (London, Routledge, 1994) p. 3.
14 See the criticisms made by S. Alexander, A. Davin and E. Hostettler in 'Labouring women: a reply to Eric Hosbsbawm', *History Workshop Journal*, 8 (1979), pp. 174–82.
15 On the nature and meanings of work, see P. Joyce (ed.) *The Historical Meanings of Work* (Cambridge, Cambridge University Press, 1987); J. Rule, *The Experience of Labour in Eighteenth-century Industry* (London, Croom Helm, 1981); R. W. Malcolmson, *Life and Labour in England 1700–1800* (London, Hutchinson, 1981); R. E. Pahl (ed.), *On Work: Historical, Comparative and Theoretical Approaches* (London, Basil Blackwell, 1988). For the cultural aspects of early modern work, see the interesting research by Michael Roberts, 'Women and work in sixteenth-century English towns', in P. J. Corfield and D. Keene (eds.), *Work in Towns 850–1850* (Leicester, Leicester University Press, 1990) pp. 86–102; Roberts, 'Another letter from a far country: the pre-history of labour or the history of work in preindustrial Wales', *Llafur*, 2 (1989), pp. 93–106; Roberts, 'The empty ladder: work and its meanings in early modern Cardiganshire', *Llafur*, 4 (1995), pp. 9–29.
16 See L. Gowing, *Domestic Dangers: Women, Words and Sex in Early Modern London* (Oxford, Oxford University Press, 1996).

17 M. Prior, 'Women in the Urban Economy: Oxford 1500–1800', in M. Prior (ed.), *Women in English Society 1500–1800* (London, Routledge, 1985), pp. 93–117; S. Wright, 'Churmaids, huswyfes and hucksters: the employment of women in Tudor and Stuart Salisbury', in L. Charles and L. Duffin (eds.), *Women and Work in Pre-industrial England* (London, Croom Helm, 1985), pp. 100–21, and S. Wright, '"Holding up half the sky": women and their occupations in eighteenth-century Ludlow', *Midland History*, 14 (1989), pp. 53–74.

18 See, for example, H. Barker, 'Women, work and the Industrial Revolution: female involvement in the English printing trades, *c.* 1700–1840', in H. Barker and E. Chalus, *Gender in Eighteenth-Century England* (London, Longman, 1997); F. Hunt, 'Opportunities Lost and Gained: Mechanization and Women's Work in London Bookbinding and Printing Trades', in A. V. John (ed.), *Unequal Opportunities: Women's Employment in England 1800–1918* (Oxford, Oxford University Press, 1986); S. Reynolds, *Britannica's Typesetters* (Edinburgh, Edinburgh University Press, 1989).

19 On women's work in two areas of the early modern farming economy, see A. Hassell-Smith, 'Labourers in late-sixteenth century England: a case study from north Norfolk', *Continuity and Change* (1989), Part 1, 4.1, pp. 11–52; Part 2, 4.3, pp. 367–94; C. Shammas, 'The world women knew: women workers in the north of England during the seventeenth century', in R. S. Dunn and M. M. Dunn, *The World of William Penn* (University of Pennsylvania Press, Philadelphia, 1986).

20 C. Morris (ed.), *The Journeys of Celia Fiennes* (London, Cresset Press, 1947), p. 46.

21 B. A. Holderness, 'Widows in pre-industrial society: an essay upon their economic functions', in R. M. Smith (ed.), *Land, Kinship and Life-cycle* (Cambridge, Cambridge University Press, 1984), pp. 423–42; O. Hufton, 'Women without men: widows and spinsters in Britain and France in the eighteenth century', *Journal of Family History*, 9:4 (1984), pp. 355–74; P. Sharpe, 'Literally spinsters: a new interpretation of local economy and demography in Colyton in the seventeenth and eighteenth centuries', *Economic History Review*, 44 (1991), pp. 46–65; D. Weir, 'Rather never than late: celibacy and age of marriage in English cohort fertility 1541–1871' *Journal of Family History*, 9 (1984), pp. 340–54; R. Wall, 'Women alone in English society', *Annales de Démographie Historique* (1981), pp. 303–20.

22 Pinney Papers, Bristol University Library.

23 E. A. Wrigley and R. S. Schofield, *The Population History of England, 1541–1871* (Cambridge, Cambridge University Press, 1981), pp. 262–3.

24 P. Griffiths, 'Masterless young people in Norwich, 1560–1645', in P. Griffiths, A. Fox and S. Hindle (eds.), *The Experience of Authority in Early Modern England* (London, Macmillan, 1996), pp. 146–86.

25 I. Krausman Ben-Amos, *Adolescence and Youth in Early Modern England* (New Haven, Yale University Press, 1994); A. Kussmaul, *Servants in Husbandry in Early Modern England* (Cambridge, Cambridge University Press, 1981); D. Simonton, 'Apprenticeship: Training and Gender in Eighteenth-century England', in M. Berg (ed.), *Markets and Manufacture in Early Industrial Europe* (London, Routledge, 1991), pp. 227–60; P. Sharpe, 'Poor children as apprentices in Colyton 1598–1830', *Continuity and Change*, 6 (1991), pp. 253–70.

26 L. A. Tilly and J. W. Scott, *Women, Work and Family* (London, Routledge, 1987); Bridget Hill, *Women, Work and Sexual Politics in Eighteenth-Century England* (London, UCL Press, 1994; Oxford, Blackwell, 1989).

27 See, for example, M. Hunt, *The Middling Sort: Commerce, Gender and the Family in England 1680–1780* (Berkeley, University of California Press, 1996).

28 See K. D. M. Snell, *Annals of the Labouring Poor* (Cambridge, Cambridge University Press, 1985), pp. 270–319. Valuable on early modern women's lives in general are: S. D. Amussen, *An Ordered Society: Gender and Class in Early Modern England* (New York, Columbia University Press, 1988); A. Laurence, *Women in England 1500–1760: A Social History* (London, Weidenfeld and Nicolson, 1994) and P. Crawford, 'From the woman's view: preindustrial England 1500–1750', in P. Crawford (ed.), *Exploring Women's Past* (Sydney, Allen and Unwin, 1983), pp. 49–85.

29 N. Z. Davis, 'Women in the crafts in sixteenth-century Lyon', in B. A. Hanawalt (ed.), *Women and Work in Preindustrial Europe* (Bloomington, Indiana University Press, 1986), p. 184. Also relevant is J. Quaraert, 'The shaping of women's work in manufacturing: guilds, households and the state in central Europe 1648–1870', *American Historical Review*, 90 (1985), pp. 1122–48.

30 G. Walker, 'Expanding the boundaries of female honour in early modern England', *Transactions of the Royal Historical Society,* 6 (1996), p. 236.

31 E. Shorter, 'Women's work: what difference did capitalism make?' *Theory and Society*, 3 (1976), pp. 485–512; N. McKendrick, J. Brewer and J. H. Plumb, *The Birth of a Consumer Society: the Commercialization of Eighteenth-Century England* (London, Hutchinson, 1983).

32 P. Sharpe, *Adapting to Capitalism: Working Women in the English Economy* (London, Macmillan, 1996).

33 E. Sanderson, *Women and Work in Eighteenth-Century Edinburgh* (London, Macmillan, 1996). On women and trade more broadly, see Hunt, *The Middling Sort* and E. Kowaleski-Wallace, *Consuming Subjects: Women, Shopping and Business in the Eighteenth Century* (New York, Columbia University Press, 1997).

34 L. Weatherill 'A possession of one's own: women and consumer behaviour in England 1660–1740', *Journal of British Studies*, 25 (1986), pp. 131–56; B. Lemire, *Dress, Culture and Commerce: The English Clothing Trade before the Factory 1660–1800* (London, Macmillan, 1997); A. J. Vickery 'Women and the World of Goods: a Lancashire Consumer and her Possessions 1751–81', in J. Brewer and R. Porter (eds.), *Consumption and the World of Goods* (London, Routledge, 1993), pp. 274–301.

35 Viktoria Masten, 'Women in the trades and professions of eighteenth-century Ipswich and Bath'. Unpublished paper presented at 'Women, Trade and Business Conference in Exeter University', July 1996.

36 A. Wilson, *The Making of Man-Midwifery: Childbirth in England 1660–1770* (Cambridge, Cambridge University Press, 1995); J. Donnison, *Midwives and Medical Men: A History of the Struggle for Control of Childbirth* (London, Heinemann, 1988); H. Marland, *The Art of Midwifery: Early Modern Midwives in Europe* (London, Routledge, 1993); O. Moscucci, *The Science of Woman* (Cambridge, Cambridge University Press, 1990); B. B. Schnorrenberg, 'Is childbirth any place for a woman? The decline of the midwife in eighteenth century England', *Studies in Eighteenth-Century Culture* 10 (1981), pp. 393–408; M. Versluysen, 'Old wives tales? Women healers in English history', in C. Davies (ed.), *Rewriting Nursing History* (London, Croom Helm, 1980), pp. 175–99; A. L. Wyman, 'The surgeoness: the female practitioner of surgery 1400–1800', *Medical History*, 28 (1984), pp. 22–41.

37 O. Saito, 'Who worked when: life-time profiles of labour force participation in Cardington and Corfe Castle in the late eighteenth and mid-nineteenth centuries', *Local Population Studies*, 22 (1979), p. 23.

38 For recent background surveys, see P. Hudson, 'Women and industrialisation', and J. Humphries, 'Women and paid work', in J. Purvis (ed.), *Women's History: Britain, 1850–1945* (London, UCL Press, 1995), pp. 23–50 and pp. 85–106.

39 In addition to the bibliography provided in Reading 1 which includes important works on women and common rights, see J. Gielgud, 'Nineteenth-century farm women in Northumberland and Cumbria: the neglected workforce' (unpublished D.Phil. thesis, University of Sussex, 1992); P. Horn, *Victorian Countrywomen* (Oxford, Oxford University Press, 1991); E. Hostettler, 'Women farm workers in eighteenth and nineteenth-century Northumberland', *North East Labour History*, 16 (1982), pp. 40–1; J. Kitteringham, 'Country work girls in nineteenth-century England', in R. Samuel (ed.), *Village Life and Labour* (London, Routledge and Kegan Paul, 1975), pp. 75–138; P. Sharpe, 'The women's harvest: straw-plaiting and the representation of labouring women's employment *c.* 1793–1885', *Rural History*, 5:2 (1994), pp. 129–42.

40 Contemporary comment is worth reading on this subject which became part of the debates on the 'condition of England question' in the mid-nineteenth century. See, for

example, the piece by journalist Harriet Martineau, 'Female industry', *Edinburgh Review* (1859) reprinted in S. Hamilton (ed.), *Criminals, Idiots, Women and Minors: Victorian Writing by Women on Women* (Peterborough, Ontario, Broadview Press, 1995), pp. 29–73. In addition to the extensive references in Reading 1, see D. Busfield, 'Skill and the Sexual division of labour in the West Riding textile industry 1750–1914', in J. A. Jowitt and A. J. MacIvor (eds.), *Employers and Labour in the English Textile Industries 1850–1939* (London, Routledge, 1988); J. Humphries, 'From work to dependence? Women's experience of industrialisation in Britain', *Refresh*, 21 (1995), pp. 5–8; D. Valenze, *The First Industrial Woman* (New York, Oxford University Press, 1995); S. Walby, *Patriarchy at Work* (Cambridge, Polity, 1986). For a controversial view of wage levels, see J. Burnette, 'An investigation of the female–male wage gap during the Industrial Revolution in Britain', *Economic History Review*, 50 (1997), pp. 257–81.

41 A. Clark, *The Struggle for the Breeches* (London, Rivers Oram, 1995); J. Schwarzkopf, *Women in the Chartist Movement* (London, Macmillan, 1991); B. Taylor, *Eve and the New Jerusalem* (London, Virago, 1983); D. Thompson, 'Women and radical politics: a lost dimension', in D. Thompson (ed.), *Outsiders: Class, Gender and Nation* (London, Verso, 1993), pp. 77–102. For comparison, see the important essays in L. L. Frader and S. O. Rose, *Gender and Class in Modern Europe* (Ithaca, Cornell University Press, 1996).

42 E. Roberts, *A Woman's Place: An Oral History of Working Class Women 1890–1940* (Oxford, Blackwell, 1984; reprinted 1995); A. Davin, 'Imperialism and motherhood', *History Workshop Journal*, 5 (1978), pp. 12–66; W. Seccombe, 'Patriarchy stabilized: the construction of the male breadwinner wage norm in nineteenth-century Britain', *Social History*, 11 (1986), pp. 53–76. For specific case studies, E. Garrett, 'The trials of labour: motherhood versus employment in a nineteenth-century textile centre', *Continuity and Change*, 5 (1990), pp. 121–54; D. Jones, 'Counting the cost of coal; women's lives in the Rhondda 1881–1911', in A.V. John (ed.), *Our Mothers' Land: Chapters in Welsh Women's History* (Cardiff, University of Wales Press, 1991), pp. 109–33; L. Davidoff, 'The separation of home and work? Landladies and lodgers in nineteenth and twentieth-century England', in L. Davidoff (ed.), *Worlds Between* (Cambridge, Polity, 1995), pp. 151–79; J. Bourke, 'Working women: the domestic labor market in Rural Ireland 1890–1914', *Journal of Interdisciplinary History*, 21 (1991), pp. 479–99; C. Evans, 'Unemployment and the making of the feminine during the Lancashire cotton famine', in P. Hudson and W. R. Lee (eds.), *Women's Work and the Family Economy in Historical Perspective* (Manchester, Manchester University Press, 1990) pp. 248–70.

43 There is now an extensive literature on this subject. See, for one example, S. Pennington and B. Westover, *A Hidden Workforce, Homeworkers in England 1850–1985* (London, Macmillan, 1989).

44 For the direct personal experience of an activist in a Crewe clothing factory, see Ada Nield Chew, *The Life and Writings of a Working Woman* (London, Virago, 1982).

45 M. Anderson, 'The social position of spinsters in mid-Victorian Britain', *Journal of Family History*, 9 (1984), pp. 377–93; D. Gittins, *Fair Sex: Family Size and Structure 1900–39* (London, Hutchinson, 1982).

46 F. Finnegan, *Poverty and Prostitution: a Study of Victorian Prostitutes in York* (Cambridge, Cambridge University Press, 1979); B. Littlewood and L. Mahood, 'Prostitutes, magdalenes and wayward girls', *Gender and History*, 3:2 (1991), pp. 160–75; L. Mahood, *The Magdalenes: Prostitution in the Nineteenth Century* (London, Routledge, 1990); P. McHugh, *Prostitution and Victorian Social Reform* (London, Routledge, 1980); J. Walkowitz, *Prostitution and Victorian Society: Women, Class and the State* (Cambridge, Cambridge University Press, 1980); J. Walkowitz, 'Male vice and feminist virtue', *History Workshop Journal*, 13 (1982), pp. 77–93; M. Luddy, 'Prostitution and rescue work in nineteenth-century Ireland', in M. Luddy and C. Murphy (eds.), *Women Surviving: Studies in Irish Women's History in the Nineteenth and Twentieth Centuries* (Dublin, Poolbeg, 1989), pp. 51–84.

47 B. Corrado Pope, 'The influence of Rousseau's ideology of domesticity', in M. J. Boxer and J. H. Quartaert (eds.), *Connecting Spheres* (New York, Oxford University

Press, 1987), pp. 136–55; C. Hall, 'The early formation of Victorian domestic ideology', in C. Hall (ed.), *White, Male and Middle Class* (Cambridge, Polity, 1992), pp. 75–93; J. Rendall, *The Origins of Modern Feminism* (London, Macmillan, 1985).

48 F. K. Prochaska, *Women and Philanthropy in Nineteenth-Century England* (Clarendon, Oxford, 1980); A. Summers, 'A home from home: women's philanthropic work in the nineteenth century', in S. Burman (ed.), *Fit Work for Women* (London, Croom Helm, 1979), pp. 33–63.

49 A. J. Hammerton, *Emigrant Gentlewomen: Genteel Poverty and Female Emigration 1830–1914* (London, Croom Helm, 1979); K. Hughes, *The Victorian Governess* (London, Hambleton, 1993); P. Jalland, 'Victorian spinsters: dutiful daughters, desperate rebels and the transition to the New Woman', in P. Crawford (ed.), *Exploring Women's Past* (Sydney, Allen and Unwin, 1983); M. Vicinus, *Independent Women: Work and Community for Single Women 1850–1920* (London, Virago, 1985).

50 J. Lewis, 'Women and society: continuity and change since 1870', *Refresh*, 1 (1985), reprinted in A. Digby and C. Feinstein (eds.), *New Directions in Economic and Social History* (London, Macmillan, 1989), pp. 130–42; L. Holcombe, *Victorian Ladies at Work* (Newton Abbot, David and Charles, 1973); P. Hollis, *Ladies Elect: Women in English Local Government 1865–1914* (Oxford, Clarendon, 1987).

51 The material for this paragraph was drawn from Sheila Rowbotham, *A Century of Women* (London, Viking, 1997).

52 G. Braybon, *Women Workers in the First World War* (London, Routledge, 1989); G. Braybon and P. Summerfield, *Out of the Cage: Women's Experiences in Two World Wars* (London, Pandora, 1987); A. Marwick, *Women at War 1914–18* (London, Fontana, 1977); A. Woollacott, *'On Her Their Lives Depend': Munitions Workers in the Great War* (Berkeley, University of California Press, 1994).

53 *Guardian Supplement with Virago*, June 1997: 'Wayward girls and wicked women'.

54 *Guardian Weekend*, 29 November 1997, Maggie O'Kane, 'A holy betrayal' pp. 39–45.

55 A. Kessler-Harris, 'The just price, the free market and the value of women', *Feminist Studies*, 14 (1988), pp. 235–50.

SECTION
I

DEBATING WOMEN'S WORK

Commentary

The three readings in this section focus on women's work, and wider questions of women's experience through a broad swathe of time. My own piece (Reading 1) provides an overview of research thus far and reflects my conviction of the need for history 'from the bottom up'. It also shows that we need to place case studies within 'the big picture' and that this should form the basis of the search for synthesis about women's lives that is presently under way. The larger framework for women's work engages Hill and Bennett in Readings 2 and 3. They debate whether 'continuity' or 'change' are the most relevant contexts in which to explore women's lives. Bridget Hill, the author of a broad survey of women's work in eighteenth-century England,[1] writes in reply to a review article by Judith Bennett, a medievalist who has written extensively on women's work in rural medieval England, as well as considering broad influences on women's work in later time periods. Bennett argued for analysing continuity as a major problematic in women's history with the recognition that 'Women were as clustered in low skilled, low status, low paying occupations in 1200 as in 1900.'[2] As she propounded in an expanded version of some of the central points of the review article, women's history might be described as 'a history of small shifts, short term changes and enduring continuities'.[3]

If we accept Bennett's argument, it is evident that there has never been a 'golden age' of approximate equality between the sexes in terms of work, as some historians following Alice Clark have claimed. In examining the persistence of a raw deal for women, Bennett suggests that we must explore the history of patriarchy.[4] This is not a concept to be taken at face value and Bennett would be the first to agree that we need to historicise and contextualise male domination.[5] In the heated debate between Bennett and Hill, the latter expresses the view that such a pursuit threatens to confine women's history to a ghetto. Her article is also a critique of Goodman and Honeyman who have asserted the key role of patriarchy in the long-run economic history of women's work.[6] Hill believes that it is possible for historians to analyse change in the position of women with regard to work. Taking women's work as an indicator of their status, she argues that one major change was the impact of the destructive role of capitalism in the eighteenth century. To some extent, of course, this is a question of examining women's work within specific local settings. Hill writes mainly of the rural experience of women, whereas Bennett's view concerned women in the differing contexts of European towns and cities. While the debate is useful in the sense of pointing out the ways in which women's history has become more nuanced since the 1970s, some of the thrust of their arguments finds echo in recent work. In particular, Anna Clark's recent book attempts to put gender into the story of the development of the British working class and stresses the force of both patriarchy and capitalism.[7] Like Hill, she identifies in this piece a 'sexual crisis' in the first half of the nineteenth century. My own work would also suggest that we cannot privilege either continuity or change in understanding women's experience. We are simplifying historical understanding if we do not attempt to unravel the multiple influences in a given situation.

The classic works of Clark and Pinchbeck did not attempt to integrate the history of women into mainstream historical debates. Louise Tilly, writing in 1989, argued that, while women's history had vastly increased our knowledge of women's experience through the many descriptive case studies that had appeared, in the future this history needed to become more problem-solving.[8] She called for connecting the findings of women's history to the questions already on the agenda of all historians. She also felt that feminist history implied the existence of a separate agenda for change and action – a commitment to make scholarship work on women's behalf. In the dialogue in print which followed, Bennett suggested that Tilly had not gone far enough, and that women's history must critique the assumptions behind pre-existing historical debates.[9] The creativity and power of women's history must command interest in its own questions. As suggested in the introduction, this is perhaps another echo of a debate which has been ongoing for women's rights for most of this century: can equality be best achieved through separate development based on gender difference or by demanding an equivalence with men in all spheres? In the specific case of women's history, is this best pursued as a separate discipline, or as part of an integrated historical pursuit within the academy? If the balance of interest is moving towards gender issues, can the concerns of women's historians be maintained? As the history of work is increasingly examined through the lens of gender, it is to be hoped that the very significant achievements of women's history remain firmly in the spotlight.

Notes

1 B. Hill, *Women, Work and Sexual Politics in Eighteenth-Century England* (Oxford, Basil Blackwell, 1989; London, UCL Press, 1994).

2 J. M. Bennett, 'History that stands still': women's work in the European past', *Feminist Studies*, 14:2 (1988), p. 278.

3 J. M. Bennett, 'Medieval women, modern women: across the great divide', in D. Aers (ed.), *Culture and History 1350–1600: Essays on English Communities, Identities and Writing* (Brighton, Harvester Wheatsheaf, 1992), p. 164.

4 For a more detailed outworking of these ideas see J. M. Bennett, 'Misogyny, popular culture and women's work', *History Workshop Journal*, 31 (1991), pp. 166–88, and her *Ale, Beer and Brewsters in England: Women's Work in a Changing World 1300–1600* (Oxford, Oxford University Press, 1997).

5 Much ongoing work is attempting to do this. For a survey, see A. Fletcher, *Gender, Sex and Subordination in England 1500–1800* (New Haven and London, Yale University Press, 1995).

6 As well as the article cited by Hill, Jordan Goodman and Katrina Honeyman have produced a textbook, *Gainful Pursuits: The Making of Industrial Europe 1600–1914* (London, Edward Arnold, 1988).

7 A. Clark, *The Struggle for the Breeches: Gender and the Making of the British Working Class* (London, Rivers Oram Press, 1995). Anna Clark is not to be confused with Alice Clark!

8 L. A. Tilly, 'Gender, women's history and social history', *Social Science History*, 13:4 (1989), pp. 439–62.

9 J. M. Bennett, 'Comment on Tilly: who asks the questions for women's history?', *Social Science History*, 13:4 (1989), pp. 471–7.

1

Continuity and change: women's history and economic history in Britain

PAMELA SHARPE

Women's history in Britain, while less politicized than in North America, is in a healthy state. Conferences on the subject proliferated in 1993 and 1994. New journals such as *Gender and History* and *Women's History Review* are flourishing and there are courses in universities at both undergraduate and graduate level. Women's history is part of a wider project concerning the historical construction of gender. Indeed, men's history is now a growth area.[1] Yet in the field of economic history, gender is still rarely considered. There is a sense in which we still need to concentrate on research about women in the economic past before moving to a more comprehensive analysis. One would look in vain for more than a handful of papers concerning women's economic history at any of the recent gender conferences. Thus while a gendered approach is now very much integral to social history, economic history lags seriously behind – perhaps only in the area of history of technology is gender a topical issue.[2]

'The economic history of women is a neglected field', wrote Richards in 1974, in the conclusion to an article about the patterns of women's employment in the industrial revolution.[3] Is this still true? Research and writing from a number of quarters has certainly been growing over the last 20 years. Awareness of the importance of gender is an increasingly important part of many economic historians' work. In a sense, however, the ingredients have been collected but the cake has yet to be mixed. Recovery of 'invisible women' has dominated the agenda. The paucity of sources is a problem, yet many new sources and fresh approaches to them have appeared over the last two decades. It is when synthesis takes place that debate is engendered. We are moving to an 'add and stir' stage in the process, with potentially delicious results.

Much of the research carried out on this subject falls into a broad 'social history' category and economic historians are only just beginning to reap the benefits of this. Social history has come of age in the past 20 years, adding vastly greater sophistication to the analysis of social categories. In some areas of history, gender is taken as a point of departure with enormous explanatory and interpretative potential. In the older, and now relatively

Maxine Berg, Amy Louise Erickson, Pat Hudson, and Christine MacLeod made helpful comments on an earlier version of this article. Eleanor Gordon provided me with references for Scotland.

more traditional discipline of economic history, recent methodological developments have been less conducive to including women. Over the last 20 years the major change in this field has been the application of fresh approaches to quantification.

Statistical analysis is an entirely justifiable means of extending our historical knowledge. But great care is required in the use of the data. This is particularly true of the labour market where the data have too often left out a major part of the labour force – women.[4] The historian's problems with data are well known. For example, investigation of census material has now revealed it to be a poor tool for use in analysing Victorian women's employment participation.[5] Higgs has demonstrated that, setting aside problems created by seasonality and the prejudices of enumerators, the imperative of the early national censuses was a picture of medical and public health aspects of the workforce; censuses were in no sense an employment record and are thus quite unreliable for an assessment of the amount and timing of work women were doing, particularly for agricultural work. Indeed this has been proved by Miller who found that there was no comparison between records of women workers' activities in farm accounts and their occupational designation in the censuses of late nineteenth-century Gloucestershire.[6]

Much recent historiography points to women's role as an adaptable part of the labour force – something crucial to an industrializing nation yet difficult to quantify or even 'catch' in documents. Berg has argued that one major role of women in the industrial revolution was their ability to take up reorganized trades which otherwise would have been hidebound by old artisan traditions.[7] How did the existence of a group with the capacity to grease the wheels of the labour market affect the shaping of economic processes? Such adaptability makes women's work even less amenable to quantification. This apart, the history of women's employment throws up characteristics which are difficult to measure – built-in customary and ideological factors affecting their work patterns – for which quantitative methods may be less suited.

Further, we need to write the history of economies with an appreciation that categories are not in themselves neutral. It is not only statistics that contain their own hidden meanings. As Scott has written, using the French employment record, the 1848 Statistique de l'industrie, taking a document at face value,

> perpetuates a certain vision of the economy and of statistical science as an essentially objective enterprise; it makes the historian an unwitting party to the politics of another age. An alternative approach situates any document in its discursive context and reads it not as a reflection of some external reality but as an integral part of that reality, as a contribution to the definition or elaboration of meaning, to the creation

of social relationships, economic institutions, and political structures. Such an approach demands that the historian question the terms in which any document presents itself and thus ask how it contributes to constructing the reality of the past.[8]

In raising these points, Scott's entreaty is for us to be better historians. However, as yet women's history and economic history seem to be following separate paths which are only beginning to intersect. How might they usefully come together? My operating premise is that there are vast unrealized possibilities in this area. Recent research on women's employment, for example, throws up some puzzles for conventional economic analysis. According to Berg, women in certain areas of the industrial revolution economy could be paid wages in excess of what the supply and demand conditions would predict,[9] perhaps suggesting some limitations to the application of neo-classical economic theory.

Yet writing gender into the analysis raises its own problems. The work done on the economic history of women suggests that marxist-feminist explanations of subordination to patriarchy are too sweeping. An increasing amount of literature has recently employed the idea that notions of 'separate spheres' subjected women to a 'domestic ideology' in the industrializing era.[10] A critique of this literature has now been instigated by Vickery; indeed this may represent the first significant departure from a unified feminist project of women's history. Associated with theories about either patriarchy or other ideological formulations are notions of continuity or change.[11] Indeed ideas of continuity or change underlie much of the literature which is concerned with women's economic history. Both tend to suggest women's impotency to deal with their situations; continuity implying that the forces of subordination are too powerful to be overturned, whereas change is unilinear – the position of women is seen as worsening as a result of industrialization, for example.

In counteracting the 'separate spheres' theory, Vickery dispels the view that change is necessarily important when analysing women's history. Indeed she believes that we must resist theories which suggest that capitalism resulted in women's marginalization and, rather, stress the broadly unchanging nature of women's working lives through time. Bennett has also argued that continuity is the prevailing picture when women's employment is placed in a very long-term perspective. In a seminal review article, Bennett argued for the history of women's work as a 'history that stands still'.[12] She believes that the circumstances of women's employment were little changed in modern from medieval times. However, recent scholarship (undertaken in the last 20 years) on women's economic history suggests that neither change nor continuity is satisfactory as either an explanatory or a descriptive scheme.

The main work in women's economic history has been on women's employment and this has been reinforced by more recent attention to women's demography, as well as their circumstances regarding property and consumption. In fact, these subjects need to be considered in conjunction with employment to help to broaden an undue emphasis on women's market-oriented involvement. Women's access to economic resources did not always readily translate into wages. Indeed, controlling resources can be concerned with budgeting, looking after children or the sick, or managing a piece of land. None of these is readily measurable in terms of economic indicators. Instead we need a much broader definition of 'employment' for women than for men. The problem with using either 'continuity' or 'change' to explain the history of women's employment is the nebulous character of the benchmarks for comparison. How can we compare adequately the value of all the varying constituents of women's lives in 1700 with those in 1900?

Perspectives of 'continuity' or 'change' need *la longue durée*. However, despite Bennett's cue, recent scholarship has been patchy. Far more new research has appeared on women's employment in the medieval than in the early modern period. Syntheses by Bennett and Goldberg have been supported by a number of case studies, which reflected wider issues raised in European literature.[13] By contrast, the early modern period is still dominated by Clark's *Working life of women in the seventeenth century*, published in 1919.[14] In the introduction to a new edition, Erickson has shown how scholarship has developed since Clark wrote, but highlights the lacunae where no new research has been carried out.[15] Attempts to consider the amount of work, type of work, and sexual division of labour in the industrial revolution founder on this problem of lack of information regarding the early modern period.

I

Research in the last 20 years has tended to stress that women's position has been contingent on economic forces, thus setting up a 'change' framework. Turning first to agriculture, the view of the change in women's employment from the early modern to the modern period which is now firmly installed in conventional accounts of economic and social history is based on the work of Snell.[16] He argues that the eighteenth century saw an increase in the sexual specialization of agricultural work. Women's role in the south-east of England, which concentrated largely on arable farming, became more confined and less well paid as the century advanced. From a situation with a reasonably equitable sharing of tasks, Snell argued, drawing on Robert's work, that women were excluded from harvest technology when farmers began to make more use of scythes than sickles.[17] The result was that by the middle of the nineteenth century, women had little role in agriculture, although the pastoral west presented a different case due to female work opportunities in dairying, usually on smaller farms which used family labour.[18] Despite their widespread acceptance, these views cannot go without question. First, there is no certain case for the equitable sharing of household tasks by men and women in the early modern economy.[19] Secondly, the mid nineteenth-century picture is questionable if we consider Higg's reinterpretation of the census figures. Thirdly, although Snell's arguments concern farm servants, they have been used to describe work patterns of the entire female agricultural workforce. There are other discrepancies here. For example, the reluctance of women to work in the harvest may be associated with the simultaneous activity of gleaning: King has produced evidence of the importance of this to the labouring family's budget.[20] Allen also departs from Snell in considering prosperity in the dairying sector. He argues that this saw a process of deskilling: 'Yeomen's wives had run dairies and performed many tasks on the farm; by the nineteenth century they had no trade'.[21] De Vries, on the other hand, suggests that a move to market-oriented arable would actually increase women's and children's work in weeding, pruning, and labour-intensive picking of crops.[22]

All these approaches suffer from a lack of detailed case studies to back them up. We still need more specific studies of women's employment in different areas. We have not yet progressed from a situation where in the early 1970s Richards had to deal 'mainly in aggregates in a subject where even local studies are sparse'.[23] Allen, for example, attempts to construct wage data for eighteenth-century women workers in straw-plaiting and lace-making using scarcely a handful of reference points derived from Pinchbeck and contemporary writers. For agricultural workers themselves a wealth of detail can be gathered in local archives using household and farm accounts.[24] It is necessary to build up a corrective picture at the local level by developing new sources, in which, as far as is possible, we can discover the feminine aspect. What women actually did needs to be established from the bottom up, paying attention to localized differences and to such factors as seasonal change, age-specificity, and marital status. Going beyond the locally constructed case study, the research must be placed in a comparative framework.[25] My own research on Essex indicates that while women are generally absent from harvest operations from the early modern through to the modern era, they disappear from some sectors but find more work in others. In other words, both continuity and change are applicable to different groups of women, yet the usefulness of these terms as descriptions of what is happening to women in general is limited.[26]

A key project of future studies should be examination of the relationship between women's involvement in agricultural and industrial sectors of the economy and whether they shifted their labour between the two. The work of Allen and of de Vries is important here. This may also be a way of breathing some life into the increasingly sterile 'proto-industry debate'. It has the potential to be the most significant area of economic history to highlight women's work in the eighteenth century and earlier. As a cheap and abundant source of labour, women were the obvious resort for those establishing 'industries in the countryside'. Theoretical work such as that of Tilly and Scott on women's employment and the family economy is now classic.[27] However, with the exception of Levine's work on demography,[28] scholars have produced few local studies stressing women's role in British proto-industrial manufacture as Gullickson has done for Auffay in France and Ogilvie for Württemberg in Germany.[29] In Britain women remain marginal and functional even in this debate. A recent special issue of *Continuity and Change* devoted to 'Proto-industrialization in Europe' gave short shrift to women.[30]

However, de Vries has developed the concept of a demand-driven 'industrious revolution' taking place in regions all over Europe in the period 1500 to 1800.[31] This preceded the more conventional supply-driven industrial revolution. The model suggests that work effort was intensified by the use of more child and female labour. The increased consumer demand was also primarily female. De Vries's arguments place women in a far more central position in economic development and are a powerful suggestion that women's work in manufactures and in agriculture cannot be viewed separately. Yet, Allen's argument, based largely on evidence from the English south midlands, indicates little connection between the industrial and agricultural revolutions. Allen argues that a shift to large arable farms in the eighteenth century changed the sex balance of rural employment towards men. He finds that proto-industry failed to absorb much of the surplus labour, and that 'There can be little doubt that the employment opportunities of women were brighter in 1676 than in 1831.'[32] Humphries's argument that access to commons, which provided much women's work, declined in the eighteenth century, thus aiding proletarianization, supports Allen's case.[33] However, the dynamic yeoman farms of the seventeenth century, which Allen describes, fit de Vries's model.

Both de Vries's and Allen's views are complex and controversial, and provide differing echoes of the effect of economic change on women. Past economies experienced uneven development and some different areas of expansion and retraction apply. As a result, there were growth areas such as agricultural services,[34] along with highly paid women's work in certain new areas such as the potteries and metalware,[35] at the same time as some of the poorest strata fell victim to a labour surplus economy and the meanest forms of servicing, such as laundering or charring, often for people just above them in wealth. Specialization created opportunities for some women while denying them to others.

II

By reaching back in time from the industrial revolution, we gain little support for linear explanations, regardless of the direction they take. Much of the literature on women's employment in the industrial revolution has been concerned with either the direction of change or the underlying continuities. The classic text on women's role in the industrial revolution, Pinchbeck's *Women workers*, was written in 1930 and badly needs a successor. Pinchbeck drew largely on national sources – nineteenth-century Parliamentary Papers and contemporary writers – to form a picture of women's work in agriculture, trade and industry, and in various businesses. She put together a vast amount of information to argue that women's position was, in the long term, improved by industrialization, which, by taking women outside the home, 'resulted in better conditions, a greater variety of openings and an improved status'. This view has not stood the test of time. It is indicative that the areas of women's work Pinchbeck chose *not* to detail, 'Domestic servants, and such workers as dressmakers, milliners, slop sewers, frame-work knitters and boot and shoe makers, whose industries continued without alteration until later in the nineteenth century', have provided the focus of much feminist scholarship during the last 20 years.[36]

The overall effects of industrialization on women in terms of wages, conditions, and opportunities remain an open question. They are the focus for most of the 'change' narratives. Two historians who broached the subject in 1974, Richards and McKendrick, came to differing conclusions.[37] Richards, heavily reliant on the censuses, argued that a diminution in women's opportunities during the industrial revolution produced a U-shaped curve of employment participation. Decline through the loss of traditional employment in manual sectors outweighed the gain from new factories. McKendrick, whose concern was with consumption, based his argument on the assumption of increasing opportunities for women in factories and in service combined with rising wages; this put them in a position to consume more goods. Twenty years on, the position is little clearer. Whereas Berg and Hudson see industrialization as bringing growing opportunities for women's employment, Humphries is inclined to see more doors closing than opening.[38] In fact, the historical project has often considered the amount of women's employment as part of a larger debate about the standard of living rather than focusing directly on employment.[39] Most recently, Nicholas and Oxley have produced new evidence, on the height of female convicts, to support the underlying assumption that industrialization limited women's living standards.[40]

Collating heights, like assimilating wage data – whether from Snell's settlement examinations or in Horrell and Humphries's new research based on household budgets – provides us with a quantifiable measure of women's experience in industrialization, which is all too elusive in national statistics.[41] It does not prevent us from questioning the representativeness of these statistics, however. Humphries argues that the low earnings of women during the industrializing time period, and the decline of spinning and other rural industries, saw their increasing marginalization in the labour market and argues for a somewhat earlier domesticity for working-class women than has so far been suggested by those who have looked at the 'family wage'. The problem here is the extent to which low and falling wages suggest falling work opportunities in industrialization when cheap labour was of the essence. Indeed, Humphries and Horrell's own figures show the importance of outwork, particularly in the 1820s and 1830s. Far from some rural industries such as lace, silk, and straw-plait contracting at this time, they were undergoing expansion which, although sometimes seasonal, could be vigorous. Humphries's analysis is also concerned with the labour force participation of wives, whereas nineteenth-century employers looked towards young single women as their primary labour force, as classic texts on the industrial revolution have emphasized. Most of the evidence we have suggests that relative to women's income, children's earnings rose in early industrialization. Again, the extent to which these earnings represent economic demand is questionable.

Humphries and Horrell's family budgets certainly do point to occupational and regional differences. Research on women's work in industry during the industrial revolution has been built up from local case studies, and some syntheses have appeared.[42] Women's employment in factories has been reassessed by marxist-feminist historians: rather than offering 'independence', it is seen as putting women into patriarchical situations little different from those preceding factory employment, along with the strengthening of the sexual division of labour.[43] Far more manufacture took place as outwork rather than inside factories, offering work conditions which, it has been argued, were little changed with industrialization. The continuity implicit here does not mean that there is nothing to say. Schwarz, using insurance records, has recently presented new information about women's employment in London. He has shown that women were overwhelmingly concentrated in service and needlework trades, a situation which does not change in the industrial revolution, and has pointed out the extent to which the London labour market was both casual and acutely seasonal.[44]

We are presented with a major problem for examining patterns of both agricultural and industrial employment in our lack of knowledge about domestic service in the period 1750–1850. In contrast to France, few studies have been addressed to this problem in Britain.[45] Yet with an increasing middle-class population we would imagine that service opportunities expanded greatly. Since it concerns the most numerically significant sector of female employment in the industrial revolution era, this problem urgently needs attention. Some historians have characterized service as 'disguised unemployment'; is this accurate or does it contain unwarranted conceptions of surplus women, side-stepping rather than being integral to the industrialization process? A chronologically patchy yet growing literature on prostitution is connected with the literature on service since prostitution was often also a lifecycle stage and could be either an alternative or a successor to service.[46]

III

Further information can be fed into these debates from recent research on women in medical 'professions', and work in demography and the history of childhood. Developments in the relatively new field of social history of medicine have produced research on areas of women's work such as nursing, midwifery, and in other forms of healing, but also in women's work in the care and upbringing of their own and other people's children.[47] Wet-nursing, for example, was a well-paid employment for women until the early nineteenth century.[48] In the context of an eighteenth-century 'medical marketplace' these areas deserve greater recognition.

Demography is one field of quantification which has enlightened more than it has obscured, as Hufton and Zemon Davis pointed out in early assessments of women's history.[49] Demography by its very nature is concerned with the behaviour of both sexes and has produced a lifecycle picture for women.[50] The average age at which women marry and their likelihood of remaining single is of crucial importance in considering their working lives, especially as their demographic behaviour was more variable than men's. How many children women might have, the likelihood of their survival, the age at which they might leave home, and the number of years a woman might live after childbearing are also at issue.[51] However, the failure to link demographic patterns and socio-economic aspects of past communities remains quite striking. The emphasis within demography has been on 'household' or 'family', thus masking differences within these groups. Yet while the history of the family and women's history may be related and mutually supportive, they are not identical historical pursuits with the same interests.

The contribution of historians of childhood in the industrial revolution to debates which look at women's employment should not be overlooked, since women's and children's employment opportunities were certainly related. Cunningham has recently argued that children's employment opportunities may have been insufficient prior to industrialization.[52] He approaches the question from a different angle to Nardinelli, who stresses the economic value of children in industrialization compared with their pre-industrial counterparts.[53]

IV

Property and consumption – neither an entirely new field – currently attract most attention from economic historians of women in the industrial revolution. Perhaps it is not coincidental that such concerns should grow out of the 1980s. Controversially, Erickson argues that in the early modern period ordinary women, married or unmarried, controlled property on a scale which has not hitherto been recognized and that this had far-reaching effects on many aspects of life, such as the upbringing of children.[54] Legal loopholes, which allowed this, declined over the course of the eighteenth century. Berg examined women's property holding in the rising towns of Birmingham and Sheffield in the early nineteenth century,[55] and also found that women controlled far more property than the historical analysis to date would have suggested. Berg also stresses women's role as trust-holders which could have been a family business strategy.

The latest work on property, then, while not arguing along completely identical tracks, reinterprets the position of women with regard to property law to give them far more economic influence. Recent research on women and consumption in the eighteenth century also suggests that they were active decision makers. Both Vickery, in her study of a Lancashire woman and the control of her household, and Weatherill, in an analysis of women's possessions in probate inventories, indicate that women's spending decisions must be viewed as historically important factors.[56] This again lends support to de Vries's 'industrious revolution'.

V

Bennett has recently argued that the enduring patterns of women's subordination across centuries force us to look beyond economic structures.[57] We certainly must incorporate social, cultural, and ideological factors into the economic history of women in more constructive ways. By considering other influences on the supply and demand curves for women's labour we may gain some insight into why the wage levels are unpredictable. Evidence is emerging that women could, in certain contexts, be independent economic agents. Humphries argues that 'women's subordination seems to have been interwoven with their economic activities so that it moulded the economic self and not simply the terms and conditions under which women took part'.[58] At the same time, thought should be given to the ways in which the strands might or might not be synthesized into gender history, and how the results can be integrated into mainstream economic history. Rethinking the constraints imposed by 'continuity' or 'change' narratives is essential to this.

In 1974, Richards argued that with the notable exception of Pinchbeck, 'economic historians have not felt justified in discussing the work of women as an analytically significant element in the process of economic growth'.[59] In 1995 this situation *has* changed. Women's position as a major part of the workforce of the industrial revolution is beginning to be reinforced, particularly by due recognition of their role as pre-industrial producers, as property holders, and as consumers. It is clear that in the central question for economic historians of the industrial revolution era – how resources kept ahead of population in an industrializing country – we cannot afford to ignore women. As de Vries put it, 'The household strategies that fostered the industrious revolution placed the wife in a strategic position, located as it were, at the intersection of the household's three functions: reproduction, production and consumption.'[60] Single women and widows were just as important. Reproduction is essentially woman-centred; so – we see from increasing amounts of research – are production and consumption.

Immense strides have been made in the last 20 years in establishing women's economic importance in the past. We must now rewrite economic history texts to reflect a different set of priorities. In doing so we no longer need to be hampered by overarching narratives of 'continuity' versus 'change'. Both are keeping women in a contingent position. In a multi-faceted economy like that of the eighteenth and nineteenth centuries, some women's lives saw continuities, others changed. What must concern us now is understanding these individual experiences within the broad framework of the economic past. In doing so we will certainly learn more about the complex characteristics of the economies and societies in which women – and men – lived and worked.

Notes

1 Roper and Tosh, *Manful assertions.*
2 Cockburn, 'Material of male power;' Cockburn, *Brothers*; Freifeld, 'Technological change'; Rose, 'Gender antagonism'; Rose, *Limited livelihoods.*
3 Richards, 'Women in the British economy', p. 356.
4 For example, Lindert and Williamson, 'English workers' living standards'.
5 Higgs, 'Occupational censuses'; Higgs, 'Women, occupations and work'; Hill, 'Women, work and the census'. See also Williams and Jones, 'Women at work'.
6 Miller, 'Hidden workforce'.
7 Berg, 'What difference did women's work make?'
8 Scott, *Gender and the politics of history*, pp. 137–8.
9 Berg, 'What difference did women's work make?', pp. 32–3.
10 Davidoff and Hall, *Family fortunes*; Hall, *White, male and middle class.* Additionally Davidoff, 'Role of gender'; Davidoff, 'Separation of home and work?'; Rose, 'Gender at work'; Rose, *Limited livelihoods.* For some different views see Rendall, *Origins of modern feminism.*
11 Vickery, 'Golden age'. This debate has surfaced recently in Hill, 'Women's history' and Bennett, 'Women's history'. Hill stresses the discontinuity of capitalism while Bennett affirms the endurance of patriarchy.
12 Bennett, 'History that stands still'.
13 Bennett, 'Medieval women, modern women'; Bennett, *Women in the medieval English countryside*; Goldberg, *Women, work and lifecycle.* The literature on women and work in medieval England is now extensive. Apart from the classic Power,

Medieval women, see Bennett, 'Public power and authority'; Bennett, 'Village ale-wife'; Goldberg, 'Women's work, women's role'; Goldberg, ed., *Woman is a worthy wight*; Hanawalt, 'Peasant women's contribution'; Hilton, 'Women traders'; Hutton, 'Women in fourteenth-century Shrewsbury'; Kowaleski, 'Women's work'; Kowaleski and Bennett, 'Crafts, gilds'; Lacey, 'Women and work'; Middleton, 'Familiar fate'; Penn, 'Female wage earners'.

14 Clark, *Working life of women.*

15 For contributions in this area see Amussen, *Ordered society*; Cahn, *Industry of devotion*; Earle, 'Female labour market'; Prior, 'Women in the urban economy'; Rappaport, *Worlds within worlds*, pp. 36–42; Roberts, 'Words'; Roberts, 'Women and work'; Thwaites, 'Women in the marketplace'; Wright, 'Churmaids'; Wright, 'Holding up'. On Scotland see Houston, 'Women in the economy'. For Ireland, MacCurtain and O'Dowd, eds., *Women in the early modern Ireland*. A recent addition is Laurence, *Women in England*.

16 Snell, *Annals*, pp. 15–66; Ankarloo, 'Agriculture', for an earlier and broader conception.

17 Roberts, 'Sickles and scythes'.

18 See for example the different picture given by Hassell-Smith, 'Labourers'.

19 See also Valenze, 'Art of women'.

20 King, 'Customary rights'.

21 Allen, *Enclosure*, p. 289.

22 Richards, 'Women', p. 338.

23 de Vries, 'Between purchasing power'.

24 Gilboy, 'Labour at Thornbough'; Hassell-Smith, 'Labourers'; Shammas, 'The world women knew'; Sharpe, 'Time and wages'.

25 For example, by the late nineteenth century female agricultural labour was far more common in Scotland and Ireland than in England. See Morgan, 'Agricultural wage rates'; Hostettler, 'Gourlay Steell'; Devine, 'Women workers'. On Ireland, see Bourke, 'Women and poultry'; Bourke, 'Dairywomen'; Bourke, *Husbandry to housewifery*.

26 Sharpe, *Adapting to capitalism.*

27 Tilly and Scott, *Women, work and family*; see also Rose, 'Proto-industry'; Hudson and Lee, *Women's work and the family economy*, pp. 14–19.

28 Levine, *Family formation.*

29 Gullickson, *Spinners and weavers*; Ogilvie, 'Women and proto-industrialisation'.

30 *Cont. & Change*, 8:2 (1993).

31 de Vries, 'Between purchasing power', p. 119.

32 Allen, 'Growth of labor productivity'; Allen, *Enclosure*, p. 251.

33 Humphries, 'Enclosures'.

34 Wrigley, 'Urban growth and agricultural change'.

35 Berg, 'What difference did women's work make?'

36 Pinchbeck, *Women workers*, p. 4. An earlier, much less illustrious text was Tickner, *Women in English economic history.*

37 Richards, 'Women in the British economy'; McKendrick, 'Home demand'.

38 Berg, 'What difference did women's work make?'; Berg and Hudson, 'Rehabilitating'; Humphries, 'Lurking'. As Thomas, 'Women and capitalism', has shown, the aims of enquiring into the connections between women's employment and industrialization have not simply been historical. They have been concerned with a political agenda regarding the effect of industrial development in developing countries.

39 Horrell and Humphries, 'Old questions'; Snell, *Annals*, pp. 15–66.

40 Nicholas and Oxley, 'Living standards'.

41 The literature on nineteenth-century industrial work for women is now prodigious. See, for example, Alexander, 'Women's work'; Humphries, 'Protective legislation'; Humphries, 'The most free from objection'; John, *By the sweat of their brow*; Jordan, 'Exclusion'; Malcolmson, *English laundresses*; Morgan, 'Women, work'; Schmiechen, *Sweated industries*; Taylor, *Eve and the new Jerusalem*; Valverde, 'Giving the female'. On office work, Silverstone, 'Office work'; Thane, ' "Herstory" in accounting'. Relevant essays are found in John, ed., *Unequal opportunities*; Lewis, ed., *Labour and love*. New studies of Welsh, Scottish, and Irish women's work have recently been

completed.. See Gordon, *Women and the labour movement*; Gordon and Breitenbach, *The world is ill-divided*; Gordon and Breitenbach, *Out of bounds*; Reynolds; *Britannica's typesetters*. On Wales see essays in John, ed., *Our mother's land*. On Ireland, Brenda Collins has been working on women and the textile industry: see, for example, Collins, 'Sewing and social structure'; Daly, 'Women in the Irish workforce'; also the essays collected in Luddy and Murphy, eds., *Women surviving*.

42 For example, Alexander, Hostettler, and Davin, 'Labouring women'; Berg, 'Women's work'; Berg, *Age of manufactures*; Lewis, *Women in England*; Rendall, *Women in an industrialising society*; Roberts, *Women's work*; for Scotland, Gordon, 'Women's sphere'.

43 Bradley, *Men's work, women's work*; Lown, *Women and industrialisation*; Phillips and Taylor, 'Sex and skill'.

44 Schwarz, *London in the age of industrialisation*.

45 See Davidoff, 'Mastered'; McBride, *Domestic revolution*; Horn, *Victorian servant*. For France: Maza, *Servants and masters*; Fairchilds, *Domestic enemies*. On early modern English servants see Holmes, 'Domestic service in Yorkshire', and work in progress by Tim Meldrum.

46 Finnegan, *Poverty and prostitution*; Walkowitz, *Prostitution*; Mahood, *Magdalenes*; Littlewood and Mahood, 'Prostitutes'; Luddy, 'Prostitution and rescue work'.

47 Davies, ed., *Rewriting nursing history*; Dingwall, Rafferty, and Webster, eds., *Social history of nursing*; Donnison, *Midwives and medical men*; Forbes, 'Regulation of English midwives'; Marland, ed., *Art of midwifery*; Moscucci, *Science of woman*; Pelling and Webster, 'Medical practitioners'; Pelling, 'Occupational diversity'; Pelling, *Strength of the opposition*; Pelling, *Poverty, health and urban society*; Schnorrenberg, 'Is childbirth any place for a woman?'; Witz, *Professions and patriarchy*; Wyman, 'Surgeoness'.

48 Fildes, *Breasts, bottles and babies*; Fildes, *Wet nursing*; Maclaren, 'Nature's contraceptive'; Newall, 'Wet-nursing'.

49 Hufton, 'What is women's history?'; also Zemon Davis, 'Women's history in transition'.

50 Anderson, 'Emergence of the modern lifecycle'.

51 For literature relating to women and demography, see Hill, 'Marriage age of women'; Hufton, 'Women without men'; Sharpe, 'Literally spinsters'; Shorter, 'Female emancipation' and rejoinder by Tilly, Scott, and Cohen, 'Women's work and European fertility'; Wall, 'Women alone'.

52 Cunningham, 'Employment and unemployment'; Cunningham, *Children of the poor*.

53 Nardinelli, *Child labor*; also Bolin-Hort, *Work, family and the state*.

54 Erickson, *Women and property*; Erickson, 'Common law'; Holderness, 'Widows in preindustrial society'; Staves, *Married women's separate property*; Todd, 'Freebench'; Todd, 'Remarrying widow'; on the nineteenth century, Holcombe, *Wives and property*.

55 Berg, 'Women's property'.

56 Vickery, 'Women and the world of goods'; Weatherill, 'A possession'. Earlier work on consumption was carried out by Thirsk, 'Fantastical folly of fashion'. Lemire, *Fashion's favourite*, examines women both as consumers and as vendors of secondhand clothing.

57 Bennett, 'Medieval women'; Bennett, 'Misogyny'.

58 Humphries, 'Lurking', p. 32.

59 Richards, 'Women', p. 338.

60 de Vries, 'Between purchasing power', p. 119.

References

Alexander, S., 'Women's work in early nineteenth-century London', in A. Oakley and J. Mitchell, eds., *The rights and wrongs of women* (1976), pp. 59–111.

Alexander, S., Hostettler, E., and Davin, A., 'Labouring women: a reply to Eric Hobsbawm', *Hist. Workshop*, 18 (1979), pp. 174–82.

Allen, R. C., 'The growth of labor productivity in early modern English agriculture', *Exp. Econ. Hist.*, 25 (1988), pp. 117–46.

Allen, R. C., *Enclosure and the yeoman* (Oxford, 1992).

Amussen, S., *An ordered society: gender and class in early modern England* (Oxford, 1988).

Anderson, M., 'The emergence of the modern lifecycle in Britain', *Soc. Hist.*, 10 (1985), pp. 69–87.

Ankarloo, B., 'Agriculture and women's work: directions of change in the west, 1700–1900', *J. Fam. Hist.*, 4 (1979), pp. 111–20.

Bennett, J. M., 'The village ale-wife: women and brewing in fourteenth-century England', in B. A. Hanawalt, ed., *Women and work in pre-industrial Europe* (Bloomington, 1986), pp. 20–36.

Bennett, J. M., *Women in the medieval English countryside: gender and household in Brigstock before the plague* (Oxford, 1987).

Bennett, J. M., 'History that stands still: women's work in the European past', *Fem. Stud.*, 14 (1988), pp. 269–83.

Bennett, J. M., 'Public power and authority in the medieval English countryside', in M. Erler and M. Kowaleski, eds., *Women and power in the middle ages* (Athens, Ga., 1988), pp. 18–36.

Bennett, J. M., 'Misogyny, popular culture and women's work', *Hist. Workshop*, 31 (1991), pp. 166–88.

Bennett, J. M., 'Medieval women, modern women: across the great divide', in D. Aers, ed., *Culture and history, 1350–1600: essays on English communities, identity and writing* (1992), pp. 147–75.

Bennett, J., 'Women's history: a study in continuity and change', *Women's Hist. Rev.*, 2 (1993), pp. 173–84.

Berg, M., *The age of manufactures, 1700–1820* (1985).

Berg, M., 'Women's work, mechanization and the early phases of industrialisation in England', in P. Joyce, ed., *The historical meanings of work* (Cambridge, 1987), pp. 94–98, reprinted in R. E. Pahl, ed., *On work* (Oxford, 1988), pp. 61–94.

Berg, M., 'What difference did women's work make to the industrial revolution?', *Hist. Workshop*, 35 (1993), pp. 22–44.

Berg, M., 'Women's property and the industrial revolution', *J. Interdisc. Hist.*, XXIV (1993), pp. 223–50.

Berg, M. and Hudson, P., 'Rehabilitating the industrial revolution', *Econ. Hist. Rev.*, XLV (1992), pp. 24–50.

Bolin-Hort, P., *Work, family and the state: child labour and the organisation of production in the British cotton industry, 1780–1920* (Lund, 1989).

Bourke, J., 'Women and poultry in Ireland', *Irish Hist. Stud.*, XXV (1987), pp. 293–310.

Bourke, J., 'Dairywomen and affectionate wives: women in the Irish dairy industry', *Agric. Hist. Rev.*, 38 (1990), pp. 149–64.

Bourke, J., *Husbandry to housewifery: women, economic change and housework in Ireland, 1890–1914* (Oxford, 1993).

Bradley, H., *Men's work, women's work* (Oxford, 1989).

Cahn, S., *Industry of devotion: the transformation of women's work in England, 1500–1660* (New York, 1987).

Clark, A., *Working life of women in the seventeenth century* (1919; 3rd edn., 1992, intro. A. L. Erickson).

Cockburn, C., 'The material of male power', *Feminist Rev.*, 6 (1981), pp. 41–58.

Cockburn, C., *Brothers: male dominance and technological change* (1983).

Collins, B., 'Sewing and social structure: the flowerers of Scotland and Ireland', in R. Mitchison and P. Roebuck, eds., *Economy and society in Scotland and Ireland, 1500–1939* (Edinburgh, 1988), pp. 242–54.

Cunningham, H., 'The employment and unemployment of children in England, *c.* 1680–1851', *P. & P.*, 126 (1990), pp. 115–50.

Cunningham, H., *The children of the poor: representations of childhood since the seventeenth century* (Oxford, 1991).

Daly, M., 'Women in the Irish workforce from pre-industrial to modern times', *Saothar*, 7 (1981), pp. 74–82.

Davidoff, L., 'Mastered for life: servant and wife in Victorian and Edwardian England', *J. Soc. Hist.*, 7 (1974), pp. 406–28.

Davidoff, L., 'The separation of home and work? Landladies and lodgers in nineteenth- and twentieth-century England', in S. Burman, ed., *Fit work for women* (1979), pp. 64–97.

Davidoff, L., 'The role of gender in "the first industrial nation": agriculture in England, 1780–1850', in R. Crompton and M. Mann, ed., *Gender and stratification* (Cambridge, 1986), pp. 190–213.

Davidoff, L. and Hall, C., *Family fortunes: men and women of the English middle class, 1780–1850* (1987).

Davies, C., ed., *Rewriting nursing history* (1980).

Devine, T. M., 'Women workers, 1850–1914', in Devine, ed., *Farm servants and labour in lowland Scotland* (Edinburgh, 1984), pp. 98–123.

Dingwall, R., Rafferty, A. M., and Webster, C., eds., *An introduction to the social history of nursing* (1988).

Donnison, J., *Midwives and medical men: a history of the struggle for control of childbirth* (1988).

Earle, P., 'The female labour market in London in the late seventeenth and early eighteenth centuries', *Econ. Hist. Rev.*, 2nd ser., XLII (1989), pp. 328–53.

Erickson, A. L., 'Common law versus common practice: the use of marriage settlements in early modern England', *Econ. Hist. Rev.*, 2nd ser., XLIII (1990), pp. 21–39.

Erickson, A. L., *Women and property in early modern England* (1993).

Fairchilds, C., *Domestic enemies: servants and their masters in old regime France* (Baltimore, 1984).

Fildes, V., *Breasts, bottles and babies* (Edinburgh, 1986).

Fildes, V., *Wet nursing: a history from antiquity to the present* (Oxford, 1988).

Finnegan, F., *Poverty and prostitution* (Cambridge, 1979).

Forbes, T. R., 'The regulation of English midwives in the sixteenth and seventeenth centuries', *Medic. Hist.*, 8 (1964), pp. 235–44.

Freifeld, M., 'Technological change and the "self-acting" mule: a study of skill and the sexual division of labour', *Soc. Hist.*, ii (1986), pp. 319–45.

Gilboy, E. W., 'Labour at Thornbough: an eighteenth-century estate', *Econ. Hist. Rev.*, III (1932), pp. 388–98.

Goldberg, P. J. P., 'Women's work, women's role in the late medieval north', in M. A. Hicks, ed. *Profit, piety and professions in late medieval England* (Gloucester, 1990), pp. 34–50.

Goldberg, P. J. P., *Women, work and lifecycle in a medieval economy* (Oxford, 1992).

Goldberg, P. J. P., ed., *Woman is a worthy wight: women in English society, c. 1200–1500* (Stroud, 1992).

Goodman, J. and Honeyman, K., 'Women's work, gender conflict and labour markets in Europe, 1500–1900', *Econ. Hist. Rev.*, XLIV (1991), pp. 608–28.

Gordon, E., 'Women's sphere', in W. H. Fraser and R. J. Morris, eds., *People and society in Scotland*, II: *1830–1914* (Edinburgh, 1990), pp. 206–35.

Gordon, E., *Women and the labour movement in Scotland, 1850–1914* (Oxford, 1991).

Gordon, E. and Breitenbach, E., *The world is ill-divided: women's work in Scotland in the nineteenth and early twentieth centuries* (Edinburgh, 1990).

Gordon, E. and Breitenbach, E., *Out of bounds: women in Scottish society, 1800–1945* (Edinburgh, 1992).

Gullickson, G. L., *Spinners and weavers of Auffay* (Cambridge, 1986).

Hall, C., *White, male and middle class: explorations in feminism and history* (Cambridge, 1992).

Hanawalt, B. A., 'Peasant women's contribution to the home economy in late medieval England', in Hanawalt, ed., *Women and work in pre-industrial Europe* (Bloomington, 1986), pp. 3–17.

Hassell-Smith, A., 'Labourers in late sixteenth-century England: a case study from north Norfolk', *Cont. & Change*, 4 (1989), pp. 11–52, 367–94.

Higgs, E., 'Women, occupations and work in the nineteenth-century censuses', *Hist. Workshop*, 23 (1987), pp. 59–80.

Higgs, E., 'Occupational censuses and the agricultural workforce in Victorian England', *Econ. Hist. Rev.*, XLVIII [(1995), pp. 706–16].

Hill, B., *Women, work and sexual politics in eighteenth-century England* (Oxford, 1989).

Hill, B., 'The marriage age of women and the demographers', *Hist. Workshop*, 28 (1989), pp. 129–47.

Hill, B., 'Women, work and the census: a problem for historians of women', *Hist. Workshop*, 35 (1993), pp. 78–94.

Hill, B., 'Women's history: a study in change, continuity or standing still?', *Women's Hist. Rev.*, 2 (1993), pp. 5–22.

Hilton, R. H., 'Women traders in medieval England', *Women's Stud.*, II (1984), pp. 139–55.

Holcombe, L., *Wives and property: reform of the married women's property law in nineteenth-century England* (Oxford, 1983).

Holderness, B. A., 'Widows in pre-industrial society; an essay upon their economic functions', in R. M. Smith, ed., *Land, kinship and lifecycle* (Cambridge, 1984), pp. 423–42.

Holmes, J., 'Domestic service in Yorkshire, 1650–1780' (unpub. D. Phil. thesis, Univ. of York, 1989).

Horn, P., *The rise and fall of the Victorian servant* (1975).

Horrell, S. and Humphries, J., 'Old questions, new data and alternative perspectives: the standard of living in the British industrial revolution', *J. Econ. Hist.*, LII (1992), pp. 849–80.

Horrell, S. and Humphries, J., 'Women's labour force participation and the transition to the male-breadwinner family, 1790–1865', *Econ. Hist. Rev.*, XLVIII (1995), pp. 89–117.

Hostettler, E., 'Gourlay Steell and the sexual division of labour', *Hist. Workshop*, 4 (1977), pp. 95–100.

Houston, R. A., 'Women in the economy and society of Scotland, 1500–1800', in R. A. Houston and I. D. Whyte, eds., *Scottish society, 1500–1800* (Cambridge, 1989), pp. 118–47.

Hudson, P. and Lee, W. R., eds., *Women's work and the family economy in historical perspective* (Manchester, 1990).

Hufton, O., 'Women without men: widows and spinsters in Britain and France in the eighteenth century', *J. Fam. Hist.*, 9 (1984), pp. 355–76.

Hufton, O., 'What is women's history?', in J. Gardiner, ed., *What is history today?* (Basingstoke, 1988), pp. 82–5.

Humphries, J., 'Protective legislation, the capitalist state and working-class men: the case of the 1842 Mines Regulation Act', *Fem. Rev.*, 7 (1981), pp. 1–32.

Humphries, J., 'The most free from objection . . .: the sexual division of labour and women's work in nineteenth-century England', *J. Econ. Hist.*, XLVII (1987), pp. 929–50.

Humphries, J., 'Enclosures, common rights and women: the proletarianization of families in the late eighteenth and early nineteenth centuries', *J. Econ. Hist.*, L (1990), pp. 17–42.

Humphries, J., 'Lurking in the wings . . . women in the historiography of the industrial revolution', *Bus. & Econ. Hist.*, 20 (1991), pp. 32–44.

Hutton, D., 'Women in fourteenth-century Shrewsbury', in L. Charles and L. Duffin, eds., *Women and work in pre-industrial England* (1985), pp. 83–99.

John A. V., *By the sweat of their brow: women workers at Victorian coal mines* (1980).

John A. V., ed., *Unequal opportunities: women's employment in England, 1800–1918* (Oxford, 1986).

John A. V., ed., *Our mother's land: chapters in Welsh women's history* (Cardiff, 1991).

Jordan, E., 'The exclusion of women from industry in nineteenth-century Britain', *Comp. Stud. Soc. Hist.*, 31 (1989), pp. 309–26.

King, P., 'Customary rights and women's earnings: the importance of gleaning to the rural labouring poor, 1750–1850', *Econ. Hist. Rev.*, XLIV (1991), pp. 461–76.

Kowaleski, M., 'Women's work in a market town: Exeter in the late fourteenth century', in B. A. Hanawalt, ed., *Women and work in pre-industrial Europe* (Bloomington, 1986), pp. 145–64.

Kowaleski, M. and Bennett, J. M., 'Crafts, gilds and women in the middle ages: fifty years after Marian K. Dale', *Signs*, 14 (1989), reprinted in J. M. Bennett, E. A. Clark, J. F. O'Barr, B. A. Wilen, and S. Westphal-Wihl, eds., *Sisters and workers in the middle ages* (Chicago, 1989), pp. 11–38.

Lacey, K. E., 'Women and work in fourteenth- and fifteenth-century London', in L. Charles and L. Duffin, eds., *Women and work in pre-industrial England* (1985), pp. 24–82.

Laurence, A., *Women in England, 1500–1760: a social history* (1994).

Lemire, B., *Fashion's favourite: the cotton trade and the consumer in Britain, 1660–1800* (Oxford, 1991).

Levine, D., *Family formation in an age of nascent capitalism* (New York, 1977).

Lewis, J., *Women in England, 1870–1950* (Brighton, 1984).

Lewis, J. ed., *Labour and love: women's experience of home and family, 1850–1940* (Oxford, 1986).

Lindert, P. H. and Williamson, J. G., 'English workers' living standards during the industrial revolution: a new look', *Econ. Hist. Rev.*, 2nd ser., XXVI (1983), pp. 1–25.

Littlewood, B. and Mahood, L., 'Prostitutes, magdalenes and wayward girls', *Gender & Hist.*, 3 (1991), pp. 160–75.

Lown, J., *Women and industrialisation: gender at work in nineteenth-century England* (Oxford, 1990).

Luddy, M., 'Prostitution and rescue work in nineteenth-century Ireland', in M. Luddy and C. Murphy, eds., *Women surviving: studies in Irish women's history in the nineteenth and twentieth centuries* (Dublin, 1989), pp. 51–84.

McBride, T. M., *The domestic revolution* (1976).

MacCurtain, M. and O'Dowd, M., eds., *Women in early modern Ireland* (Edinburgh, 1991).

McKendrick, N., 'Home demand and economic growth: a new view of the role of women and children in the industrial revolution', in McKendrick, ed., *Historical perspectives: studies in English thought and society* (1974), pp. 152–210.

Maclaren, D., 'Nature's contraceptive: wet nursing and prolonged lactation; the case of Chesham, Buckinghamshire, 1578–1601', *Medic. Hist.*, 23 (1979), pp. 427–41.

Mahood, L., *The magdalenes: prostitution in the nineteenth century* (1990).

Malcolmson, P., *English laundresses: a social history, 1850–1930* (Urbana, 1986).

Marland, H., ed., *The art of midwifery* (1993).

Maza, S. C., *Servants and masters in eighteenth-century France* (Princeton, 1983).

Middleton, C. 'The familiar fate of the famulae: gender divisions in the history of wage labour', in R. E. Pahl, ed., *On work* (Oxford, 1988), pp. 21–47.

Miller, C., 'The hidden workforce: female field workers in Gloucestershire, 1870–1901', *Southern Hist.*, 6 (1984), pp. 139–61.

Morgan, C. E., 'Women, work and consciousness in the mid nineteenth-century English cotton industry', *Soc. Hist.*, 17 (1992), pp. 23–41.

Morgan, V., 'Agricultural wage rates in late eighteenth-century Scotland', *Econ. Hist. Rev.*, 2nd ser., XXIV (1971), pp. 181–201.

Moscucci, O., *The science of woman* (Cambridge, 1990).

Nardinelli, C., *Child labor and the industrial revolution* (Bloomington, 1990).

Newall, F., 'Wet-nursing and childcare in Aldenham, Hertfordshire, 1596–1726: some evidence in the circumstances and effects of seventeenth-century childrearing practices', in V. Fildes, ed., *Women as mothers in pre-industrial England* (1990), pp. 122–38.

Nicholas, S. and Oxley, D., 'The living standards of women during the industrial revolution, 1795–1820', *Econ. Hist. Rev.*, XLVI (1993), pp. 723–49.

Ogilvie, S., 'Women and proto-industrialisation in a corporate society: Württemberg woollen weaving, 1590–1760', in P. Hudson and W. R. Lee, eds., *Women's work and the family economy in historical perspective* (Manchester, 1990), pp. 76–103.

Pelling, M., 'Occupational diversity: barbersurgeons and the trades of Norwich', *Bull. Hist. Medic.*, 56 (1982), pp. 484–511.

Pelling, M., *The strength of the opposition: the College of Physicians and unlicensed medical practice in early modern London* (Oxford, 1993).

Pelling, M., *Poverty, health and urban society in England, 1500–1700* (Harlow, forthcoming, 1995) [now entitled: *The Common Lot: Sickness, Medical Occupations and the Urban Poor in Early Modern England* (Harlow, 1998)].

Pelling, M. and Webster, C., 'Medical practitioners', in C. Webster, ed., *Health, medicine and mortality in the sixteenth century* (Cambridge, 1979), pp. 165–235.

Penn, S. A. C., 'Female wage earners in late fourteenth-century England', *Agric. Hist. Rev.*, (1987), pp. 1–14.

Pennington, S. and Westover, B., *A hidden workforce: homeworkers in England, 1850–1985* (1989).

Phillips, A. and Taylor, B., 'Sex and skill: towards a feminist economics', *Fem. Rev.*, 6 (1980), pp. 79–88.

Pinchbeck, I., *Women workers and the industrial revolution, 1750–1850* (1930, new edn. 1981).

Power, E., *Medieval women* (Cambridge, 1975).

Prior, M., 'Women in the urban economy: Oxford, 1500–1800', in Prior, ed., *Women in English society, 1500–1800* (1985), pp. 93–117.

Rappaport, S., *Worlds within worlds: structures of life in sixteenth-century London* (Cambridge, 1989).

Rendall, J., *The origins of modern feminism* (1985).

Rendall, J., *Women in an industrialising society: England, 1750–1880* (Oxford, 1990).

Reynolds, S., *Britannica's typesetters: women compositors in Edwardian Edinburgh* (Edinburgh, 1989).

Richards, E., 'Women in the British economy since about 1700', *Hist.*, LIX (1974), pp. 337–57.

Roberts, E., *Women's work, 1840–1940* (1988).

Roberts, M., 'Sickles and scythes: men's work and women's work at harvest time', *Hist. Workshop*, 7 (1979), pp. 3–28.

Roberts, M., ' "Words they are women, and deeds they are men": images of work and gender in early modern England', in L. Charles and L. Duffin, eds., *Women and work in pre-industrial England* (1985), pp. 122–80.

Roberts, M., 'Women and work in sixteenth-century English towns', in P. J. Corfield and D. Keene, eds., *Work in towns, 850–1850* (Leicester, 1990), pp. 86–102.

Roper, M. and Tosh, J., eds., *Manful assertions: masculinities in Britain since 1800* (1991).

Rose, S., 'Gender at work: sex, class and industrial capitalism', *Hist. Workshop*, 21 (1986), pp. 113–32.

Rose, S., 'Proto-industry, women's work and the household economy in the transition to industrial capitalism', *J. Fam. Hist.*, 13 (1988), pp. 181–93.

Rose, S., 'Gender antagonism and class conflict: exclusionary strategies of male trade unionists in nineteenth-century Britain', *Soc. Hist.*, 13 (1988), pp. 191–208.

Rose, S., *Limited livelihoods: gender and class in nineteenth-century England* (1992).

Schmiechen, J. A., *Sweated industries and sweated labor: the London clothing trades, 1860–1914* (Urbana, 1984).

Schnorrenberg, B. B., 'Is childbirth any place for a woman? The decline of the midwife in eighteenth-century England', *Stud. Eighteenth-Cent. Cult.*, 10 (1981), pp. 393–408.

Schwarz, L. D., *London in the age of industrialisation* (Cambridge, 1992).

Scott, J. W., *Gender and the politics of history* (New York, 1988).

Shammas, C., 'The world women knew: women workers in the north of England during the seventeenth century', in R. S. Dunn and M. M. Dunn, eds., *The world of William Penn* (Philadelphia, 1986), pp. 99–114.

Sharpe, P., 'Literally spinsters: a new interpretation of local economy and demography in Colyton in the seventeenth and eighteenth centuries', *Econ. Hist. Rev.*, XLIV (1991), pp. 46–65.

Sharpe, P., 'Time and wages of west country workfolks in the seventeenth and eighteenth centuries', *Loc. Pop. Stud.* [LV (1995), pp. 66–8].

Sharpe, P., *Adapting to capitalism: working women in the English economy, 1700–1850* (1996).

Shorter, E., 'Female emancipation, birth control and fertility in European history', *Amer. Hist. Rev.*, LXXVIII (1973), pp. 605–40.

Silverstone, R., 'Office work for women: an historical review', *Bus. Hist.*, 18 (1976), pp. 98–110.

Snell, K. D. M., *Annals of the labouring poor: social change and agrarian England, 1660–1900* (Cambridge, 1985).

Staves, S., *Married women's separate property in England, 1660–1833* (Cambridge, Mass., 1990).

Taylor, B., *Eve and the new Jerusalem* (1983).

Thane, P., 'The history of the gender division of labour in Britain: reflections on "herstory" in accounting: the first eighty years', *Accounting, organisations and society*, 17 (1992), pp. 299–312.

Thirsk, J., 'The fantastical folly of fashion: the English stocking knitting industry, 1500–1700', in N. B. Harte and K. Ponting, eds., *Textile history and economic history* (Manchester, 1973), pp. 50–73; reprinted in J. Thirsk, *The rural economy of England* (Oxford, 1984), pp. 235–57.

Thomas, J., 'Women and capitalism: oppression or emancipation? A review article', *Comp. Stud. Soc. Hist.*, 30 (1988), pp. 534–49.

Thwaites, W., 'Women in the market place: Oxfordshire, c. 1690–1800', *Midland Hist.*, 9 (1984), pp. 23–42.

Tickner, F. W., *Women in English economic history* (1923).

Tilly L. A. and Scott, J. W., *Women, work and family* (New York, 1978).

Tilly, L. A., Scott, J. W., and Cohen, M., 'Women's work and European fertility patterns', *J. Interdisc. Hist.*, VI (1976), pp. 447–76.

Todd, B. J., 'The remarrying widow: a stereotype reconsidered', in M. Prior, ed., *Women in English society, 1500–1800* (1985), pp. 54–92.

Todd, B. J., 'Freebench and free enterprise: widows and their property in two Berkshire villages', in J. Chartres and D. Hey, eds., *English rural society, 1500–1800* (Cambridge, 1990), pp. 175–200.

Valenze, D., 'The art of women and the business of men: women's work and the dairy industry, c. 1740–1840', *P. & P.*, 130 (1991), pp. 142–69.

Valverde, M., 'Giving the female a domestic turn: the social, legal and moral regulation of women's work in British cotton mills, 1820–1850', *J. Soc. Hist.*, 21 (1987), pp. 619–34.

Vickery, A. J., 'Golden age to separate spheres? A review of the categories and chronology of English women's history', *Hist. J.*, 36 (1993), pp. 383–414.

Vickery, A. J., 'Women and the world of goods: a Lancashire consumer and her possessions, 1751–81', in J. Brewer and R. Porter, eds., *Consumption and the world of goods* (1993), pp. 274–301.

de Vries, J., 'Between purchasing power and the world of goods: understanding the household economy in early modern Europe', in R. Porter and J. Brewer, eds., *Consumption and the world of goods* (1993), pp. 85–132.

Walkowitz, J., *Prostitution and Victorian society: women, class and the state* (Cambridge, 1980).

Wall, R., 'Women alone in English society', *Annales de Démographie Historique*, 18 (1981), pp. 303–20.

Weatherill, L., 'A possession of one's own: women and consumer behaviour in England, 1660–1740', *J. Brit. Stud.*, 25 (1986), pp. 131–56.

Williams, L. J. and Jones, D., 'Women at work in nineteenth-century Wales', *Llafur*, 3:3 (1982), pp. 20–9.

Witz, A., *Professions and patriarchy* (1992).

Wright, S., ' "Churmaids, huswyfes and hucksters": the employment of women in Tudor and Stuart Salisbury', in L. Charles and L. Duffin, eds., *Women and work in pre-industrial England* (1985), pp. 100–21.

Wright, S., ' "Holding up half the sky": women and their occupations in eighteenth-century Ludlow', *Midland Hist.*, 14 (1989), pp. 53–74.

Wrigley, E. A., 'Urban growth and agricultural change: England and the continent in the early modern period', *J. Interdisc. Hist.*, 15 (1985), pp. 683–728.
Wyman, A. L., 'The surgeoness: the female practitioner of surgery, 1400–1800', *Medic. Hist.*, 28 (1984), pp. 22–41.
Zemon Davis, N., 'Women's history in transition: the European case', *Fem. Stud.*, 2 (1976), pp. 83–103.

2

Women's history: a study in change, continuity or standing still?

BRIDGET HILL

Recent work on European women in the early modern period as indeed in the eighteenth and nineteenth centuries has increasingly stressed continuities. Much that we once thought of as representing the effects on women of the emergence of capitalism or of industrialisation, it is claimed, was already present long before the advent of either. Some have drawn the conclusion therefore that capitalism and industrialisation have played no part in the developing work roles of women and that the 'great change' theory of women's history is outdated. What is needed, it has been argued, is for feminist historians to abandon traditional periodisation of history and invent their own. At the same time there has been a long drawn-out and passionately waged controversy among feminist historians about the relative importance of class and gender in the history of women. No historian of women today would deny that gender has been a crucial shaping influence in the history of women. But currently there is a tendency to push both theses to their limits. What has resulted is a proposed approach to women's history, and more particularly to the history of women's work that is, I believe, both wrong and a-historical. The fact that it comes from scholarly historians with deservedly high reputations makes it particularly insidious.

The argument often starts with an attack on the notion of so-called 'golden ages' for women. The idea of better times in the past runs throughout history and it is not just confined to the elderly. But has there ever been a 'golden age' for women? There may have been periods when one class of women, often an élite, has had a marginally better life experience, but no golden age for women as a whole and certainly no golden age for the great mass of labouring women. Frequently in the past women have expressed a belief in a golden age as a way of making bearable their own

A reply by Judith Bennett to this article appeared in *Women's History Review* (Volume 2, Number 2, 1993) [Reading 3 of the present volume].

intolerable lives – surely, they have argued, it cannot always have been like this for women, it must once, at some unspecified time in the past, have been different. There must have been a period when a more equal society existed and women's worth was recognised on a par with that of men. Mary Collier, the washerwoman poet of the eighteenth century, from the moment in childhood when her mother died and her education ceased, lived a life of drudgery: washing, charing, brewing in other people's houses. Little wonder then that the injustice of relations with her rich and leisured mistresses raised questions of what Edward Thompson has called 'the humanity of class divisions'.[1] Mary Collier was over 50 when she started to write poetry. The drudgery of her work seemed endless but she recognised that it was not merely her lot but that of all 'poor Woman-kind'. She questioned whether it had always been like this for women:

> Oft have I thought as on my bed I lay,
> Eas'd from the tiresome Labours of the day.
> Our first Extraction from a Mass refin'd
> Could never be for Slavery design'd,
> Till Time and Custom by degrees destroy'd
> That happy state our Sex at first enjoy'd.
> Why men had used their utmost care and toil,
> Their Recompense was but a Female Smile;
> When they by Arts or Arms were rendered great,
> They laid their Trophies at a Woman's Feet.
> They, in those days, unto our Sex did bring
> Their Hearts, their All, a free-will Offering,
> And as from us their Being they derive,
> They back again should all due homage give.[2]

Other women have believed with equal conviction in a millennium in the future when women would experience a golden age. Female prophetesses have appeared throughout history claiming equal rights with men to express their views. As Mary Cary wrote in 1651 'the time is coming when not only men but women shall prophesy'.[3] There has been a recurring belief in the coming of a female messiah that would signal the dawn of a new and better era for women. Such ideas may have been based on myth but the myths were powerful and we should ask ourselves why at certain periods it became necessary for women to create them.

But this is very different from historians claiming for any one period of the past a 'golden age' for women and it is they who are the focus of recent criticism. 'The tempting specter of a "golden age"', Judith Bennett has claimed, 'has haunted the study of pre-industrial woman since the earliest decades of this century'. Such a ghost must be exorcised. If more particularly concerned with the tendency among medievalists, she also

accuses modern historians of creating 'an idyllic image of women in
preceding eras' as a 'convenient starting point . . . against which to contrast
their own findings and conclusions'.[4] It is assumed that their findings will
reveal women's situation as less than idyllic. But the contrast – if that is
really what modern historians are seeking – would be achieved if their
findings revealed a marked improvement in the situation of women. There
are many historians who see the present as a 'golden age' in relation to the
past, and history as the story of ever-upward progress. Many feminist
historians believe the criteria of modern feminism are appropriate in judging
women of the past. We are warned of the danger of romanticising the past,
and this danger is real, but it is also possible to romanticise the present,
which is something feminist historians are just as prone to. There is indeed
'a need to disabuse our students of the comfortable notion that they live
in a post-feminist "best-of-all-possible-worlds" for women'.[5] There are
historians who regard the past with a measure of contempt. They cannot
bear the thought that in any way the lives of men or women in earlier ages
had advantages over those of later and present times.

Bennett's thesis that historians have located such 'golden ages' in pre-
industrial times has a wider thrust. Pre-industry covers a very long time
indeed. One consequence of such a thesis is that many centuries, and the
women within them, get concertina-ed into a homogeneous mass. Moreover
historians of women of any period from medieval to modern times are
dismissed on the same grounds – a tendency to see their own period as one
of decline from earlier, and better, times. Generalisation, argues Bennett,
'need not lead to crude universal statements, instead it can point out trends,
possibilities, areas of common and divergent experience . . . we can (and
should) generalize about women'.[6] 'Generalizations', writes Merry Wiesner
with equal conviction, 'which lump all women together are very
dangerous'.[7] Particularly, she might have added, when covering women in
very different periods in different cities and countries. Recently, it has been
as much against historians of the seventeenth and eighteenth century as
against medievalists that the accusation of creating 'golden ages' has been
levelled. For example 'feminists like Clark and . . . Pinchbeck – or more
recently . . . Tilly . . . and Scott' are accused of favourably comparing
'women's place in the pre-industrial family-based economy to women's
place in the modern capitalist and industrial economy'.[8] The implication is
that 'favourable comparison' amounts to the creation of a 'golden age'.
Peter Earle has singled out Alice Clark as most responsible for creating the
myth of the *bon vieux temps*.[9] Often in apportioning blame, it is the first-
wave historians of women – Eileen Power, Clark, Dorothy George and Ivy
Pinchbeck – who are held mainly responsible. There is a tendency to treat
them as holding identical views 'loosely informed by the ideas of Friedrich
Engels who identified the roots of modern female subjection in the
emergence of monogamy, private property and a money economy'.[10] But is

this right? Did they all identify a golden age for women in pre-industrial times? Were they even in agreement in their conclusions? I think not.

Dorothy George's *London Life in the Eighteenth Century* (1925), while not focussing exclusively on women, does contain a great deal of information on working women. It specifically makes the point that London does not fit into social historians' idea of the late eighteenth century 'as the beginning of a dark age, in which there was a progressive degradation of the standard of life, under the blight of growing industrialism, while the earlier part of the century is considered a golden age'. For London, she wrote, 'it is improvement, not deterioration, which can be traced about 1750 and becomes marked between 1780 and 1820'. But she goes out of her way to stress how London was exceptional. As the century progressed it became less not more industrialised. 'It underwent a transformation, indeed a revolutionary one, in the course of the century, but the direct results of what is called the industrial revolution were not conspicuous there'. So she concluded: 'London to a great extent escaped both the torrent of pauperization which deluged the greater part of agricultural England, and the catastrophic fall in wages which occurred in many places'.[11] There can be no doubt that George was opposed to any 'golden age' theory for London. *England in Transition* (1931) was even less concerned with women, but in it she confronted head-on the question of whether the Industrial Revolution brought 'distress and degradation to the workers' or whether it meant 'a step forwards'. Her answer was that 'it was a real advance in social status' and 'a material advance' but that there had been victims. She singled out women in rural areas 'where there was little or no work for women' and as she added, available employment for wives could make all the difference to a family's enjoying 'a tolerable plenty' or penury. But in sharp contrast to Alice Clark's analysis she believed 'the first half of the eighteenth century was a more prosperous time for working people than the seventeenth century'. But on whether it was a golden age and how it compared to the 60 years that followed she was cautious; a golden age for the squirearchy and 'the great' perhaps, but little changed for the small farmer and the agricultural labourer (and, she might well have added, their wives and daughters).[12]

With Dorothy George's work on London in mind Peter Earle's recent research on the female labour market in late seventeenth- and early eighteenth-century London looks rather different. It is a revealing analysis, but London, as Dorothy George reminds us, was exceptional.[13] Clark was unsure about when exactly a decline for women in opportunities for working partnerships with their husbands began. She hazarded a guess that it was at the end of the seventeenth century but thought such women were probably still outnumbered by those that could work within their husbands' business. In contrast Earle argues that from 1695 to 1725 very few wives in fact worked in their husbands' business. 'Widows proved unlikely to pursue their late husband's business', he added, 'if the trade was an uncongenial one'.[14] Earle shows 'women *already* clustered in the so-called feminine trades'.[15] But where women are concerned can we see London as representative of the occupational structure of the country as a whole? It had little agriculture and the results of the industrial revolution, as Dorothy George said, 'were not conspicuous there'.[16] Both cotton and wool spinning, so central to the early stages of industrialisation, were virtually absent. Earle concludes that the general structure of women's occupations in London during this period is very similar to that revealed by the 1851 occupational census for London although with higher participation rates. In 1851 the first four occupations were the same as in the earlier occupational sample for London. But this is a somewhat dangerous comparison as a third of Earle's total sample of women in any employment were part-time and would not have been included in the nineteenth-century census anyway, and as he admits, the census recorded relatively few working wives. There is, he concludes, little evidence of the narrowing of women's employment opportunities. Earle does not deny the possible existence of a *bon vieux temps* but concludes only that if it existed it must have been before the end of the seventeenth century. Is this really so different from Alice Clark's conclusion? Clark was writing of the whole century and of the whole country. Where women's occupations are concerned Earle covers five years of the century and focusses exclusively on London. What would have been useful – and gone some way to resolve the question of whether there had been a decline, and if so when – is some comparison with the occupations of women in London at an earlier date, say the beginning of the seventeenth century.

What of Ivy Pinchbeck's classic *Women Workers and the Industrial Revolution, 1750–1850* (1930)? It has been accurately described as subscribing 'to a somewhat unproblematic and optimistic interpretation of the effects of industrial capitalism on women'.[17] Any belief in a pre-industrial 'golden age' for women is not to be found in its pages. Rather there is a rugged determination to see the best in industrialisation in its effect on women. But, like George, Pinchbeck was conscious that as a result of change many women – particularly married women – lost out as far as work opportunities were concerned. Lacking the mobility of single women they could not move to where work opportunities existed. Notable was the effect of agricultural change. Productive work for women declined. The effect of enclosures in eroding the land occupied by tenant farms and cottages meant that the wives concerned lost opportunities of supporting themselves and their families. The situation was aggravated by the decline of some of the domestic industries, particularly hand-spinning. Many became wholly dependent on their husbands. Later change created a class of female wage labour but as Pinchbeck concludes 'the wage-earner was at a considerable financial disadvantage as compared with the cottager's wife under the old system, since the wages that could be earned were barely sufficient for the most inadequate standard of individual subsistence'.[18] It is difficult to see any other way of describing the lot of such women than as 'worse off'. In the long term the consequences of such change may have been different. Undoubtedly new work opportunities for women developed. But in the short term they lost out. Even so, Pinchbeck managed to find some good in such developments. 'Many women', she wrote, 'were able for the first time in the history of the industrial classes, to devote their energies to the business of home making and the care of their children'.[19]

Of all the first-wave historians of women in the seventeenth and eighteenth centuries it is Alice Clark who comes closest to creating a 'golden age' model; although it is not a term she ever uses. She set out to explore the influence of industrialisation on the productivity of women in the seventeenth century which she saw as a period of transition between feudal and modern society. Her verdict was pessimistic. The 'triumph of capitalistic organisation' coincided with a restriction of women's productive capacity. It 'tended to deprive them of opportunities for sharing in the more profitable forms of production, confining them as wage earners to the unprotected trades'. But Clark, while suggesting that an approximation to economic equality existed within the family economy, never claimed that women were 'equal members' of seventeenth-century society. Nor would she have favoured putting the clock back.[20] It was not the sharpening of class divisions, nor the free sway of the profit motive that she attacked in capitalism but its destruction of creativity; and she was not just thinking of it in economic terms. Over 70 years have passed since she wrote. It would be extraordinary – and rather shameful – if in all those years there had not been work done, initially often inspired by her, that requires some amendment of her conclusions. Her work suffers from the defects of any attempt to generalise, even about the same kind of women in the same period. It tends to underestimate the exceptions, to omit regional and local diversity, to simplify the complexity of factors influencing women's changing work roles. But without the generalisation much of the present work on particular industries, towns and localities would never have got started. There has yet to be written anything on the seventeenth century with the scope and vision of her work.

There is then little ground for lumping these first-wave historians of women together. They differed both in their analysis and in their conclusions. Not one of them talked of a 'golden age' for women, most of them firmly rejected the notion, but all of them used words like 'better' and 'worse', 'improvement' and 'decline' to describe the changing position of women in relation to work. For all were concerned with change in women's work role, the nature of that change, and when and how it had come about. All of them frequently compare the position of women in one period with that of another; the difference between women in Elizabethan times with

those of the Restoration; the position of medieval women as compared with
women under modern industrial capitalism, of women in the early and late
eighteenth century, of women before and after the Industrial Revolution.
There would certainly be disagreement between historians about what
makes an age more or less 'golden' for women (and for which women?),
and, more realistically, how 'better off' and 'worse off' are interpreted. Are
they to be seen in terms of higher real wages, more employment, husbands
in better paid jobs, happier lives, more independent or self-fulfilled
existences, or, as for Bennett, does a 'golden age' mean one thing and one
thing only; sexual equality? But it seems that mere rejection of the notion of
a 'golden age' is not enough. For behind the apparent issue of 'golden ages'
there lies the assumption that comparisons are bad, as are the use of words
like 'more' or 'less', 'better' or 'worse'. Women's history, writes Bennett
'must eschew simplistic notions of times getting "better" or "worse" '.[21] But
if the women we are studying thought times were getting 'better' or 'worse'
can we as historians ignore them? And it is not only the old who look back
to earlier and happier times. Women who lost the means of contributing to
their family income when commons were enclosed and cottages pulled
down, or when agricultural change meant there was no longer the same
demand for their labour, or when new machinery made handicraft industry
redundant and took industry from the home to the factory, might
understandably feel things were getting worse for them. A recent review of
a work on women in Europe explained how the authors 'reject the golden
age' theory that women were better off 'before modern society further
stratified class and gender'. But, the review continues, 'they also wisely
repudiate the notion that modernity was an unmixed blessing for women by
providing new access to property, education, and occupations'.[22] We might
note the discriminating choice of words like 'modern society' and
'modernity', but where exactly does such a statement leave the reader?
What else can a 'mixed blessing' mean except that women were in some
respects better off, and in others worse?

Often Olwen Hufton has been quoted in support of the critics of the so-
called makers of pre-industrial golden ages.[23] But not always does the use to
which her work is put fully relate to what she actually wrote. 'One problem
for the early modernist is that feminist writing on the nineteenth century has
tended to force upon historians of the early modern period one unenviable
task', Hufton writes, 'that of locating a *bon vieux temps* when women
enjoyed a harmonious, if hard-working, domestic role and social
responsibility before they were downgraded into social parasites or factory
fodder under the corrupting hand of capitalism'. 'So far', she concluded,
'the location of this *bon vieux temps* has proved remarkably elusive'.[24] In
other words it was new interpretations of the nineteenth century –
interpretations which suggested that the view of things getting better and
better for women under industrialisation, of industrialisation as a great

liberating force for women, was in dire need of revising – which has made the eighteenth century, in relative terms and in some respects, appear better. it is historians of women in the nineteenth century, Hufton implies, who have moved the goal posts of the debate.

Some of the same criticisms on the grounds of representativeness that Earle's article invites, can be directed at examples quoted by Bennett in support of her vision of the thesis of continuity in women's history. All are concerned with urban women in a variety of towns – twelfth- and thirteenth-century Castilian towns, fourteenth-century Shrewsbury, fifteenth- and sixteenth-century Leiden and Cologne, south German towns from the fifteenth to the seventeenth century – in periods it needs emphasising when the overwhelming majority of women still lived and worked in the countryside.[25] All are scholarly studies yielding valuable new evidence about the work of urban women in Europe. Both Wiesner and Howell in their studies of towns in Renaissance Germany and in fifteenth- and sixteenth-century Cologne and Leiden, respectively, conclude that working options for women declined in the late medieval period. They give different explanations of such decline. Is this surprising, since they are dealing with very different cities in which a great diversity of factors operated over different periods? To use the word 'disagree', as Bennett does, about their explanations of decline would seem inappropriate.[26] You can only disagree in discussing the same thing. Both authors, moreover, are criticised for 'sharing with Clark a tendency to exalt the working experience of women in the centuries that preceded the changes they describe'. While welcoming the evidence they provide that at different moments of time in different cities in Europe there can be found similar situations as far as the work options for women are concerned, the authors' choice of the word 'decline', their belief, and one shared by Alice Clark, it is claimed, 'that something terrible happened to the working opportunities for women at the end of the middle ages', is mistaken. The situation of women, it is argued, had not changed, nor did it change fundamentally from the seventeenth century to the present day. 'Many of the basic disadvantages faced by modern working women', she concludes, 'existed in medieval towns'. From these examples Bennett sees the 'descriptions of women's work in seventeenth-century German cities as just as easily describing fourteenth-century Exeter and nineteenth-century Paris'. Women's work in the countryside is summarily dismissed, at least for the medieval period. There was 'no economic equality in the medieval countryside'.[27] But the nature of women's work in the countryside in the periods covered by her examples is not addressed.

Rather than an argument about whether or not there ever existed a 'golden age' for women, what the argument is really about is 'great change', about whether significant watersheds exist in women's history. If words like 'industrial revolution', 'capitalism', 'industrialisation' or even just 'economic change' are seen as no longer of great relevance to women's changing experience, if you believe that rather there is a great continuity of that experience stretching from medieval to modern times and nothing has made much difference to it, then you will not like interpretations that attach importance to economic factors, and see capitalism and the whole process of industrialisation in both countryside and town as crucial, if not the only, factors in shaping changes in women's work role and the sexual division of labour. The thesis of an unchanging role for women is not only mistaken but plays into the hands of those male historians who have long argued that women's experience has no part in history because everyone knows their role has been unchanging – a view that was hotly contested by the early women's movement. Such a view suggests there have been no significant developments over time, yet some would say change and the reasons for change is what history is all about. The view of women 'as a static factor in social developments, a factor which, remaining itself essentially the same, might be expected to exercise a constant and unvarying influence on society' was firmly rejected by Alice Clark as long ago as 1919.[28] The 'fundamental continuities' that Bennett finds in the period 1200 to 1900 lead her to conclude that 'some of the standard explanations of women's subordination as workers – especially the dual villains of capitalism and industrialism – are incorrect'.[29] They are not found 'inadequate', as most historians of women would now agree, but 'incorrect'. It is not just economic change that is of secondary importance, but also class and race, among factors making any crucial difference to women's work role. No feminist historian today would deny that explanations of female subordination that ignore gender are totally inadequate but so are those that ignore everything except gender. In some aspects of her thesis Bennett is far from alone. 'Much recent literature on Britain in the eighteenth and nineteenth centuries', writes Stana Nenadic, 'has downplayed the significance of the industrial revolution, stressing the existence of continuities and modifying interpretations of the impact of the new'.[30] Merry Wiesen [*sic*], while not denying that major changes occur in history, nevertheless insists that 'because of the kinds of occupations women did, even major economic changes may not have made a significant difference to them'. The nature of their work was 'unvarying'.[31] But few have taken the thesis to the extremes to which Bennett has pushed it.

Let us be clear that her thesis of continuity is to be distinguished from the belief – now generally held – that such periods of change, the development of capitalism, industrialisation or industrial revolution, for example, stretched out over a far longer period of time than we once thought. We now recognise that agricultural and industrial change came at different periods and proceeded at different rates in different areas and within those areas to different industries and different kinds of agriculture. In England ' "industrial work" and "capitalist organisation" ', Joan Thirsk has written, 'are deceptively simple terms, masking a complex reality'. 'England', she argues, 'was a collection of highly varied regions, whose distinctive farming economies accommodated industrial work and capitalist enterprise in many different guises, and at different levels of intensity. Different rural environments were matched by others equally varied in large towns, mean market towns, and fishing ports, and in new manufacturing centres that were transforming themselves from villages into towns'.[32] Recently David Levine and Keith Wrightson have shown how a combination of factors led to the transformation of Whickham on the Durham coalfield into a fully capitalist economy in the space of less than a century. The 'peculiar precocity' of the region is in marked contrast to theories of slow development and continuity with earlier times. As the authors comment, their study 'is concerned primarily with change'.[33] But if the changes we associate with an Industrial Revolution began much earlier and continued for a much longer period of time than we once thought, there is no doubt that 'the time did seem epoch-making to those who lived in it, and in fact was epoch-making'.[34]

Recently the Bennett thesis has been echoed in an article on 'Women's work, gender conflict, and labour markets in Europe, 1500–1900'.[35] In exploring women's changing work roles its efforts to avoid granting any influence to the development of capitalism leads its authors into strange contortions. The article is also concerned with the work of urban women – women's work in agriculture is excluded. Emphasis is placed on 'periods of gender conflict' with the same dismissal of economic factors such as capitalism or industrialisation as playing any significant role in women's changing position in labour markets. The need to avoid assigning any importance to economic factors leads them into difficulties. The two most significant periods of gender conflict are identified as occurring from the late fifteenth to the end of the sixteenth century and from the early nineteenth century. The consequences of both crises were 'a more clearly specified gendering of jobs, new restrictions on the employment of women, and a reduction in the value placed on women's work associated with a greater emphasis on their domestic position in the family'.[36] Those of us who know no better might remark on the coincidence of such crises with periods of capitalist development and change.

Such crises could arise, we are told, 'for a number of reasons' but 'apparently ... because artisans and other skilled men believed their position of economic strength and thus patriarchal power to be under threat'. From the late fifteenth century urban guilds began systematically to attack women as workers either by marginalising their participation in guilds or by totally excluding them, by carefully defining the restricted areas of work in which women were allowed, and by barring women from entry to certain trades. Apprenticeship for women was restricted to an ever narrowing range of trades. On why guilds suddenly began to act with such hostility to women's work it is conceded that it was not unrelated to the undermining of guilds as a consequence of industry moving from towns into the countryside to escape the restrictiveness of guild and state regulations. In the countryside they found an abundant source of cheap labour of which women formed a substantial part. Not surprisingly guild opposition became focussed on rural women's work in domestic industry. With all this we can agree but the conclusion reached, surprisingly, is that 'gender rather than industrial organization, became the determining factor'. The origins for such hostility to women shown by guilds are, we are told, 'very poorly understood. It was part of a complex process ... but its precise location is unclear'.[37]

Many years ago Dunlop and Denman wrote that such guild hostility to women workers in England 'was not because they were women but because they broke guild regulations'.[38] The original motive behind the ordinances and regulations governing certain occupations was, Merry Wiesner writes, 'to make sure those practising an occupation had been properly trained'. The restrictions introduced by Lubeck dyers, for instance, excluded untrained men as well as women. Such restrictions 'were not perceived as directed specifically against women'.[39] Nevertheless in practice it was women who were most affected because it was they who were most consistently denied approved training. They were unskilled, more often than not had served no apprenticeship, and were often in the eyes of the guilds illegal workers. 'Where there was a fear that qualified men would be thrown out of employment by women, the work of the latter was forbidden'.[40] The beginning of such hostility was not only related to the move into the countryside of industry, as Honeyman and Goodman suggest, but dated from the time when certain industries began increasingly to resent the curbs put on greater profitability and expansion by the guilds and moved into the countryside in search of freedom from restriction and cheap labour. Some might venture to call this the early development of capitalism. It was not so much 'the guild which provoked gender conflict in the workplace' but changed economic circumstances in which demand for skilled craftsmen declined and where rural women as a source of cheap labour were increasingly employed in domestic industry.[41] Capitalism has always exploited gender conflict for its own purposes.

With Wiesner and Howell, but unlike Bennett, the authors believe that although there were wide differences between towns, 'prior to this subordination' women had enjoyed better times with some access to high-status occupations. But if earlier there had been decline, continuity marked the position of women in the labour market from the late seventeenth century. Industrial development in nineteenth-century Europe, they argue, did little to change things. Beginning in the 1820s another gender conflict erupted. 'Anti-female sentiments, akin to those prominent in early modern guild politics, resurfaced.' Now it 'embraced novel social concerns' – 'protective legislation', arguments for a family wage, and 'the ideology of domesticity'.[42] But if the strategies men used to defend their position were different the basic cause of the crisis remained the same; wherever male workers have seen their jobs threatened by the cheap labour force represented by women, when they have seen their own wages depressed by competition from low-waged women, gender conflict results. The emergence of the 'women's place is in the home' doctrine, working men's support for all protective legislation aimed at women and children, their demand for a family wage that would allow them to support their wives at home, the determination of many unions not to admit women – were indeed intimately linked to the threat women were seen as posing to working men's employment. It could lead to the paradoxical situation of capitalists and women opposing such protective legislation while working men supported it. The way the labour movement embraced the notion of a family wage was characteristic of an increasingly conservative attitude. Wally Secombe has written how it reacted 'in a narrow exclusionist fashion to the very real threat which the mass employment of women as cheap labour, represented to the job security and wage levels of skilled tradesmen'.[43]

The consequence of this second period of gender conflict, it is argued, was the establishment of a hierarchical division of labour. That women's position in the labour market remained subordinate 'in a context of economic and social change ... was more the result of a number of interacting forces' which, the authors assert with confidence, 'were patriarchal in character'.[44] Most feminist historians are now agreed that the sexual division of labour was not created by capitalism but existed long before within the family economic unit. But capitalism strengthened it, further segregating the occupations of men and women, further accentuating the inferior, unskilled nature of women's work. The subordination of women meant capitalism could count on a ready-made supply of cheap, docile, mostly unorganised labour. Today that labour is neither as cheap nor as docile nor as unorganised as it was. The consequence is that capitalism is looking further and further afield for its labour force to the abundant, still docile, cheap labour that women of the Third World represent.

Curiously, in the light of their unequivocal denial of any role to industrial capitalism and their unwillingness to admit economic change as a factor on a par with gender, it is admitted that 'what identified gender and work was the intersection of the economic and gender systems'.[45] Many have found such a concept useful. Howell, for example, sees women's work 'as the product of an intersection between two interconnected but analytically distinguishable systems', the 'sex-gender system' and the economic system.[46] Hartmann has seen it quite simply as an interaction between capitalism and patriarchy.[47] 'Female work patterns and domestic preoccupations', Honeyman and Goodman conclude, 'were not solely or primarily determined by economic forces'. Rather they were the result of 'complex relationships between patriarchy and economic materialism'.[48] What exactly is meant here by 'economic materialism' and how it might relate to economic forces or capitalist development is not stated but it is precisely this complex interaction of economic factors with patriarchy that makes it difficult if not impossible to separate them out as causal factors. And while the concept of interaction between two autonomous systems is fine as a theoretical concept it has decided drawbacks in practice. For what historians of women confront is a whole and not a segmented reality and if they must be aware of its different elements – and there are many besides gender and class – it is impossible and unrealistic to attempt to separate them out.

It is possible to find paragraphs in history textbooks purporting to describe very different periods widely separate in time which are virtually identical. Nor is this necessarily to be summarily dismissed as bad history. There are moments in the history of quite different centuries when apparently similar things were happening although often in very different contexts and for very different reasons. Anyone who has studied the changing work role of women in some Third World countries today is aware of the echoes it sets up of eighteenth- and nineteenth-century European women's experience. Their existence, however, is no ground for the creation of models of development or industrialisation. But according to Bennett's thesis, history, as far as women's work in Europe is concerned, has stood still. The task of women's history is thus to 'grapple . . . with the pressing problem of overall constancy in the [low] status of women'.[49] Does this thesis leave any room for history? It would seem not, but Bennett insists that, despite the continuities, it does. The 'particular constraints and boundaries that have framed women's work have varied in important ways', she writes. There remains a history to be written 'of new designs embroidered on a cloth of oppression and deprivation'. In other words a history of patriarchy.[50] And of course this is the real object of Bennett's thesis. If women's subordination in work is not primarily influenced by economic change, if class and race are of secondary importance, then the unchanging nature of women's work role that is claimed must relate, or so it is argued, to something women over the ages have all suffered in common: patriarchal oppression. Yet Bennett acknowledges that an approach to women's history based on a study of 'the intersection of race, class and gender' has advantages. 'By placing race and class on equal footing with gender' and 'by treating gender as part of a complex of factors', she writes, 'we can better approximate the real experiences of women, whose identities are formed not by sex alone'. But for Bennett such a concept also presents difficulties. It is 'both unnecessarily exclusive and potentially hierarchical'. But it is the latter that most concerns her. Some 'nonfeminist historians often use this tool in appalling ways, talking about race, class and gender and then ranking gender beneath the others'. Bennett's problem is not really the hierarchy as such but which particular hierarchy is chosen. Patriarchy is her choice as 'the central issue of feminism' and 'the central subject of women's history'.[51]

A historical study of patriarchy, it is admitted, is 'unappealing' in its concern for 'the mechanisms through which women have been oppressed, kept down, put in "their place" '. It is not 'an inspiring history either to research or to teach'. It is also 'a history that focuses more on men than women'.[52] But much more importantly such an approach to the history of women is mistaken. It will distort the history of women. Historians of women who adopt such a thesis will no doubt find what they are looking for – examples of the way in which patriarchal power has operated in the past to oppress women – but it will be at the cost of missing the subtlety of the complex interaction of the many other factors that have shaped women's history. It will be to ignore the fact that it is not only men who have wielded power and that women have been oppressors and exploiters as well as oppressed and exploited. 'Moral identification with female subordination in the past', Lyndal Roper has said, 'allows us to write of women as victims, acted upon and martyred'. It may be, she suggests 'a response to the confusions we feel when it is uncomfortable to admit to our own power'. Then any attempt to regain the feminist impulse that initially inspired the women's movement and the history it produced is bound to fail. Feminism has changed. To insist that only those historians of women who keep patriarchal oppression central to their work are of any worth is, as Lyndal Roper has said, 'a recipe for conservatism, a holding on to the moral certainties of a past historical moment'.[53]

Some of the criticisms such arguments invite have now been recognised by Bennett. The 'greatest insufficiency ... is that they seem to account inadequately for change over time and seem, therefore, to be a-historical'. The fault, however, is seen as lying not with the arguments but without perception of causation, of the kind of change that has affected women's lives. Rather than looking at economic or political factors for explanations, it is argued, we need to look at 'factors new to history in general because they are largely specific to women and women's history'. And the factors mentioned – including misogyny, rape, violence towards women, attitudes towards female sexuality – are indeed factors that need addressing by historians of women as well as, not instead of, others. The argument has shifted slightly. The importance of change is now acknowledged although the nature of that change, it is suggested, needs more cautious and careful reassessment. The pace of change, it is implied, has been so slow as to be virtually indistinguishable from continuity. A distinction should be made, it is argued, between change in women's experiences and continuity in their status. And it is the continuities in women's history that have yet to be fully recognised. Changes have occurred within a context of 'long-term continuities'.[54]

Would the acceptance of such a thesis (for the main thesis remains unchanged) result in the 'revitalisation' of women's history Bennett seeks?

The thesis of 'overall constancy in the [low] status of women' combined with the belief in the supremacy of patriarchy over all other factors in women's history suggests otherwise. It promises to be an arid study. Will it do anything to reverse the 'ghettoisation' of women's history?[55] As a thesis that turns its back on many of the assumptions of social, labour and economic history it can only result in greater isolation, a decided (and what will be seen as a deliberate) move away from the possibility of ever achieving integration. As a thesis that emphasises the continued oppression of women by men as of central – and supreme – importance to women's history it may well alienate the very allies – and there are many – we have won in the years since the 1960s. And is our objective as feminists only the liberation of our own sex, or should it not also embrace 'the possibility of equal relations ... between (among others) women and men'?[56] As women we will never achieve real equality and the enrichment that equality could bring to relationships without carrying men with us. This does not mean compromising our position. Certainly we must keep patriarchy firmly within both our own sights and theirs. The process of re-educating men must continue but perhaps this is not best done by constantly harping on about them as the sole offenders. They are not the only guilty parties. Will this thesis, as Bennett also hopes, re-politicise women's history?[57] 'Politicise' is used here to mean not politics but ideology. It is a thesis that devalues politics as a factor in the history of women – by emphasising the ideology of the supreme importance of the subordination and oppression of women by men.

Notes

1 Stephen Duck, *The Thresher's Labour*, Mary Collier, *The Women's Labour*, Introduction by E. P. Thompson (London, 1989), p. xii.
2 Collier, *The Woman's Labour: an epistle to Mr Stephen Duck in answer to his late poem, called* The Thresher's Labour (1739), lines 10, 11–24.
3 Mary Cary (1651) *The Little Horns Doom and Downfall*, p. 238.
4 Judith Bennett (1988) History that stands still: women's work in the European past, Review Essay, *Feminist Studies*, 14(2), pp. 269–83, *vide* 269, 270.
5 Judith Bennett in a paper delivered at the Berkshire Conference to a panel on 'What should women's history be doing?', later published in *Conference Group on Women's History Newsletter*, 21(v), November 1990, pp. 18–20, *vide* 20.
6 Judith Bennett (1989) Feminism and history, *Gender and History*, 1, pp. 251–72, *vide* 265.
7 Merry Wiesner (1986) *Working Women in Renaissance Germany*, p. 35. New Brunswick: Rutgers University Press.
8 Bennett, 'History that stands still', p. 270.
9 Peter Earle (1989) The female labour market in London in the late seventeenth and early eighteenth centuries, *The Economic History Review*, 2nd series, 42, pp. 328–53, *vide* 328.
10 Amanda Vickery (1991) The neglected century: writing the history of eighteenth-century women, *Gender and History*, 3, pp. 211–19, *vide* 211–12.
11 Dorothy George (1925, reprinted 1966) *London Life in the Eighteenth Century*, pp 15, 31.
12 Dorothy George (1931, reprinted 1953) *England in Transition*, pp. 144, 134, 105.

13 George, *London Life*, p. 15.
14 Earle, 'The female labour market', p. 339.
15 Earle, 'The female labour market', p. 339.
16 George, *London Life*, p. 15.
17 *Unequal Opportunities* (ed. by Angela John, 1986), Introduction, p. 1.
18 Ivy Pinchbeck (1930, reprinted 1981) *Women Workers and the Industrial Revolution, 1750–1850*, p. 29.
19 Pinchbeck, *Women Workers*, p. 307.
20 Alice Clark (1919, reprinted 1982) *Working Life of Women in the Seventeenth Century*, pp. 13, 299, 308.
21 Bennett, 'Feminism and history', p. 266.
22 Theresa McBride of Bonnie S. Anderson and Judith P. Zinsser (1988) *A History of Their Own: women in Europe from pre-history to the present*, Vol. I (New York), cited in Thematic reviews: integration or separation? Constructing the history of European women, *Gender and History*, 1, pp. 213–18, *vide* 214.
23 Olwen Hufton (1983) Women in history: early modern Europe, *Past and Present*, 101, pp. 125–41, *vide* 126.
24 Hufton, 'Women in history'.
25 Merry E. Wiesner *Working Women in Renaissance Germany*; Martha C. Howell (1986) *Women, Production and Patriarchy in Late Medieval Cities* (Chicago: University of Chicago Press); Maryanne Kowaleski (1966) Exeter, in Barbara A. Hanawalt (Ed.) *Women and Work in Pre-Industrial Europe* (Bloomington: Indiana University Press); Diane Hutton (1985) Women in fourteenth century Shrewsbury, in Lindsey Charles and Lorna Duffin (Eds) *Women and Work in Pre-Industrial England* (London); Heath Dillard (1984) Daughters of reconquest, in *Women in Castilian Town Society, 1100–1300* (Cambridge: Cambridge University Press).
26 Bennett, 'History that stands still', p. 274.
27 Bennett, 'History that stands still', pp. 272, 274, 275, 279.
28 Clark, *Working Life*, p. 1.
29 Bennett, 'History that stands still', p. 279.
30 Stana Nenadic (1991) Businessmen, the urban middle classes, and the 'dominance' of manufacturers in nineteenth-century Britain, *Economic History Review*, 44, pp. 66–85, *vide* 82.
31 Merry Wiesen [*sic*] as quoted in Theresa McBride (1987) Thematic reviews: integration or separation? Constructing the history of European women, a review of Marilyn J. Boxer and Jean H. Quataert (Eds) *Connecting Spheres: women in the western world* (Oxford: Oxford University Press), in Renate Bridenthal, Claudia Koontz and Susan Stuard (Eds) *Becoming Visible: women in European history*, 2nd edn (Boston); *Gender and History*, 1, p. 215.
32 Mary Prior (Ed.) (1985) *Women in English Society, 1500–1800*, Introduction by Joan Thirsk, p. 12.
33 David Levine and Keith Wrightson (1991) *The Making of an Industrial Society, Whickham, 1560–1765*, p. viii.
34 George, *England in Transition*, p. 106.
35 Katrina Honeyman and Jordan Goodman (1991) Women's work, gender conflict, and labour markets in Europe, 1500–1900, *The Economic History Review*, 44, pp. 608–28. [This article is reprinted in another Arnold Reader, Robert Shoemaker and Mary Vincent (eds.). *Gender and History in Western Europe* (London, 1998), pp. 352–76.]
36 Honeyman and Goodman, 'Women's work', pp. 608, 609; see also P. J. P. Goldberg (1986) Female labour, service and marriage in the late medieval urban north, *Northern History*, 22, pp. 18–38, particularly 35 where there is a somewhat different explanation given for the marginalisation of women's work in late fifteenth-century York.
37 Goldberg, 'Female labour', pp. 608, 612.
38 O. Jocelyn Dunlop and R. D. Denman (1912) *English Apprenticeship and Child Labour, A history*, p. 144.
39 Wiesner, *Working Women*, pp. 189, 191.

40 Dunlop and Denman, *English Apprenticeship*, p. 145.
41 Honeyman and Goodman, 'Women's work', p. 613.
42 Honeyman and Goodman, 'Women's work', p. 515.
43 Wally Secombe (1986) Patriarchy stabilised: the construction of the male breadwinner wage norm in nineteenth-century Britain, *Social History*, 11, pp. 53–76, *vide* 55.
44 Honeyman and Goodman, 'Women's work', pp. 618–19.
45 Honeyman and Goodman, 'Women's work', p. 613.
46 Howell, *Women, Production and Patriarchy*, p. 5.
47 Heidi Hartmann (1976) Capitalism, patriarchy, and job segregation, *Signs*, 1, pp. 137–69.
48 Honeyman and Goodman, 'Women's work', pp. 609, 624.
49 Bennett, 'Feminism and history', p. 266.
50 Bennett, 'History that stands still', p. 280.
51 Bennett, 'Feminism and history', pp. 257, 267.
52 Bennett, 'Feminism and history', p. 262.
53 Roper, 'What should women's history be doing?', p. 25.
54 Bennett, 'What should women's history be doing?', p. 18.
55 Bennett, 'Feminism and history', pp. 252, 266.
56 Sheila Rowbotham (1981) 'The trouble with patriarchy', in Raphael Samuel (Ed.) *People's History and Socialist Theory*, p. 369 (London).
57 Bennett, 'Feminism and history', p. 256.

3

Women's history: a study in continuity and change

JUDITH BENNETT

I have read Bridget Hill's essay on Women's history: a study in change, continuity or standing still?' with great interest, and despite her often harsh criticism of my own work, I welcome the dialogue that her essay opens.[1] As she has set up the contrast between her perspective and mine, we represent in perhaps acute forms the dual origins of women's history as it re-established itself in the 1960s and 1970s. In her emphasis on the importance of economic change in women's history, Hill reflects the critical influence of left and socialist ideologies in the development of feminism and women's history. In my own emphasis on patriarchal continuities in women's history, I reflect radical feminist theories which, while not uninfluenced by left and socialist thought, nevertheless have focussed more exclusively on gender relations and women's oppression. Needless to say, both feminism and women's history have developed far beyond this original dualism, and our field is now much enriched by (among others) black feminist thought, psychoanalytic feminism, postmodernism, studies of difference and equality, postcolonialism, and queer theory.[2] Yet Hill's essay suggests that at a basic level, we are still tussling over the old battles of the 1960s and 1970s: what matters more, sex oppression or class oppression?

Of course, what really matters is oppression in its many forms – by gender and class, to be sure, but also by race, ethnicity, sexual orientation, world region, age, and the many other ways in which Western cultures have constructed privileged norms and unprivileged deviations. These oppressions matter not only in the lived experiences of women and men today but also in our analyses of the past.[3] We must learn to juggle many differences in our studies of past societies, and we must learn, as Elsa Barkley Brown has recently argued so effectively, to write about these differences in new ways that show both relationality and equivalency.[4] These are critical new challenges that face women's history, and I wish to foreground them here, before turning to the other important challenges that shape the disagreements between Hill and me.

As I understand Hill's essay, it contains three main criticisms of my suggestion that the history of women has displayed much more continuity than historians have yet been prepared to admit. She objects to this thesis on historiographic grounds; she objects to the generalization entailed in tracing continuities across centuries, locales, and classes; and she objects to the historical study of patriarchy *per se*. I would like to deal with each of these criticisms in turn, but I must begin by emphasizing that Hill's essay presents an incomplete view of my own arguments about both continuity in women's history and the need to historicize patriarchy. Two facets of my position are absent from her presentation. First, Hill criticizes me for failing in 'History that stands still' to consider the circumstances of rural women who were, after all, the vast majority of women in pre-industrial Europe.[5] This criticism overlooks both the context of that essay and my own published work. 'History that stands still' was a review essay, and none of the books under review dealt with rural women. Nevertheless, I did address in this review the possibility that we might find 'economic equality in the countryside outside medieval towns', and in rejecting this possibility, I briefly alluded to my own book (which, of course, I could not review) on *Women in the Medieval English Countryside*.[6] To judge from Hill's own footnotes, she has either not read this book or has chosen to ignore it. In any case, I wish to emphasize that it is only Hill's incomplete treatment of my research and writing that allows her to suggest that I have 'summarily dismissed' women's work in the countryside.[7] Quite the opposite is true.

Second, Hill ignores a critical component of my argument about continuity in women's history. In an article published early in 1992, I systematically defended my position by carefully analyzing four indicators of women's work in England *c.* 1200–1700: the family economy; occupational segregation; guilds; and wage-work. Since Hill had this new article in hand before completing her critique, it is unfortunate that she decided to argue with my old work rather than to engage with my current work. 'Medieval women, modern women: across the great divide' sets out in considerable detail my observations about continuities in patterns of women's work, but I shall not repeat myself here. Instead, I urge readers of this exchange to read this article and to judge my position on that basis.[8]

Hill's first set of criticisms addresses the historiographical significance of my argument that historians have under-appreciated continuities in women's history. Hill is primarily concerned that this argument unfairly amalgamates the work of earlier historians, and in this regard, she has provided us with a useful summary of the divergent historical viewpoints of Dorothy George, Ivy Pinchbeck, and Alice Clark. Unfortunately, she does not examine closely the work of earlier medievalists such as Eileen Power, Annie Abram, and Marian Dale, nor does she consider current historians such as Caroline Barron and Susan Cahn who speak unhesitatingly of a medieval 'golden age' or 'paradise' for women.[9] I have no wish to 'lump' historians of any generation into a single category, but the full historiography of women's work in the European past shows incontrovertibly that the idea of change-for-the-worse has a strong and powerful sway over the field. Hill's own book on *Women, Work, and Sexual Politics in Eighteenth-century England* is a good example; she concludes in this study that 'there seems little doubt that women lost out as far as opportunities for work are concerned'.[10]

Two other historiographical concerns run more subtly through Hill's essay. Hill implies that historians like me cavalierly ignore the testimony of women in earlier times who thought that the conditions of their lives were worsening.[11] As a medievalist studying ordinary women through the restricted sources extant for that time, I seldom have the opportunity to assess the words of women themselves. When I do, I take such testimony seriously, but not at face value. Experience is neither unmediated nor pure; we understand what happens to us (and hence, arguably, even *experience* such happenings) through the lenses of our own histories, ideologies, and cultures. How women in the past interpreted their experiences is interesting and telling, but it is not necessarily the final word. Joan Scott has recently given us a postmodernist twist on the evidence of experience, but even without the insights of postmodernism, historians have long treated first-hand evaluations with skepticism and care.[12]

Hill also argues that my interpretations threaten to disempower women's history within the profession at large. Hill fears that if we emphasize continuity in women's history we will de-legitimize women as historical subjects. This is a fair concern, especially since some early opponents of women's history argued that women's lives were so unchanging that women have no history. But my arguments about continuity in the history of women are very different from the old view of women as 'a static factor in social developments, a factor which, remaining itself essentially the same, might be expected to exercise a constant and unvarying influence on society'.[13] Women have certainly not been a static factor in history, for as the research of the last century has shown again and again, women's lives have been very diverse, and women's lives have changed over time. Instead of advocating an absurd notion of women as static and unvarying, I have argued that – despite these diversities and these changes in experiences – the *overall status* of women has not changed nearly as much as we might like to imagine. As I put it in my analysis of women's work across the medieval/ early modern divide, 'Women's work certainly changed over these centuries, but it was not transformed'.[14] Indeed, as Hill herself acknowledges at one point, I do not assert that there has been no change in women's lives; I have instead suggested that the pace of change, the motors of change, and the realities of change differ for women and men.[15]

Moreover, are we to react to this now old and hackneyed charge that 'women have no history' by being afraid to talk about continuity as well as change? History, after all, is not just about change; it is about continuity too.[16] And if women's history has a larger measure of continuity than the histories of some other groups, that is intriguing but certainly not de-historicizing. Hill says that 'some would say change and the reasons for change is [*sic*] what history is all about', and as I understand her argument, she would include herself in this camp. If so, I disagree with her. An exclusive emphasis in historical writing on change reflects the partial perspectives caused by focussing on élites and their politics; this is one of the fundamental critiques of traditional history associated with the *Annales* school (with their proposed distinction between *événements conjunctures*, and *structures*). If we merely match the periodization of history written with a focus on men (and/or élites), we will write a colonized history. Hence, when Hill objects to the argument that feminist historians should 'abandon traditional periodisation of history and invent their own', she might be locking women's history into a march of change-over-time that is more suited to the history of privileged men than it is to the history of ordinary women. In other words, in response to Hill's question, 'Does this thesis leave any room for history?' I would have to answer 'Yes, indeed, it makes room, for a better and diversified history that encompasses more people'.[17]

In suggesting that my interpretations harm the professional placement of women's history, Hill also asserts that a focus on historicizing patriarchy will remove women's history from the mainstream of history and exacerbate the problem of its ghettoization within the larger discipline. No one will deny that the history of women still needs to be better integrated into older historical fields, but there are many strategies to achieve this objective. Louise Tilly argues that historians of women must address the central issues of social history; Joan Scott argues that we must use gender as a 'signifier of power' to bring feminist scholarship into all sectors of history (including political history); I argue that we must develop our own historical traditions so that we can meet other historical fields on equal terms.[18] None of these strategies alone is the right one; all of them (and doubtless others as well) will help us reach our goal.[19] In other words, we need to mount a multi-pronged attack against the biases of traditional history; the historical study of patriarchy is, I would argue, a critical element of this complex strategy.

Hill's second main criticism concerns generalization; both implicitly and explicitly, she argues throughout the article that I (and anyone who would seek to historicize patriarchy) treat women as a 'homogeneous mass'.[20] There is, however, a critical inconsistency in Hill's position on this score. Although she maligns me for generalizing too readily, she praises Alice Clark for the 'scope and vision' of her work 'without [whose] generalization much of the present work on particular industries, towns, and localities would never have got started'.[21] I submit that in this instance what was good for history in 1919 is good for history in 1993 as well; we need broad overviews – such as Clark's assertion of a decline in women's work with the advent of industrial capitalism and such as my assertion of extraordinary continuities in women's work across the centuries – to stimulate further research. As historians, we work always on two levels; we seek to understand the particularities of past lives, but we also quite rightly seek to place those lives in broader context. At this second level of work, generalization might be risky, but it is also (as Hill herself admits) both proper and useful.[22]

Yet how should this generalization occur? Since 1919, we have learned a great deal about differences among women, and we have slowly come to appreciate that these differences are not mere divergences from a white, middle-class, heterosexual, female norm. The differences that matter (e.g. race, class, sexual orientation, world region) are differences signified by vast imbalances of power, and we must not replicate these power imbalances in our own writing of history.[23] How, then, do we generalize without also re-colonizing the less powerful? Elsa Barkley Brown has suggested that we begin to write history less as if it were a classical music score and more like jazz, more like 'various voices in a piece of music [that] may go their own ways but still be held together by their relationship to each other'.[24] This is easier said than done, but we must try.

Nevertheless, as we study the relationality inherent to differences among women, we must not forget the relationality inherent to differences between women and men. And while jazz might be appropriate to the former, perhaps a classical composition – containing a single but complex theme – remains best for the latter.[25] Some women have more capital or status than some men; some women wield more political power than some men; some women enjoy racial or sexual privileges denied to some men. But within each group of men and women – whether the group is structured by commonalties of race, class, sexuality, or whatever – women as a group are disempowered compared to *men of their group*. Peasant women in the middle ages held much less land in their villages than did men; African-

American women under slavery were subject to more violence and sexual harassment than were African-American men; lesbian households today are much poorer than the households of gay men. We might argue about whether this disempowerment of women *vis-à-vis* comparable men has always been the case, but certainly it has *usually* been the case. Indeed, it has been the case so usually and so often that it is, I would argue, a continuous problem worthy of hard historical study and worthy of careful historical generalization.[26] In so doing, I might be highlighting a difference between women and men, but I am not thereby obscuring differences among women. Indeed, differences among women are (as I argued in 'Feminism and history') 'absolutely crucial to our understanding of historical patriarchy'.[27]

In her third objection to my work, Hill attacks my advocacy of the feminist project to historicize patriarchy. As Hill tells it, our disagreement amounts to a simple dichotomy; she thinks economic changes have transformed women's lives in the past, and I think (in her view) that patriarchal forces have kept women in unvarying subordination, and oppression. This dichotomy rests, however, on a simplistic rendering of my arguments (and the work of others who have built on these arguments).[28] First, Hill suggests that my perspective ignores 'everything except gender' and seeks to create a 'hierarchy' in which gender is ranked above race and class.[29] Second, she suggests that my focus on historicizing patriarchy places all blame on men and all virtue on women. Third, she suggests that my viewpoint completely ignores economic forces. And fourth, she suggests that my focus on patriarchal continuity treats women's experiences as static and unchanging.

I object to all of these characterizations (as well as to others too minor and numerous to mention), and I ask that readers consult my article on 'Feminism and history' to reach their own conclusions on what I argue there about the historicizing of patriarchy. You will find that I discuss in that article a need for better consideration of the diversity of women's experiences – consideration that not only encompasses differences beyond those of 'race, class and gender' but also avoids ranking any characteristic above another.[30] You will find that I consider at length how women have co-operated and colluded in our own oppression and how '[w]omen's agency *per se* is a part of the strength of patriarchy'. You will find that I advocate looking at how patriarchal structures have interacted with economic systems, even going so far as to suggest that 'we might someday be able to distinguish analytically, say, "feudal patriarchy" from "capitalist patriarchy" from "socialist patriarchy" '. And you will find that I explicitly reject the idea that patriarchy is a static force, arguing instead that 'patriarchy clearly has existed in many forms and varieties, and its history will, in fact, be a history of many different historical patriarchies'.[31]

Perhaps more telling than Hill's specific misreadings of my argument in 'Feminism and history' is the vehemence of her objection to the project of historicizing patriarchy.[32] Why does it provoke such mis-representations from a distinguished scholar? Why can't it be tolerated as yet another approach to women's history? Why must it be attacked again and again with the same old hoary arguments?[33] I might just be cantankerous, but when I encounter such strong reactions to a feminist project (and Hill is certainly not alone in the intensity of her reactions), I think, 'Well, I really might be on to something'. Patriarchy seems to be a lightning rod, a concept that attracts so much fear and loathing that it cannot, for some people, be treated in a rational and moderate fashion. As long as this is the case, we will treat the historical study of patriarchy as taboo, we will fail to understand its workings, and we will be subject to its power. In other words, the power of patriarchal forces in our lives today rests, in part, on our failure to historicize it. As long as we are afraid to name patriarchy and to study its workings (afraid because it seems to blame men, or suggests more continuity than we would like, or deemphasizes the traditional power of economic change in history), we will not understand critical aspects of the subordination of women in the past, present, and future. And as long as we do not fully understand the subordination of women in the past, present, and future, the lives of both women and men will continue to be twisted by the perverse power of patriarchal institutions.[34]

I do not think that I will convince Bridget Hill by my arguments here, but I hope I have clarified for readers my own position. History is always imperfect, always unfinished, always unended. Recognizing the inevitable fallibility of our common work as historians, I hope that this exchange between Bridget Hill and me, although perhaps more discordant than harmonious, takes all of us on to new and better studies of women in past times. We will do this best, I think, if we recognize that our feminist colleagues are seldom 'wrong' or 'a-historical' or 'insidious' or inspired by 'contempt' for the past; they are merely, like all of us, articulating ideas that are always, at best, just partial truths.[35]

Acknowledgements

I would like to thank Cynthia Herrup and Nancy Hewitt for careful readings of an early draft of this reply. Needless to say, the opinions expressed here are my own, not theirs.

Notes

1 B. Hill (1993) Women's history: a study in change, continuity or standing still?, *Women's History Review*, 2, pp. 5–22 (hereafter cited by author alone). Although I shall focus in this response on Hill's specific remarks about my own work, I do not mean to suggest thereby either that Hill's essay was directed against me alone or that

I agree with Hill's criticisms of other historians. Yet as her essay seems to be directed largely against some of my arguments (what she at one point labels 'the Bennett thesis'), it seems fair to respond specifically to these critiques.

2 Of course, feminism in the 1960s and 1970s was also influenced by other ideologies, especially (in the USA) liberalism. Queer theory, as a very recent and largely US-based phenomenon, might not yet be widely known elsewhere. For an introduction to some of the work pursued under this rubric, see the special issue of *Differences: a journal of feminist cultural studies* edited by Teresa de Lauretis, 3(2), 1991.

3 It is, I believe, dangerously easy for historians working in pre-industrial or pre-modern societies to conclude that although we need to be sensitive to issues of class and gender, we can ignore other factors – such as race. We should beware of such easy dismissals. For a useful corrective on this score, see Tessie Liu (1991) Teaching the differences among women from a historical perspective, *Women's Studies International Forum*, 14, pp. 265–76. Needless to say, all of these modern forms of oppression must be historically situated and historically understood. For example, I am not suggesting that theories derived from modern race relations in the West can be readily applied to the European middle ages, but I am suggesting that historians need to consider more fully the influence of race in medieval society.

4 Elsa Barkley Brown (1991) Polyrhythms and improvisation: lessons for women's history, *History Workshop Journal*, 31, pp. 85–90 and (1992) 'What has happened here': the politics of difference in women's history and feminist politics, *Feminist Studies*, 18, pp. 295–312.

5 Hill, p. 12 [p. 49 of the present volume].

6 Quote from J. M. Bennett (1988) 'History that stands still': women's work in the European past, *Feminist Studies*, 14, p. 279. J. M. Bennett (1987) *Women in the Medieval English Countryside: gender and household in Brigstock before the plague* (New York: Oxford University Press).

7 Hill, p. 12 [p. 49]. It is difficult to gauge the extent of Hill's charge of a summary dismissal. On the one hand, she suggests in this paragraph that she is writing about all of my work, about my 'thesis of continuity'. On the other hand, she treats only my first discussion of this possibility, i.e. my review essay on 'History that stands still'. In any case, I think that most readers would conclude from Hill's remarks that I have ignored rural women not only in this review essay but throughout my work; this would be an erroneous conclusion.

8 J. M. Bennett (1992) Medieval women, modern women: across the great divide, in D. Aers (Ed.) *Culture and History, 1350–1600: essays on English communities, identities and writing*, pp. 147–75 (London: Harvester Wheatsheaf). An abridged version of this essay is forthcoming in A. L. Shapiro (Ed.) *Feminists (Re)vision History* (New Brunswick: Rutgers University Press).

9 E. Power (1926) The position of women in C. G. Crump and E. F. Jacob (Eds) *The Legacy of the Middle Ages*, pp. 403–33 (New York: Oxford University Press). A. Abram (1916) Women traders in medieval London, *Economic Journal*, 26, pp. 276–85. M. K. Dale (1933) The London silkwomen of the fifteenth century, *Economic History Review*, 1st series, 4, pp. 324–35. C. Barron (1989) The 'golden age' of women in medieval London, *Medieval Women in Southern England* (Reading: Reading Medieval Studies, 15), pp. 35–58. S. Cahn (1987) *Industry of Devotion: the transformation of women's work in England, 1500–1660* (New York: Columbia University Press).

10 B. Hill (1989) *Women, Work and Sexual Politics in Eighteenth-century England*, p. 263 (Oxford: Basil Blackwell).

11 Hill, pp. 5–6, 11 [pp. 42–3, 48].

12 J. W. Scott (1991) The evidence of experience, *Critical Inquiry*, 17, pp. 773–97.

13 Hill, quoted Alice Clark objecting to this view, p. 13.

14 Bennett, 'Medieval women, modern women', p. 164. My point here might best be appreciated by considering the origins of the title for my original review essay about continuity. I borrowed the notion of 'history that stands still' from Emmanuel Le Roy Ladurie's inaugural lecture at the Collège de France. In that lecture, Le Roy Ladurie – looking primarily at the demographic and agricultural history of France between

1300 and 1700 – argued that despite much change and much fluctuation, 'For all the apparent movement, things had really stayed much the same'. He added later that 'Virtual stability does not mean immobility'. See E. Le Roy Ladurie (1978) History that stands still, *The Mind and Method of the Historian*, esp. pp. 21–2 (Chicago: University of Chicago Press).

15 Hill, pp. 18–19 [p. 54].

16 'Continuity' is an important theme in historical writing of all types; indeed, it is often paired with 'change' to create what is probably the most popular dyad in historical titles. In the library catalogue at my university, for example, I found this dyad in two journals (*Continuity and Change* and *Change and Continuity in Africa*) and in more than 50 books published in the last 30 years alone.

17 Quotes from Hill, pp. 13, 5, 17 [pp. 50, 42, 54]. For an early discussion of traditional periodization and women's history, see J. Kelly (1976) The social relation of the sexes: methodological implications of women's history, *Signs: Journal of Women in Culture and Society*, 1, pp. 809–23.

18 J. Tilly (1989) Gender, women's history and social history, *Social Science History*, 13, pp. 439–62 (see also comments by Gay Gullickson and me and a response by Tilly on pp. 463–80 of the same issue). J. W. Scott (1988) *Gender and the Politics of History* (New York: Columbia University Press). J. Bennett (1989) Feminism and history, *Gender and History*, 1, pp. 251–72.

19 In this regard I would like to correct two misrepresentations contained in Hill's statement (p. 18) [p. 55], 'To insist that only those historians of women who keep patriarchal oppression central to their work are of any worth is, as Lyndal Roper has said, "a recipe for conservatism, a holding on to the moral certainties of a past historical moment"'. First, I have never argued that only historians who study patriarchy are 'of any worth'. I think I am now more tolerant of different approaches than when I wrote 'Feminism and history', but even then I stated quite clearly my hope that historians not 'quit studying the historical intersection of race, class, gender, and other related factors, or cut short their search for the meanings of gender, or curtail their efforts to deal with general historical questions'. Bennett, 'Feminism and history', p. 259. Second, Roper does not necessarily agree with my arguments, but in the section quoted by Hill she was talking about feminism in general, not feminist history, not my own particular take on it, and certainly not the notion that women's historians must study only patriarchy. Roper wrote, 'Implicitly, feminists now are exhorted to maintain feminist conviction, as if by an effort of will the women's movement can be kept alive. But this can also be a recipe for a politics of conservatism, a holding on to the moral certainties of a past historical moment'. As I read Roper, her comments are not directly relevant to Hill's point. See Roper's contribution to a discussion about 'What Should Women's History Be Doing?' *Newsletter of the Conference Group on Women's History*, 21 (1990), p. 25.

20 Hill, p. 7 [p. 44].

21 Hill, p. 10 [p. 47].

22 Let me add two further points about Hill's discussion of generalization in history. First, when Hill (p. 7) [p. 44] cites Wiesner as stating that 'generalizations which lump all women together are very dangerous', she does not provide the full context. In the same paragraph, Wiesner goes on to conclude that 'More often, however, no matter how much variation there was among women, the fact that they were women was the most important determinant of what work they would do'. M. Wiesner (1986) *Working Women in Renaissance Germany*, p. 35 (New Brunswick: Rutgers University Press). (Hill mis-represents Wiesner's work a second time on p. 13 [p. 50] where she identifies Wiesner as Wiesen and attributes to her a quotation that actually belongs to Teresa McBride.) Second, Hill also rather inconsistently argues that behind my work lies 'the assumption that comparisons are bad' (p. 11) [p. 48]. Obviously, in order to generalize, I have had to compare; indeed, comparison is at that very heart of my argument about continuity in women's history. In fact, Hill later maligns me for comparing the conclusions of Merry Wiesner and Martha Howell since, in her view, they are not 'discussing the same thing' (p. 12)

[p. 49]. This is a specious objection; as the titles of their books suggest, Wiesner and Howell both formulated from their specific studies general conclusions about the history of *women's work* in *European cities* during the *medieval/modern transition;* these general conclusions can quite properly be compared and contrasted. Hill's cavil suggests that Wiesner and Howell do not generalize their findings (which, of course, they do) and then asserts that my comparison of their generalizations is illegitimate (which, of course, it is not).

23 Two essays I have found to be particularly useful in this regard are: R. R. Pierson (1991) Experience, difference, dominance and voice in the writing of Canadian women's history, in K. Offen, R. R. Pierson and J. Rendall (Eds) *Writing Women's History*, pp. 79–106 (Bloomington: Indiana University Press), and C. T. Mohanty (1991) Under western eyes: feminist scholarship and colonial discourses, in C. T. Mohanty, A. Russo and L. Torres (Eds) *Third World Women and the Politics of Feminism*, pp. 51–80 (Bloomington: Indiana University Press).

24 Lawrence Levine as quoted in Barkley Brown, 'Polyrhythms', p. 85.

25 Barkley Brown has characterized classical music as requiring 'silence – of the audience, of all the instruments not singled out as performers in this section, even of any alternative visions than the composer's'. I do not want to indulge in an argument about musical metaphors with Barkley Brown, but the classical compositions I envision are different from her characterizations – they are more various and more accommodating of alternatives, but they are nevertheless composed around a central theme. I think that we must learn to talk about differences between women and men (differences that are, I would argue, characterized by patriarchal domination) while remaining attuned to the diverse meanings and relationalities of differences among women.

26 I wish to emphasize that in generalizing about the oppression of women, I am not disagreeing with Barkley Brown's statement in 'Polyrhythms' that 'all women do not have the same gender' (p. 88). A woman's gender – what it *means* to be a woman – has varied enormously across time, place, social stratum, sexuality, and even personality. This is, of course, the point made so forcefully in Denise Riley (1988) *Am I that Name? Feminism and the Category of 'Women' in History* (London: Macmillan). I agree with Barkley Brown and Riley about these important differences among women and these important different meanings of 'women', but I also see a common ground in the positioning of all these female genders against male genders. In this sense, there is a very important difference between generalization and totalization.

27 Bennett, 'Feminism and history', p. 266.

28 Hill's essay includes, of course, a long critique of an essay by Honeyman and Goodman which she considers to be an 'echo' of my own work (p. 14) [p. 51]. I do not know these authors, and I am not, of course, responsible for their findings (which both build on and also reject my own work). In any case, although I think that Hill's explication of their argument is not entirely fair, I will not deal here with that essay and Hill's comments on it.

29 Hill, pp. 13, 18 [pp. 50, 54].

30 As I understand Hill's argument on this score, she conflates two discrete issues: (1) whether factors such as race, class, and gender should be ranked analytically and (2) whether the study of patriarchal oppression should be central to women's history. I reject the former and embrace the latter. I would like to emphasize that my advocacy of historicizing patriarchy does not mean, as Hill claims, that I believe that class and race are of 'secondary importance . . . among factors making any crucial difference to women's work role' (p. 13, [p. 50] a charge repeated on p. 17 [p. 54]).

31 For specific points and quotes, see Bennett, 'Feminism and history', pp. 257–58, 263, 261.

32 See, for example, Hill's characterization of a focus on patriarchy as 'harping on about [men] as the sole offenders' (p. 19 [p. 56]).

33 For example, Hill cites Sheila Rowbotham's objections to the study of patriarchy made in 1979, i.e. a very long time ago in terms of the development of feminist theory. Rowbotham's concerns were immediately answered by Sally Alexander and Barbara

Taylor in a response not cited by Hill. See their (1979) In defence of patriarchy, reprinted in 1981 in R. Samuel (Ed.) *People's History and Socialist Theory*, pp. 370–73 (London: Routledge & Kegan Paul).

34 In contrast to Hill, I think that this project can be undertaken not only with subtlety and complexity but also without ignoring economic forces. Some of the best theorizing about patriarchy to date has been done by S. Walby (1990) *Theorizing Patriarchy* (Oxford: Basil Blackwell). See also G. Lerner (1986) *The Creation of Patriarchy* (New York: Oxford University Press).

35 Hill, pp. 5, 7 [pp. 42, 44]. J. Hall (1989) Partial truths, *Signs: Journal of Women in Culture and Society*, 14, pp. 902–11.

EXAMINING FEMALE LABOUR MARKETS

Commentary

This section moves from the wider questions of women's work over long time periods to a detailed examination of female labour markets from the second half of the seventeenth century to the mid-nineteenth century. The fact that women were vital to the early industrial economy is not a new discovery but it is one that has recently been given renewed emphasis. It was apparent to the earliest writers about industrialisation that mills and factories relied on cheap female labour.[1] The remark has been made, *pace* Joan Kelly, that 'women may not have had a Renaissance, but men didn't have an Industrial Revolution'.[2] These four readings suggest that women's roles were conditional; locality, timing, their marital status and stage in the life-cycle all affected women's access to the labour market. Nevertheless, Berg in Reading 6 argues in evangelical tone that 'in terms of their proportionate contribution to the manufacturing labour force, women workers played a greater part over the whole course of the eighteenth century than they had done previously or were to do in the later stages of industrialisation'. Berg's own work has been vastly influential in placing women and children at the centre of 'the first industrial nation' by arguing that the increased input of women and children's labour was one of the key characteristics of an Industrial Revolution. This moves the emphasis away from the gradual onset of economic change for which econometric historians have recently argued. Women's labour was not only cheap and malleable but, as Berg argues in this piece, there were often institutional and social reasons why females were employed.

The other three pieces in this section all make innovative use of sources to extract information about women's labour. Keith Snell uses a large sample of settlement examinations, which provide a potted biography of the working careers of labouring men and women, to chart changing wage rates and seasonal employment patterns for men and women. The regional patterns show increasing sexual division of labour over the course of the 'long' eighteenth century and a diminution of work for women in arable areas, but a growth of work opportunities in pastoral farming areas. Snell's aim is not just to produce data on changing female work patterns. He situates his material within the context of a much wider debate about the standard of living in the Industrial Revolution time period. Snell is undoubtedly a 'pessimist' in terms of the impact of capitalism on the working lives of ordinary people. This debate has been conducted in microcosm with those who stress that as the economy developed women were being confined to a secondary and increasingly poorly paid sector of the labour market. As sweated trades proliferated in urban areas from the 1820s, they exploited increasing amounts of underpaid labour. Only a few optimists, such as Edward Shorter or Neil McKendrick, have argued that increasing women's work brought independence and spending power to unmarried women.[3]

The standard-of-living debate also underlies Horrell and Humphries' article (Reading 7). They have collected family budget information from a variety of sources to produce a dataset which reveals patterns of women's work in different areas of the country. Like Berg's, their results suggest that estimates of labour productivity in the Industrial Revolution, which are limited to men, are inaccurate. But Horrell and Humphries' data make them generally more guarded than Berg in seeing both openings and closures for females: both demand for female labour and un- and underemployment can in addition be seen as a major feature of women's experience of industrialisation. This result contrasts the eighteenth and nineteenth centuries. While (as might be suggested by Snell's data) the first three-quarters of the eighteenth century may have offered unprecedented levels of work opportunity for women, by the end of the century and into the nineteenth century women's work was already contracting. Before the mid-nineteenth century protective legislation served to underline elite and middle-class attitudes that women's place was in the home.

Earle uses the depositions of women at London's ecclesiastical courts for a micro-examination of wage levels, literacy and the types of work women did. The courts have been described as 'women's courts' by other historians, as the majority of people bringing cases and acting as witnesses were females.[4] Earle's evidence counters assumptions of an early modern 'golden age' and ideas that work in the city took place in the family economy. Most wives worked in different sectors from their husbands and the general profile of female employment looked little different in the late seventeenth century from the picture that can be obtained from nineteenth-century censuses. Most women's work in London through time could be characterised as poorly paid, servile and, often, ephemeral.

Snell argues firmly that it is economic factors, not social attitudes, which marginalise women in areas like the south-east of England. Drawing on the research of Michael Roberts, he particularly highlights the replacement of the sickle with the scythe in grain harvesting. Many feminist historians would part company with Snell's interpretation and give a much greater weight to attitudinal factors. Karen Sayer's recent book on the representation of female farm workers in nineteenth-century England argues that they were increasingly degraded as the century advanced.[5] Deborah Valenze, in a major work about women's employment in the Industrial Revolution, also undertakes a sophisticated analysis of attitudes to women workers, arguing that the values associated with political economy subordinated labouring women.[6]

Notes

1 See, for example, F. Engels, *The Condition of the Working Class in England* (London, 1845).
2 Joan Kelly wrote a famous article entitled 'Did women have a Renaissance?' in R. Bridenthal and C. Koonz (eds.), *Becoming Visible: Women in European History* (Boston, Houghton Mifflin, 1977), pp. 175–202, and reprinted in J. Kelly (ed.), *Women, History and Theory* (Chicago, University of Chicago Press, 1984), pp. 19–50.
3 E. Shorter, 'Women's work: what difference did capitalism make?' *Theory and Society*, 3 (1976), pp. 485–512; N. McKendrick, 'Home demand and economic growth: a new

view of the role of women and children in the Industrial Revolution', in N. McKendrick (ed.), *Historical Perspectives: Studies in English Thought and Society* (London, Europa, 1984).
4 T. Meldrum, 'A women's court in London: defamation at the Bishop of London's consistory court', *London Journal* 19:1 (1994), pp. 1–20.
5 K. Sayer, *Women of the Fields: Representations of Rural Women in the Nineteenth Century* (Manchester, Manchester University Press, 1995).
6 D. Valenze, *The First Industrial Woman* (New York, Oxford University Press, 1995).

4

Agricultural seasonal unemployment, the standard of living, and women's work, 1690–1860

K. D. M. SNELL

I

It is common for historians working on changes in the standard of living and real wage trends to acknowledge the importance and the intractibility of the problem of changing levels of unemployment.[1] Questions relating to the extent, regionality, and changes over time of yearly or seasonal unemployment have almost invariably been seen as unanswerable. M. W. Flinn, for example, reconsidering the problems of real wages for the standard of living debate, has argued to this effect:

> What matters from the point of view of the assessment of secular trends in the standard of living is secular trends in the short-run variation of levels of unemployment . . . Changes in the levels of unemployment and underemployment are probably doomed to remain among the imponderables of this problem . . . There were, of course, in this period, some groups among the working classes whose employment, and even wage-rates, fluctuated according to a fairly regular annual pattern. Given that this pattern remained fixed, the earnings of these groups would move in sympathy with wage-rates of those in permanent employment. It is possible, however, that one consequence of the not inconsiderable changes in the nature and pattern of employment over the whole period

I am grateful to Tony Wrigley, in particular, Natalie Davis, and Peter Laslett for their comments. This chapter is an extended version based on additional research of an article published in the *Economic History Review* (1981), and I would like to thank Barry Supple for his helpful editorial advice.

1750–1850 was some disruption to the patterns of employment-distribution of the seasonally or irregularly employed. At the present time it is doubtful whether it would be possible to generalize with any confidence about any trends in this aspect of seasonal movements.[2]

I want to present evidence here which enables us to do precisely that, and to consider long-term changes in male and female seasonal distributions of unemployment in agriculture, predominantly in the southern and eastern counties of England, although some attention will also be paid to wider regional variations in these patterns. This issue will be closely related to trends in male and female agricultural wages, both to provide supportive and explanatory evidence for long-term changes in the seasonal distribution of unemployment, and to draw out some implications which these changes may carry for an assessment of trends in familial income. In discussing these issues, I will develop an argument on the changing roles of men and women in the agricultural work force between 1690 and 1860, and point to its significance for the 'standard of living debate', for the study of the history of women, and of the family. I hope in doing this to contribute an answer to those questions which concern the causal connections between economic and attitudinal changes – in this case by re-assessing the importance of nineteenth-century attitudes to femininity in bringing about a diminution of female work in agriculture.

II

To consider these issues I shall use rural settlement examinations and removal orders, which, under the Settlement Act of 1662,[3] were intended to enquire into and instruct the parish of settlement of applicants for poor relief, or of those felt to be a potential burden on the poor rates. For much of our period these documents allow the analysis of seasonal distributions of unemployment as they provide the exact seasonal date at which those who were examined preparatory to relief came to require parochial aid. In the course of the examination as to settlement, other details (for example sex, marital status and occupation) were given which allow very specific geographical, occupational and sexual location of the patterns of seasonal unemployment. The application for relief, followed by the examination to find where the applicant was eligible for it, and any removal order that followed shortly afterwards, provide the indication of 'unemployment'. (This is not dissimilar in some ways to the paperwork that underpins modern seasonal unemployment figures, although the older concept and definition of settlement as 'the right to relief' has now gone.) This brief account above describes the post-1795 situation, when there was a very direct and obvious connection between these documents and 'unemployment' of the kind that concerns me here. Looking back further in time, the longer-term use of this evidence is complicated to some extent by the 1795 settlement legislation,[4] which laid down that removal could take place only when a person became chargeable to the parish, and so ended the powers given under the 1662 Settlement Act for removal when a person was thought 'likely' to become chargeable. For our purposes, before 1795 examinations could be conducted on newly arrived parish inhabitants, on inhabitants felt likely to become chargeable, and of course on those who had just become chargeable, as after 1795. This legislative change, however, does not appear to call into question the utility of this source before 1795 – newly arrived examinants would have experienced recent unemployment, possibly in their old parish, and certainly over the past week, or however long it had taken them to journey from the old parish to the new, and would probably still be unemployed in their new parish (given the rapidity of local authorities' action against those felt to be a potential encumbrance on the rates). Such action would not be taken if they had moved to take up already arranged employment. The perception of local overseers and constables, in closely tied rural communities, of who might soon become a burden on the parish, mediated by the disincentive to examine posed by the high fees charged for an examination by the parish or petty session clerk,[5] is probably a good second best to the exact date of chargeability. And the examination immediately following chargeability, very common before 1795, gives the precise seasonal date we require, as does the removal order. (All those subject to removal in any period were classed as 'paupers', and they were ordered to be accepted and cared for under the poor law by the receiving parish's overseers.) In short, the 1795 Act does not appear to mark a significant discontinuity of policy for the purposes of using these records as an indicator for long-term patterns of seasonal unemployment, and the material extracted from them would support this, showing no break for example, in the clear-cut male patterns before and after 1795.

It should be noted that this source can tell us nothing about the relative size of the male and female work force in different periods, or of the total numbers seasonally unemployed. These problems, particularly for the eighteenth century, will probably remain largely beyond the reach of historians. We shall be discussing here only long-term changes in the seasonal distribution, or patterns, of unemployment, and considering the probable implications of these changes. The method adopted has been to take the surviving examinations in different parishes (for both married and unmarried labour), and to plot the percentage of these which occurred in each calendar month. (The figures have been adjusted to eliminate the effects of irregularity in the number of days in each month.) This has been done for Cambridgeshire, Bedfordshire, Huntingdonshire, Norfolk, Suffolk, Essex, Hertfordshire, Northamptonshire, Buckinghamshire and Berkshire in Figures 4.1 and 4.2 – that is, for those counties which, when analysed in isolation from each other, very clearly showed the male pattern of seasonal unemployment which I shall associate with regions where grain growing predominates. I have excluded urban parishes, although have included some obvious cases of farm-servants and agricultural labourers out of work and examined in towns where hiring fairs were held. Most rural parishes in Cambridgeshire, Bedfordshire, Huntingdonshire, Suffolk, and Hertfordshire are represented, and many rural parishes in the other counties. Examinations resulting from illness, old age, familial desertion, and bastardy have been excluded. The two figures have been subdivided into five chronological categories, between 1690 and 1860, which are intended to demonstrate the seasonal pattern before the rising wheat prices of the second half of the eighteenth century, during that rise, during the Napoleonic Wars, after the war until the New Poor Law, and after the New Poor Law.[6]

Figure 4.1 gives the male long-term changes, and represents the grain-growing pattern of seasonal unemployment, with high employment during

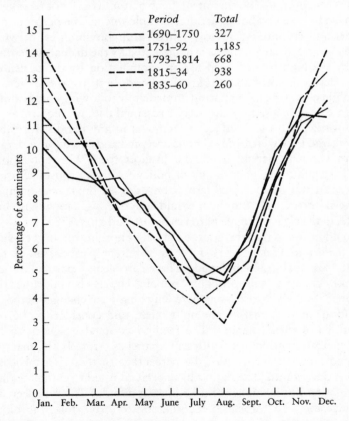

Figure 4.1 Male seasonal distribution of unemployment, 1690–1860
Camb, Beds, Hunts, Norf, Suff, Ess, Herts, Berks, Bucks and N'hants (3 month moving average)

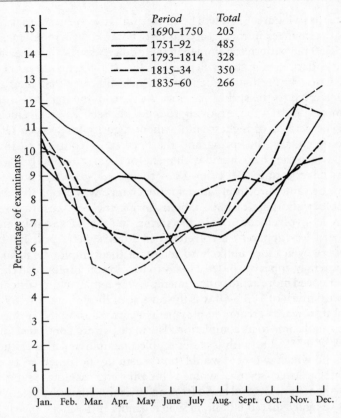

Figure 4.2 Female seasonal distribution of unemployment, 1690–1860
Camb, Beds, Hunts, Norf, Suff, Ess, Herts, Berks, Bucks and N'hants (3 month
moving average)

the harvest and high winter unemployment. Comparable agricultural
distributions for the region are of course found today. The extent to which
grain growing was supplemented by livestock can be seen in the slight rise
of unemployment occurring just after the calving and dairying season, that
is, for the months of April and May before 1793. In the western pastoral
region we will consider later, this was often the point of highest employment
insecurity during the year, and the hiring fair commonly took place in May
(as in the north-west) when the agricultural year was felt to have ended. In
the east the hiring fair was in Michaelmas (29 September), coinciding with
the immediate post-harvest period. Figure 4.1 is remarkable for the
continuous pattern of male seasonal unemployment which it presents, for
the disappearance of any such later spring unemployment by 1793, with the
periods 1793–1814 and after showing no signs of it, and for the more acute
pattern of the early nineteenth century.

If one turns to Figure 4.2, it will be apparent that women experienced much more drastic changes in their seasonal distribution of unemployment. From 1690 to 1750 the pattern for women in these counties was almost exactly that which we find for men in the earlier period. In 1751–92, however, there was a marked change in the females' pattern, which indicates that their role was being transferred to the spring activities away from the harvest, at the same time as men appeared to be moving to a greater relative involvement in the harvest. The periods of highest employment security for women (1751–92) had become equally the spring and the harvest, in contrast to the earlier tendency, which they had shared with men, for them to retain their jobs most readily in harvest time. By 1793–1814 the female pattern had proceeded further in the same direction, although the change was probably delayed by the temporary shortage of male labour during the war, ensuring relatively equal female involvement in both the spring and the harvest. By this period men showed less apparent involvement in March and April. By 1815–34 women were even more unlikely to maintain their employment during the harvest, and they appear to be least likely to become unemployed in the spring. Men experienced more acute winter unemployment than in the earlier periods. The female pattern of 1835–60 was the reverse of the pattern for 1690–1750, and the shift towards greater employment security during the spring than in the harvest had come to its completion. The male pattern continued much as it was in 1690–1750, but with less noticeable unemployment after the spring activities, in which women would now seem to be much more heavily concentrated. After spring, women became increasingly vulnerable to unemployment until December. So from an environment with a relatively high degree of sexually shared labour, in which gender differences appear to have been almost a matter of indifference to employers, we have moved to a situation indicating an unprecedently marked sexual specialisation of work. Women had come to be most secure from unemployment during a period of the year characterised in the east by relatively slight labour costs and by a low demand for labour.[7] The change was long-term, and its origin can certainly be dated from a period before 1793 – almost certainly between 1750 and 1790. This description of change affecting female work and the sexual division of labour, with its implications of a decline in annual female participation rates and potential earning capacity, can be well supported by long-term trends in male and female money wages, and by early nineteenth-century literary evidence for the region. We will turn now to evidence on wages to support this argument, and to develop an explanation of it.

III

The evidence is provided in Figures 4.3, 4.4, 4.5, 4.6, 4.7, 4.8 and 4.9. This is derived again from settlement examinations, from rural parishes in

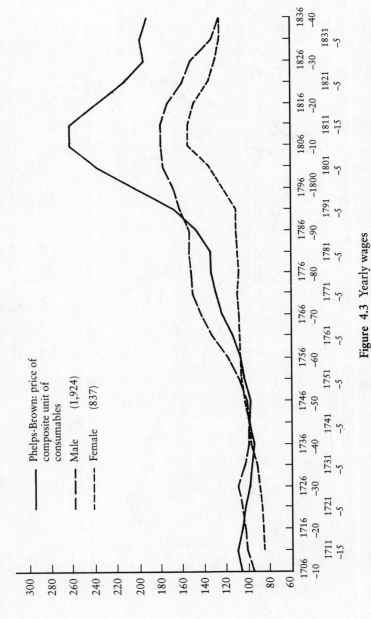

Figure 4.3 Yearly wages

Camb, Beds, Hunts, N'hants, Surr, Kent, Ess, Herts, Norf, Suff, Bucks, Berks, Oxon and Hants (1741–5 = 100)

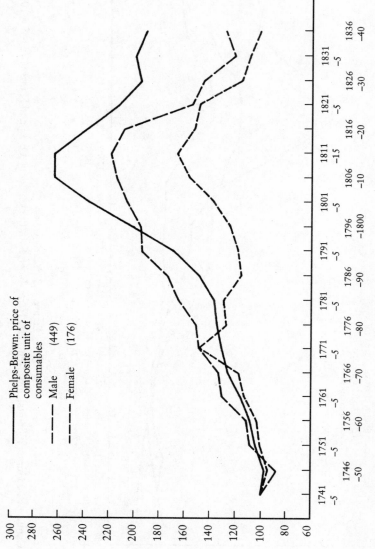

Phelps-Brown: price of
composite unit of
consumables

Male   (449)

Female   (176)

Figure 4.4 Yearly wages
Suff (1741–5 = 100)

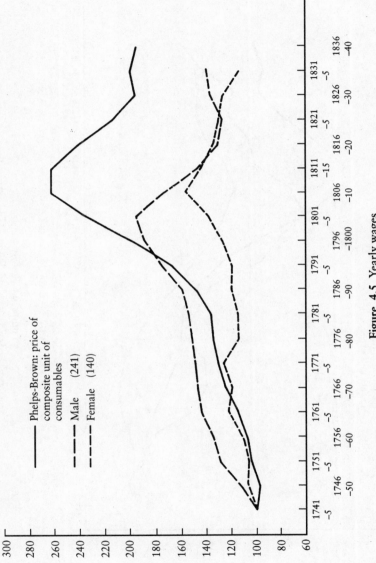

Figure 4.5 Yearly wages
Norf (1741–5 = 100)

Phelps-Brown: price of composite unit of consumables

Male (241)

Female (140)

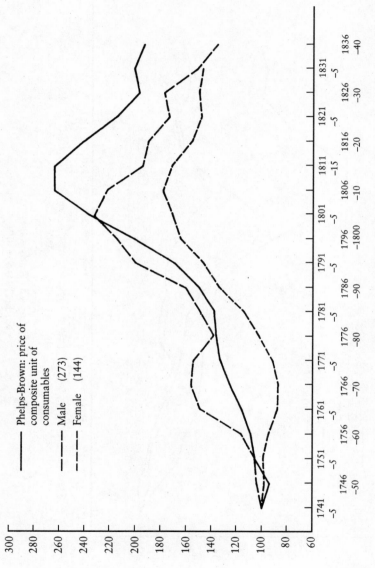

Figure 4.6 Yearly wages
Camb, Beds, Hunts and N'hants (1741–5 = 100)

Phelps-Brown: price of
composite unit of
consumables

Male   (273)

Female   (144)

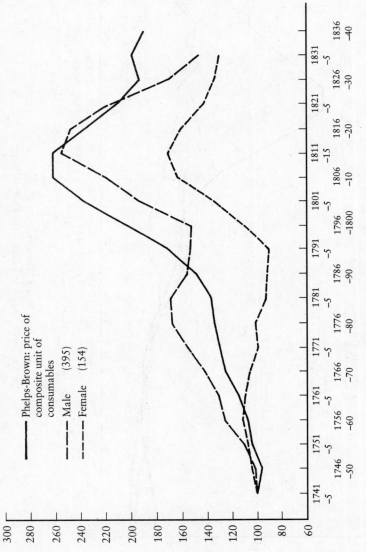

Figure 4.7 Yearly wages
Surr, Kent, Ess and Herts (1741–5 = 100)

Phelps-Brown: price of
composite unit of
consumables

Male   (395)
Female (154)

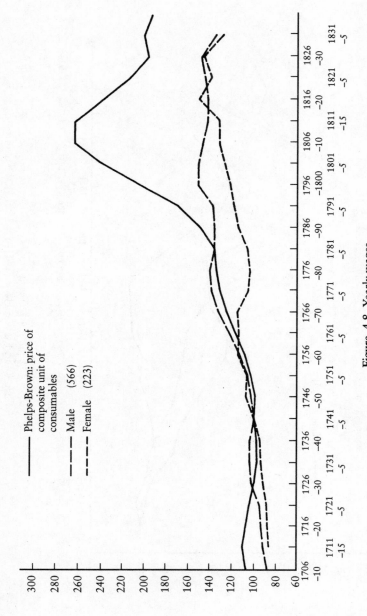

Figure 4.8 Yearly wages
Bucks, Berks, Oxon and Hants (1741–5 = 100)

Phelps-Brown: price of
composite unit of
consumables

Male   (566)

Female (223)

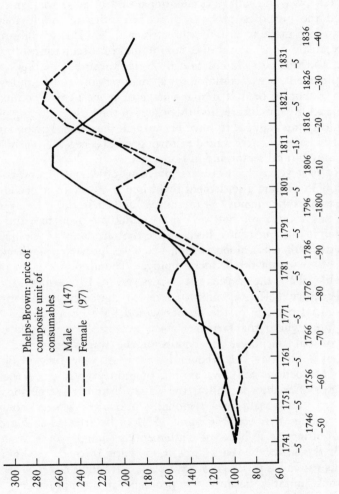

Figure 4.9 Yearly wages
London and Msx (1741–5 = 100)

Phelps-Brown: price of
composite unit of
consumables

Male   (147)
Female (97)

southern and eastern counties. It refers to unmarried men and women, hired by the year, and can be taken to reflect the yearly wages paid at hiring fairs in these counties to agricultural 'farm-servants' and domestic servants.[8] The wages are predominantly agricultural, with a greater emphasis on domestic servants for London and Middlesex. Because of the high degree of movement between purely agricultural employment and employment in small market-town and village occupations, and because the same hiring fairs served the purposes of both these categories of employment, no attempt has been made to distinguish between them. This would probably be an unrealistic task, given the combining of occupations by many employers, and this close interaction of agricultural and market-town or village employment. It was common for a 'farm-servant' to be employed for a year by a publican, or in a similar village or market-town context, and then move back to agriculture, and the wages of the hirings (taking place at the same hiring fair) appear to have been much the same. For our present purposes they have been combined to form general series for yearly hirings within the agricultural sector and in London.

Details of past yearly hirings were given in settlement examinations in connection with gaining a settlement by hiring for a year. The account was from the examinant's memory of the hiring, and there does not appear to have been any motive for him or her to under- or over-state the wages earned. Examinants must have been aware that accounts of the hiring by which a settlement was gained would, whenever possible, be checked by the parish officers with the former employer. The accounts given may be more reliable than the details of wages given by farmers to early nineteenth-century Select Committees, or to agricultural investigators, where the social prestige of the farmer would have been affected by his statement, and where the farmer chosen may in any case have been atypical. For our purposes, the details of the wages contained in the examinations (and they are frequently given in very full detail, with accounts of deductions for days absent, of money given 'in earnest', or rises during or after the year) allow the wages of unmarried persons to be located exactly temporally and regionally, and some general long-term patterns of change between 1662 and 1834 to be seen. (The New Poor Law ended hiring as a head of settlement, although some wages are available in the first few years after it, perhaps through the failure of parish clerks to realise this.) They have some advantages over other wage material, most notably because the problem of unemployment, which affects any consideration of agricultural weekly wage rates, was absent; because they were available every year during this period (rather than only in 1767–70, 1795, 1824, and 1833, as for Bowley's data); and because full details were given alongside other particulars as, for example, the nature of employment, the length and conditions of hiring, or the sex and marital status of the examinant.[9] But because the series presented here are for yearly hirings of unmarried people, inclusive of board and lodging, they have some disadvantages compared to labourers' wage rates. It seems likely that short-term trends in the latter, however, were closely paralleled by trends in wages paid for yearly hirings, and for the purpose of generalising about agricultural wages for married people this assumption has been made. One must be aware, however, that the balance of yearly hirings, and hirings for a shorter time, began to change after 1780,[10] and that generalisations from these wage series about the long-term movement of weekly real wages must be made more tentatively. But the short-term changes (that is for periods of up to about twenty years) in wages of both types of hiring probably followed each other closely.[11] And it is unlikely that the types of work of the weekly and yearly hired were sufficiently dissimilar to render the sexual wage differentials of the latter unrepresentative of the long-term sexual differentials for the weekly hired labourers.

While some general conclusions do emerge from these series, we must also note that most examinations did not go into details of wages, and that the numbers of citings of wages presented here, while almost representing the complete availability of examinations for these counties, are at times nevertheless small. In this regard they have much in common with other series covering the eighteenth and early nineteenth centuries, as compiled by Bowley or Gilboy, which were frequently based on smaller numbers of cases.[12] They are less open to the charge of being very irregularly located in time, which might be made of some of Bowley's figures, particularly for agriculture. His figures were based on discontinuous, and often polemical, evidence, as provided by Arthur Young (1767–70), Sir Frederick Eden (1795), the Report of the Commission on Paying Labourers' Wages out of the Poor Rates (1824), and the Poor Law Report of 1834. This evidence provided Bowley with his 'pivot years', for which he had evidence, and the trends between them were then 'interpolated' in an unclarified manner. Nevertheless, the trends for the eastern counties considered here are in agreement with the impression given by Bowley's figures for this region, which pointed to very low agricultural weekly wage rates in the early nineteenth century. It should be stressed that we are dealing with a group of counties in the south-east which were notoriously badly paid, and that their wage trends should not be taken as generally typical of other areas, particularly in the north.

It might also be claimed that the figures represent going rates of yearly payment prevalent at the regional hiring fairs in different periods, and in this sense have a regularity and representativeness which would be conspicuously lacking for hirings arranged for a shorter period on a more individual basis, away from the institutional context of the statute fairs. The wages varied more by age than by regionality within the compass of individual fairs, and some examinations indeed gave lengthy past details of wages, including those obtained when the examinant was in his or her teens. Such early wages have generally been excluded, to help remove the problem of variation through age-specific earnings. It was of course only the last yearly hiring which conferred settlement, and this would normally take place shortly before marriage, after which 'farm-servants' in this region normally became 'labourers' and moved outside this system of hiring. In consequence, most examinations were concerned only with the last hiring, and the figures may be taken to indicate the mean 'adult' wage of farm-servants, usually aged in their early twenties. Information in the examinations indicated a mean marriage age for men and women of twenty-six and twenty-four respectively, which remained reasonably constant over time. The 'adult' wage was reached by about the age of nineteen and remained steady thereafter, and it seems unlikely that any possible changes in the marriage age could have influenced the trends presented. Nevertheless, despite these supportive comments, it must be noted that these wage series are in some instances based on small numbers, and should be handled tentatively. They are presented as bearing directly on the regions and labour force which concern us, being largely derived from the same settlement documents on which the seasonal unemployment data is based, and as providing the most satisfactory evidence available.[13]

It is necessary to make a few further introductory points on these wage series. The hirings and their details recorded in the examinations were past biographical events of those examined, and so the wages paid cannot be held to be atypical as a consequence of the immediate circumstances of the examinant on examination. In addition, rural poverty in this period had a particular life-cycle, with family men aged about thirty-four with three or more children as yet economically unproductive, and the aged being particularly prone to dependence on the poor rates. Many also came under examination because of illness, familial desertion, or the death of a spouse. While such cases have been eliminated in the consideration of seasonal unemployment, their accounts of past wages are included here. The marked seasonality of eastern agricultural employment also made it very likely that agricultural workers would be examined at some point in their lives. In addition, estimates of relief dependency were very high, particularly in the late eighteenth and early nineteenth centuries, varying between a quarter and a half of village populations requiring assistance.[14] And in the numerous cases where a labour rate or roundsman system was used, it was possible for 'unemployment' among the labour force to become total, with free labour having to become pauperised to find employment.

Furthermore, as we shall see elsewhere, there were many apprenticed artisans examined as to settlement, particularly in urban parishes, who (as for those claiming settlement by renting more than £10 per annum) were in a higher social and economic category than the agricultural labour covered here. And examinants would either sign or make their mark at the end of examinations, making it possible to compare illiteracy rates for examinants with occupationally specific material uncovered by Schofield from parish marriage registers. He found that male illiteracy for servants and labourers (1754–1844) varied between 59 and 66 per cent.[15] During the same period, male illiteracy in examinations, for a sample of two thousand for this occupational group, was 63 per cent. (For male examinants regardless of occupation it varied by county between 40 and 58 per cent. Bedfordshire had the highest illiteracy – also found by Schofield.[16]) It is therefore most unlikely that we are dealing with an unrepresentative sample of the (increasingly homogeneous) agricultural labouring class – those referred to by contemporaries as the 'labouring poor'.

Nor, one should note, is it likely that the localised mobility of examinants makes the settlement data in any way unrepresentative of yearly wages (or of the seasonal unemployment patterns of agricultural labour). Such mobility was a general characteristic of farm-servants, and the high turnover of village populations is now well documented. In addition, a significant proportion of examinations were purely intra-parochial affairs, concerned to check eligibility to relief upon chargeability, and these would not be followed by removal. This proportion settled in their parish of examination varied according to such factors as the size of parish population or administrative efficiency, and normally ranged from between 20–55 per cent, most commonly around 30 per cent. Many examinants who were to be removed had of course been long resident parochially before becoming chargeable. In short, it seems that the immediate conditions which produced an examination do not render this source unreasonably atypical of the standard hiring fair wages in different periods for the unmarried class of 'farm-servants'.

For the purposes of the argument here this introduction can suffice, as I will be mainly concerned with only one feature of these wage statistics – the long-term relative movements of male and female wages, and in particular with the marked tendency for male and female wages to move in inverse correlation at some point between 1750 and 1800 in all the groups of counties covered. In Figure 4.6, for Cambridgeshire, Bedfordshire, Huntingdonshire, and Northamptonshire, the period was 1755 to 1780. In Figure 4.7, for a group of counties immediately circling London, it was 1755 to 1800. In London and Middlesex (Figure 4.9) we can see this between 1765 and 1790. In Norfolk (Figure 4.5) it was after 1765. In Suffolk (Figure 4.4) it was between 1770 and 1800. In Buckinghamshire, Berkshire, Oxfordshire and Hampshire (Figure 4.8) a similar movement occurred after 1760. The same tendency can be seen in the large overall grouping of counties featured in Figure 4.3, between 1755 and 1795, although here, as one would expect, it is less chronologically specific than in the other figures.[17] From the 1790s male and female wages moved more closely in unison, responding to the price rises of the Napoleonic Wars. The inverse correlation was largely a pre-1800 phenomenon, but one that was clearly marked. In virtually all these eastern counties, female real wages were falling from about 1760, which is from when I am dating the changes in female work during the agricultural year.

Some further points might also be noted. Male real wages rose, notably in the thirty years after 1740, and then stabilised. But this gain was lost in the Napoleonic Wars. There was little recovery after 1815, when real wages frequently continued to fall, in the context of agricultural depression, disbanding of the forces, high poor rates, intensified structural unemployment, and widespread, largely unprecedented, agrarian unrest in the east. This general trend can be seen in Figure 4.3. Figure 4.7 for the circle of counties around London, shows a decline in male real wages from 1780, a recovery between 1811 and 1825, but then another decline. A long-term fall is clearly apparent in Norfolk and Suffolk, strikingly so in Buckinghamshire, Berkshire, Oxfordshire, and Hampshire, and there appears to have been little recovery in Cambridgeshire, Bedfordshire, Huntingdonshire, or Northamptonshire. The London and Middlesex wages (Figure 4.9) can be supplemented with the urban wages of St Clement Danes, Middlesex (Figure 4.10). They give the most optimistic picture with their tendency to rise after 1820, but even here there was a decline between 1795 and 1820. These London and Middlesex series are also remarkable for the manner in which female wages kept up with male wages, after (in Figure 4.9) the inverse movement of 1765 to 1790. There is much evidence on the awareness of single women of their possibilities in London, particularly in domestic service, and the series would seem to support this.[18] Furthermore, London and Middlesex money wages were far higher than those of the surrounding counties, which is, of course, a difference well known from other wage series. The counties immediately surrounding London had the next highest money wages, with Norfolk and Suffolk's structural unemployment, high poor rates, and depressed rural industries producing the lowest money wages in the early nineteenth century of all south-eastern counties examined, which is what Bowley's figures would lead us to expect.[19] The major point to stress in regard to these eastern wage series, however, is the tendency (especially outside London and Middlesex) of female real wages to fall continuously from about 1760; but for there then to be a period when male money wages continued to rise, and male real wages either to rise or to remain steady (in inverse correlation to the female trend), until about thirty years later, when they too underwent what appears to be a long-term decline. We shall return to this for its implications for real familial income at a later point. For the present I shall be concerned to explain the post-1750 sexual division of labour, which these wage series appear nicely to substantiate.

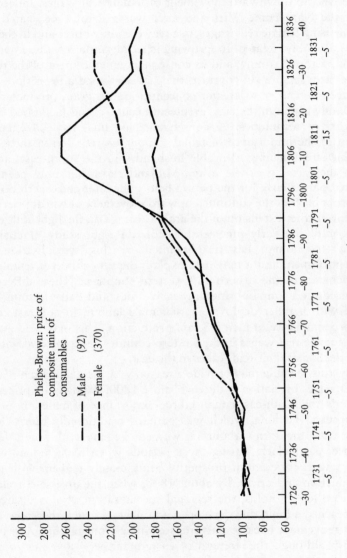

Figure 4.10 Yearly wages
St Clement Danes, Msx (1741–5 = 100)

Phelps-Brown: price of
composite unit of
consumables

Male (92)

Female (370)

IV

In doing this, let us turn to the very different pattern of female wages in the more pastoral west, as seen in Figures 4.11, 4.12, 4.13, and 4.14. In this area there was no downward movement of female real wages. Indeed, the period of the Napoleonic Wars and after was generally associated with buoyant or rising female real wages, in a way certainly not found in the east. This was probably related to growing specialisation of these western counties in pastoral farming, and its consequent enhancement of the role of the female farm-servant. In contrast, the east continued a transition in the later eighteenth century to greater concentration on grain production – a trend probably begun in the late seventeenth century, and facilitated by the new husbandry techniques. A consequence of this may have been a diminution of the importance of female labour, as reflected in their wage trends. This strengthening of arable husbandry in the south-east, and its effects on the farming of the heavy Midland clays, has now been well documented particularly for the period before the later eighteenth century. It seems probable that the continued upward movement of wheat prices was conducive to further extension of the arable acreage on the light soils of the south-east until the early nineteenth century. Recent study of changing agricultural technology has also pointed to this specialisation and employment of men, and it may help explain the very different female real wage movements of the eastern and western counties.[20] These differences may be based on a simple formula: that livestock and dairy farming were associated with a fuller deployment of female labour, in contrast to the growing predominance of men in grain production. This may help explain the rise of female real wages in the western counties, as compared with the long-term decline of their real wages in the east.

Similarly, this formula may provide a reason why male and female wages moved in inverse correlation in the east before 1800. Rising grain prices and production in the south-east enhanced the importance of male labour, and reduced pastoral farming, which was perhaps traditionally more closely associated with the farm labour of women. Female real wages fell in consequence, particularly during those periods when male money wages were rising, with agricultural prosperity being closely tied up with rising cereal production and prices. By about 1800, when the inverse correlation in the east no longer holds, the regional specialisation of agriculture had probably reached a limit, and developed no further. Indeed, there may have been some movement back to pasture, stemming from falling grain prices after 1813,[21] although the strength of eastern farmers' loyalties to grain production by then may have hindered such a development on a wide scale. It is my contention here that the periods of inverse correlation of male and female wages saw the most rapid specialisation in cereal production. As the corn output of the south-east continued to expand after the mid-eighteenth

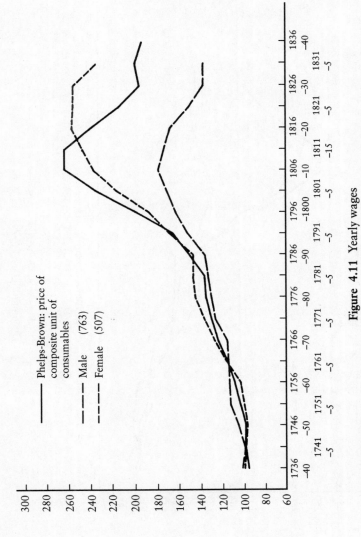

Figure 4.11 Yearly wages

Mon, Heref, Worcs, Salop, Glos, Brecons, Glam, Som, Wilts, Devon and Dorset (1741–5 = 100)

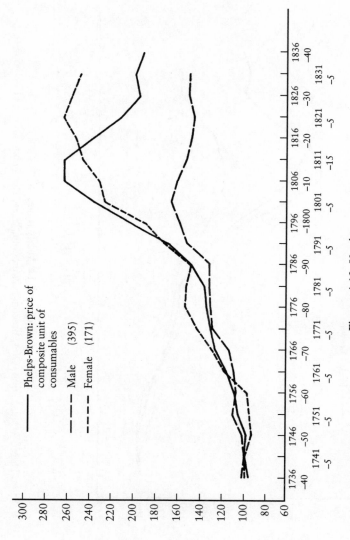

Figure 4.12 Yearly wages
Devon and Dorset (1741–5 = 100)

Phelps-Brown: price of
composite unit of
consumables

––– Male   (395)
- - - Female   (171)

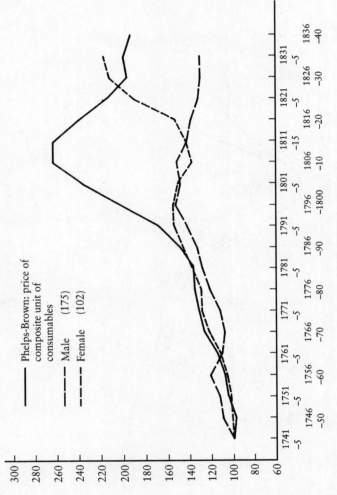

Figure 4.13 Yearly wages
Wilts and Som (1741–5 = 100)

Phelps-Brown: price of
composite unit of
consumables

Male   (175)

Female (102)

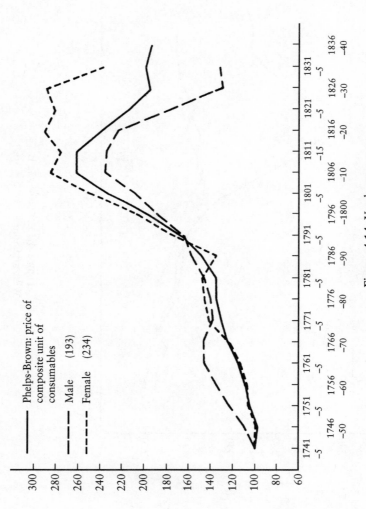

Figure 4.14 Yearly wages
Mon, Heref, Worcs, Salop, Glam, Brecons and Glos (1741–5 = 100)

century, in the context of growing structural unemployment, so female agricultural labour became less in demand, and their money wages fell relative to men. The growing sexual specialisation of labour further depressed female wages, at a time when the involvement of women in the region's increasingly heavy grain production was declining in favour of their participation in the increasingly insignificant dairy and calving season, in spring weeding, and in early summer haymaking. The seasonality of their employment had become more obviously aligned with forms of pastoral agriculture now more firmly associated with the Midlands and areas to the west. As the eighteenth century progressed, this simple formula – of female involvement in pastoral activities and of men in the harvest – became more applicable.[22]

This account can be substantiated further by considering male and female wages in the Midland counties of Leicestershire, Nottinghamshire, and Rutland (Figure 4.15), and the counties of Buckinghamshire, Berkshire, Oxfordshire, and Hampshire (Figure 4.8). For most of these counties were significantly enclosed during the first phase of parliamentary enclosure, before 1790, when there was generally an intensification of pasture and livestock rearing, and reduction of arable farming, most particularly in Leicestershire, Nottinghamshire, and Rutland.[23] Given the changes in the west, one might therefore expect female wages here to keep up with male more than occurred to the south and east. The figures (notably Figure 4.15) show this to have been the case. There were comparatively slight inverse movements of male and female wages after about 1760, with again a tendency for female real wages to fall rather earlier than male. But over the long-term male and female wage trends were quite similar, with the eastern disparities less in evidence. Real wages fell in the later eighteenth century in both groups of counties, but most markedly in the more southern counties.[24]

We can briefly supplement the western wage data with seasonal distributions of unemployment for some border counties with Wales (Figure 4.16). The figure also gives the pastoral pattern for men and women together, which is similar to that found in these counties taken separately, although some indicate greater insecurity of employment around May.[25] The seasonally regular distribution of unemployment may be taken as a standard pattern for most of the region (with its common May hiring fairs), in the way that the eastern pattern is representative of the general seasonality of the south-eastern counties dealt with here. Preliminary research suggests that this western seasonality of employment would be that frequently found in the rural north-west and extreme north, and it helps to explain why yearly hiring survived longer in the west and north than in the east. Both the male and female patterns indicate that employment was spread comparatively evenly over the year. There are suggestions of a distinct sexual division of labour in this period (men are clearly more involved in the harvest), but it was one which (given a relatively constant

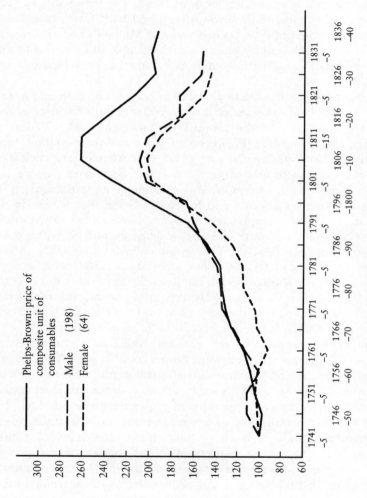

Figure 4.15 Yearly wages
Leics, Notts and Rut (1741–5 = 100)

Phelps-Brown: price of
composite unit of
consumables

Male (198)

Female (64)

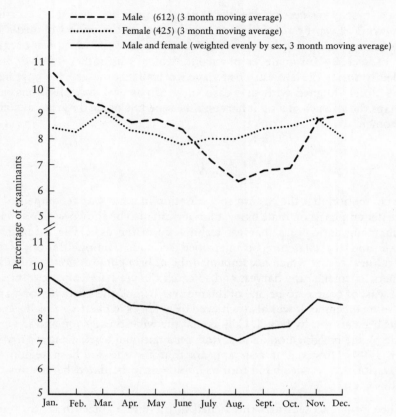

Figure 4.16 Seasonal distribution of unemployment, 1780–1834
Mon, Heref, Worcs, Salop and Glos

level of female activity during the year) seems to be mutually complementary, and probably had favourable implications for familial income.[26]

This comparison of east and west raises the possibility that female specialisation in livestock, dairying, and haymaking, while adversely affecting women in the east, may have been more favourable for them in the west, and so raises problems concerning the emergence, or perpetuation, of sexual attitudes. Without detracting from the importance and complications of this issue, we can simply note such problems here. For example, did the west see livestock and dairying increasingly become the preoccupation of men, as they became more markedly the area's dominant agricultural feature? The assumptions underpinning some feminist historiography might carry this implication, by seeing long-held attitudes of male dominance as being imposed on the changing economic structure of the area. Yet the rising female money wages of the west would question such a theoretical framework. Even by the early nineteenth century, the period immediately after the spring calving and dairying season in the west was not noticeably one of security for male employment, which was rather located most evidently during the harvest. The female work allocation seems to have been more closely aligned with the seasonality of pastoral specialisations, and perhaps the absence of a tight harvest time schedule made these better suited to women.

V

The contention that the eastern specialisation in grain was accompanied by a greater emphasis on male harvest labour can also be shown with reference to changing agricultural harvest technology in the east. The rising grain prices, and the changing or intensified economic rationalisation of the agricultural sector which accompanied them, brought a desire from tenant farmers to quicken the harvest and so catch the pre-harvest peak of prices. This was, of course, to be one of the motives behind the introduction of the threshing machine. It was also achieved by changes in hand-tool technology. It has been argued by E. J. T. Collins that the widespread supplanting of the sickle by the bagging hook and scythe, on a national level, occurred mainly after 1790. However, it also appears that for the southern region the innovations of heavier hand-tool technology can be dated before this. As Collins says:

> The status quo was first threatened in the mid eighteenth century at about which time the practice of 'bagging' with the heavy hook began to replace hand reaping in the London area, Devon, and the English Marcher counties ... Yet by 1790 the impact of these innovations was confined to just a few districts of southern Britain. The corn scythe, which had become established in southern England in the medieval period, had by this late stage failed to penetrate much beyond the Humber.[27]

It seems clear that there was much regional variation in the adoption of heavier tools, with some southern areas experiencing their introduction from the mid-eighteenth century. We might expect that the south-eastern areas most strongly manifesting the grain-growing pattern of seasonal unemployment were those in which such changes took place relatively early. Given the sharp fluctuations of grain prices during the year, peaking immediately before the harvest, it was economically rational for the regions most dependent on grain to lead the way. In this connection, we can draw upon Michael Roberts' interesting discussion of harvest technology. With the surplus grain production of the early eighteenth century, concern with wastage became (he argued) less important, and the scythe was extended from its traditional use for barley, oats, peas, and beans to the harvesting of wheat and rye. Women never used the scythe, and so: 'as the male-dominated corn scythe became more popular the value of men's wages was enhanced and women had to start looking elsewhere for well-paid employment'.[28] This statement is exactly reflected in the figures for the changing sexual division of labour from the mid-eighteenth century, and is further substantiated by the inverse correlations of male and female wages. The chronology of the hand-tool innovations, and the regional specialisations of farming which underlay it, continues to be debated. But it seems likely that such innovations were an important cause of the changing sexual division of labour after about 1750, being accompanied by greater demand for male harvesters. But these factors must also be supplemented as explanations by the effects of male vulnerability to unemployment (an enabling factor for, and consequence of, cereal specialisation), which also excluded female competition; and perhaps also by the employing motivations of farmers concerned with rising familial dependence on the poor rates. I shall return to these points later.

VI

As I am using a previously untested source, it seems appropriate now to consider what literary evidence there is to support the argument for an intensified sexual specialisation of agricultural work after the mid-eighteenth century; and to develop the suggestion that this specialisation brought with it a declining participation of women within the agricultural work force. The large pamphlet literature on eighteenth- and nineteenth-century poor relief, the Annals of Agriculture, and the County Surveys in the early nineteenth century are generally unhelpful, although all these sources frequently mention female unemployment. The major evidence presented in the unfortunately rather late Poor Law Report of 1834, in the subsequent Poor Law Reports, and in the 1843, 1867–8, and 1868–9 Reports on the Employment of Women and Children in Agriculture provide numerous indications of the increasingly insignificant role of female agricultural labour in this region. But the evidence usually fails to provide any background to the change, which could help identify its origins and causes. Hence historians have concerned themselves with the tail-end of the process, and have missed both its regional variations and long-term character.[29]

Nevertheless, if one approaches these reports with the views advanced earlier in mind, a great deal emerges which suggests that change in the sexual division of labour and, indeed, in the extent of female participation, had already taken place to a large degree, and that it cannot in consequence be seen as initially stemming from particular Victorian moral sentiments regarding the 'proper' roles of women. The strength of these by the 1860s cannot be doubted, and they are well represented in these reports. But they reflected the relative absence of female labour in this region by then, rather than being significantly instrumental in its decline.[30] As Thomas Lawrence of Childry (Berkshire), a labourer aged eighty-two, told the 1868–9 Commission: 'The women don't work so much as they used to, they don't employ them . . . my master employed as many as the whole parish does now, and so the farms ain't kept so clean now. The young men that are out of work won't go elsewhere to look for it.'[31] Two implications emerge from this statement: that even in Lawrence's younger days women were mainly engaged in 'cleaning' land for corn and then in weeding it (during the spring), and that male unemployment was a major factor excluding female labour. We shall return to this latter theme shortly.

What is striking about the earlier evidence of the 1843 Select Committee is the limited role women had when compared to the early eighteenth century, or the seventeenth century, when their work was very similar in its seasonality to that of men, and the differential between male and female wages was much less notable. There is abundant supportive evidence for a very wide range of female participation in agricultural tasks before 1750 in the south-east, when their work extended to reaping, loading and spreading dung, ploughing, threshing, thatching, following the harrow, sheep shearing, and even working as shepherdesses.[32] In other regions similar work continued more noticeably into the nineteenth century (particularly in parts of the north, where the 'bondage' system was practised), but there is almost nothing in the 1843 Report to suggest such a range of female participation for this district. In the area around Bury St Edmunds, for example, our earlier description of female work by this period is reinforced by being told that they work mainly in March, April, and May, at stone-picking, weeding and dropping corn, and in gleaning after the harvest in August. 'In other months they are generally unemployed.' They were not even employed significantly in haymaking in late May in this area.[33] Around Hadleigh 'out-door labour for women is confined to a little weeding of corn in spring; occasional labour in the hay-time; gleaning at harvest; and for children and young women, dropping wheat about Michaelmas'.[34] At Lavenham: 'Women are not much employed on the land on the whole, not more than four months in the year.'[35] And around Hunston it was 'the want of employment, and I may almost say complete idleness, during a great part of the year (particularly with women and girls), that increases the bastardy list, among other evils'.[36]

If we turn to the most valuable, and earliest, systematic evidence open to us – the answers to questions 11, 12, and 13 of the Poor Law Commission of 1832–4, on the extent of female agricultural labour, the same conclusion is strongly borne out. In Great Shelford in Cambridgeshire, for example, it was the case that 'We have no employment for women and children but haymaking and weeding'.[37] In Caddington (Bedfordshire) 'the women and children are rarely, if ever, employed in field labour'.[38] And 'Women are scarcely ever employed in agriculture', in Lidlington, also in Bedfordshire.[39] At Gestingthorpe (Essex) 'We have no employment for women.'[40] It was said of Kelveden (Essex) that 'The parish being entirely agricultural, and the number of labourers more than equal to the demand (about five Men, besides Boys, to the 100 acres) there is little employment for Women and Children.'[41] Once again, structural unemployment seemed to contribute to the diminution of female agricultural work. In Great Waltham, there was 'Scarcely any [employment for women or children]; a few are occasionally employed in picking stones off the land.'[42] At Thorpe le Soken, there was 'very little [female employment]. At particular seasons, as Spring and Autumn, some employment is afforded for Women and Children on the land.'[43] Or at Bassingbourne (Cambridgeshire) there was 'A little, only for a short time, in the Spring, in field work.'[44] As for the role of women in the harvest by this date, it was usually limited to the very short-term work of gleaning. This was so, for example, in Wisbech St Mary (Cambridgeshire): 'in Harvest a few are able to reap, but the major part who are not confined with a large family go gleaning'.[45] In Holy Trinity (Isle of Ely) it was said that 'Women's time in harvest is generally employed in gleaning.'[46] There were many other statements to this effect throughout the counties which concern us. Examples include Clavering, in Essex ('Not any except harvest gleaning'),[47] Standen Massey, in Essex ('But little, except stone and twitch picking, haymaking, and gleaning in harvest time'),[48] Witham, in Essex ('They glean corn after the harvest, but they do nothing in it'),[49] Welwyn, in Hertfordshire ('The women of Hertfordshire seldom work at corn harvest'),[50] and All Saints, in Suffolk ('Women and Children are not much employed, either in Summer or Winter, or in Harvest, except gleaning').[51]

An analysis of all the parishes returning answers to the Poor Law Commission (in the counties covered by my seasonal unemployment figures) provides a wider picture of the agricultural events mentioned most frequently as involving female participation. The female occupation most commonly reported was that of spring weeding, essentially of corn, with ninety-eight parishes mentioning this. It was clearly the main factor making for the high security of female spring employment found in the nineteenth-century patterns of Figure 4.2. Haymaking was noted by seventy-three parishes, gleaning by fifty-eight parishes, stone-picking by forty-three parishes, 'the harvest' (which could of course mean gleaning only) by thirty-three parishes, reaping by nineteen parishes, wheat planting (in October) by fifteen parishes, and the pulling and topping of turnips by seven parishes.[52] Bean-setting was mentioned by four, 'burning' by four, and all other agricultural tasks by only two or less parishes.

David Davies, in the *Case of the Labourers in Husbandry* (1795) – among the most famous contemporary publications on rural poverty, and probably the most reliable – argued that the two most needed remedial measures were an increase of wages to counteract falling real wages, and a revival of employment for women. Previously, he argued, there had been many opportunities for women and children to work, 'whereas now, few of *these* are constantly employed . . . so that almost the whole burden of providing for these families rests upon the *men*' (his italics). The result had been a fall in familial income, and 'the consequence is universally felt in the increased number of the dependent poor'. The measures, he continued, 'which appear most necessary to be immediately adopted, are the two following; viz. that of *raising wages*, and that of *providing employment for women and girls*. These two measures should go together' (his italics).[53]

Thus, as Figure 4.2 suggested, female labour in the east by the 1830s had become heavily limited to the spring work of weeding corn, and to haymaking, with a subsidiary involvement in the harvest as gatherers and tyers, and particularly as gleaners. There is little evidence in government reports which would lead us to question the long-term pattern and timing of change outlined earlier from the settlement material, and much also to support the contention, made with reference to female wages, that the concentration of women on a few specific tasks was accompanied by a tendency for them to be excluded from a traditionally fuller and more sexually equal participation in agriculture. This development was a Victorian phenomenon only in the sense that the Victorian period saw the completion of the process. It cannot be held to have been primarily a product of Victorian morality and middle-class assumptions regarding the roles of women. It is indeed more tempting to see the economic rationality of this sexual differentiation as lying behind these attitudes and morality.[54]

VII

Some concluding remarks can now be made on the long-term changes I have outlined. The implications of the eastern patterns of seasonal unemployment for the standard of living debate lie in the increased acuteness of the male pattern in 1815–34, though we may note that their general pattern continued much the same over the whole period.[55] The acuteness of this early nineteenth-century pattern questions the capacity of enclosure and the new, improved, agricultural practices to provide greater and more regular employment throughout the year for the growing male labour force, particularly in seasons previously characterised by high employment insecurity.[56] Because of a tendency under the New Poor Law for there to be a greater reluctance to apply for relief, the pattern after 1835 is not readily comparable to those which preceded it. The greater availability of piecework in the nineteenth century may have lessened the problem of winter unemployment, or prevented any further intensification of it.

Alternatively, such piecework may have represented a more calculating use of labour, and may have replaced more permanent forms of employment. The pattern for the later nineteenth century may appear less extreme only because of the changes in poor law administration of 1834, and the well-documented hostile attitudes of the poor to those changes.[57]

That the nineteenth-century male patterns were not more acute was partly a result of the eighteenth-century fall-off of female employment, which I have suggested accompanied the sexual specialisation of agricultural work. Had women continued with their pre-industrial agricultural involvement, male employment would probably have become even more seasonally precarious. In assessing implications for *familial* income (a more important consideration for the 'standard of living' than male wage trends alone), one should see the male pattern in relation to the deterioration of employment possibilities for women which accompanied and helped determine it.[58] When one considers in conjunction with this the falling male real wages of the period after about 1780, through to the New Poor Law (and arguably thereafter, as an effect of that law),[59] and the even more extreme long-term depression of female real wages from about 1760, the effects on familial income seem clear – effects compounded of course by the rising demographic dependency ratio: the fertility changes of the period produced much larger family sizes. Female labour was not diverted elsewhere in the east. Against the widespread decline of cottage industry in the region after the Napoleonic Wars,[60] and the reduced role of women in many apprenticed trades, and in family-based artisan production,[61] one can mainly set work in the straw-plait industry in parts of Bedfordshire, Buckinghamshire, and Hertfordshire, and in the silk mills of some Essex parishes. Domestic service, especially in London, for the unmarried only, and some other more poorly paid London occupations (such as dressmaking and millinery, or 'slop-shop' tailoring), were other female economic options open by the early nineteenth century.[62] And demand for domestic servants in the early nineteenth century probably helped hold up female wages then. But these south-eastern counties, besides paying notoriously low agricultural wages, lacked the developing sectors providing alternative female employment and the steady or rising female real wages which characterised other regions in the west or north.

A wide range of factors was responsible for the extremity of the early nineteenth-century pattern of male unemployment, and for the fall in real wages, which came in marked contrast to the trends for male real wages in the period between 1740 and about 1780. Such factors would certainly include the eastern specialisation in grain, demographic pressure and its associated structural unemployment, the agricultural depression caused by falling prices after 1813, and perhaps a failure of farming profits to rise commensurate with rents after enclosure. And as we shall see elsewhere, enclosure was a major factor in parishes enclosed by act. Real wages may also have been hit by a possible shift back to pasture when prices fell in the early nineteenth century. While it is not clear how extensive such a reversion was, it would certainly have reduced general demand for a labour force by now over-abundant even for the intensive, but short-term, requirements of cereal production. This pessimistic picture of the early nineteenth-century south-eastern agricultural sector could be amply supported by evidence from parliamentary or newspaper enquiries; by the evidence of Speenhamland and the wide range, and short-term variability, of alternative poor relief measures;[63] by the changing depiction of the agricultural labourer in the poetry and painting of the eighteenth and early nineteenth centuries;[64] by the rising poor rates of the later eighteenth century, and their very high level during the high price years, after the Napoleonic Wars, and in the later 1820s; by changes in hiring practices, and the growing difficulty in gaining settlements as employers increasingly hired for periods a few days under the full year;[65] by the causes and consequences of the decline of apprenticeship in the south-east, outside London, after 1750;[66] and by the well-documented evidence of continual agrarian unrest from 1795 through to 'Swing', and thereafter. All were witnesses to the problem of unemployment.[67] Lack of employment provision may, in the period after 1850, have been the major factor behind outward mobility from the land,[68] but an almost opposite situation may have obtained in the early nineteenth century, when lack of agricultural capital, a reluctance of rents to fall commensurate with prices, and structural unemployment produced widespread periodical reliance on a still highly localised settlement and poor relief system, which tended to hinder outward mobility in the east. This set up a depressing circularity of cause and effect which was broken only with the mid-century revival of agricultural profitability.[69]

As was suggested earlier, the sexual specialisation of work in the east is only partly to be explained as a consequence of the region's expansion of grain production, bringing a more extensive use, by employers, of male harvest labour and heavier technology. Male vulnerability to periodical unemployment, an associated feature of cereal production, may also have produced measures, originating from within the labour force, to reduce female competition.[70] We have noted literary indications which suggest this, and while the scythe may have been a major excluding factor in relation to the harvest, male structural unemployment probably led to pressure against women working in other tasks, such as ploughing, dung-spreading, or threshing. Such unemployment was increasingly in evidence after 1760, as the well-documented rising parish poor rates would suggest. Employers may have cooperated in this, and may have been inclined to limit employment to men to guard against familial dependence on the poor rates. No doubt an effect of the resulting decline of female participation was to soften the potential vulnerability of men to unemployment and to the experience of falling real wages, but it did so at the expense of real familial income.[71]

One must also consider the possibility that a decline of a pre-industrial 'family economy' may have contributed to the changes analysed – by which term I mean the synonymity of home and work place for husband and wife. In the early eighteenth century, access to the commons, a greater prevalence of owner-occupiers and small tenants, and less dependence on weekly wage labour away from the home place, may have laid the groundwork for a more equal sexual division of labour than that which became increasingly apparent after 1760. The argument for the east has, indeed, suggested that the model of the 'pre-industrial family economy', with more equally shared sex roles, may have been a real feature of the period from 1690 to the mid-eighteenth century. While the early eighteenth century certainly already had a significant agricultural proletariat, it was probably the case that the decline then of both small tenants and owner-occupiers reduced the potential for a wide participation of women within the family economy.[72] Such a development may also have brought a re-assessment of the roles of women within the wage-dependent labour force. Certainly such a decline of a 'family economy' form of production made men more vulnerable to the effects of unemployment; and in this sense the decline, with its associated separation of male place of work and home place, may have limited the possibilities for fuller female participation at the same time as its closely related effect on employment security produced pressures against female competition from the male labour force itself. But at this point it seems premature to develop more fully this line of explanation, and its significance for the history of the family. Insofar as the seasonal unemployment figures relate mostly to partially or wholly wage-dependent labour, rather than to families of owner-occupiers, it would have to be demonstrated that female work in the family economy created a social acceptance of similar work roles for more wage-dependent women, before an argument for a relatively shared sexual division of labour being based on the family economy could become fully convincing. This may depend on an assessment of the degree to which owner-occupier families were partially dependent on wage labour, and such an assessment is not currently accessible. Neither are we yet in a position to be entirely certain that a larger degree of sexually shared labour was a common characteristic of the 'pre-industrial' period. While a greater predominance of family-economy production earlier would suggest this, it may also have been to some extent an associated feature of population stagnation.[73] Earlier periods, as, for example, the late sixteenth and early seventeenth centuries, may have witnessed limited changes in the sexual division of labour parallel to those discussed here, because of demographic influences on the labour market.

The divergence of the female pattern of seasonal unemployment away from that of men after the mid-eighteenth century, to a concentration of work during a less labour-intensive period of the year, with low labour costs, and the associated long-term decline of female wages, implies a fall-off from their earlier participation rates, and a decline of their annual earning capacity. This seems well supported by early nineteenth-century literary evidence for the region. It is also likely that these changes brought an associated decline of women as a percentage of the total labour force, although one can only deduce this from the evidence provided, which cannot directly confront this more intangible problem. The definition of a 'female agricultural work force' in a period and region so characterised by seasonal fluctuations in labour demand is in any case problematic; and it may be unrealistic to pose the discussion in these terms, and of greater value to limit generalisation to the more certain effects on familial income of the changes analysed. We might, however, recall Eric Richards' argument in this context that: 'in the pre-industrial framework women were absorbed in a broad range of activity which was subsequently narrowed by the structural changes associated with the Industrial Revolution'.[74] The progressive domination of the economy by men, which he stressed, seems reinforced by the eastern evidence, although it is doubtful if this was so marked in the pastoral west. The availability of relatively highly paid agricultural and alternative female employment in many areas of the north, coupled with the much greater continuity of northern agricultural employment practices (in particular, the 'bondage system', and yearly hiring[75]), and the relative absence of structural and acute seasonal unemployment, make it likely that these regions witnessed more prolonged and fuller female economic participation and greater buoyancy of real familial income than in the south and east.[76]

One might take this point further and emphasise the regional variety of male and female wage trends, patterns of unemployment, and differences in the sexual division of labour. Such diversity could be demonstrated more extensively by incorporating material for northern or south-western regions lying outside the groups of counties I have considered. Even if one takes only the southern agricultural sector, seasonal distributions of male unemployment existed (for example, in Sussex, or in parts of the south-west) which are unlike the dominant patterns contrasted here. And this is to say nothing of the different and varying patterns of unemployment experienced by men and women in the apprenticed trades in the south-east, or of how the decline of apprenticeship affected these. The same diversity is clearly apparent in rural and other wage trends. To a limited extent this has been shown by a few excellent regional studies of the standard of living. But it would be dubious to suppose that the wage data currently available for the eighteenth and nineteenth centuries (which lack *any* indicators of unemployment), is anything other than highly localised and sparse, and barely hints at the regional diversity which existed. That diversity becomes all the more complex when one takes into account the regionality and changes of seasonal unemployment and the sexual division of labour, with their implications for familial income. It may be the case that attempts to generalise discussion of the standard of living, or of the extent and continuity of the home market, are as yet premature, and that the immediate aim of research should be to delineate much more sharply the regional differences and changes of the period. When this is more adequately achieved it is possible that the resulting appreciation of a wide variety of regional and occupational experience may reduce the importance of drawing conclusions at a national level; and one hopes then for a much more accurate and specific understanding of the local economic, demographic, and social processes involved, of their interrelation with cultural attitudes, and for a sensitive understanding of how they affected the labouring classes.

The problems of structural unemployment and cereal specialisation in the east have pointed my discussion primarily to the inadequacy of demand for labour. The surplus population (especially female) of the region has made a consideration of labour supply relatively unimportant. However, the significance of the changes in female employment may also bear directly on the question of provision of labour for cottage industry (as indeed may the two regional employment seasonalities I have contrasted). In the eastern counties covered here one thinks particularly of lace and straw-plait. The way the agricultural changes affecting women provided a labour force for such activities will be readily apparent, and it may also be the case that the attractiveness of such industries in the mid- and late eighteenth century contributed to the agricultural division of labour. But one can only stress the short-term significance of this in the east, given the decline of most cottage industries after 1815. The decline of female spinning in particular, probably most marked after 1800, and much commented on in early nineteenth-century government reports for the region, may have aggravated female unemployment and depressed familial income. The importance of these changes for the provision of domestic servants may be especially noted, and I would have no quarrel with the characterisation of nineteenth-century domestic service (in the south-east) as a form of 'disguised underemployment'.[77]

Finally, a main theme of this chapter can be re-emphasised: the historical determinants of women's economic and domestic roles would appear to be located primarily in seemingly autonomous changes in the structure of the economy, rather than in shifts of social attitudes. Moral sentiments antagonistic to female labour in the nineteenth century may have reinforced the pattern of change described here, and contributed to the process begun in the mid-eighteenth century. But insofar as they cannot readily be dated from before 1800, at the very earliest, their significance seems heavily undercut by the evidence that the major sexual division of labour began at least fifty years before such 'middle-class' attitudes towards the roles of women can have had influence. Insofar as economic change and its accompanying motivations alone probably began that process in the south-east, there is a need to re-evaluate the origins and effects of Victorian attitudes to femininity. This would reveal with greater clarity their causal dependency on, and compatibility with, changes in the economic structure, particularly in relation to the factors acting on male employment, and would attempt a fuller understanding of their origins in the poorly documented and elusive eighteenth-century background. Such an exercise would also contribute to a fuller and more instructive understanding of the formation and relativity of social attitudes to concrete, but changing, social and economic environments.

Notes

1 For a bibliography of literature dealing with the debate on living standards, see M. W. Flinn, 'Trends in real wages, 1750–1850', *Econ. Hist. Rev.*, XXVII (1974), 412–13. See also T. R. Gourvish, 'Flinn and real wage trends in Britain, 1750–1850: a comment', *Econ. Hist. Rev.*, XXIX (1976); M. W. Flinn, 'Real wage trends in Britain, 1750–1850: a reply', *Econ. Hist. Rev.*, XXIX (1976); G. N. von Tunzelmann, 'Trends in real wages, 1750–1850, revisited', *Econ. Hist. Rev.*, XXXII (1979); N. F. R. Crafts, 'National income estimates and the British standard of living debate: a reappraisal of 1801–1831', *Explorations in Economic History*, XVII (1980); E. H. Phelps-Brown and S. V. Hopkins, *A Perspective of Wages and Prices* (1981); and for an overview of the work of P. H. Lindert and J. G. Williamson, see their 'English workers' living standards during the Industrial Revolution: a new look', *Econ. Hist. Rev.*, XXXVI (1983). On unemployment in the pre-industrial period, see D. C. Coleman, 'Labour in the English economy of the seventeenth century', *Econ. Hist. Rev.*, VIII (1956). On the problem of agricultural unemployment in the early nineteenth century, see in particular N. Gash, 'Rural unemployment, 1815–1834', *Econ. Hist. Rev.*, VI (1935); E. L. Jones, 'The agricultural labour market in England, 1793–1872', *Econ. Hist. Rev.*, XVII (1964); G. E. Fussell and M. Compton, 'Agricultural adjustments after the Napoleonic Wars', *Econ. Hist.*, IV (1939); A. Digby, 'The labour market and the continuity of social policy after 1834: the case of the eastern counties', *Econ. Hist. Rev.*, XXVIII (1975); M. W. Flinn, 'The Poor Employment Act of 1817', *Econ. Hist. Rev.*, XIV (1961); D. C. Barnett, 'Allotments and the problem of rural poverty, 1780–1840', in E. L. Jones and G. E. Mingay (eds.), *Land, Labour and Population in the Industrial Revolution* (1967); E. J. T. Collins, 'Harvest technology and labour supply in Britain, 1790–1870', *Econ. Hist. Rev.*, XXII (1969), and his 'Migrant labour in British Agriculture in the nineteenth century', *Econ. Hist. Rev.*, XXIX (1976); M. Blaug, 'The myth of the old poor law and the making of the new', *Jnl of Econ. Hist.*, XXIII (1963), and his 'The Poor Law Report re-examined', *Jnl of Econ. Hist.*, XXIV (1964); D. A. Baugh, 'The cost of poor relief in south-east England, 1790–1834', *Econ. Hist. Rev.*, XXVIII (1975); D. N. McCloskey, 'New perspectives on the Old Poor Law', *Explorations in Economic History*, X (1972–3); J. R. Poynter, *Society and Pauperism: Ideas on Poor Relief, 1795–1834* (1969); M. E. Rose, 'The allowance system under the New Poor Law', *Econ. Hist. Rev.*, XIX (1966); F. G. Emmison, 'Relief of the poor at Eaton Socon, Bedfordshire, 1706–1834', *Beds Hist. Rec. Soc.*, XV (1933); A. Digby, 'The rural poor law', in D. Fraser (ed.), *The New Poor Law in the Nineteenth Century* (1976); A. J. Peacock, *Bread or Blood; a Study of the Agrarian Riots in East Anglia in 1816* (1965). For two excellent discussions of the rural standard of living, see: D. R. Mills, 'The quality of life in Melbourn, Cambridgeshire, in the period 1800–1850', *International Review of Social History*, XXIII (1978); and T. L. Richardson, 'Agricultural labourers' standard of living in Kent, 1790–1840', in D. J. Oddy and D. Miller (eds.), *The Making of the British Diet* (1976). For the relation of unemployment to the introduction of the threshing machine, see: S. Macdonald, 'The progress of the early threshing machine', *Agricultural History Review*, XXIII (1975); N. E. Fox, 'The

spread of the threshing machine in central southern England', *Agric. Hist. Rev.*, XXVI (1978); S. Macdonald, 'Further progress with the early threshing machine: a rejoinder', *Agric. Hist. Rev.*, XXVI (1978); E. J. T. Collins, 'The diffusion of the threshing machine in Britain, 1790–1880', *Tools and Tillage*, II (1972). And, of course, see E. J. Hobsbawm and G. Rudé, *Captain Swing* (1969, 1973 edn).

2 Flinn, 'Trends in real wages', 410–11.

3 13 & 14 Car II c. 12. And see 1 Jac II c. 17; 3 Wm & Mary c. 11; 8 & 9 Wm III c. 30; 12 Anne c. 18; 9 Geo I c. 7; 3 Geo II c. 29. For further discussion of the use of settlement documentation for these purposes, see K. D. M. Snell, 'Settlement, poor law and the rural historian: new approaches and opportunities', *Rural History: Economy, Society, Culture*, 3:2 (1992), 145–72.

4 35 Geo III c. 101. Some groups earlier could not be removed until chargeable, such as holders of settlement certificates, soldiers, sailors, and their families, and friendly society members. See 8 & 9 Wm III c. 30; 24 Geo III c. 6; 33 Geo III c. 54.

5 This fee could be between 3s. and 7s. for one examination in the late eighteenth century, and would be considerably more for extra copies made and removal orders drawn up, with notices of pending removal sent. The removal itself would usually cost over £8 and if attended by legal expenses would go well over £20. Such a sum would maintain a single pauper continuously for about three years.

6 The counties represented in these figures indicate a reasonable continuity of their proportional contribution over the five periods, and the explanation for the figures does not appear to be bound up with a temporal change in their geographical incidence. Discontinuities of emphasis were small, and the agricultural specialisation of these counties was sufficiently homogeneous to make these insignificant. All these counties very clearly indicate the male grain-growing pattern when analysed separately, and the descriptions of women's work presented in the 1834 Poor Law Report were very similar for each county.

The removal orders which went with examinations sometimes give occupations, and such cases are incorporated here, alongside a relatively small number of orders for people examined in heavily agricultural parishes. The order was intended to follow the examination through the post (to the parish to which removal was to take place) by two weeks, but was commonly drawn up by the clerk (and even sent) on the same day. Any slight time lag becomes insignificant when using a three month moving average. Orders usually lack the occupational specificity of examinations, although this problem can largely be obviated by careful choice of agricultural parishes, leaving aside centres of cottage industry. The information given by parish in the 1801 census on numbers engaged in agriculture and handicraft manufacturing is a helpful guide for this. A very large majority of rural examinants commonly worked in agricultural occupations. The advantages of orders are their consistent precision on chargeability, marital status, family size, and ages of children. The addition here makes no significant difference to the distributions from examinations, and usefully supplements them; no cases of removal for which the examination survives are included. Further figures were also calculated using a much larger number of rural removal orders only, and this produced similar distributions and changes to those presented here.

These figures should not be used to generalise further on the changing sex ratios of applicants for relief over time, as additional sex-specific research provided a stronger numerical basis for some of the distributions.

7 The monthly wage payments made by farmers in the east were, of course, in direct inverse correlation to the male seasonal unemployment patterns of Figure 4.1. See, for example, W. Marshall, *Review and Abstract of the County Reports to the Board of Agriculture. Vol. III: The Eastern Department* (1811, York, 1818 edn), p. 256; Rev. C. D. Brereton, *A Practical Inquiry into the Number, Means of Employment and Wages of Agricultural Labourers* (Norwich, 1824), p. 74, giving the monthly wage expenditure for a large Norfolk farm between 1805 and 1824.

8 The wages are for full fifty-two week hirings. Wages for other variants of service (fifty-one weeks, nine months, provision of 'board' wages, etc.) are not included. Such variants on the full yearly hiring are discussed in chapter 2 [K. D. M. Snell, *Annals of the Labouring Poor: Social Change and Agrarian England, 1660–1900* (Cambridge

University Press, 1985)]. I have also included yearly wages from other sources besides examinations, such as diaries, farm accounts, pamphlets on agriculture and the poor law, and the like. The wage rates from other sources generally match closely those in the examinations, which comprise most of the citings aggregated here.

9 For the importance of trends in yearly wages, particularly in relation to questions of the location of the home market, and the determinants of marriage, see J. Hajnal, 'European marriage patterns in perspective', D. V. Glass and D. E. C. Eversley (eds.), *Population in History* (1965).

10 See chapter 2 [Snell, *Annals of the Labouring Poor*].

11 The correspondent for the rural districts in the *Morning Chronicle* in 1849 gave a view, which supports this, that yearly wages, arranged at the hiring fair, were closely related to weekly wage rates: 'The servants hired at this fair are generally such as are boarded and lodged on the farm, but the wages offered them were a good indication of what was likely to be the rate in vogue, so far as the ordinary farm labourer was concerned.' *Morning Chronicle*, 27 Oct. 1849. It is difficult to gauge how representative of weekly wage movements the annual wage trends were, particularly after the 1780s. From then there was a growing tendency to hire for shorter periods – necessitated, in the context of escalating poor rates, by the desire to avoid the settlements created by yearly hiring, and to ease the increasing parochial dependency of the married, who were, of course, more expensive to maintain on the rates than the single. Yearly hiring also became unsuited to the intensive, but short-term labour requirements of cereal-producing regions, which we noted in regard to Figure 4.1. The system had also probably been more compatible with the family life-cycle demand for labour of small farms and owner-occupiers in an earlier period. On the one hand, it could be held that as a consequence of the factors undercutting the viability of the yearly hiring system, yearly wage rates fell more than did weekly. On the other, it could be argued with equal weight that the categories of labour remaining hired by the year were increasingly those which were indispensable to the farmer, and who had traditionally received higher wages (e.g., carters, shepherds, and so on), and that, in consequence, these yearly figures underrepresent the actual weekly real wage decline. I do not consider Bowley's figures for weekly wage trends to be that adequate fully to resolve this problem. But we can note that my figures tend to represent rural wages as being at the same or a marginally higher level by the 1830s as they had been around 1760 (e.g., Figure 4.3). If we turn to Bowley, we find to support this that Berkshire, Buckinghamshire, Cambridgeshire, Essex, Suffolk, and Norfolk all had wages as late as 1850 which were within 6d. of their 1767–70 level (A. L. Bowley, 'Statistics of wages in the United Kingdom during the last hundred years', pt I, 'Agricultural wages', *Jnl of the Royal Statistical Society*, LXI (1898), 704). Further weekly wage data which I have collected could also be introduced here to make the same point.

There was also no doubt among contemporaries that weekly real wages fell in the southern (and many Midland) counties. For example, see: D. Davies, *The Case of the Labourers in Husbandry* (1795), e.g., pp. 25ff, 56–7, 68–74, 87ff, 124–5, 156ff; S.C. [Select Committee] on Agricultural Labourers' Wages, VI (1824), p. 22; S.G. and E.O.A. Checkland (eds.), *The Poor Law Report of 1834* (1974), p. 284; Marshall, *Review and Abstract*, p. 304; *Annals of Agriculture*, XXV (1795), 609 (communication from Rev. J. Howlett, claiming that real wages had been falling since 1756); G. Dyer, *The Complaints of the Poor People of England* (1792), p. 100; W. Frend, *Peace and Union recommended to the associated Bodies of Republicans and Anti-Republicans* (Cambridge, 1793), pp. 47–9; A. Smith, *The Wealth of Nations* (1776, Harmondsworth, 1977 edn), p. 177: 'The high price of provisions during these ten years past has not in many parts of the kingdom been accompanied with any sensible rise in the money price of labour'; C. Vancouver, *General View of the Agriculture of the County of Devon* (1808, 1969 edn), p. 362: 'The price of labour has certainly not kept pace with the depreciation in the value of money within the last 20 years'; G. D. H. and M. Cole (eds.), *The Opinions of William Cobbett* (1944), pp. 86, 181; G. Glover, 'Observations on the state of pauperism', *The Pamphleteer*, X (1817), 389; T. P. MacQueen, *Thoughts and Suggestions on the Present Condition of the Country* (1830), p. 9; R. Pashley, *Pauperism and the Poor Laws* (1852), pp. 254ff;

T. Postans, *Letter to Sir Thomas Baring on Causes which have produced the Present State of the Agricultural Labouring Poor* (1831), p. 8; Rev. J. Howlett, *An Examination of Mr. Pitt's Speech in the House of Commons, Feb. 12, 1796* (1796); Arthur Young (Board of Agriculture), *General Report on Enclosures* (1808), p. 19; J. Wedge, *General View of the Agriculture of the County of Warwick* (1794), p. 24. The list could be considerably extended, and there were virtually no contrary opinions. Bread purchases probably constituted about 44 per cent of total family expenditure in the 1760s, but this had risen to about 60 per cent by 1790. See R. N. Salaman, *The History and Social Influence of the Potato* (Cambridge, 1949), p. 497. The point has also been well made that the bread scale was much reduced in the early nineteenth century, implying falling real familial income. See Blaug, 'Myth of the old poor law', in Flinn and Smout, *Essays in Social History*, pp. 131–3; J. L. and B. Hammond, *The Village Labourer* (1911, 1978 edn), pp. 129–31, 173; Hobsbawm and Rudé, *Captain Swing*, p. 31. The downward trend of agricultural real wages for the east after about 1790 is also well supported by Mills, 'Quality of life in Melbourn, Cambridgeshire', and Richardson, 'Agricultural labourers' standard of living in Kent'.

12 See in particular Bowley, 'The statistics of wages', pt 1, 'Agricultural wages', 702–22; A. L. Bowley, 'The statistics of wages in the United Kingdom during the last hundred years', pt IV, 'Agricultural wages – concluded. Earnings and general averages', *Jnl Roy. Stat. Soc.*, LXII (1899), 555–70; E. W. Gilboy, *Wages in Eighteenth-Century England* (Cambridge, Mass., 1934).

13 1741–5 has been chosen as a base for these series as price fluctuations for these five years appear to balance each other out, and produce a mean which is neither exceptionally high nor low. It is at the start of the general upswing of food prices, and so also a convenient point from which to consider the effects of that price rise.

The figures have been calculated by taking five year means of the data available for each group of counties, and then producing a three point moving average of these five year means to give an effect which would be similar to a fifteen year moving average of the data. [. . .] This was felt to be appropriate as some hirings can only be located to within about three years of their actual date. This was also done to the Phelps-Brown price index. The latter was chosen as it is one of the few price indices which spans the requisite period, rather than through any particular suitability which it was felt to have for the wage data. The London bread price series, which also extends over the entire period, was also tried, and produced a trend which was almost exactly interchangeable with that of the Phelps-Brown index. This was felt to justify the use of the latter here. We can also recall M. W. Flinn's argument for the 'quite remarkable degree of agreement' of price indices in this connection (Flinn, 'Trends in real wages', 402). Indeed, I calculate a multiple correlation coefficient between the Exeter, Eton, and Winchester price series of 0.9927 (1700–1820). It has been suggested that prior to the mid-eighteenth century greater regional price variations existed, and that these appear to have levelled off in the course of the eighteenth century. See A. H. John, 'The course of agricultural change, 1660–1760', in L. S. Pressnell (ed.), *Studies in the Industrial Revolution* (1960), pp. 125–56; C. W. J. Granger and C. M. Elliott, 'Wheat prices and markets in the eighteenth century', *Econ. Hist. Rev.*, XX (1967). But the yearly fluctuations of prices, at any rate, were very similar by region in 1700–50: the multiple correlation coefficient between the Exeter, Eton, and Winchester price series was still very high, at 0.9797.

The high price years of 1795–6, 1800–1, and 1812–13 have been included in the formulation of the Phelps-Brown index presented. It was appreciated that such inclusion would have the effect of accentuating the appearance of falling real wages after about 1790, and so the index was also recalculated by omitting these years, and substituting instead a mean of the two years immediately before and after each of the three very high price periods. This produced a trend the peak of which was only ten points down from the original index including the high price years, and gave an intersection of the male wage index with the price index which was only about five years later for Figure 4.3. In view of these very minor differences, which certainly will not affect the general argument, the six high price years were incorporated. It would in any case have been a 'rather dubious procedure' to have omitted them.

14 I would agree with C. R. Oldham, who pointed out that experience of the poor law must have been almost universal for labourers in Oxfordshire. See his 'Oxfordshire poor law papers', *Econ. Hist. Rev.*, V (1934–5), 94. There are reasons for believing that some counties to the east were even more highly pauperised than Oxfordshire. On the high levels of rural poverty or poor law dependency, giving estimates of between 25 and 51 per cent, see: Hobsbawm and Rudé, *Captain Swing*, pp. 50–3; J. D. Chambers, 'Enclosure and labour supply in the Industrial Revolution', in D. V. Glass and D. E. C. Eversley (eds.), *Population in History* (1965) pp. 321–2, n. 45; J. M. Martin, 'Marriage and economic stress in the Felden of Warwickshire in the eighteenth century', *Population Studies*, XXXI (1977), 528; G. Edwards, *From Crow-Scaring to Westminster* (1922), p. 16; Emmison, 'Relief of the poor at Eaton Socon', 1–9, 48–50, 54–5, and n. 136; W. Hasbach, *The History of the English Agricultural Labourer* (1908), pp. 188–90; A. H. John (ed.), *Enclosure and Population* (Farnborough, 1973), intro., p. 3; R. Williams, *The Country and the City* (St Albans, 1973), p. 185; Mills, 'Quality of life in Melbourn, Cambridgeshire', 383ff; R. Jefferies, *The Hills and the Vale* (1909, Oxford, 1980 edn), p. 159; C. S. Orwin and B. I. Felton, 'A century of wages and earnings in agriculture', *Jnl Roy. Agric. Soc.*, XCII (1931), 242ff. The S.C. on Agricultural Labourers' Wages, VI (1824), pp. 3, 34, reported that it was 'impossible' to avoid parish assistance. A labourer is 'identified altogether with the rates'. And see William Cobbett, *Advice to Young Men* (1830, Oxford, 1980 edn), pp. 320ff, on the unfortunate and unpredictable nature of pauperism, affecting ex-ratepayers, ex-overseers of the poor, and so on: 'How many thousands of industrious and virtuous men have, within these few years, been brought down from a state of competence to that of pauperism!' It is also worth noting that total poor relief (1815–20) was slightly over 3 per cent of the national income of England and Wales – a figure as high as the percentage of national income spent on unemployment relief in the 1930s. Of course, the figure of 3 per cent conceals large regional differences, and the much more acute problems of the south. See K. N. Raj, 'Towards the eradication of poverty – an European precedent', in K. S. Krishnaswamy *et al.* (eds.), *Society and Change. Essays in Honour of S. Chaudhuri* (Oxford, 1977), p. 63.

15 R. S. Schofield, 'Dimensions of illiteracy, 1750–1850', *Explorations in Econ. Hist.*, X (1973), 450.

16 Schofield, 'Dimensions of illiteracy', 447. See also Hobsbawm and Rudé, *Captain Swing*, p. 42, on high illiteracy in Bedfordshire. D. Jones, 'Thomas Campbell Foster and the rural labourer: incendiarism in East Anglia in the 1840's', *Social History*, I (1976), 7, reports male illiteracy of 74.5 per cent for labourers in four Suffolk parishes (1837–51). Female farm-servant/ex-farm-servant illiteracy from examinations was 73.3 per cent. The only comparable figure is that given by Jones, 'Thomas Campbell Foster', 7, of 78.5 per cent illiteracy among rural labourers' wives. (Illiteracy figures from examinations are of course subject to the usual precautionary remarks on the usefulness of a signature as a test of literacy.)

17 The use of some counties in this figure not covered by Figures 4.1 and 4.2 could be dropped for the purposes of consistency, but this would have no significant effect on the male and female trends as presented.

18 See, for example, D. C. Coleman, *Courtaulds, an Economic and Social History*, vol. 1 (Oxford, 1969), pp. 96–101, 236–44; A. Young, *A Farmer's Letters to the People of England* (1767), pp. 353–4. ('Young men and women in the country fix their eye on London as the last stage of their hope . . . The number of young women that fly there is incredible.')

19 Bowley, 'Statistics of wages', pt I, 'Agricultural Wages' (1898), 704–7, and 711–22. See also E. H. Hunt, *Regional Wage Variations in Britain, 1850–1914* (Oxford, 1973), pp. 62–4; Coleman, *Courtaulds*, vol. 1, pp. 244–5; and D. C. Coleman, 'Growth and decay during the Industrial Revolution: the case of East Anglia', *Scandinavian Econ. Hist. Rev.*, X (1962).

20 See Collins, 'Harvest technology'; and M. Roberts, 'Sickles and scythes: women's work and men's work at harvest time', *History Workshop*, VII (1979).

21 See Fussell and Compton, 'Agricultural adjustments', 202; M. Turner, *English*

Parliamentary Enclosure (Folkestone, Kent, 1980), p. 93. But see also A. R. Wilkes, 'Adjustments in arable farming after the Napoleonic Wars', *Agric. Hist. Rev.*, XXVIII (1980).

22 It was, of course, true that there were enclaves of pastoral farming in the east – most notably in the east Suffolk parishes lying in the area within Coddenham, Hacheston, Cookly, Metfield, Trandeston, Wyverstone, Stonham – and my Suffolk material is heavily representative (perhaps significantly so) of the more strictly arable parishes lying outside this area. The division of cereal and pastoral farming, made only with reference to the eastern and western counties covered here, is necessarily crude; local exceptions can readily be made to it, and it serves the purpose only of general explanation. It is felt to be justified through being indicated strongly in the contrasts of the eastern 'cereal' pattern of seasonal unemployment (with its sharp 'V' shape – Figure 4.1), and the much flatter pattern of the western counties, with more noticeable insecurity of employment during May (Figure 4.16). The very marked constancy of these patterns within separate eastern and western counties in the eighteenth and nineteenth centuries, and the use of the division by J. Caird (*English Agriculture in 1850–1* (1951)) was held to justify the division of farming as used. This division is also very clearly apparent in the regional seasonality of marriages, peaking in October–November in the south-east (outside Sussex, or north-west Norfolk before the innovations there), and in May–June in the western counties taken here – after the south-eastern Michaelmas hiring fairs, and those of May in the west. Such marriage seasonality provides a rough indication of regional agricultural specialisation by positing high frequency of marriage immediately following payment of yearly wages to 'farm-servants', and, in other words, by pointing to the dominant hiring period of yearly labour in each region. It provides only a general picture of agricultural specialisation, of course, as there could still be much variation of agriculture in regions having either May or Michaelmas hiring fairs; and there were obvious religious factors affecting the seasonality of marriage. See E. A. Wrigley and R. S. Schofield, *The Population History of England, 1541–1871* (1981), pp. 302–4. The research of Ann Kussmaul on changes in regional marriage seasonality should significantly advance our understanding of shifts in agricultural specialisation. And see also D. B. Grigg, 'An index of regional change in English farming', *Trans. Inst. Brit. Geog.*, XXXVI (1965).

23 For discussion of cropping changes in these counties, see chapter 4 [*Annals*].

24 Similar changes occurred in the seasonal distributions of female unemployment for the south Midlands as for the east. See chapter 4 [*Annals*].

25 Examinations for Monmouthshire have been supplemented by removal orders for heavily agricultural parishes, which provide very similar distributions.

26 The relation of these two eastern and western patterns to the regionality of nineteenth-century agricultural unrest will be immediately apparent. There was very little unrest in the western counties covered here, while the eastern counties, and regions within them, which were most affected by the 'Bread or Blood' riots in 1816 and by 'Swing' unrest, were notably those with the most acute seasonality of unemployment (Hobsbawm and Rudé, *Captain Swing*, p. 158). I will deal with this issue, and with the relation of these patterns to the situation of cottage industry, more extensively elsewhere.

For discussion of seasonal distributions in the south-west and Midlands, see chapters 4 and 8 [*Annals*]. I will discuss distributions for northern and other Midland counties in a later publication.

27 Collins, 'Harvest technology', 456–7.

28 Roberts, 'Sickles and scythes', 19. And see A. Young, *The Farmer's Kalendar; Containing the Business Necessary to be Performed on Various Kinds of Farms during Every Month of the Year* (1771, 1778 edn), pp. 231–9, for a detailed assessment of the contemporary debate on the advantages of mowing over reaping wheat – 'a subject that has been much discussed within a few years, and with great warmth'. In an earlier period, the harvest had been gathered in a few days, by very large numbers of male and female workers, rather than by a smaller group of skilled male scythe users, taking a couple of weeks. See for example, G. E. Evans, *The Farm*

and the Village (1969), pp. 64–5, quoting Sir John Cullum and Langland; Brereton, *Practical Inquiry*, pp. 46–7. See also K. Thomas, 'Work and leisure in pre-industrial society', *Past and Present*, XXIX (1964), 52–3, on English bye-laws from the thirteenth century requiring *all* villagers (regardless of sex) to work in the harvest. This was re-enacted by the Statute of Artificers.

29 For the usual views on this question, see for example: I. Pinchbeck, *Women Workers and the Industrial Revolution, 1750–1850* (1930); G. E. Mingay, *Rural Life in Victorian England* (Glasgow, 1979), pp. 73, 217–18; E. Hostettler, 'Gourlay Steell and the sexual division of labour', *History Workshop*, IV (1977), 95–101; J. Kitteringham, 'Country work girls in nineteenth-century England', in R. Samuel (ed.), *Village Life and Labour* (1975), pp. 127–33; P. Horn, *Labouring Life in the Victorian Countryside* (Bristol, 1976), pp. 117, 125; J. D. Chambers and G. E. Mingay, *The Agricultural Revolution, 1750–1880* (1966, 1978 edn), p. 189. I suspect that the problem has been complicated by the immediate effects of the New Poor Law, which probably led to some resurgence of female and child labour to supplement falling familial income, resulting from the measures of 1834, but this should not obscure the long-term character of the change. On this immediate effect of the New Poor Law see, for example, Hasbach, *English Agricultural Labourer*, pp. 223–6; Pinchbeck, *Women Workers*, pp. 54–8, 67; Orwin and Felton, 'A century of wages', 241.

30 Here, for example, is an opinion cited by George Culley to the 1868–9 Commission:

> Farm labour is the certain ruin of the female character; they become bold, impudent, scandal-mongers, hardened against religion, careless of their homes and children, most untidy, given to drink, coarse-minded, debased, depravers of any virtuous girls who work with them, having no pride in their home or their children, and few home feelings. Their children are ragged and quite untaught, and a dirty home often drives the husband to the public house.

Report on the Employment of Children, Young Persons, and Women in Agriculture, XIII (1868–9), p. 158.

31 Report on the Employment of Children, p. 619.

32 See, for example, n. 28 above, and A. Clark, *Working Life of Women in the Seventeenth Century* (1919), pp. 57, 66–7, 73, 87; Pinchbeck, *Women Workers*, pp. 16–18, 55; Roberts, 'Sickles and scythes', 7, 17–20; C. Middleton, 'The sexual division of labour in feudal England', *New Left Review*, CXIII–CXIV (1979), 153, 160–1:

> arrangements were generally flexible and sexually non-exclusive, and there is evidence of women being engaged in most male tasks – such as reaping, binding, mowing, carrying corn, shearing sheep, thatching, and breaking stones for road maintenance ... Women were hired to carry out virtually the whole gamut of agricultural routes ... women's role in the reserve labour force of feudalism differed hardly at all from that of men – a strong indication that the housewife role was but weakly developed in the poorest strata.

P. Laslett, *The World We Have Lost* (1973), pp. 115–16 (quoting John Locke); J. Barrell, *the Dark Side of the Landscape* (Cambridge, 1980), pp. 50–1; J. Turner, *The Politics of Landscape* (Oxford, 1979), p. 177; E. Richards, 'Women in the British economy since about 1700: an interpretation', *History*, LIX (1974), 337–57; Sir A. Fitzherbert, *Book of Husbandry* (1534), ed. by W. W. Skeat (1882), pp. 97–8; James Thomson, *The Seasons* (1744), Autumn, lines 151ff; B. H. Putnam, 'Northamptonshire wage assessments of 1560 and 1667', *Econ. Hist. Rev.*, I (1927), 133. And more generally, see also P. Laslett, 'Les Rôles des femmes dans l'histoire de la famille occidentale', in E. Sullerot (ed.), *Le Fait feminin* (Paris, 1977), pp. 447–65; E. Boserup, *Women's Role in Economic Development* (1970); J. W. Scott and L. A. Tilly, 'Women's work and the family in nineteenth-century Europe', *Comparative Studies in Society and History*, XVII (1975); A. Macfarlane, *The Origins of English Individualism* (Oxford, 1978), pp. 78–82, 91, 131–5; and especially B. Ankarloo, 'Agriculture and women's work: direction of change in the west, 1700–1900', *Jnl of Family History*, IV (1979), 114–15, 119: in Sweden 'the direction of change was towards a more pronounced preference for males in the agrarian labor force ... Advanced areas ... were moving in the direction of excluding women from the labor force as early as the end of the eighteenth century.' See also the interesting discussion by Hunt, *Regional Wage Variations*, pp. 121–3, where he argues that women worked most where male wages were highest. (Chapter 6 below [*Annals*] covers similar long-term changes affecting the apprenticed trades.)

33 Report on the Employment of Women and Children in Agriculture, XII (1843), p. 247.
34 Report on the Employment, p. 247.
35 Report on the Employment, p. 244.
36 Report on the Employment, p. 234. If this is so, the argument may be of relevance to the problems of the eighteenth-century rise of illegitimacy, and changes in nuptiality and female marriage age, stressed by Wrigley and Schofield, *Population History of England*. One would expect the diminution of female employment to necessitate a younger female marriage age, and reduce both their ability and inclination to delay marriage. It seems probable that this occurred. See in particular M. Anderson, 'Marriage patterns in Victorian Britain: an analysis based on registration district data for England and Wales', *Jnl of Family History*, I (1976). He stresses the low proportion unmarried in East Anglia and the East Midlands in 1861; the effect of female employment in service as a major factor delaying marriage, where such employment persisted; and the influence of the sex ratio on marriage chances, such that where women considerably outnumbered men (i.e., 'less agricultural areas', because of female rural out-migration) they were marrying on average eighteen months later, and nearly twice as many would ultimately remain spinsters than in areas (such as East Anglia and the East Midlands) where this sex ratio was reversed. It can therefore be suggested that rural out-migration (because of the changes documented in this chapter) produced a rural sex ratio conducive to higher female marriage chances, leading to relatively early marriage and a high proportion of women marrying, with obvious consequences for fertility. This effect of female unemployment on marriage (via out-migration and the sex ratio) was compounded by the necessity of early marriage for women when they had so little ability to delay. Anderson comments that: 'as female employment increases, non-marriage and late marriage increases' (p. 69).

When one considers the growing attention being focussed by English demographers on the determinants of marriage, and the near universality of yearly hiring as a life-cycle stage before marriage in the early eighteenth-century agricultural sector, the importance of changes in this hiring system will be apparent. For further discussion of marriage age and nuptiality, see in particular chapters 2, 4, and 7 below [*Annals*].

37 Poor Law Report, XXX (1834), p. 64.
38 Poor Law Report, p. 3.
39 Poor Law Report, p. 5.
40 Poor Law Report, p. 175.
41 Poor Law Report, p. 180.
42 Poor Law Report, p. 188.
43 Poor Law Report, p. 190.
44 Poor Law Report, p. 49.
45 Poor Law Report, p. 72.
46 Poor Law Report, p. 67.
47 Poor Law Report, p. 171.
48 Poor Law Report, p. 188.
49 Poor Law Report, p. 190.
50 Poor Law Report, p. 226.
51 Poor Law Report, p. 447.
52 The association of women with the root crop is unexpectedly slight, but this was nevertheless an additional aspect of their spring work. The gang system in particular grew up in the mid-1820s because of demand for labour essentially for turnip husbandry and the spring weeding of corn in newly drained and enclosed Fen parishes, and in closed parishes. That the system developed at all was, we should note,

partly attributable to the acute female and child unemployment of the surrounding parishes. The relatively slight appearance of female labour in connection with turnip husbandry in the 1834 Report may be associated with the very regional incidence of the gang system at this time – limited to the immediate parishes around Castle Acre, and a few other Fen parishes. The system had expanded into parts of surrounding counties where similar conditions obtained by the time of the reports of the 1860s, but the controversy it aroused appears to have been significantly disproportionate to its extent, particularly in the 1830s and 1840s. It was reported in the 1843 Report, for example, that: 'I am rejoiced to find my own county, Suffolk, free from such unhappy proceedings as those around Castle Acre. I had never heard of it, nor can I find any one in this neighbourhood that has; and I feel assured that Norfolk landowners and farmers, as a body, are not aware of it' (p. 226). And we should note also the young age of gang labour: 'There are but few grown-up women, and those of the worst characters, who join the gangs' (p. 279). Outside the gang parishes the employment of women in turnip husbandry does not seem to have been that marked, and typical parochial comments on female employment at this were: 'There is very little turniping here' (p. 252), or 'not much done in this district' (pp. 227–8).

53 Davies, *Case of the Labourers*, pp. 65–7, 69–74, 87ff, 124–5, 156ff. Significantly, he also stressed the need for fuller employment to be provided during the winter. Many poor law measures, such as the roundsman system or labour rate, were aimed only to help male labourers, and either assumed female unemployment or restricted it further. (Parish lists made up of labour to be employed would be of men.) And such measures certainly accentuated sexual disparities of income. See, for example, the Labour Rate Act, 2 & 3 Will. IV c. 96; Brereton, *Practical Inquiry*, pp. 75–90; Rose, 'The allowance system under the New Poor Law', 619–21.

54 One correspondent to the Society for Bettering the Condition of the Poor (III, 1806, pp. 75–7), complained of the lack of female agricultural employment, of women becoming 'a burthen upon the father of the family, and in many cases upon the parish', and continued:

> The wife is no longer able to contribute her share towards the weekly expenses . . . In a kind of despondency she sits down, unable to contribute anything to the general fund of the family, and conscious of rendering no other service to her husband, except that of the mere care of his family.

The occupational censuses are, of course, too late to document these changes being argued for, but the earliest (1841) fully supports them. Women in the eastern counties included in Figures 4.1 and 4.2 constituted only 2.9 per cent of the total agricultural labour force of those counties (they would be only 2.2 per cent if one discounted Cambridgeshire and Berkshire). In Bedfordshire they were as low as 0.6 per cent by this date. This is, we should note, *despite* the fact that the occupational census was taken in the months of March and April, which we noted as having the highest employment security for women in the east during the year. In the western counties of Monmouthshire, Herefordshire, Worcestershire, Wiltshire, and Gloucestershire, by contrast, women constituted 9.1 per cent of the total agricultural labour force in 1841, supporting the suggestion that such a region saw greater continuity and involvement of women in agriculture than the east. We should also note that the census months coincided with the period of greatest female *insecurity* of employment in the west, and that the regional disparity of female participation has been minimised to the maximum possible extent by the choice of months in which the census was taken. Such greater involvement also seems possible for the south-west, as in Dorset and Devon in the late eighteenth and early nineteenth centuries male and female patterns of unemployment were almost identical, in a way certainly not found in the east (see chapter 8 [*Annals*]). And literary evidence is available for this region in the early nineteenth century suggesting a much wider range of female work than existed in the later nineteenth century, when female work had become more strictly limited to dairying activities (chapter 8 [*Annals*]).

While these regional differences certainly existed, they should not be overstressed, as women in England as a whole only made up 3.9 per cent of the agricultural labour force in 1841 (4.6 per cent if one excludes the eastern counties treated here); suggesting that the argument for significant diminution of female labour having already taken place by the early nineteenth century has a wider applicability than just to the eastern counties, although it seems that in this region it had been earliest and most extreme. Comparable research under way on the north and Midlands will soon permit the pattern of rural change elsewhere to be outlined in detail.

55 The growing seasonal acuteness of unemployment can also be shown by using overseers' accounts. See chapters 2 and 4 [*Annals*].

56 For the influential contrary view, see Chambers, 'Enclosure and labour supply'. For the effects of enclosure, see chapter 4 [*Annals*].

57 A. Digby, *Pauper Palaces* (1978), ch. 12; U. Henriques, 'How cruel was the Victorian poor law?', *Hist. Jnl.* XI (1968); and chapter 3 below [*Annals*]. See also Collins, 'Diffusion of the threshing machine', 28, on changes in winter unemployment after 1835. He suggests that this probably diminished, using the point that employers now had greater motivation to employ in the winter because of the high costs of maintaining families in the workhouse; one of the arguments made at the time in defence of the New Poor Law. Without developing the point, one should recall, however, that there was some continuity of out-relief (mainly to the married) after 1835, partly for this reason, which may have made such employing motivations unnecessary; that statements to this effect were made by defenders of the New Poor Law in a period of intense controversy, and that many contrary opinions could be juxtaposed against them; and that the extreme animosity of the poor to the new law makes relief figures after 1835 a dubious comparative index of actual improvement or deterioration in winter provision of employment. And if the law did indeed force tenant farmers to employ surplus labour during the winter on a significant scale, its widespread popularity among them might in retrospect seem rather odd. The view that the law had increased winter employment in this way was put to Rev. Huxtable by the 1847 S.C. on Settlement and Poor Removal (XI, p. 561). He was then asked: 'Does that accord with your experience?' He replied: 'No, certainly not.' Nevertheless, between about 1850 and the later 1870s, at any rate, it seems almost certain that employment provision improved; and there may also have been improvement in the later 1830s, although I doubt that this was a direct effect of the law.

58 It is almost certain that changes in single women's employment and wages also affected married women – single and married women's work in agriculture was very similar, as descriptions in the government reports make clear.

59 See chapter 3 [*Annals*].

60 Pinchbeck, *Women Workers*, pp. 210–39. Of course, William Cobbett had his own forthright views on the loss of cottage-industrial employment:

> One of the great misfortunes of England at this day is, that the land has had taken away from it those employments for its women and children which were so necessary to the well-being of the agricultural labourer. The spinning, the carding, the reeling, the knitting; these have been all taken away ... But let the landholder mark how the change has operated to produce his ruin. He must have the labouring MAN and the labouring BOY; but, alas! he cannot have these, without having the man's wife and the boy's mother, and little sisters and brothers. Even Nature herself says, that he shall have the wife and little children, or that he shall not have the man and the boy. But the Lords of the Loom, the crabbed-voice, hard-favoured, hard-hearted, puffed-up, insolent, savage and bloody wretches of the North have, assisted by a blind and greedy Government, taken all the employment away from the agricultural women and children.

See his *Cottage Economy* (1822, Oxford, 1979 edn), pp. 180–1.

61 See chapter 6 [*Annals*].

62 Prostitution was another. London, the main destination for female out-migrants from these eastern counties, had 80,000 to 120,000 'prostitutes' by the mid-nineteenth century. R. Pearsall, *The Worm in the Bud: The World of Victorian Sexuality* (1972), p. 313. William Cobbett complained in 1830 of the rise of illegitimacy and of growing numbers of prostitutes in southern country villages. See his *Advice to Young Men*, p.

226. The Victorian prostitution problem is of course a major issue in its own right, and I have not the space to discuss it here. But its historiography might usefully take more account of changes in women's work. See S. Marcus, *The Other Victorians* (1966); F. Henriques, *The Immoral Tradition: Prostitution and Society* (1965); Pearsall, *Worm in the Bud*; B. Harrison, 'Underneath the Victorians', *Victorian Studies*, X (1967); J. R. and D. J. Walkowitz, '"We are not beasts of the field": prostitution and the poor in Plymouth and Southampton under the Contagious Diseases Act', in M. Hartman and L. W. Banner (eds.), *Clio's Consciousness Raised* (New York, 1974); F. Finnegan, *Poverty and Prostitution: A Study of Victorian Prostitution in York* (Cambridge, 1979). And see the following contemporary accounts: M. Ryan, *Prostitution in London with a Comparative View of that of Paris and New York* (1839); W. Tait, *An Enquiry into the Extent, Causes, and Consequences of Prostitution in Edinburgh* (Edinburgh, 1840); R. Wardlaw, *Lectures on Female Prostitution: its nature, extent, effects, guilt, causes, and remedy* (Glasgow, 1842); W. Logan, *An Exposure, from Personal Observation, of Female Prostitution in London, Leeds and Rochdale, and especially in the City of Glasgow* (Glasgow, 1843); J. B. Talbot, *The Miseries of Prostitution* (1844); W. Acton, *Prostitution considered in its Moral, Social and Sanitary Aspects, in London and other large Cities* (1857); T. C. Newby, *Our Plague Spot* (1859); W. Logan, *The Great Social Evil* (1871).

63 See for example, Poynter, *Society and Pauperism*; Emmison, 'Relief of the poor at Eaton Socon'; E. M. Hampson, *The Treatment of Poverty in Cambridgeshire, 1597–1834* (Cambridge, 1934).

64 See the inspired argument of Barrell, *Dark Side of the Landscape*.

65 See chapter 2 [*Annals*].

66 See chapter 5 [*Annals*].

67 And see Peacock, *Bread or Blood*; Hobsbawm and Rudé, *Captain Swing*; J. P. D. Dunbabin, *Rural Discontent in Nineteenth-Century Britain* (1974). For supportive discussion of the standard of living in this area, see: Mills, 'Quality of life in Melbourn, Cambridgeshire'; and Richardson, 'Agricultural labourers' standard of living in Kent'.

68 J. Saville, *Rural Depopulation in England and Wales, 1851–1951* (1957).

69 For an interesting contrary argument to this last statement, see J. P. Huzel, 'The demographic impact of the Old Poor Law: more reflexions on Malthus', *Econ. Hist. Rev.*, XXXIII (1980). Huzel argues, for rural parishes in Kent, that high poor rates were positively correlated with out-migration. It is possible, however, that he has picked the county where one would most expect such a finding – given the immediate proximity of the south London labour market, and the well-established links between this and Kent, via the migration routes through north Kent. For a discussion of this, and the way it affected wages in south London and Kent, see E. J. Hobsbawm, 'The nineteenth-century London labour market', in R. Glass (ed.), *London: Aspects of Change*, ed. by the Centre of Urban Studies (1964).

70 For similar developments in the artisan trades, see chapter 6 [*Annals*].

71 This argument concentrates on the probable significance of sexual divisions of labour, and male and female wage trends, for real familial income. The issue has another equally important but more problematical dimension in relation to the standard of living: the qualitative assessment of how these changes affecting familial relations, and earlier forms of production based more on the family unit, were subjectively experienced by the poor themselves. This can await later discussion.

72 In this respect, the diminution of female agricultural participation could be dated back to the mid- or late seventeenth century, rather than only to the mid-eighteenth century. There is a wide historiography on these landownership changes, but see the bibliography in G. E. Mingay, *Enclosure and the Small Farmer in the Age of the Industrial Revolution* (1968); and chapter 4 below [*Annals*].

73 For strong suggestions that we are dealing with change from the 'pre-industrial' pattern, see all the references in n. 32 above.

74 See his excellent discussion, 'Women in the British economy', 347.

75 See for example, Dunbabin, *Rural Discontent*, chs. 6 and 11.

76 Compare the interesting discussion by T. M. Devine, 'Social stability and agrarian

change in the eastern lowlands of Scotland, 1810–1840', *Social History*, III (1978),
335: 'The social effects of agrarian change in a mixed-farming region were almost the
reverse of those in a specialist cereal zone.' A similar point is constantly made by W.
Cobbett, *Rural Rides* (1830, Harmondsworth, 1967 edn), pp. 81, 206, 215, 258:
'Invariably have I observed . . . the more purely a corn country, the more miserable the
labourers.'

We may note, with reference to the related question of the location and continuity
of the home market, that this material points to unexpected buoyancy of male and
female demand in the south-eastern agricultural sector before about 1770 (most
apparent in the rising male real wages after 1740, and in the evidence of fuller female
participation and relatively low sexual wage differentials before the later eighteenth
century); but for there then to have been a collapse of that demand in the south-east
outside London (although not of female demand in the west), suggesting that the
continued course of industrialisation was increasingly dependent upon exports, and
the northern and middle-class market. I hope soon to develop this further, partly on
the basis of more regionally disparate wage material also covering the north, and in
more class-specific detail. For the role of female demand, see N. McKendrick, 'Home
demand and economic growth: a new view of the role of women and children in the
Industrial Revolution', in his (ed.) *Historical Perspectives. Studies in English Thought
and Society in Honour of J. H. Plumb* (1974). And on the important role of farm-
servant spending on marriage, see Hajnal, 'European marriage patterns', 132.

77 Richards, 'Women in the British economy', 348.

5

The female labour market in London in the late seventeenth and early eighteenth centuries

PETER EARLE

One problem for the early modernist is that feminist writing on the
nineteenth century has tended to force upon historians of the early
modern period an unenviable task, that of locating a *bon vieux temps*
when women enjoyed a harmonious, if hard-working, domestic role
and social responsibility before they were downgraded into social
parasites or factory fodder under the corrupting hand of capitalism. So
far the location of this *bon vieux temps* has proved remarkably elusive.[1]

Much of the responsibility for the hypothesis of this *bon vieux temps* must
rest with Alice Clark whose pioneering book, *The working life of women in
the seventeenth century*, was first published in 1919. Clark's study ranges
across the whole of the seventeenth-century English economy, but much of
it relates to the working life of women in London which is the subject of this
article. She saw the London trades as characteristic of 'family industry', a

My thanks are due to Vanessa Harding who read the article in draft.

stage in the development of manufacturing when 'the wife of every master craftsman ... could share his work.'[2] However, family industry was to be undermined by the rise of 'capitalism' which led to an increase in the scale of business, with the result that fewer journeymen could afford to set up in business for themselves and so had to leave home each day to work on a master's premises where there was no place for their wives to work.

Clark's evidence for this hypothesis was sketchy and she was not too sure when the developments she described took place. However, she seems to have identified the later seventeenth century as a period which saw an increase in the number of women who were deprived of the opportunity of partnership with their husbands. 'The immediate result is obscure', she wrote, 'but it seems probable that the wife of the prosperous capitalist tended to become idle, the wife of the skilled journeyman lost her economic independence and became his unpaid domestic servant, while the wives of the wage earners were drawn into the sweated industries of that period. What were the respective numbers in each class cannot be determined, but it is probable that throughout the seventeenth century they were still outnumbered by the women who could find scope for productive activity in their husbands' business.'[3]

Today, 70 years after the publication of Clark's book, we have made little or no progress in determining the truth or otherwise of her basic hypothesis, let alone in determining 'the respective numbers' of wives who were 'idle', 'unpaid domestic servants', or engaged in 'the sweated industries of that period'. Indeed, it would be fair to say that we know virtually nothing about the female labour force in early modern London except in the most unstructured and superficial way.[4] This article will attempt to throw some light on this subject by examining the depositions of female witnesses before the London church courts in the late seventeenth and early eighteenth centuries. Such records are well known for providing insights into migration patterns and literacy and these two subjects will be considered in sections II and III. It is less well known that, for a brief period between about 1695 and 1725, the depositions also provide quite detailed information on women's employment and thus open a window on the topics just discussed.[5]

I

The records of three courts have been employed for this study. The most important was the Consistory Court of the bishop of London which dealt mainly with suits relating to defamation, divorce, or the legality of marriages.[6] Other material has been gathered from the Commissary Court, whose surviving records for the period relate almost entirely to testamentary cases, and from the Court of Arches. This last court had an appellate function but also operated as a court of first instance for the 13 City parishes which were peculiars of the archbishop. This jurisdiction was loosely defined and in fact most cases were first instance suits brought by Londoners not resident in these parishes on similar issues to those dealt with by the Consistory Court.[7]

Cases in all three courts were conducted on the basis of written material. Plaintiffs appointed a proctor who presented their case in a written libel and the defendant did the same, his or her answer being known as an allegation. For the evidence from witnesses, numbered interrogatories were drawn up and the witnesses were examined on these by the registrar 'in some private room, from which all other persons . . . are removed . . . and he reduces to writing their answers . . . and he reads them over distinctly to each witness' who then signed or marked the deposition.[8]

The interrogatories contained questions relating not only to the matter in dispute but also to the witnesses themselves and these latter are what concern us. Such questions could take any form thought fit and were designed to give some idea of the status and dependability of the witness. The answers can provide a mass of information – age, marital status, place of birth, residence and changes of residence over several years, length of marriage, occupation of husband, wealth, regularity of attendance at church, relationship to the parties, etc. Between about 1695 and 1725 witnesses were also quite often asked some such question as 'How and by what meanes doe you gett your liveing and are you maintained?' and it is the answers to such questions that provide the information on employment.[9] Although the same interrogatory was used for the examination of all witnesses in a case, not all the questions were put to all the witnesses, nor did all the witnesses answer all the questions that were put to them. The bias seems to be that female witnesses were asked and answered personal questions more often than male witnesses and, as it happens, they tended to give more interesting answers.

The church courts were closed during the 1640s and 1650s and their records start again around 1665. What has been done here is to collect two samples from the depositions of female witnesses resident in London. The first, the 'origins' sample, consists of all witnesses whose place of birth is stated in the introductory section of their deposition, the information collected comprising the year of the deposition, the age of the deponent, her place of birth, and whether she signed or marked the deposition. There were just over 2,000 of these cases between 1665 and 1725 and they have been used for an analysis of female migration and literacy patterns. The second sample, the 'employment' sample which has been studied in more detail, consists of 851 female witnesses who gave evidence between 1695 and 1725 which included information as to how they were maintained or employed.[10]

Witnesses in most cases were those who knew the parties or who had happened to be present when defamatory words were spoken and there is little obvious bias in their selection.[11] There also seems little motive for deceit on the subjects discussed here, except perhaps for witnesses to make themselves out as rather more distinguished than they actually were. Naturally, discretion meant that the whole truth was not likely to be disclosed to the registrar of the court, despite the awe-inspiring surroundings and the frequent reminders of the final resting place of those who committed perjury. No one, for instance, said that she gained her livelihood from prostitution or theft, though other witnesses claimed that more than one of the sample was a common whore or the mistress of a bawdy-house. Leaving this aside, it seems probable that if someone said that she had been born in Newcastle, was 26, had been married two years and earned her livelihood by selling fish, then all four statements were accurate, though ages and lengths of marriages were probably not exact for the older women.[12]

It is clearly desirable to test the representativeness of these 'samples', though this is difficult since so little is known about the population from which they were drawn. Table 5.1 examines the age structure of the 'origins' sample, focusing on those over 15 since very few young girls appeared as witnesses, and using Wrigley and Schofield's back-projection age structure for 1696 as a control. At first glance, the sample seems to under-represent both the younger and the older age groups but this may well be merely a reflection of the realities of a London population. The shortage of deponents in their late teens probably reflects the fact that there were proportionately fewer female teenagers in London than elsewhere since such a high proportion of Londoners were immigrants who typically arrived in their early twenties,[13] while the shortage of deponents aged 45 and over probably reflects the lower expectation of life for adults in London.

The age structure of the sample may be representative but there was clearly a considerable area bias as can be seen in table 5.2. The City and the East End have roughly the same proportion of witnesses as a proxy of their

Table 5.1 Age structure of sample

Age group	London born %	Immigrants %	Whole sample %	Men and women 1696 %
15–19	12.8	4.7	7.1	12.2
20–24	19.3	12.5	14.6	12.0
25–34	31.2	30.6	30.8	21.3
35–44	19.6	24.9	23.3	18.4
45–54	9.7	15.5	13.8	16.4
55 and over	7.4	11.8	10.4	19.7
	100.0	100.0	100.0	100.0

Source: All members of 'origins' sample (see text p. 123 and n. 10) aged 15 or more (N = 2,106); men and women 1696 calculated for these age-groups from Wrigley and Schofield, *Population history*, p. 218.

Table 5.2 Distribution of sample by area

Area	Employment sample		Burials in bills	
	N	%	N	%
City within walls	92	10.9	2,674	11.5
Western suburbs[a]	462	54.9	8,089	34.8
Eastern suburbs[b]	194	23.0	5,295	22.8
Northern suburbs[c]	59	7.0	3,749	16.2
Southern suburbs[d]	35	4.2	3,414	14.7
	842	100.0	23,221	100.0
Unknown	9			
	851			

Notes:
[a] St. Andrew Holborn, St. Bride, and all parishes west;
[b] St. Botolph Bishopsgate, St. Botolph Aldgate, and all parishes east;
[c] all parishes north between St. Andrew Holborn and St. Botolph Bishopsgate;
[d] all parishes south of river.
Source: 'employment' sample (see text p. 123 and n. 10); average burials in Bills of Mortality for 1695–7 and 1723–5 from *Collection.*

relative populations would suggest; the West End, however, is over- and the northern and southern suburbs under-represented. It is easy to explain the shortage of witnesses from south of the river since this area came under the jurisdiction of the bishop of Winchester whose Consistory Court records for Surrey do not seem to have survived. However, it is difficult to think of a reason why there should be relatively few witnesses from the northern suburbs.

How well does the sample reflect the social structure of London? This is, of course, far harder to define or measure but the sample is probably somewhat biased towards the poorer women of London.[14] There are very few wives of merchants, wholesalers, or the upper echelon of the professions, though the lower middle class of shopkeepers, manufacturers, solicitors, and government officials such as customs house officers is well represented. The divorce cases also ensure that there is quite a good representation of the leisured members of West End society. Below the middle class, the sample seems to reflect very well the artisan and working-class population of London and it is the women of that class, whether wives, daughters or widows, who make up the bulk of the numbers. Just how far down the social scale the sample goes is difficult to say. There are some very poor women, including some supported by their parishes, but the sample probably excluded an unrespectable substratum who were not thought suitable to give evidence to the Church courts.

II

Early modern London was a city whose population was dominated by immigrants and the sample provides no surprise in this respect, just under 70 per cent being born outside the metropolis.[15] In table 5.3 their origins are compared with Elliott's sample of deponents in the Commissary Court between 1565 and 1644 and also with Glass's analysis of the origins of the freemen of 1690.[16] The two samples of church court deponents, in the first two columns, display a strikingly similar regional distribution, the only major anomaly being the difference in the proportion of migrants from the eastern counties. There is little evidence here of that considerable contraction in the migration field during the seventeenth century which has been found from analysis of apprentice and freemen lists.[17] There are only

Table 5.3 Migration patterns

Region of origin	Deponents (1565–1644) N = 1315 %	Women (1665–1725) N = 2121 %	Freemen (1690) N = 1548 %
Home counties[a]	17.8	18.9	20.3
South midlands[b]	13.4	14.4	22.9
North midlands[c]	11.4	10.6	14.3
Western counties[d]	14.6	16.8	18.0
Eastern counties[e]	12.4	6.1	5.8
South[f]	2.6	3.8	4.6
North-east[g]	9.3	7.0	4.8
North-west[h]	11.4	10.0	6.3
Wales	3.3	3.3	2.2
Scotland and Ireland	1.4	5.7	0.6
Abroad	2.4	3.4	0.2
	100.0	100.0	100.0
Total migrants	78.1	69.4	72.2
London	21.9	30.6	27.8
	100.0	100.0	100.0

Notes:
Regions as in Elliott
[a] Middlesex, Herts, Surrey, Kent, Essex;
[b] Bucks, Beds, Oxon, Berks, Northants;
[c] Warwicks, Notts, Derbys, Staffs, Leics;
[d] Gloucs, Wilts, Somerset, Dorset, Devon, Cornwall, Worcs, Hereford;
[e] Cambs, Lincs, Rutland, Hunts, Suffolk, Norfolk;
[f] Sussex, Hants;
[g] Yorks, Northumberland, Durham;
[h] Lancs, Cheshire, Shropshire, Cumberland, Westmorland.
Source: deponents (1565–1644) from Elliott, thesis, p. 169; women (1665–1725) from 'origins' sample (see table 5.1); freemen (1690) from Glass, 'Socio-economic status', p. 387.

slight increases in the proportion of migrants from the home counties and the south midlands and not a very big decrease in those from the north which is more than cancelled out by the large increase in immigrants from Scotland and Ireland.[18]

However, when we compare the female witnesses of 1665–1725 with the freemen of 1690 (second and third columns), we discover quite considerable differences in the origins of migrants. The proportion of female witnesses from anywhere outside England is over 9 per cent higher and the proportion from the two northern regions nearly 6 per cent higher, while the proportion from the home counties and the south midlands is nearly 10 per cent lower. These are not huge differences, but they do show that the female witnesses tended to travel further than the freemen and suggest that the migration experience of the two groups was not identical.

III

The literacy of London women has already been studied by Cressy using the same church court depositions but with a random sample of cases. He found a remarkable improvement in literacy in the seventeenth century, 10 per cent or less of women being able to sign their name in the decades up to 1640 but 36 per cent in the 1680s, 48 per cent in the 1690s and 56 per cent in the 1720s. He suggested two hypotheses to explain this growth in literacy, 'an educational revolution among late Stuart and early Hanoverian women in the metropolis', and a creaming off by London of people who had learned their literacy elsewhere.[19]

These hypotheses are tested in tables 5.4 to 5.6 where the immigrants and London-born are distinguished and literacy is tabulated by decade of birth rather than decade of deposition, a more appropriate method since witnesses were of all ages and the ability to write is likely to have been learned at a similar age in most people's lives. Improvement was apparent

Table 5.4 Literacy of London women

Witnesses born	London born		Immigrants		All witnesses	
	N	% sign	N	% sign	N	% sign
Before 1640	104	32.7	311	34.7	415	34.2
1640–9	90	51.1	241	42.7	331	45.0
1650–9	67	55.2	233	43.8	300	44.8
1660–9	83	62.7	272	54.8	355	56.6
1670–9	125	60.0	200	58.0	325	58.8
1680 and after	174	67.2	215	58.6	389	62.5

Source: 'origins' sample (see table 5.1).

Table 5.5 Literacy of London-born women

Witnesses born	City within walls		Western suburbs		Other suburbs	
	N	% sign	N	% sign	N	% sign
Before 1640	31	58.1	32	37.5	41	9.8
1640–9	28	71.4	23	47.8	39	38.5
1650–9	19	73.7	22	54.5	26	42.3
1660–9	19	68.4	26	65.4	38	57.9
1670–9	23	82.6	50	64.0	52	46.2
1680 and after	42	69.0	73	65.8	59	67.8

Note: areas of London as in table 5.2.
Source: 'origins' sample (see table 5.1).

Table 5.6 Literacy of female immigrants

	Witnesses born before 1660		Witnesses born 1660 and after	
Region of origin	N	% sign	N	% sign
Home counties	150	38.7	128	50.8
South midlands	117	38.5	95	63.2
North midlands	80	48.7	77	64.9
Western counties	144	36.8	104	64.4
Eastern counties	55	47.3	35	62.9
Southern counties	31	41.9	25	76.0
North-east	47	40.4	56	46.4
North-west	82	35.4	65	47.7
Others	80	37.5	102	60.8

Note: regions as table 5.3.
Source: 'origins' sample (see table 5.1).

everywhere, especially for Londoners born in the 1640s and for immigrants born in the 1660s. Such findings certainly seem to indicate an improvement in the education of London girls, but in the middle of the seventeenth century rather than in the late Stuart and Hanoverian period. They also suggest that migrants were the 'cream' of provincial girls. Houston calculated decadal percentages of between 7 and 14 for the literacy of female witnesses on the Northern Circuit Assizes between the 1604s and 1690s, rising to 26 per cent for the 1720s and 1730s, figures which may be compared with the literacy rates of witnesses from the north-east and north-west in table 5.6. Cressy found similar percentages to those of Houston for East Anglia, an area whose female migrants to London were even more literate than those from the north.[20]

However, it is quite possible that the high literacy of London women has little to do with either of Cressy's hypotheses. If the ability to sign a document was something learned as a child and the general level of literacy was rising, one would expect literacy rates to show a linear decline with age of deponent. In fact, as table 5.7 shows, the pattern of literacy when analysed by age-group takes the form of an inverted U-curve rather than a linear decline. Literacy rates were relatively low for young deponents, rose to a peak in the late twenties for Londoners and in the early thirties for immigrants, and only began to fall off in the late age-groups. Such findings suggest that a fairly high proportion of deponents learned to write their name as adults and not at school or from their parents, thus casting doubt on any direct link between improvements in literacy and improvements in education.[21] They also throw some doubt on the use of signatures as a test of literacy, since their signature may well have been all that these adult women had actually learned. The prevalence of very shaky, misspelt and virtually illegible signatures among female deponents certainly suggests that many of them had learned very little else.[22]

Table 5.7 Literacy by age-groups

Age-group	London-born		Immigrants	
	N	% sign	N	% sign
19 and under	88	48.9	69	36.2
20–24	121	58.7	184	43.5
25–29	105	63.8	210	50.0
30–34	99	60.6	241	53.5
35–44	127	62.2	367	51.8
45–54	60	51.7	228	47.8
55 and over	48	27.1	174	39.1

Source: 'origins' sample (see table 5.1).

IV

We now turn to the question of what the female population of London did for a living, starting by seeing whether they engaged in any paid employment at all. When witnesses were asked how they were maintained, they naturally gave a wide range of answers, but these can be categorized under seven different heads – by the woman's own employment; by her husband's employment or fortune; by her relatives or friends; by her own means; by taking in lodgers;[23] by the parish; or by a pension from the Crown, the last being paid to the widows of army officers and to several Huguenot women. Many women were also maintained from two or more of these sources, from both their own and their husband's employment, for instance; or from their own employment with some assistance from the parish.[24]

Table 5.8 sets out the proportion of female deponents who were or were not gainfully employed. 'Wholly maintained by employment' means that no other source of support was given in the deposition. 'Partly maintained' means that some other category of support was also mentioned. It is clear from the table that a very high proportion of London women were wholly or partly dependent on their own earnings for their living. Only 28 per cent of the sample mentioned no employment for which they received payment, a proportion which might be compared with the 57 per cent of all London women aged 20 or over who were listed as being without occupation in the 1851 census.[25] This gives some substance to Richards's hypothesis of a U-shaped curve of women's employment in Britain – high in 1700 and today, low in Victorian times – though the 1851 census seriously undernumerated the employment of wives.[26]

Table 5.8 Proportion of women employed

	Wholly maintained by employment		Partly maintained by employment		No paid employment	
	N	%	N	%	N	%
Spinsters	187	77.6	14	5.8	40	16.6
Wives	139	32.6	117	27.4	171	40.0
Widows	134	73.2	22	12.0	27	14.8
Total	460	54.0	153	18.0	238	28.0

Source: 'employment' sample (see table 5.2).

Some idea of the status of the women with no paid employment may be gained from their comparative literacy; 67 per cent of them signed their depositions compared with 45 per cent of the employed. The occupations of husbands, which are listed in appendices A and B, also provide a clue.[27] No woman whose husband was described as a master said that she worked for her living. The same holds true for the wives of most of the gentlemen, the professionals, the more skilled artisans and the more distinguished and better paid generally though there were many exceptions. The wives of the less skilled and the poorly paid, on the other hand, normally needed paid employment to help to keep the family going, especially in London where both male and female occupations were often notoriously seasonal.

A further indication of the characteristics of wives in paid employment can be seen in table 5.9 which describes the age structure of employment. The pattern is strikingly different from that of today, the level of employment rising through the family-raising years and declining thereafter.

Table 5.9 Age structure of employed wives

Age-group	N employed	Total	% employed
24 and under	17	40	42.5
25–34	96	157	61.2
35–44	90	131	68.7
45–54	43	76	56.6
55 and over	10	23	43.5
	256	427	

Source: 'employment' sample (see table 5.2).

The logic seems obvious. Paid work was something done for the most part by poor women and most women were poor but they got poorer as they struggled to raise their families, an inevitable feature of the poverty cycle, made worse by the fact that husbands had the unfortunate habit of deserting, falling sick, failing in their business, or being sent to a debtors' prison.

V

What did London women actually do for a living? The first point to note is that it was unusual for husband and wife to work together at the same trade.[28] Only 26 of the 256 employed wives stated that they worked with their husbands and few of these engaged in what might be called 'male' trades as can be seen in appendix A. The commonest shared occupation was running a food and drink outlet, no less than 11 of the 26 working in a tavern, victualling house, cook-shop, or strongwater shop, while another 3 were bakers or pastry-cooks. It is possible that other wives helped their husbands, but received no money for their help and so did not think that such work was relevant.[29] However, the jobs that wives actually said that they did provide little support for Clark's claim that the majority of wives found 'scope for productive activity in their husbands' business.'[30]

Given the fact that wives rarely shared their husbands' occupation, it is no surprise that few widows carried on their husbands' trade after his death and that some who did do so gave up fairly quickly, such as Jane Wright who followed her husband's trade as a master tailor for two years after his death but then gave up the business and 'now works to a slop shop', a job description which we can tell from another description meant that she worked at home making seamen's jackets and drawers.[31] Other widows were more successful in carrying on their husbands' business; there were two butchers, a tallow-chandler, a linen-draper, a wholesale stocking dealer, a goldsmith, and an engraver on stone among the widows in the sample.[32]

However, these 'male' occupations or businesses represent only a very small proportion of the 156 working widows, the great majority of whom (like the great majority of all other London women) did 'women's work' as is made abundantly clear by table 5.10.

Table 5.10 Occupations of London women, 1695–1725

Occupation	Numbers employed				% of total
	Spinsters	Wives	Widows	Total	
Domestic service	124	14	18	156	25.4
Charring/laundry	9	43	16	68	11.1
Nursing/medicine	3	26	27	56	9.1
Textile manufacture	8	15	5	28	4.6
Making/mending clothes	34	60	30	124	20.2
Hawking/carrying	2	28	14	44	7.2
Shopkeeping	12	19	16	47	7.7
Catering/victualling	3	32	18	53	8.7
Misc. services	3	8	7	18	2.9
Misc. manufacture	2	6	4	12	2.0
Hard labour/daywork	1	5	1	7	1.1
	201	256	156	613	100.0

Source: 'employment' sample (see table 5.2).

The table ignores the additional occupations mentioned by some witnesses and tabulates only the first occupation named by the witness. There is space only for a few brief observations about the occupational distribution revealed by the table. Domestic servant, as one would expect, was the commonest and was also normally the first occupation of women working in London. Most servants had a wide experience of different places before they finally quit service to get married or to take up another occupation. The length of time in one place ranged from a few days to 30 years, but the median was about one year with the lower quartile serving six months or less and the upper quartile two years or more.[33] Girls did not necessarily go straight from place to place; many varied their lives by taking a different type of job between places. Many also broke their employment with visits of varying length to parents. Migration to London did not necessarily mean permanent exile. Servants did much the same sort of work as those listed under 'charring and laundry' which really consists of three different types of occupation – 'going out a washing and scowering', i.e. as a charwoman on daywork wages; taking in washing to do in one's own home; and specialist cleaning services such as starching linen and cleaning silks or gloves.

Most of the women under 'nursing and medicine' described themselves as nurses or more commonly nursekeepers, a word which the *O.E.D.* defines as people who nursed the sick. Some deponents specialized in nursing women who were lying in and some in nursing children, either as children's nurses in the modern sense or as wet nurses, though few women gave their first occupation as wet nurse. Nursing the sick normally meant living in somebody else's house for a period of time, often several months, and the expression commonly used was 'goeing out a nursekeeping'. On the more strictly medical side, there were eight midwives and three women who engaged in alternative medicine, one who cured cancers, one who cured the pox, and one who provided physic for the poor.

Much the biggest group under 'textile manufacture' were the silk-winders. This was a big industry in the East End, providing much employment for women and girls and especially for the wives of sailors.[34] There were only seven spinsters in the literal sense of the word and only two women engaged in weaving. 'Making and mending clothes' was the second biggest occupational group after domestic service and was also the most complex, consisting of some general and some very specialist occupations. The biggest group were the sempstresses, though this was a word rarely used by the deponents who normally described themselves as being employed in plainwork or sewing, or who simply said that they were maintained by working at their needle. The next largest group were the mantuamakers or dressmakers, an occupation which had developed rapidly from the 1670s and 1680s as a result of changes in women's fashions which meant that fewer of their clothes were made by the normally male tailors,[35] though there are four female tailors in the sample. Apart from mantuamakers, there were large numbers of women who made particular sorts of clothes, sometime bespoke but often as stock items for shops. We have already mentioned the slopshops who put out material to be made into garments for sailors; in the sample there were also staymakers, bodice-makers, cap-makers, glovers, button-makers, periwig-makers, women who made up linen into shirts and smocks, and specialists who made fustian frocks, scarves, riding hoods, children's coats and hooped petticoats as well as some who specialized in making such things as fringes and tassels for the upholsterers. Finally, there were embroiderers, specialist 'flourishers' who embroidered muslin and gauze, quilters, one or two lacemakers, and a handful of knitters, though most of this work had been engrossed by the male framework knitters.[36]

'Hawking and carrying' comprises the market women and those who hawked foodstuffs and other products about the streets, though a few worked from a fixed point of sale such as a cellar and so were virtually shopkeepers. The biggest group were those who sold fruit and vegetables, followed by fishwives and old clothes dealers, while other products sold in the streets included bread, pies, baked puddings, butter and eggs, sausages, tea, linen and muslins, earthenware and water.

Much the commonest shops kept by women were chandlers' and milliners' or haberdashers' shops which account for 29 of the 47 women engaged in shopkeeping, though several of the milliners should really be placed under 'making clothes' since they were either apprentices or journeywomen who would have spent most of their time at their needles making up the stock of the shops. There were also potters' shops, picture shops, perfumers, grocers, and a few pawnbrokers. 'Catering and victualling' is dominated by the 24 women who ran an establishment variously described as a victualling, public, or ale-house and the eight who kept strongwater or brandy shops. There were also keepers of coffee-shops and cook-shops, pastry-cooks and pie-makers, two bakers, one milkwoman, and one who bred up poultry.

There remains the miscellaneous section. The manufacturers included two chair-caners, two fanmakers, one engraver on stone, and one each who made bellows, bricks, flasks, pipes, pottery, sacks, and sieves. Miscellaneous services includes six schoolteachers, one of whom doubled as a professional letter-writer, five women who worked for their local church or parish as clerk, sextoness, pewkeeper, or vestrywoman, Maria Margaretta Galli, a 22-year-old Italian who 'since her being in England hath maintained herself by singing and teaching to sing', the mistress of a company of comedians normally based at Epsom, a ladies' hairdresser, a woman who discounted seamen's 'tickets' (i.e. acknowledgements of wages due), a woman who earned her living by running errands for the prisoners in the Savoy, a turnkey in the King's Bench prison, and even a proto family historian, the widow Jane Vyse who lived 'upon a small estate of her own and upon searches made in the Fleet Registry'.[37]

How can one generalize about these female occupations? First of all, the general structure of occupations is very similar to that revealed by the 1851 census, though with higher participation rates. In 1851, the first four occupations for London women were domestic service, making and mending clothes, charring and laundry, and nursing, the same as in our sample, though they accounted for an even greater proportion of employment in London than they had in the earlier period. The narrow range of other employments was also common to both periods.[38] The comparison should not be pressed too far since it is clear that the 1851 census omits much of women's employment, but there is certainly little evidence of a narrowing of women's employment opportunities as a result of the industrial revolution or of Victorian mores. Employment opportunities were already narrow in 1700 and the only real difference seems to be that more women worked for their living in the earlier period than they did in the 1850s, probably because more women were poor. Neither men nor women worked in 1700 if they did not have to, any more than was the case in Victorian times.

The second obvious point about women's occupations is that a high proportion of them were casual, intermittent, or seasonal and that few people except servants and those running shops or victualling outlets would have expected to be employed the whole year through. Thomas Firmin wrote in 1678 of 'a poor woman that goes three dayes a week to wash or scoure abroad, or one that is employed in nurse-keeping three or four months in a year, or a poor market-woman who attends three or four mornings in a week with her basket, and all the rest of the time these folks have little or nothing to do.' The accuracy of his figures may be debatable, but the general picture seems obviously right.[39]

Our data suggest that the great majority of women were unable to work in 'male' trades and, since nearly three-quarters of women wanted to or had to work for a living, they necessarily competed intensely for the work which was left, much of it of a casual nature and none of it organized by gilds or livery companies. The result, naturally, was that they got very poor wages. To set these in context, we can look at the pensions paid by City parishes in our period. The normal top pension, designed to support the recipient completely, seems to have been £5 4s. a year or 2s. a week, though some people got 2s. 6d. a week. So, 2s. can perhaps be taken as a proxy for the 'poverty line'.[40] Most men's wages ranged from just under 10s. a week to £1 a week or more. A few women, such as specialist needle-workers, were paid 10s. or even 12s. a week, i.e. above the minimum level of male pay, but the great majority only earned between 4s. and 10s. a week, most of them at the lower end of this scale, 5s. a week being about the norm.[41] Such wages were certainly low but, at twice the subsistence rate, they were adequate to provide a living for a single woman and were also valuable supplements to family incomes, though life would obviously have been hard for a widow or woman living on her own who had to support children on such wages.

Two other characteristics of the female labour market are illustrated in tables 5.11 and 5.12. Table 5.11 analyses the age structure of broad occupational groups and shows that young women were mainly domestics,

Table 5.11 Age structure of occupations (number in occupation as percentage of all employed women in age-group)

Occupation	24 and below	25–34	35–44	45–54	55 and over
Domestic service	60.7	28.0	8.4	2.2	2.4
Needle trades	13.6	23.5	19.6	19.1	7.3
Char/laundry/nursing	5.0	18.0	28.7	21.3	24.4
Hawking/shop/victualling	10.0	18.0	30.7	40.5	31.7
Other occupations	10.7	12.5	12.6	16.9	34.2
	100.0	100.0	100.0	100.0	100.0

Source: 'employment' sample (see table 5.2).

Table 5.12 Literacy of working women

Occupation	Sign	Total	% sign
Winding silk	0	18	0
Char/washerwoman	6	57	11
Hawkers	8	44	18
Nursing	16	46	35
Domestic servants	62	156	40
Needle trades	80	114	70
Shopkeepers	38	47	81
Midwives	7	8	87
Schoolteachers	6	6	100

Source: 'employment' sample (see table 5.2).

those in the next higher age-group clustered in the needle trades, while charring, washing, nursing, and hawking tended to be the preserve of older women whose declining eyesight and arthritic fingers prevented them from maintaining themselves 'by their needle'. Table 5.12 describes the literacy of working women and shows that there were considerable occupational differences, ranging from the totally illiterate silk winders of the East End to the full literacy of the schoolteachers, though one of the latter clearly did not use a pen very often. This hierarchy of literacy reflects the status hierarchy of women's jobs, though not necessarily their pay, and in this respect the high score of the needle trades is significant. Contemporary comment suggests that such jobs as mantuamaker, milliner and sempstress were just about the only ones thought suitable for the daughters of respectable people. This tended to cause these occupations to be particularly overcrowded and their pay accordingly low, one reason perhaps for the contemporary view that prostitution was particularly rife among girls in the needle trades.[42]

VI

At what age did girls start work in London? A good idea of this can be obtained from the resumé of lodgings and employment over the last 3, 5, 7 or some other period of years which witnesses were often required to give. Such data suggest that the earliest age at which London-born girls entered service or apprenticeship was 10, though it is possible that East End girls engaged in silk-winding started somewhat earlier and that the same was true of parish apprentices.[43] Most London girls, however, started work much later, the commonest ages being 15 to 17 while some were still living at home, 'designing to go into service' at 20, and many of course never worked for their living, staying in their comparatively prosperous homes and being maintained by their parents or guardians till marriage.[44]

Many immigrants already had experience of work, normally of domestic service, before they came to London. A common experience was for a girl to leave home in her late teens or very early twenties, work for a year or two as a servant with a country family or in the nearby market town, and then make the move to London. Arrival in London was cushioned for many immigrants by the fact that they had relatives in the metropolis with whom they could stay while they found their first place. The age of arrival in London can be worked out for 58 immigrant deponents, 14 of whom were in their teens, 28 between 20 and 25 inclusive, and the remaining 16 over 25, the oldest being a 47-year-old widow from Northumberland who opened a cook-shop in Piccadilly out of the savings of many years of service in the north country. The average age of arrival in London was 23 and the median 22.[45]

This different pattern of starting work in London is reflected in the ages at which immigrants and Londoners got married, as Elliott has shown for the early seventeenth century.[46] Many witnesses were required to state how long they had been married to their current husbands. The answers only occasionally say whether this husband was the first and, since widowhood was a fairly common state for women in their twenties and even in their teens, the ages at marriage which can be calculated are higher than they would be if first marriages could be confidently identified. Despite this, the London-born still demonstrate the comparatively early age which Elliott has shown from the evidence of those who bought marriage licences. The median age of the 46 for whom it was possible to make this calculation was 21, while the median for the 133 immigrant cases was, at 25, similar to the rest of the country.[47]

Leaving home, the first job, and marriage were clearly important landmarks in the life-cycle of a woman. The other end of the cycle can also be studied by seeing how the 41 women in the sample aged 60 or over were maintained, a group consisting of 13 wives and 28 widows. Nine of the wives were maintained by their husbands, though one had kept school until she was 60, and the other four worked, two as washerwomen, one as a charwoman and one as vestrywoman to Trinity Chapel where her husband was clerk. Four widows were maintained from a private income, presumably inherited from their husbands, and three were supported by family or friends. Two other widows, one aged 74 and the other 66, were supported entirely by their parishes and one received 1s. 6d. a week from the parish in addition to what she could earn from making bone-lace edgings.[48] The other 18 widows still worked for their living, three of them with some assistance from inherited money. There was no let up for these poor old women, six of whom were still working in their seventies – two washerwomen, a nurse, a midwife, a teacher, and a publican – and one who was still supporting herself by selling fruit and vegetables from a Bloomsbury cellar when she was 86.[49]

What can we conclude from this brief survey of the older women in the sample? There is perhaps a tendency to think of the parish as the main support of poor old women, understandable since parish records are normally the only means of learning much about them and women certainly made up the majority of elderly pensioners. It is more likely, however, that, although the parish was an option, it was not by any means the typical support of elderly widows. It also seems to have been fairly unusual, in London at least, for the elderly to be supported by their children. Most women therefore were forced to rely on their husbands if still alive or on themselves, the latter being much the more frequent.

VII

The maintenance questions asked by the church courts between 1695 and 1725 open up a fascinating window on the lives of London women through which we can see a world which does not perhaps match our preconceptions. This is certainly not the world of the *bon vieux temps* which once again proves elusive. If it ever did exist, it must have been before the late seventeenth century.[50] The London of Queen Anne was not a place where the majority of women worked with their husbands in a harmonious domestic setting. Most women certainly worked for their living but were barred by custom, law, or their own inclinations from sharing in 'men's work' and so were forced to compete as individuals for the 'women's work' that remained.[51] Most of them seem to have managed to do so successfully, despite the handicaps they faced, and one can only salute their perseverance in the harsh capitalist world of the metropolis.

Contemporaries do not seem to have had any moral objection to women working for their living, quite the opposite in most cases, and one does not read in this period that a woman's place is in the home. Women were expected to work for their living, in addition to their multifarious domestic duties, and indeed the low productivity and low earnings of the society made their earnings imperative if families were to survive in any comfort. In this respect, the London of Queen Anne may have been a rather different place from the London of Queen Victoria but, in most other respects, the working lives of women in the London of 1700 were remarkably similar to those exposed by Mayhew and the mid-Victorian censuses a century and a half later.

Notes

1 Hufton, 'Women in history', p. 126.
2 Clark, *Working life*, p. 10.
3 Clark, *Working life*, p. 235.

4 Much the best discussion of the subject is to be found in the scattered references to women's employment in George, *London life*.

5 The same source provides similar information on men's employment, but it would be difficult to use this to duplicate the analysis in this article. There are too few male witnesses who answered questions on maintenance in relation to the number of different male occupations, and the distribution of occupations is also distorted by the fact that a sizeable proportion of male witnesses were called to give professional evidence – clergymen, lawyers, scriveners, apothecaries, surgeons, and parish clerks.

6 The records are kept in the Greater London Record Office (hereafter GLRO). Some idea of the distribution of cases can be seen from an analysis of two deposition books, DLC 245 (1697) and DLC 249 (1705–7). The depositions related to 157 suits of which 92 were defamation suits, 61 related to marriage and 4 to other subjects, mainly parish business. There were 256 witnesses in the defamation cases and 406 in the marriage cases which had on average over twice as many witnesses. Altogether, there were 683 deponents in these two books of whom 382 (56 per cent) were women.

7 The Commissary Court records are in the Guildhall Library (hereafter GHMS) and the records of the Court of Arches in Lambeth Palace Library (hereafter LPL). My assumption that most London cases were first instance and not appeal cases rests on the fact that there is very little duplication between the witnesses appearing in the Consistory Court and the Court of Arches in the same period. On the records of the Court of Arches see Slater, *Lists*; Slater, 'The records'; Barber, 'Records of marriage'. Most studies of the church courts relate to the period before the Civil War, though many of these are still valuable for an understanding of the period after 1660. See Owen, *Records of the established Church*, especially ch. 6; Wunderli, *London church courts*; Houlbrooke, *Church courts*; Marchaunt, *Church under the law*; Sharpe, *Defamation*; Ingram, *Church courts*.

8 Law, *Forms of ecclesiastical law*, p. 225. For this section on the practice of the courts I have relied on the above; Consett, *The practice*; and Owen, *Records of the established church*, especially pp. 36–8.

9 GLRO DLC 152, fo. 95, Long v. Hutchins.

10 The 'origins' sample consists of all female deponents who gave place of birth in GLRO DLC 236–62, 631–4; GHMS 9065A/8–11; LPL Eee 1–11. The 'employment' sample consists of all female deponents who gave information on maintenance in GLRO DLC 244–62, 631–4; GHMS 9065A/9–11; LPL Eee 8–11.

11 The most likely bias would be a superfluity of servants since these were often called to give evidence in divorce cases. However, the bias is slight since their evidence often related to events many years in the past and, by the time they gave it, they had left service, married, and were often engaged in some other occupation.

12 The reported ages of the 'origins' sample were tested for inaccuracy by the Smith Index which enumerates the number of stated ages ending in 1, 3, 7, 9 and expresses them as a percentage of 40 per cent of the total reported ages. The scores were: ages 20–29 = 94.7; 30–39 = 75.4; 40–49 = 53.5; 50–59 = 37.7; 60–69 = 51.9; all ages 20–69 = 71.0. The London-born scored considerably higher than the immigrants, 81.7 compared with 66.8. The scores for women over 30 are fairly low, a fact which will clearly affect the accuracy of calculations based on counting back from recorded ages, such as the brief discussion of age at marriage on p. 137.

13 See below, p. 137.

14 Further support for this impression of the social structure of the sample can be obtained from witnesses' statements of their worth or fortune, though it is difficult to come to firm conclusions since less than a fifth of the sample answered such a question and many answers were fairly meaningless. Just under half these deponents stated that they were worth 'nothing', 'very little', 'not much' or 'only what she works for', about a quarter estimated their net fortune at up to £50 with the remaining quarter being worth more, less than 10 per cent being worth over £500.

15 For estimates of the number of immigrants required to enable the metropolitan population to grow as it did in different periods see Wrigley, 'Simple model' and Finlay, *Population and metropolis*, pp. 8–9.

16 Elliott, thesis, pp. 166–7; Glass, 'Socio-economic status', p. 387. The analysis of Glass's data omits the 'illegible and not known' and takes London as 430, Middlesex as 71, and Surrey as 54, i.e. removing the 'Londoners' from Middlesex and Surrey.

17 For a summary of a number of studies on this subject see Wareing, 'Changes in geographical distribution'. See also Patten, *Rural-urban migration*; Kitch, 'Capital and kingdom'; Elliott, thesis, pp. 158–9. In a study based on depositions from the church courts, Souden, 'Migrants', p. 148 finds no contraction in the migration field of women moving to provincial towns in the seventeenth century. He also suggests (p. 135) that the deposition evidence provides the best opportunity to examine patterns of migration. There seems little doubt that this is true, especially from the later seventeenth century when such traditional sources for migration studies as apprentice and freedom records reflect only a fairly small and privileged section of the urban population. For another provincial study using deposition evidence, see Clark, 'Migration'.

18 The increase in immigrants from Scotland, Ireland, and abroad is particularly striking in the second half of the period studied, rising from 5.3 per cent of all immigrants to 12.5 per cent before and after 1695. France was much the biggest source of immigrants from abroad with 26; small numbers also came from Holland, 'Belgium', Germany, Portugal, Spain, Italy, New England, India, and the West Indies.

19 Cressy, *Literacy*, pp. 147–9. Experts on this subject suggest that the ability to sign roughly reflects fluency in reading but may not reflect fluency in writing. See Cressy, *Literacy*, pp. 54–5; Schofield, 'Dimensions of illiteracy', pp. 440–1.

20 Houston, 'Development of literacy', p. 204; Cressy, *Literacy*, p. 144.

21 For a similar pattern in a sample of indentured servants whose literacy rates rose with their age see Galensen, 'Literacy and age'.

22 The standard of signatures among male witnesses was much higher. So was their general level of literacy. An examination of all witnesses, male and female, in three deposition books covering the middle of the reign of Queen Anne (GLRO DLC 249–51) showed that 51 per cent of the women and 89 per cent of the men signed their depositions.

23 Unfortunately, earning money by taking in lodgers was not reported consistently by the witnesses. Many women referred to lodgers in the text of their deposition, but failed to mention their earnings from this source when asked a question on maintenance.

24 E.g. GLRO DLC 250 fo. 313; DLC 260 fo. 43.

25 Alexander, *Women's work*, p. 12.

26 Richards, 'Women in the British economy'; on the shortcomings of the 1851 census see, among others, Alexander, *Women's work* and Higgs, 'Women, occupations and work'. Two main problems have been identified: (a) husbands as householders who provided information to the enumerators neglected to mention their wives' paid employment; (b) the guidance as to the treatment of part-time work was ambiguous. In both respects, the depositions used here are probably more reliable than the census since it was the women themselves who provided the information on oath and they certainly do not seem to have been reluctant to mention part-time employment.

27 See appendix B for a list of the occupations of husbands of 'unemployed' wives and appendix A for a list of the occupations of married couples.

28 See appendix A for more details.

29 Some of the wives listed in appendix A may well have helped their husbands occasionally when not engaged in their own jobs. Some of the 'unemployed' wives in appendix B may also have been unpaid assistants, especially those listed under shopkeepers, clothing, and food/drink. However, the available evidence suggests that it was unusual for a wife to work at the same occupation as her husband.

30 Clark, *Working life*, p. 235.

31 LPL Eee 9 fos. 295, 523.

32 LPL Eee 8 fo. 697; GLRO DLC 250 fo. 493. For a general discussion of women in business see Earle, *English middle class*, ch. 6.

33 Based on 114 cases. This high rate of turnover should be compared with Elliott's study of early seventeenth-century London. She found the average length of service with one household to be over four years, while only 13.5 per cent of servants stayed for less than one year. Elliott, thesis, p. 225. In general on domestic servants in the period covered by this article see Hecht, *Domestic servant class* and Earle, *English middle class*, pp. 76 and 218–29.

34 On this industry see Wadsworth and Mann, *Cotton trade*, pp. 106–7; Rothstein, thesis, pp. 131–2; Stern, 'Silk throwers'.

35 Ginsburg, 'Tailoring'.

36 Narrow silk-weaving was another important occupation for women which had largely been lost to men in the course of the seventeenth century. See Clark, *Working life*, pp. 102–6, 138–41.

37 The last six cases can be found in GLRO DLC 249 fo. 383v; DLC 252 fos. 130–2; DLC 256 fo. 23; LPL Eee 9 fos. 644 and 730; Eee 10 fo. 173.

38 *Census, 1851* (P.P. 1852–3, LXXXVIII, pt. I), table xxviii: 85 per cent in these four groups in 1851; 66 per cent in our sample. The biggest change is in domestic service (which had risen from 25 to 40 per cent of the total) but this may simply reflect the fact that this was an occupation which was normally recorded in 1851, while many other women's jobs were not. Snell, *Annals*, ch. 6 argues that the opportunities for women were much wider in the eighteenth than in the nineteenth century and puts together an impressive list of occupations which were sometimes undertaken by women. However, one could list many more such occupations from the 1851 census, including Queen, but women engaged in such jobs were the exception rather than the rule. Most London women from the late seventeenth century right through to Victorian times were engaged in a narrow range of occupations.

39 Firmin, *Some proposals*, p. 18.

40 Macfarlane, thesis, pp. 149–55. GLRO DLC 255 fo. 242. See also Firmin, *Some proposals*, pp. 4, 7 who claimed that his scheme to enable poor women to take flax home to spin would earn them some 3d. or 4d. a day. 'There is no fear that any person who can wind silk, stitch bodies, or almost any other work that you can name, will leave these if they can have them to spin flax, the price whereof is so very low.'

41 Information on women's wages is hard to come by and, in any case, one faces the usual problem of just what the wage meant. Figures from Campbell, *London tradesman* suggest the following women's wages: milliner: 5s. to 6s. a week 'out of which she is to find herself in board and lodging' (p. 208); capmaker: 9s. to 12s. a week (p. 210); quilter: 3s. to 4s. a week 'and their diet' (p. 213); 'a good glover may get ten or twelve shillings a week' (p. 223); staymaker: 'a woman cannot earn above a crown or six shillings a week, let her sit as close as she pleases' (p. 225); bodicemaker: 'women that can apply themselves, and refrain from gin, may get from five to eight shillings a week' (p. 226). It seems probable that women's wages, like men's wages, had risen in London between 1700 and 1747 so that the rates in our period would have been somewhat lower.

42 On the 'gentility' of the needle trades see Snell, *Annals*, pp. 293–4 and for some snide comments on the morals of women engaged in them, see Campbell, *London tradesman*.

43 Apprenticeship seems to have been fairly unusual for girls. Only 17 witnesses in the 'employment' sample were either apprentices when they gave their evidence or referred to a previous apprenticeship. Ten were apprenticed to various forms of needlework and nearly all the rest to shopkeepers or to 'housewifery'. All but one were under 25 and they represent 9 per cent of all witnesses under 25 in the sample, a minimum proportion since some of those out of their time might not have mentioned an earlier apprenticeship. Snell analysed early eighteenth-century female apprenticeship in five counties from the Inland Revenue data and found that girls were only 5 per cent of the total of male and female apprentices and that 62 per cent of the girls were apprenticed to various forms of needlework. Snell, *Annals*, pp. 293–3.

44 Based on 47 cases. There were 37 spinsters supported by relatives in the sample, 10 aged 16 or less, 15 aged 17–20, and 12 aged 21 or more.

45 These ages should be compared with Elliott, thesis, p. 221 who found average ages of arrival for immigrant girls in the early seventeenth century some four or five years younger.
46 Elliott, thesis, p. 282.
47 For ages at first marriage from reconstitutions, mainly of villages and small towns, see Wrigley and Schofield, 'English population history'.
48 GLRO DLC 249 fo. 132 (she 'now' receives alms, suggesting that she has only recently become a pensioner); DLC 633 fo. 376 (used to take in washing and keep a herb-shop, 'now' a pensioner of St Martin's in the Fields); DLC 260 fo. 43.
49 GHMS 9065A/11 fo. 337.
50 For a survey of continental evidence which shows that, if there had been any change in this respect, it was much earlier, see Goodman and Honeyman, *Gainful pursuits*, pp. 111–13.
51 It should be noted that much of the period considered was one of war. This must affect the findings to a certain extent since more husbands than usual would have been away from home, at sea or in the army, and it seems probable that the demand for labour in some consumer industries would have been affected by the high taxation of the period. It is obvious that more wives would be forced to work in hard times than good times as Prior has shown in 'Women in the urban economy'.

References

OFFICIAL PUBLICATIONS

Census of Great Britain, 1851. Population tables (P.P. 1852–3, LXXXVIII, pt. I).

SECONDARY SOURCES

Alexander, S., *Women's work in nineteenth-century London: a study of the years 1820–50* (1983).
Barber, M., 'Records of marriage and divorce in Lambeth Palace Library', *Genealogists' Mag.*, XX (1980), pp. 109–17.
Campbell, R., *The London tradesman* (1747).
Clark, A., *The working life of women in the seventeenth century* (1919).
Clark, P., 'Migration in England during the late seventeenth and early eighteenth centuries', *P. & P.* 83 (1979), pp. 57–90.
A collection of the yearly bills of mortality from 1657 to 1758 (1759).
Consett, H., *The practice of the spiritual or ecclesiastical courts* (1685).
Cressy, D., *Literacy and the social order: reading and writing in Tudor and Stuart England* (Cambridge, 1980).
Earle, P., *The making of the English middle class: business, society and family life in London, 1660–1730* (1989).
Elliott, V.B., 'Mobility and marriage in pre-industrial England' (unpublished Ph.D. thesis, University of Cambridge, 1978).
Finlay, R.A.P., *Population and metropolis: the demography of London, 1580–1650* (Cambridge, 1981).
Firmin, T., *Some proposals for the imploying of the poor, especially in and about the City of London* (1678).
Galensen, D.W., 'Literary and age in pre-industrial England: quantitative evidence and implications', *Econ. Dev. & Cult. Change*, 29 (1981), pp. 813–29.
George, M.D., *London life in the eighteenth century* (1925).
Ginsburg, M., 'The tailoring and dressmaking trades, 1700–1850', *Costume*, VI (1972), pp. 64–71.

Glass, D.V., 'Socio-economic status and occupations in the City of London at the end of the seventeenth century', in A.E.J. Hollaender and W. Kellaway, eds., *Studies in London history* (1969), pp. 373–89.

Goodman, J. and Honeyman, K., *Gainful pursuits: the making of industrial Europe, 1600–1914* (1988).

Hecht, J.J., *The domestic servant class in eighteenth-century England* (1956).

Higgs, E., 'Women, occupations and work in the nineteenth-century censuses', *Hist. Workshop*, XXIII (1987), pp. 59–80.

Houlbrooke, R.A., *Church courts and the people during the English Reformation, 1520–1570* (Oxford, 1979).

Houston, R.A., 'The development of literacy in northern England, 1640–1750', *Econ. Hist. Rev.*, 2nd ser., XXXV (1982), pp. 199–216.

Hufton, O., 'Women in history: early modern Europe', *P. & P.*, 101 (1983), pp. 125–41.

Ingram, M., *Church courts, sex and marriage in England, 1570–1640* (Cambridge, 1987).

Kitch, M.J., 'Capital and kingdom: migration to later Stuart London', in A.L. Beier and R.A.P. Finlay, eds., *The making of the metropolis: London, 1500–1800* (1986), pp. 224–51.

Law, J.T., *Forms of ecclesiastical law; or, the mode of conducting suits in the Consistory Courts, being a translation of the first part of Oughton's Ordo Judiciorum* (1831).

Macfarlane, S.M., 'Studies in poverty and poor relief in London at the end of the seventeenth century' (unpublished D. Phil. thesis, University of Oxford, 1982).

Marchaunt, R.A., *The church under the law: justice, administration and discipline in the diocese of York, 1560–1640* (Cambridge, 1969).

Owen, D.M., *The records of the established church in England, excluding parochial records* (1970).

Patten, J., *Rural-urban migration in pre-industrial England* (Oxford University School of Geography Research Papers, 6, 1973).

Prior, M., 'Women in the urban economy: Oxford, 1500–1800', in Prior, ed., *Women in English society, 1500–1800* (1985), pp. 93–117.

Richards, E., 'Women in the British economy since about 1700: an interpretation', *History*, LIX (1974), pp. 337–57.

Rothstein, N.K.A., 'The silk industry in London, 1702–66' (unpublished M.A. thesis, University of London, 1961).

Schofield, R.S., 'Dimensions of illiteracy, 1750–1850', *Exp. Econ. Hist.*, X (1972–3), pp. 437–54.

Sharpe, J.A., *Defamation and sexual slander in early modern England: the church courts at York* (York University, Borthwick Papers, no. 58, 1981).

Slater, M.D., *Lists of the records of the Court of Arches* (1951).

Slater, M.D., 'The records of the Court of Arches', *J. Eccles. Hist.*, IV (1953), pp. 139–53.

Snell, K.D., *Annals of the labouring poor: social change and agrarian England, 1660–1900* (Cambridge, 1985).

Souden, D., 'Migrants and the population structure of later seventeenth-century provincial cities and market towns' in P. Clark, ed., *The transformation of English provincial towns, 1600–1800* (1984), pp. 133–68.

Stern, W.M., 'The trade, art or mistery of silk throwers of the City of London in the seventeenth century', *Guildhall Misc.*, VI (1956), pp. 25–30.

Wadsworth, A.P. and Mann, J. de L., *The cotton trade and industrial Lancashire, 1600–1780* (Manchester, 1931).

Wareing, J., 'Changes in the geographical distribution of the recruitment of apprentices to the London companies, 1486–1750', *J. Hist. Geog.*, VI (1980), pp. 241–9.

Wrigley, E.A., 'A simple model of London's importance in changing English society and economy, 1650–1750', *P. & P.*, 37 (1967), pp. 44–70.

Wrigley, E.A. and Schofield, R.S., 'English population history from family reconstitutions: summary results, 1600–1799', *Pop. Stud.*, XXXVII (1983), pp. 157–84.

Wrigley, E.A. and Schofield, R.S., *The population history of England, 1541–1871* (Cambridge, 1981).

Wunderli, R.M., *London church courts and society on the eve of the Reformation* (Cambridge, Mass., 1981).

Appendix A: Occupations of married couples

Occupation(s) of wife	*Occupation(s) of husband*
Domestic servant	Pewterer
Domestic servant	Joiner
Domestic servant	House-painter (deserted)
Domestic servant	Domestic servant
Domestic servant	Mason
Domestic servant	Haberdasher (deserted)
Domestic servant	Hairseller (debtors' prison)
Domestic servant	Groom to Duke of Newcastle
Domestic servant	Sailor
Domestic servant	Sailor
Domestic servant	Cook (at sea)
Domestic servant	Domestic servant
Tirewoman	Dancing-master
Washing/scouring	Shoemaker
Washing/scouring	Sailor
Washing/scouring	Smith
Washing/scouring	Tailor (now in army)
Washing/scouring	Barber/periwig-maker
Washing/scouring	Shoemaker
Washing/scouring	Shoemaker
Washing/scouring/nursekeeping	Tailor
Washing/scouring	Sawyer
Washing/scouring	Labourer
Washing/scouring/making clothes	Drummer
Charring	Chairman
Charring	Gunsmith
Glove washer	Clockmaker
Washing hoods and scarves	Soldier
Washing silks	Shoemaker
Washing silks/clearstarching	Coachman
Starcher	Shoemaker
Clearstarcher	Sailor
Clearstarcher	Shagreen case maker
Washing linen	Labourer
Washing linen	Chairman
Washing and starching linen	Waterman
Washing gents' linen/plainwork	Ostler
Washing	Shoemaker
Washing	Baker (now at sea)
Washing	Cook
Taking in washing	Tailor
Washing/other honest labour	Slater
Washing/plainwork/making sacks	Waterman
Washerwoman	Tinman
Washerwoman	Tailor
Washing clothes	Domestic servant
Washing clothes	Ropemaker
Washing clothes	Tailor (now in Hamburg)
Washing clothes	Sailor (quartermaster)
Washerwoman	Plasterer
Nursing children	Fisherman
Nursing children	Tailor
Nursing children	Labourer
Nursing parish children/charwoman	Shoemaker/Chelsea pensioner
Wetnurse	Coachman

Nursekeeping	Gentleman (Jacobite in exile)
Nursekeeping	Bricklayer
Nursekeeping/washing and scouring	Sailor
Nursekeeping	Mathematical instrument maker
Nurse	Gardener
Nursekeeping/nursing parish children	Broker
Nursekeeping	Staymaker
Nurse	Joiner
Nurse	Custom house waiter
Nursekeeping/sewing	Soldier
Nursekeeping/drover	Drover
Nursekeeping	Coachman
Nursekeeping/threadwork	Sailor
Nursekeeping/nursing parish children	Labourer/watchman
Nursekeeping	Sailor
Nursekeeping/winding silk	Cowkeeper
Midwife	Gentleman
Midwife	Feltmaker
Cures cancers	Weaver
Hair doubler	Weaver
Spinning	Shoemaker
Spinning	Sailor
Spinning shoemakers' thread	Smith
Spinning worsted/daywork	Sailor
Spinning worsted	Sailor
Winding silk	Sailor
Winding silk	Sailor
Winding silk	Sailor
Winding silk	Sailor
Winding silk	Sailor
Winding silk	Sailor
Winding silk	Sailor
Silk twisting/washing	Soldier
Silk throwster	Sailor (in Jamaica)
Knitting/sewing/washing/nursing	Sailmaker (at sea)
Knitting thread stockings	Sailor
Mending lace	Coachman
Button-maker	Smith
Plushing waistcoats	Sailor
Quilting	Grocer
Making fustian frocks	Hotpresser and packer
Making and selling old clothes	Horner
Making linen/knitting	Fellowship porter
Capmaking	Gentleman/army officer
Capmaking	Capmaker/Chelsea pensioner
Bodice-maker	Sailor
Staymaker	Staymaker
Staymaker	Staymaker
Tailor	Shoemaker (living in Jamaica)
Tailor/piecebroker	Tailor
Tailor/staymaker	Tailor
Working for slop shops	Soldier
Sewing	Goldbeater
Sempstress	Shoemaker
Needlework/nursekeeping	Labourer
Needlework	Ship's carpenter
Needlework/washing	Barber (deserted)
Needlework	Gentleman/selling drugs
Needlework	Baker

Needlework/worsted doubler	Woolcomber/astrologer
Needlework	Weaver
Needlework	Wire-drawer
Needlework	Sailor
Needlework	Tailor
Plainwork/making riding-hoods	Perfumer
Plainwork/nursing	Domestic servant
Plainwork/starching	Grocer
Plainwork/other stitching work	Chelsea pensioner
Plainwork	Drawer in tavern
Plainwork (employs other women)	Tailor
Plainwork	Sawyer
Plainwork	Vintner
Plainwork	Gentleman
Mantuamaker	Gentleman
Mantuamaker/silktwisting/sewing	Sailor
Mantuamaker/plainwork	Leather-dresser (failed)
Mantuamaker	Sailor
Mantuamaker/making children's coats	Vintner
Mantuamaker	Glass-grinder
Mantuamaker	Shoemaker
Mantuamaker/making children's coats	Limner
Mantuamaker	Sword-cutler
Mantuamaker	Staymaker
Mantuamaker/alehouse-keeper	Victualler
Making scarves and mantuas	Baker
Mantuamaker	Staymaker
Mantuamaker	Gentleman/solicitor
Mantuamaker	Gentleman
Mantuamaker	Upholsterer
Carries loads to markets	Heelmaker
Petty chapwoman	Broadsilkweaver
Selling linen	Waterman
Tubwoman/selling water/day labour	Shipwright
Delivering tobacco pipes	Sailor
Selling butter and eggs	Porter
Selling earthenware	Brewer's servant
Hawking earthenware	Shoemaker
Selling goods for pastry-cook	Joiner
Buying and selling old clothes	Throwster
Buying and selling old clothes	Drover
Selling tea, chocolate (no shop)	Sailor
Selling tea	Labourer
Selling pies in the street	Soldier
Selling bread	Soldier
Selling fish and fruit	Sailor
Selling fish and fruit	Soldier
Selling fruit from a cellar	Tailor
Selling herbs and fruit	Labourer in victualling office
Selling fruit	Blacksmith (long time ill)
Herbwoman/pewkeeper	Carpenter
Selling fruit	Sailor
Selling fruit and greens	Carpenter
Selling fruit/needlework	Vintner
Selling coal and wood	Baker/coal seller
Potter's shop	Potter
Picture shop	Bricklayer
Pawnbroker	Printseller/selling clothes
Selling lace, holland etc.	Gentleman

Sells trunks and boxes	Gentleman
Selling fine quiltings	Coachman
Cheesemonger's shop	Cheesemonger
Milliner	Gentleman
Milliner	Gentleman
Chandler's shop	Gentleman
Chandler's shop	Wine-cooper
Chandler's shop	Tailor
Chandler's shop	Coachman
Chandler's shop	Domestic servant
Chandler's shop (parish pays rent)	Sailor
Chandler's shop	Sailor
Milkwoman	Labourer
Pastry-cook	Pastry-cook
Baker	Baker
Baker	Baker
Cookshop	Roasting-cook
Cookshop	Sailor
Selling drink/making pies	Musician
Selling drink/nursing children	Carpenter
Selling spirits	Founder
Tavern-keeper	Vintner
Selling brandy, sugar, calicoes etc.	Sailor
Brandy shop	Hartshorn rapper
Strongwater shop	Strongwaterman
Strongwater shop/selling whips	Coachman
Public house	Instrument case maker
Public house	Hoop shaver
Public house	Fireworker in Queen's service
Public house/victualler	Victualler
Public house	Victualler
Public house	Sailor
Victualling house	House carpenter/victualler
Public house	Victualler
Victualler	Victualler
Public house	Victualler
Alehousekeeper	Victualler
Public house	Tailor/public house
Public house	Gardener to Lady Russell
Public house	Gentleman
Public house	Tinman
Public house	Tailor
Brickmaker/selling fish and fruit	Brickmaker
Dealing in seamen's tickets	Sailor
Running errands for prisoners	Prison turnkey
Potter	Joiner
Flaskmaker	Waterman
Pipemaker	Pipemaker
Vestrywoman to Trinity Chapel	Wiredrawer/clerk to Trinity Chapel
Chaircaner/mending clothes	Saddletree platemaker
Schoolteacher	Banker's man
Schoolmistress	Hatmaker
Schoolmistress	Gentleman
Hard labour	Sailor (now in Jamaica)
Day labourer	Labourer
Labourer	Sailor
Daywork	Shoemaker
Honest labour	Sailor

Notes: For a similar list see George, *London life*, appendix VI. This lists the occupations of married couples, mainly in the second half of the eighteenth century, using the records of witnesses, prosecutors and prisoners appearing at the Old Bailey from the *Sessions Papers*. She found the same lack of partnership between husband and wife evident in the table above. There were 86 couples, 8 of whom worked at the same trade – a saloop seller, two weavers, a shoemaker, a tailor, a butcher and an upholsterer and a couple who 'kept the fairs'. Three other wives did work very closely connected to that of their husbands, while all the rest had totally different occupations. Some of these occupations, such as thief, fence, and shoplifter, were not surprisingly not among those admitted by our sample to the registrars of the church courts.
Source: 'employment' sample (see table 5.2).

Appendix B: Occupations of husbands of 'unemployed' wives

Gentleman/professional		Sawyer	2
Gentleman/Esquire	17	Japanner	1
Army officer	5	Turner	1
Government official	4	Carver	1
Customs house officer	3		
Exciseman	2	*Food/drink*	
Surgeon	3	Public house	2
Attorney	1	Brewer	2
Clergyman	1	Vintner	2
Accountant	1	Victualler	2
Bailiff	1	Innholder	1
		Brandyseller	1
Merchants/shopkeepers		Wine-cooper	1
Merchant	3	Cook	1
Exchange broker	1	Grocer	1
Clothworker	2	Cheesemonger	1
Upholsterer	5	Tallow-chandler	1
Haberdasher	2	Gingerbread-baker	1
Hatter	2	Hog-seller	2
Stuffman	1		
Merchant-taylor	1	*Metalwork*	
Linen-draper	1	Sword-cutler	2
Jeweller	1	Blacksmith	2
Tobacconist	1	Founder	1
		Pewterer (1m)	1
Clothing		Cutler	1
Weaver (2m)	5	Anchorsmith	1
Tailor (2m)	4	Clockmaker	1
Shoemaker (1m)	2	Gunplate-worker	1
Ribbon-maker (1m)	1		
Button-maker	1	*Sea/river*	
Silk stocking-maker	1	Ship's captain/master	3
Capmaker	1	Ships' officers	4
		Sailor	9
Building/furniture		Waterman	4
Carpenter	4	Lighterman	1
Painter	4	Fisherman	1
Joiner	4	Shipwright	1
Bricklayer	3		
Plasterer	3	*Others*	
Mason (1m)	3	Barber	2

Gardener	3	Charcoalman	1
Coachman	3	Bookbinder	1
Chairman	2		
Labourer	2		
Porter	2	Unknown	5

Note: 'm' = master if this is stated; many of the others may also be masters.
Source: 'employment' sample (see table 5.2).

6

What difference did women's work make to the Industrial Revolution?

MAXINE BERG

Recent research by economic historians on patterns of economic growth during the eighteenth and nineteenth centuries has raised important questions for the significance of women's work. This research has substantially changed our views on the speed and extent of industrial change during those years classically identified with the Industrial Revolution, about 1760 to 1820. No longer is this period regarded as one of fundamental economic and technological transformation. Quantitative indicators of economic growth have challenged traditional ideas of rapid industrialization. The new indices of economic growth produced by Crafts, Lindert and Williamson, Mokyr and Wrigley point to continuity rather than discontinuity in the growth of output and of productivity during the years of England's classic Industrial Revolution.[1] This rejection of the idea of a fundamental break in the economy in the later eighteenth and early nineteenth centuries has also affected social and political history. It has brought about a dramatic change in the perspectives of social historians on work experiences and class formations. These have emphasized continuities between eighteenth-century radicalism and nineteenth-century social protest.

Whatever the intention of those responsible for such new historical views, the result has been to discard the Industrial Revolution altogether in wider historical writing. It is thus that we read Norman Stone, from the right, dismissing the 'industrial revolution' as the conceptual relic of a few outdated early twentieth-century economists. And from the left Gareth Stedman Jones has described the 'changing face of nineteenth-century Britain' as the discovery of a continuity between eighteenth and nineteenth-century class formations.[2] I believe that these new perspectives on both the economy and the workforce have entailed a flight away from the study of many of the major topics of economic history into social history. But equally social historians have readily accepted such perspectives as the general framework for their own work, rather than seriously considering their assumptions, omissions and implications. These are already the subject of debate,[3] and it is appropriate now to enquire into the effect of the single most glaring omission from this new history – women's work. There has, of course, been considerable historical writing on women's work, wages and conditions during the industrial revolution.[4] But this is a social history which runs parallel to, or provides a parenthetical paragraph to, mainstream economic history. The impact of women's labour and wages has not been considered in the construction of indices of economic change because long runs of quantitative data on occupations, labour-force participation and wages are not generally available. Women were rarely recorded in the eighteenth century in official statistics, legal records or wage books in terms other than widow or spinster. But this is not grounds for excluding descriptive and analytical consideration of their impact on current understandings of this classical phase of industrialization. Before turning to this we must look first at currently-accepted views among many historians of the economy of the eighteenth and early nineteenth centuries.

It is now apparent that the eighteenth-century economy was much more industrial than was once thought. Higher proportions of the population were occupied in industrial urban and rural crafts and in proto-industrial manufacture than Gregory King and Joseph Massie estimated at the time. But more persons occupied as industrial workers did not necessarily mean higher rates of economic growth. New estimates of England's social structure show that even before the beginning of the eighteenth century most families were occupied not in subsistence agriculture, but in commercial agriculture and in manufacture and services for the market. But the economy did not achieve any significantly high growth rates until the second quarter of the nineteenth century. Productivity grew over the whole economy very slowly: 0.2 per cent per year in 1769–1801, 0.7 per cent per year in 1801–31, and 1.0 per cent per year in the period 1831–60.[5]

Families occupied in industry, building and commerce comprised 27.7 per cent of the population in 1688, but 36.8 per cent in 1759.[6] The substantial proportions of the population engaged in these activities, however, yielded but few bonuses to overall growth rates. Indeed, if we look to productivity growth in the manufacturing sector, this was only 0.2 per cent per year between 1760 and 1801, and 0.4 per cent per year between 1801 and 1831. Most of the economic growth actually achieved up to the second quarter of the nineteenth century found its source in agriculture and in two extremely small industries: cotton and iron. These industries did experience a spectacular acceleration in their growth of output, but they were very small industries, which together contributed less than 10 per cent of value added [see note] in industry in 1770; however, this rose to approximately 30 per cent in 1831.[7] By far the greatest proportion of industrial employment was to be found in activity organized in very traditional ways and using non-mechanized and even primitive technologies. As late as 1831 only 10 per cent of the adult male workforce worked in high-productivity industries serving distant markets.[8]

The following tables indicate the characteristics in terms of productivity growth and of employment of the manufacturing sector as seen by Crafts and Wrigley.

These tables indicate that by far the highest proportion of value added in industry was provided by industries which experienced little change in technical processes or organizations. And furthermore, most industrial employment was locked into activities where productivity had remained static for generations. Only a small proportion of male employment went to high-productivity industry, and despite its contribution, it could not shift the weight imposed by the more traditional activities on the overall economy. Not until the advent of advances in the use of coal-based sources

Table 6.1 Value added in British industry[9]

Industry	% 1770	% 1801	% 1831
Cotton	2.6	17.0	22.4
Wool	30.6	18.7	14.1
Linen	8.3	4.8	4.4
Silk	4.4	3.7	5.1
Building	10.5	17.2	23.5
Iron	6.6	7.4	6.7
Copper	0.9	1.7	0.7
Beer	5.7	4.6	4.6
Leather	22.3	15.5	8.7
Soap	1.3	1.5	1.1
Candles	2.2	1.8	1.1
Coal	4.4	5.0	7.0
Paper	0.4	1.1	0.8

Table 6.2 Adult male employment in 1831 (20 years of age and over)[10]

Sector	Number	%
Agriculture	980,750	32.6
Manufacturing	314,106	10.4
Retail trade and handicraft	964,177	32.0
Capitalist, bankers, professionals	179,983	6.0
Labourers (other than agricultural)	500,950	16.6
Servants	70,629	2.3
Total	3,010,595	100.0

Table 6.3 Major employments in retail
trade and handicrafts in 1831[11]

Activity	Number
Shoemakers	110,122
Carpenters	83,810
Tailors	60,166
Publicans	52,621
Shopkeepers	49,529
Blacksmiths	45,405
Masons	31,631
Butchers	31,026
Bricklayers	28,939
Bakers	23,730
Total	516,979

of power – that is, until the spread of steam power through industry in the second third of the nineteenth century – was industrial productivity to rise substantially and so to leave behind its pre-industrial patterns.

This is the current story of the Industrial Revolution. It is a Malthusian tale based on an economy with a surplus of labour. In such an economy much of this labour was tied up in petty retailing, traditional trades, and some proto-industrial activity. A certain amount of this labour was 'disguised unemployment', in the sense that reducing numbers employed in the industry would not reduce its output. The effect of such a labour surplus according to this economic theory is to keep wages to a subsistence level. New industries offering employment at subsistence wages would have this workforce to draw on; they would also have the labour generated by an increasing population, and the labour of women and children transferred from household to commercial activities.[12]

According to current understanding, the problem of development faced by the British economy in the eighteenth century was not a large subsistence agricultural sector. On the contrary, agricultural productivity increased steadily over the century, and there was a fundamental shift of labour away from agriculture; male employment in the sector fell from 61.2 per cent of the labour force in 1700 to 32.6 per cent in 1800.[13] But manufacturing and commerce, apart from a few key but still very small industries, was over-endowed with labour relative to capital and was technologically stagnant. The evidence for this view, however, lies largely in the characteristics of the distribution of the labour force, and in this case the adult male labour force. A small proportion of the adult male labour force was to be found in progressive manufacturing industries serving distant markets. It is this above all which has led historians to ascribe Britain's relatively poor economic performance to her industrial sector.

What difference does the inclusion of women's and children's labour make to this scenario?[14] First, we cannot answer this question at the aggregate level because occupational data on women and children were not collected in the eighteenth century. Second, the historical discussion of women's industrial employment during industrialization has been given over thus far to a fruitless divide between optimistic and pessimistic positions.[15] This has failed to recognize the implications of the absence of long-run occupational data for women.

The extent to which women's employment opportunities in industry waxed or waned over the course of the eighteenth and early nineteenth centuries varied according to the industry, region, town, rural community, and time period chosen. Women's employment opportunities were also women's labour-force participation rates in rapidly changing or traditional activities. Women's labour-force participation has therefore been cut off from the whole discussion of productivity change, shifts of labour and incomes between sectors and output growth in the period. Male occupational structures, on the contrary, have formed the basic building block of all these macro-economic estimates.

Let us see what information on women's employment is available at the regional and industrial level to provide some provisional answers to the question of the difference made to the general picture by the inclusion of women. This question was raised, but immediately dismissed, by Wrigley:

> In some of the most dynamic industries, such as cotton textiles, a high proportion of the labour force was female. . . . If information were available for the whole labour force, therefore, the numbers and percentages just given would be changed somewhat, probably in the direction of raising the overall percentage in forms of employment where productivity per head was rising, but not to a degree that would greatly affect the thrust of the argument presented.[16]

The lack of aggregative data on women's employment has meant that their contributions have thus far not been acknowledged. Yet as even Wrigley has conceded, a high proportion of the labour force in the dynamic industries, such as cotton textiles, was not male, but female. Women workers were also concentrated in proto-industrial activity, in the potteries and to a lesser degree in metal goods. To what extent have our views of the low productivity of British industry in the crucial years of the Industrial Revolution been distorted because we have been looking at the industrial distribution of the wrong workforce? It was the female not the male workforce which counted in the new high-productivity industries.

The relative place of the textile industries needs to be set in the context of wider industrial output. The textile industries as a whole contributed 45.9 per cent of value added in British industry in 1770 and 46 per cent in 1831. What had changed over the period was the contribution of the individual industries. Cotton's place grew from 2.6 per cent to 22.14 per cent, and wool's declined from 30.6 per cent to 14 per cent. But the gender division of the workforce did not change: it remained predominantly female throughout the period. In 1770 fourteen men were needed to make twelve broadcloths, but an additional seventeen women and twenty-seven children were also required.[17] In the Yorkshire worsted manufacture, female spinners outnumbered woolcombers and weavers by three to one. The linen industry contributed more to value added in 1770 than did the iron industry, and only approximately 2 per cent less than it did in 1831. Adam Smith calculated that in addition to flax growers and dressers, three or four spinners were necessary to keep one weaver in constant employment.[18] Silk contributed 4.4 per cent of value added in 1770, the same proportion as coal; by 1831 the position of coal was more important at 7 per cent, but equally silk's had grown, after a dip, to 5.1 per cent. This too was a women's industry. In 1765, the proportion of women and children to men in the London trade was fourteen to one; and there were 4,000 in the Spitalfields trade.[19] In addition to this the industry was scattered by the late eighteenth century over twenty counties and fifty towns, with one mill in Stockport employing 2,000. Women were employed in both the throwing and the weaving sections of the industry, including large numbers of colliers' wives in the suburbs of Coventry. These were 'women's industries', though they also of course employed smaller proportions of men in branches such as weaving. Even in face of the technological innovation and factory organization that raised some of them by the early nineteenth century into 'dynamic' industrial sectors, they remained women's industries. For many 'dynamic' sectors, it was the distribution of the female labour force, not the male, which counted.

The cotton industry, the key 'dynamic' sector credited with much of the productivity increase of the industrial sector, employed higher proportions of women and children than of men in factories in both the eighteenth and the early nineteenth century. The few large-scale cotton mills of the eighteenth century employed roughly equal proportions of men and women, and of adults and children. The cotton factory labour force of 1818 showed that women accounted for a little over half of the workforce, and children accounted for a substantial proportion. In Scotland, these proportions were even more marked. Women and girls made up 61 per cent of the workforce in Scottish cotton mills; outside of Glasgow, the women were even more prominent, for they were also employed in throstle spinning and in spinning on short mules.[20]

Too much emphasis has been given in histories of women's work to the factories, whereas only a small amount of industry was organized in this way in the eighteenth and early nineteenth centuries. Dynamic industries might also, however, be organized as workshops or as dispersed or subcontracted units. Innovation in markets, distribution networks and

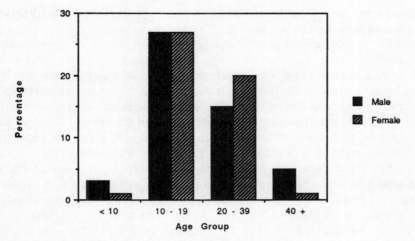

Figure 6.1 Workers in the cotton industry by age and gender, 1819
Source: Parliamentary Papers 1819 CX, Report of the State and Conditions of the Children Employed in the Cotton Manufactories of the United Kingdom. Data used in Hermann Freudenberger, Francis J. Mather and Clark Nardinelli, 'A New Look at the Early Factory Labour Force', *Journal of Economic History*, xliv (1984), pp. 1085–90.

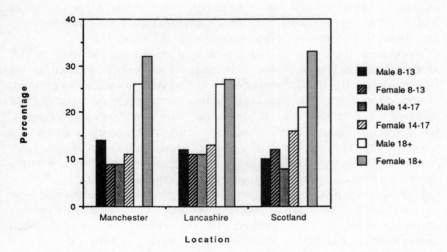

Figure 6.2 Workers in the cotton industry by age and gender, 1833
Source: Parliamentary Papers 1833 XX, First Report of . . . Commissioners [on] the Employment of Children in Factories, p. D2 107; *Parliamentary Papers* 1834 XX, Factories Inquiry Commission, Supplementary Report Part I, pp. 21–2. Data used in Per Bolin-Hort, *Work, Family and the State. Child Labour and the Organisation of Production in the British Cotton Industry, 1780–1920*, Lund, 1989, p. 54.

division and specialization of labour were equally important ingredients to a progressive industrial sector.

Other textile industries employing high proportions of women were lacemaking and stocking knitting, two decentralized or putting-out industries. Lacemaking was exclusively a female trade. From the late seventeenth century the industry was important in Devon when Honiton lace was popular, and employed approximately 4,000 in the Colyton district alone. It occupied 21 per cent of the population of the town of Colyton, and was therefore a major industry.[21] With the rise of the pillow-lace industry late in the eighteenth century, numbers employed were estimated as high as 140,000 for Buckinghamshire, Northampton and Bedfordshire.[22] Hand-knitting had ranked with spinning as the main women's industry, albeit a very traditional one, in rural areas all over the country, and continued in Scotland and the dales of the West Riding long after the introduction of framework knitting. Even after the introduction of the frame, used initially by men, women were occupied in seaming, finishing and winding. Increasingly, as apprenticeship regulations were bypassed, women also worked the frames.

Thus when we talk of industry in the eighteenth and early nineteenth centuries, we are talking of a largely female workforce. Of course there were many other predominantly male industries which also contributed substantial proportions of value added: the leather trades, building and mining. But these are also classic examples of traditional industries which underwent very little innovation over the period. Indeed the building trades and shoemaking were sponges for casual surplus labour.[23]

To be sure, there were a number of such traditional industries which absorbed excess female labour, but many of these had declined in the eighteenth century; hand spinning and knitting were notable examples. But in some regions these had been replaced by other newer manufactures – flax spinning in Scotland, silk throwing in Essex, and jennyspinning in Lancashire. In many cases, these new industries absorbed much less women's labour than had the former local industries. Women not reabsorbed into new industries were left unemployed, or moved into the fastest-growing occupational category of all, domestic service.

In the case of men, their occupations are recorded from parish and legal records, but these sources do not convey the extent of chronic unemployment of male workers in the eighteenth century. Their unemployment and underemployment were masked behind occupational categories. If women's labour has not been adequately counted, then equally it is likely that there are cases where men's labour has been double counted.

The iron industry provides the counter-example of an industry with a new technology and dominated by male labour. But if we compare its industrial significance to that of textiles, we find it contributed much smaller proportions of value added in industry: 7.4 per cent of value added in 1801 in comparison with cotton's 17 per cent; 6.7 per cent in 1831 beside cotton's 22.4 per cent. Furthermore, while men worked in iron, other contemporary metalworking industries which were also undergoing rapid innovation employed a mixed family labour force, or high proportions of women and children in home and large-scale workshops. Indeed there was a typical division of labour between women and children making small chains and nails at home while the men worked away in puddling and rolling mills. The Birmingham trades in the eighteenth century encompassed a whole range of new industries deploying new techniques with division of labour: button- and buckle-making, japanning, and 'toymaking', the manufacture of light ornamental ware and light hardwares. These industries employed a mixed labour force, and systematic data available only from the nineteenth century indicates growing proportions of women and girls, rising from 14 per cent of the labour force in the Birmingham trades in 1841 to 18 per cent in 1851.[24]

Those industries at the forefront of technological and organizational innovation were also mainly industries employing women's labour. Why was this the case at a time when there was so much disguised and real unemployment among male workers in the industrial sector? The usual

Table 6.4 Age–sex ratio within the Birmingham metal trades

Workforce	% 1841	% 1851
Men (males over 20)	71	58
Boys (males under 20)	17	24
Women (females over 20)	8	11
Girls (females under 20)	4	7
Total	100	100

Source: Clive Behagg, *Politics and Production in the Early Nineteenth Century*, London, 1990, p. 48.

Table 6.5 Age–sex ratio within the button-making trades

Workforce	% 1841	% 1851
Men	45	27
Boys	15	16
Women	24	32
Girls	16	25
Total	100	100

Source: Clive Behagg, *Politics and Production in the Early Nineteenth Century*, London, 1990, p. 48.

reason given for the employment of women rather than of men in industry is cheap labour. Women had lower wages than men, and were therefore substituted where the opportunity arose. New industries would, therefore, seek out locations where there was female unemployment, and so acquire traditionally cheap labour at an even greater discount. But this analysis is not sufficient if we assume a labour-surplus economy. If there was male unemployment, and wages at the margin at only a subsistence level, why did not entrepreneurs seek out male labour? There is evidence of stable if not falling male wage rates for the period up to 1820. There are, of course, no long-term wage trends for women, but it is generally assumed that women by custom received one third to one half the wage of men. This in itself might be enough to induce a substitution of female for male labour. But there is more data available at the regional level to indicate other factors at play. We know that there were big regional differences in male wages.[25] But so there were too for female wages.

Relatively high earnings for women in manufacturing were to be found in areas of the North and the Midlands where textiles, metalwares and potteries were expanding rapidly; and also in some southern agricultural areas where lacemaking, straw plaiting and silk spinning were growth industries. *Relative* is just as it says – women's wages were nearly always lower than men's wages in any branch of manufacture. In most cases they were also lower than the lowest local male wages, those of male agricultural labourers. But in the newer, expanding industries some women's wage rates were at least equal to those received by local male agricultural labour, and sometimes much higher. It must also be remembered that wages were not earnings. High earnings required not just high wage rates, but steady employment over the week, the seasons and the economic cycle. Earnings for women were also tied to family contributions, especially from children, and to future work expectations. 'Apprenticeship', training or experience divided the wages of young learners from the piece rates of older tradeswomen. And equally high-wage teenage labour could be a short-lived experience in the range of a woman's lifetime earnings. All of these factors must be considered to provide a profile of trends in women's earnings over the Industrial Revolution.[26] We do not yet have the data to provide this, neither do we have long-run data drawn from a large number of observations for a range of industries and regions. Before a reasonable account can be provided for more than individual towns or villages of the demand for women's labour and wage rates, substantial data must be built up from sources primarily available in local records.

On the basis of some individual observations of women's wage rates across a number of trades, we can however make some comparisons between periods of their relation to male wage rates. Wage rates rather than earnings should also provide us with at least some indication of the demand for women's labour.

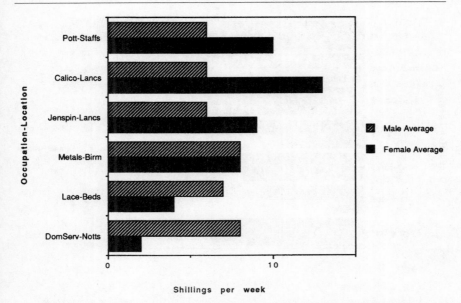

Figure 6.3 Women's wages in some occupations and regions, 1760–1770,
compared to local male wage rates in agriculture

Sources: Male agricultural wages according to region are found in Edward Hunt,
'Industrialization and Regional Inequality: Wages in Britain, 1760–1914', *Journal of
Economic History* 46, pp. 935–66, and in Edward Hunt, 'Wages', in John Langton
and Robert Morris, *Atlas of Industrializing Britain 1780–1914*, London, 1986,
p. 63.
Women's wages: Domestic service, Nottinghamshire – Bridget Hill, *Women, Work
and Sexual Politics*, Oxford, 1988, p. 133; Lace, Bedfordshire – Ivy Pinchbeck,
Women Workers and the Industrial Revolution (1930), London, 1981, p. 207;
Metals, Birmingham – Maxine Berg, 'Women's Work, Mechanization and the Early
Phases of Industrialization in England', in Patrick Joyce, *The Historical Meanings of
Work*, London, 1987, p. 83; Jenny spinning, Lancashire – Maxine Berg, 'Women's
Work', p. 76; Calico printing, Lancashire – Maxine Berg, 'Women's Work', p. 79;
Pottery painting, Staffordshire – Maxine Berg, *The Age of Manufactures*, London,
1985, p. 152; Lorna Weatherill, *Consumer Behaviour and Material Culture in
Britain 1660–1760*, London, 1988, p. 100; Robin Reilly, *Josiah Wedgwood
1730–1795*, London, 1992, p. 130.

Low wages were clearly not the only reason for employing women in new
industries. Indeed most of these occupations were gender-segregated, at least
for time and place, though these gender divisions were subject to change. In the
short run, and with no other contiguous changes, there was little possibility of
substituting female for male labour as wage differentials changed.

The lacemaking industry is a good example. Far from being an industry
developed on the feminization of poverty, it promoted the independence of

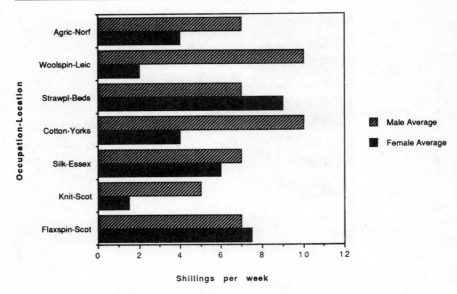

Figure 6.4 Women's wages in some occupations and regions, 1790–1797, compared to local male wage rates in agriculture

Sources: Agriculture, Norfolk – Hill, *Women, Work*, p. 54; Woolspinning, Leicestershire – Berg, *The Age of Manufactures*, p. 140; Straw plaiting, Bedfordshire – Pinchbeck, *Women Workers*, p. 216; Cotton, Yorkshire – Berg, *Age of manufactures*, p. 140; Silk, Essex – Lown, *Women and Industrialization*, Cambridge, 1990, p. 29; Knitting, Scotland – Alex Gibson and T. Christopher Smout, *Prices, Food and Wages in Scotland, 1550–1780*, Cambridge, forthcoming, chap. 9; Flax spinning, Scotland, Gibson and Smout, *Prices, Food*.

women as wage earners.[27] Wages in the seventeenth and early eighteenth century were high, higher than those for wool spinners and much higher than those for local male agricultural labour.[28] Yet despite the evident prosperity of this occupation for a time, men were not employed in it, neither did they seek to enter it. It was not wages which determined this gender divide, but the organizational and technological attributes of a women's workforce. The reason for this gender division did not lie in any physical attribute such as steady application or small fingers. For men were tailors, jewellers and makers of watch parts and scientific instruments. Old men and boys in some rural areas were also to be found stocking knitting by hand.[29]

When women workers were introduced in new industries or new settings, they usually entered these along with a whole range of organizational and technological changes.[30] A simple example was their entry into power-loom weaving. These new labour forces, technologies and organization associated together to yield substantially higher rates of profit than had been possible in other industries or under earlier manufacturing regimes. This phenomenon has not yet been investigated for eighteenth- and early nineteenth-century Britain. But it has been observed for the early nineteenth-century United States. Productivity changes have been linked to organizational and technological change, mainly in the form of the division of labour and supervised work regimes. Here larger-scale workshops and small factories yielded economies of scale at even such low-optimum plant-size levels as six to fifteen employees. The source of these economies was a division of hand-performed tasks, the use of simple tools, supervision and a more disciplined work regime. These workshops and factories also drew on higher proportions of female and child labour than similar industries organized under artisanal regimes. In industries deploying large-scale production, as in the factory textile industry and paper-making, more capital-intensive processes were introduced along with a more female and juvenile workforce. These industries were associated with gains in productivity and in wages for women over the period.[31]

This phase of development in manufacturing in the north-east of the U.S. bore many similarities to the earlier phase of industrialization in eighteenth-century Britain. If the kinds of organizational and technological changes observed in both factory and non-mechanized industry in the early nineteenth-century United States were associated both with changes in the division of labour and with gains in productivity, it seems likely that there were similar associations in eighteenth-century industry in Britain.

It is important to see the extent to which new technologies and organization were associated with a female and child labour force. For the early nineteenth-century United States, Goldin and Sokoloff see the reason for this in women's lower wages relative to men's. Means were sought to substitute women's labour for men's. But this was only part of the answer in Britain; there may also be other reasons for this use of women's labour in the United States.

It is evident in Britain that women and children were simply assumed to be the key workforce to be targeted with any novelty in manufacturing methods. Machines and processes were invented with this workforce in mind. New techniques in calico printing and spinning provide classic examples of experimentation on a child and female workforce. In calico printing, processes were broken down into a series of operations performed particularly well by teenage girls who contributed manual dexterity (learned already at home) with high labour intensity. The spinning jenny was first invented for use by a young girl, its horizontal wheel making it uncomfortable for an adult worker to use for any length of time.[32] Girls (and boys as well) were, as is well known, widely employed with the newer textile technologies in silk and cotton industries. They were used in the silk throwing mills, where they were taken on from the ages of 6 to 8, 'because their fingers are supple and they learn the skills more easily'.[33] A cotton mill at Emscote was reported to have dismissed girls after their apprenticeship because their fingers were too big to go between the threads.[34]

Patents and contemporary descriptions of new industries frequently pointed out the close connection between a particular innovation and its use of a child or female labour force.[35] The economist Dean Tucker, in 1760, described as the key attribute of the division of labour in the Birmingham trades the use of child assistants as an extra appendage of the worker; this use also trained these children to habits of industry.[36] It was widely held at the time that machines for stamping and piercing in the small metal trades extended the range of female employment, especially that of young girls.[37] Girls were specifically requested in advertisements in Birmingham's *Aris's Gazette* as button piercers, annealers and for stove and polishing work in the japanning trades.[38]

Josiah Wedgwood reported to the Children's Employment Commission in 1816 that girls were employed in 'painting on the biscuit' mainly,[39] but they also paint upon the glaze and after the second dipping. They work with 'a camel hair pencil in painting patterns upon the ware, sitting at the table.'[40] The hand-made nail trade relied largely on the labour of women and children. An early nineteenth-century innovation, the 'oliver' or foot-operated spring hammer, allowed a smith to work single-handed, but was responsible for all kinds of deformities in the teenage girls who used it.[41]

These are just some examples of the ways in which new technologies and divisions of labour were introduced, then described by contemporaries in terms of the gender and age of the workforce using them. Such gender-typing of innovation would probably have entailed two explanations. The first is that manufacturers and inventors saw the technical and profit-making advantages in using a new workforce which could be integrated with the new techniques, in such a way as to bypass traditional artisan customs and arrangements. If these latter arrangements were left in place while new techniques were introduced, the likely result was resistance by producers to the new technology.[42] Contemporary manufacturers furthermore believed that women and girls had a greater 'natural' aptitude for the manual dexterity and fine motor skills required by the new techniques, and that 'female' ways of working together were more amenable to division of labour than were 'male' work cultures.

The second way of looking at this gendered technology is that inventions and new working methods in manufacture were rather public affairs in the eighteenth century. The advantages of new projects in the seventeenth century, and of new manufacturing enterprises in the eighteenth century, were frequently presented to the state or to local communities in terms of their capacities for providing employment.[43] Though the real point of such innovation was to save labour, if it was to be profitable, nevertheless it was politically expedient to present technologies in terms of the female and child labour they would employ, rather than the male labour they would save.

The concerns of Poor Law authorities for providing manufacturing employment for women and girls, as well as industrial training for young girls in spinning and lace schools, reflected concerns not just over poor rates, but over illegitimacy and in some areas the high proportion of single women among the poor.[45] These concerns were also related to the differential effects of changing agricultural practices and declining opportunities in rural domestic industry on the gender division of the labour market. New methods were making sharp inroads on women's work in pastoral agriculture, dairying and hand spinning.[46] Robert Allen estimates the proportionate reduction of women's employment in agriculture in the South Midlands to be much higher than that of men or boys.

Table 6.6 Agricultural employment in the south Midlands[44]

Approximate date	Men	Women	Boys
Early 1600s	79,135	52,148	50,210
Early 1700s	72,801	46,144	43,128
Early 1800s	54,976	32,902	27,507

It has, indeed, been argued that rather than widespread children's and women's employment before the industrial revolution, there was a heritage going back to the sixteenth century of insufficient employment for this part of the labour force. Women in London were employed in a narrow range of badly-paid domestic work as well as in textile and clothing manufacture. Children aged less than thirteen or fourteen faced idleness, with manufacture providing the only (and very limited) hope of employment.[47]

It seems that the new industries of the eighteenth century and their innovations can be presented either as moulders of a new type of industrial workforce, or as a sponge for a traditionally cheap and even more available source of labour. What role did women and girls play in these new industries?

Labour-supply factors no doubt played a part in the characteristics of the industrial labour force in the eighteenth century. Women went in large numbers to many 'traditional' female manufactures such as needlework, just as men flocked to the building trades and shoemaking. Demographic change over the course of the eighteenth century was introducing new age and gender balances in the workforce. Children aged five to fourteen comprised approximately one-sixth of the population in the 1670s and one-quarter in the 1820s. This compares with only 6 per cent in 1951.[48] The young were thus both a potential source of labour, and the source of a high dependency ratio in society. Gender balances were also skewed towards women until late in the eighteenth century. Pamela Sharpe has shown recently the extent to which sex ratios in Colyton moved in favour of women throughout the seventeenth and the first half of the eighteenth century, and less so in the later eighteenth century.[49] Women married late, and there were higher numbers of spinsters and widows in the population than there were to be in the early nineteenth century.[50] Close associations between spinsterhood, poverty and illegitimacy prevailed over the century in Colyton.[51] Celibacy peaked at approximately one-quarter of groups reaching marriageable age in the 1670s and 1680s, and fell thereafter, until it started to rise again in the 1780s.[52]

In Colyton over twice the percentage of women from among the poor remained unmarried as among other social groups, and high celibacy and high feminine sex ratios prevailed over the whole eighteenth century. Colyton and other areas of rural industry like it experienced high feminine sex ratios, restraints on marriage, and lower rates of population growth than elsewhere.[53] High proportions of single women seeking some means of subsistence were reinforced by large numbers of widows. Between 1574 and 1821 over a quarter of households were headed by a single person; widows accounted for 12.9 per cent of households.

Historians have noted a decline in the numbers of these widows remarrying in the seventeenth and eighteenth centuries. The relationship of this to women's employment opportunities, on the one hand, or poverty on

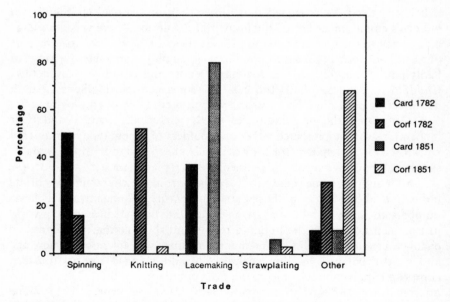

Figure 6.5 Occupations of married and widowed working women in Cardington, Bedfordshire, and Corfe Castle, Dorset, 1782 and 1851
Source: Osamu Saito, 'Who Worked When: Life-Time Profiles of Labour Force Participation in Cardington and Corfe Castle in the Late Eighteenth and Mid-Nineteenth Centuries', *Local Population Studies*, 1979, pp. 14–29, p. 25.

the other, is open to debate.[54] Our standard image of women working within the context of the family economy is a great distortion for the eighteenth century. Substantial numbers of single women, either spinsters or widows, needed to gain an independent subsistence, but in many cases, wages were pitifully inadequate or highly precarious.[55]

Labour-force participation rates varied by industry between married and widowed women, as indicated in Saito's study of listings of inhabitants in Cardington in Bedfordshire and Corfe Castle in Dorset. This shows dramatic differences in the participation rates of married women and of widows between the two communities, differences which can be explained largely by the availability of work in cottage industry. Figures 6.5 and 6.6 indicate the percentages of married and widowed women engaged in the various cottage industries in both places. Most women in Cardington in 1782 were employed in spinning and lacemaking; in 1851, the predominant industry was lacemaking. Corfe Castle's main female industry in 1790 was knitting, but by 1851 few women were employed in any of the old cottage industries.[56]

The different industrial structures were reflected in major differences in the marital status of women workers. Similar high proportions of married and widowed women worked in the eighteenth and the nineteenth centuries in Cardington; while Corfe Castle's widows dominated the cottage industries in 1790, but dwindled with those industries by 1851.[57]

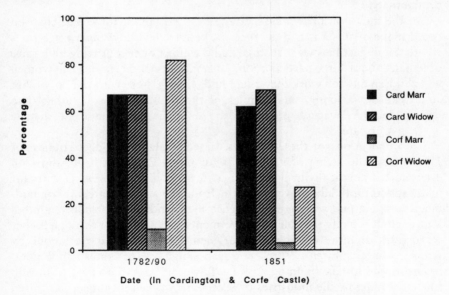

Figure 6.6 Labour force participation rates for married and widowed women in Cardington and Corfe Castle, 1782 and 1851
Source: Osamu Saito, 'Who Worked When', p. 23.

While wages for women in the newer industries could well be respectable, and, as demonstrated, were sometimes higher than those for men in agricultural labour, they were also volatile, or the wages of relatively brief 'golden ages'.[58] As such, single women and widows were certainly able to take the opportunity of an independent subsistence for a time in many of these industries, but this good fortune might be precarious and was frequently short-lived.

Where women worked within a family economy their low or fluctuating wages could become the deciding factor between crisis and stable or improving conditions for families. Even limited earnings, if pooled within a family economy, could help to put together a subsistence. This subsistence was most often based not on the traditional model of the family enterprise, but on individuals within a family or household working at a variety of activities and for a range of different employers.[59] The female silk weavers of Bedworth, Hillfields and Nuneaton in Warwickshire were the wives of miners; the female chain and nailmakers of the Black Country were the wives and daughters of ironworkers.[60]

Estimates for industrial productivity have thus far been based only on data for male labour and wages. This wage data indicates stable or falling real wages at least until 1820, although there was considerable regional variation.[61] These trends in income levels have been associated with overall slow rates of growth in productivity, and especially of industrial productivity.[62]

But the inclusion of women's wage rates and labour-force participation could make a substantial difference to these trends. Low male wage rates where family incomes were at stake had the effect of encouraging high rates of female labour-force participation.[63] Among very poor families, all women and children did any work they could find; among those who were poor, but could eke out a living, the earnings of the household head, rather than female market wages, provided the major determinant of female participation rates.[64]

The implications of these findings, based on Eden's budget studies for 1795–6 and the listing of inhabitants for Corfe Castle in 1790, show up even more dramatically in eighteenth-century Scotland. Here wage rates for male agricultural labour varied little from the mid-seventeenth to mid-nineteenth century, yet there is evidence that conditions for many families improved. It is likely that such improvement came about not through higher wage rates or more employment for men, but through more labour by women and children. With relatively high wage rates and good opportunities in flax spinning and the 'flowering' or embroidery of muslin (the expanding textile industries of Scotland), women in some areas raised their families from destitution to getting by.[65]

These features of the labour of women as individuals and as members of households affected the development of the newer industries and the technologies invented to use their labour. The gender characteristics of these industries and techniques were important to overall industrial performance, yet that performance has thus far been assessed only in terms of information on industries employing men or on male employment in industries employing women, children and men.

What effect did this combination of female labour supply and gender-based industrial expansion have on women's employment and incomes? While high proportions of the labour force employed in manufacturing were female, especially in the newer textile industries, it is also evident that the employment provided by industry was not sufficient to the task of soaking up the surplus labour left in the wake of demographic and agricultural change.

If we look at those industries and technological innovations affecting women, there is evidence of an eighteenth-century machinery question, one predating the introduction of the big power technologies and large-scale factories of the nineteenth century. The spinning jenny displaced nine in ten warp spinners and thirteen in fourteen weft spinners in the West of England.[66] Silk-throwing machinery and Heathcoat's lacemaking machinery destroyed traditional sources of domestic women's employment. The double engine loom, the Jacquard loom, the flying shuttle and framework knitting machinery displaced more. But other new processes in calico printing, the Birmingham trades and the potteries drew on more women's labour. The spinning jenny and the power loom displaced women workers, but they were still themselves worked by women, though substantially fewer of these were employed than under the older technologies. When women's work in woollen spinning in Scotland went into decline it was replaced by flax spinning, then by flowering muslin or embroidery.[67]

As long as we are dogged by the paucity of quantitative indicators on women's employment for the early industrial period, there can be no resolution of the issue of mechanization and women's work. But if we rely on current estimates of value added in industry, we see that the place of the new sectors was not sufficiently great to absorb the numbers of women displaced in agriculture and domestic spinning. The labour-surplus economy which prevailed for men by the early nineteenth century also prevailed for women in the eighteenth century. Nevertheless, in terms of their proportionate contribution to the manufacturing labour force, women workers played a greater part over the whole course of the eighteenth century than they had done previously and were to do in the later stages of industrialization. While for the most part women's work in this period was low-waged and exploitative, where this work contributed to a family economy, it lifted families above destitution. Where wages were higher for women, there were some limited possibilities of gaining an independent subsistence, and in such cases single women did work independently or in groups outside the family economy. Such work could support women as individuals, but could do so generally for only limited phases of the life cycle.

By the mid-nineteenth century, labour conditions historically specific to the Industrial Revolution had changed. As real wages rose, the proportions of occupied women fell at a rate of 0.7 per cent per decade over the last half of the nineteenth century. Other factors combined to reinforce this effect, notably a combination of factory legislation, the activities of male trade unionists and an increasingly pervasive ideology of the male breadwinner, and of fit and proper female activities. From levels recorded as high as the 67.5 per cent of married women working in Cardington in the 1780s, participation rates of married women in the whole country fell to 10 per cent in 1911.[68]

What impact does the recognition of women's employment have for our interpretations of the Industrial Revolution? Interpretations have thus far been focused mainly on data for adult male labour. The shift of labour away from agriculture would be reinforced with the inclusion of female labour. But the interpretation given to industry might be substantially altered by taking account of women's labour. The dominant parts of the manufacturing sector were employers of higher proportions of women than of men, and women rather than men were employed in the new progressive industries to which most of the productivity gain in industry has been attributed. We need to know the extent to which the sources of productivity gain which made the first Industrial Revolution can be found, in industry at least, in the deployment of a largely female workforce with attributes firstly of high labour intensity with female patterns of labour discipline along with technical dexterity, and only secondly of low wages.

If we are ever in a position to pin down these sources of productivity gain, we may well find ourselves contemplating an Industrial Revolution which did achieve significant productivity gains, by employing women's and children's labour, and by introducing the organizational and technological innovation which went with this: in other words, the Industrial Revolution as it was once familiarly understood.

Notes

1 See Nicholas Crafts, *British Economic Growth during the Industrial Revolution*, Oxford, 1985; E. Antony Wrigley, *Continuity, Chance and Change. The Character of the Industrial Revolution in England*, Cambridge, 1988; Peter Lindert and Jeffrey Williamson, 'English Workers' Living Standards during the Industrial Revolution: a New Look', *Economic History Review* 36, 1983, pp. 1–25; Joel Mokyr, 'Has the Industrial Revolution been Crowded Out? Some Reflections on Crafts and Williamson', *Explorations in Economic History* 24, 1987, pp. 293–319.

2 See, for example, Norman Stone, *Europe Transformed, 1878–1919*, London, 1983, p. 83; Gareth Stedman Jones, 'The Changing Face of 18th-Century Britain', *History Today* 41, 1991, pp. 36–40.

3 Edward H. Hunt, 'Industrialization and Regional Inequality: Wages in Britain 1760–1914', *Journal of Economic History* xlvi, 1986, pp. 935–66; Julian Hoppit,

'Counting the Industrial Revolution', *Economic History Review* 43, 1990, pp. 173–93; Maxine Berg and Pat Hudson, 'Rehabilitating the Industrial Revolution', *Economic History Review* 45, 1992, pp. 24–50; Pat Hudson, *The Industrial Revolution*, London, 1992.

4 See, for example, Jane Rendall, *Woman in Industrialising Society 1750–1880*, Oxford, 1990; Leonore Davidoff and Catherine Hall, *Family Fortunes. Men and Women of the English Middle Classes*, London, 1987; Sonya Rose, 'Gender Antagonism and Class Conflict: Exclusionary Tactics of Male Trade Unionists in Nineteenth-Century Britain', *Social History* 13, 1988, pp. 191–208; Angela John, ed., *Unequal Opportunities: Women's Employment in England, 1800–1918*, Oxford, 1985; Pat Hudson and W. Robert Lee, eds., *Women's Work and the Family Economy in Historical Perspective*, Manchester, 1990.

5 C. Knick Harley, 'British Industrialization before 1841: Evidence of Slower Growth during the Industrial Revolution', *Journal of Economic History* 42, 1982, pp. 267–89; Crafts, *British Economic Growth*, pp. 31, 81, 84.

6 Peter Lindert and Jeffrey Williamson, 'Revising England's Social Tables, 1688–1812', *Explorations in Economic History* 19, 1982, pp. 385–408.

7 Value added is the portion of the whole value paid directly to labour and capital in an industry. It excludes payments for materials or services from other sectors of the economy. The sum of all direct earnings of industries (or 'values added') is national income. The value added of one industry is therefore the measure of is 'contribution' to national income. See Donald McCloskey, 'The Industrial Revolution 1780–1860: a Survey', in Joel Mokyr, *The Economics of the Industrial Revolution*, London, 1985, p. 62.

8 Wrigley, *Continuity*, p. 85.

9 Crafts, *British Economic Growth*, p. 22.

10 Wrigley, *Continuity*, p. 85.

11 Wrigley, *Continuity*, p. 85.

12 This 'classical' model based in Malthus and Ricardo is developed in W. Arthur Lewis, 'Economic Development with Unlimited Supplies of Labour', *The Manchester School* 22, 1954, pp. 139–91, especially pp. 141–3.

13 Nicholas Crafts, 'The Eighteenth Century: a Survey', in Roderick Floud and Donald McCluskey, *An Economic History of Modern Britain*, vol. 1 (new edition), 1992.

14 I have raised some of these issues more briefly in Berg, 'Women's Work and the Industrial Revolution', *ReFresh* 12, 1991, pp. 1–4.

15 For a discussion of the many 'transitions' in women's work and their optimistic and pessimistic implications see Eric Richards, 'Women in the British Economy since about 1700: An Interpretation', *History* 59, 1974, pp. 337–47; Olwen Hufton, 'Women in History: Early Modern Europe', *Past and Present* 101, 1983, pp. 125–41; Judith Bennett, 'History that Stands Still: Women's Work in the European Past', *Feminist Studies* 14, 1988, pp. 269–83; and Jane Humphries, '"Lurking in the Wings . . .": Women in the Historiography of the Industrial Revolution', *Business and Economic History* 20, 1991, pp. 32–44.

16 Wrigley, *Continuity*, p. 87.

17 Adrian Randall, *Before the Luddites*, Cambridge, 1990, pp. 54–5, 58.

18 Adam Smith, *An Inquiry into the Nature and Causes of the Wealth of Nations* (1776), 2 vols, Oxford, 1976, Book IV, viii, vol. 1, p. 644.

19 See N. K. Rothstein, 'The Silk Industry in London, 1702–1766' (unpublished MA thesis, University of London, 1961), chap. 2; Judy Lown, *Women and Industrialisation*, Cambridge, 1991, chap. 1.

20 Hermann Freudenberger, Francis J. Mather and Clark Nardinelli, 'A New Look at the Early Factory Labour Force', *Journal of Economic History* 44, 1984, pp. 1085–90, esp. p. 1087; Per Bolin-Hort, *Work, Family and the State. Child Labour and the Organization of Production in the British Cotton Industry, 1780–1920*, Lund, Sweden, 1989, p. 54.

21 Pamela Sharpe, 'Literally Spinsters: a New Interpretation of Local Economy and Demography in Colyton in the Seventeenth and Eighteenth Century', *Economic History Review* 44, 1991, pp. 46–65, especially p. 52.

22 Ivy Pinchbeck, *Women Workers and the Industrial Revolution, 1750–1850* (1930), London, 1981, p. 204; Gordon R. Spenceley, 'The Origins of the English Pillow Lace Industry', *Agricultural History Review*, 21, 1973, pp. 81–93.

23 See J. M. Martin, 'Village Traders and the Emergence of a Proletariat in South Warwickshire, 1750–1851', *Agricultural History Review* 32, 1984, pp. 179–189. Cf. R. C. Allen, *Enclosure and the Yeoman*, Oxford, 1992, who found that shoemakers made up 15 per cent of industrial employment in the South Midlands in 1831, pp. 249–52. These trades fitted well with W. A. Lewis's petty retail trades which are enormously expanded in overpopulated economies. See Lewis, 'Economic Development', p. 141.

24 See Maxine Berg, *The Age of Manufactures*, chap. 12; Clive Behagg, *Politics and Production in Nineteenth Century England*, London, 1990, pp. 48–9.

25 See Edward H. Hunt, 'Industrialisation and Regional Inequality: Wages in Britain 1760–1914', *Journal of Economic History* 46, 1986, pp. 935–66.

26 Some of these factors are raised by Jane Humphries in her project on eighteenth- and nineteenth-century household budgets. Budgets were collected in this survey only for households containing a man and a wife, and most cases are taken from the nineteenth century. Analysis thus far, however, shows that family incomes rose more rapidly than male incomes for the period of early industrialization. This indicates that female participation rates and earnings provided greater contributions than they did in subsequent periods. See Sara Horrell and Jane Humphries, 'Eighteenth and Nineteenth Century Household Budgets', Department of Applied Economics, University of Cambridge, Mimeo, 1991. [See Reading 7]

27 Sharpe, 'Literally Spinsters', p. 55.

28 Sharpe, 'Literally Spinsters', p. 52.

29 George Walker, 'Wensley Dale Knitters', *The Costume of Yorkshire*, London, 1914.

30 For discussion of the combination of gender division and new organizational regimes in manufacturing now see Ruth Pearson, 'Women's Employment and Multinationals in the UK: Restructuring and Flexibility', in Diane Elson and Ruth Pearson, eds., *Women's Employment and Multinationals in Europe*, London, 1989, pp. 12–38.

31 Claudia Goldin and Kenneth Sokoloff, 'Women, Children and Industrialization in the Early Republic: Evidence from the Manufacturing Censuses', *Journal of Economic History* 42, 1982, pp. 752, 753, 760.

32 See Maxine Berg, *The Age of Manufactures*, pp. 139–53.

33 James Pattison, Peter Noaille, *Children's Employment Commission*, 1816.

34 Theodore Price, G. A. Lee, *Children's Employment Commission*, 1816.

35 See Christine MacLeod, *Inventing the Industrial Revolution: the English Patent System*, Cambridge, 1988, pp. 159–71.

36 Dean Tucker, cited in Roy Porter, *English Society in the Eighteenth Century*, Harmondsworth, 1982, pp. 213–14.

37 David C. Eversley, 'Industry and Trade 1700–1800', *Victoria County History of Warwickshire* vii, London, 1965, pp. 110–11.

38 See advertisements in *Aris's Gazette*, 1766–96.

39 This is a technical term for porcelain and other china after firing, but before glazing.

40 Josiah Wedgwood, *Children's Employment Commission*, vol. I, 1816.

41 E. I. Davies, 'The Handmade Nail Trade of Birmingham and District', M.Comm. Thesis, University of Birmingham, 1933, p. 142.

42 A good example of new technologies clashing with artisan customs is the finishing processes in the woollen manufacture in the early nineteenth century. See Adrian Randall, *Before the Luddites*.

43 See Joan Thirsk, *Economic Policy and Projects: the Development of Consumer Society in Early Modern England*, Oxford, 1978. This theme also appears in patent specifications in the seventeenth and eighteenth centuries. See Christine McLeod, *Inventing the Industrial Revolution*, pp. 158–73.

44 Taken from R. C. Allen, *Enclosure and the Yeoman*, Table 12-1.

45 Pamela Sharpe, 'Poor Children as Apprentices in Colyton, 1598–1830', *Continuity and Change* 6, 1991, pp. 253–7.

46 See Keith Snell, *Annals of the Labouring Poor, Social Change and Agrarian England*

1660–1900, Cambridge, 1985, chaps. 1, 6; Robert Allen, *Enclosure and the Yeoman*, chaps. 12, 13; Deborah Valenze, 'The Art of Women and the Business of Men: Women's Work and the Dairy Industry, c. 1740–1840', *Past and Present* 130, 1991, pp. 142–69; Adrian Randall, *Before the Luddites*, p. 60.

47 Some of this research is set out as a critique of the conclusions of Alice Clark, *Working Life of Women in the Seventeenth Century* (1919), London, 1981. See Peter Earle, 'The Female Labour Market in London in the late Seventeenth and early Eighteenth Centuries', *Economic History Review* 42, pp. 328–53, pp. 338, 340, 346; Jeremy Boulton, 'London Widowhood Revisited: the Decline of Female Remarriage in the Seventeenth and Early Eighteenth Centuries', *Continuity and Change* 3, 1990, pp. 323–55; David Kent, 'Ubiquitous but Invisible: Female Domestic Servants in Mid-Eighteenth Century London', *History Workshop* 28, 1989, pp. 111–29, especially, pp. 119, 125; Hugh Cunningham, 'The Employment and Unemployment of Children in England, c. 1680–1851', *Past and Present* 126, 1990, pp. 115–50, especially pp. 131, 133, 137.

48 E. Antony Wrigley and Roger S. Schofield, *The Population History of England, 1541–1871*, London, 1981, Tab. A3.1, pp. 528–9.

49 Pamela Sharpe, 'Literally Spinsters', p. 55.

50 For further discussion of this for the country as a whole, and its interpretation for the course of women's lives, see Bridget Hill, 'The Marriage Age of Women and the Demographers', *History Workshop* 28, 1989, pp. 129–47; and her *Women, Work and Sexual Politics in Eighteenth-Century England*, Oxford, 1989, chaps. 12, 13.

51 Sharpe, 'Literally Spinsters', pp. 56–7.

52 See Hill, *Women, Work*, p. 223.

53 Sharpe, 'Literally Spinsters', p. 63. Cf. Richard Wall, 'Leaving Home and the Process of Household Formation in Pre-industrial England', *Continuity and Change* 2, 1987, pp. 77–101, especially p. 86 for discussion of households in proto-industrial communities headed by women.

54 See Barbara J. Todd, 'The Remarrying Widow: a Stereotype Reconsidered', in Mary Prior, ed., *Women in English Society 1500–1800*, London, 1985, pp. 54–93. Cf. Jeremy Boulton, 'London Widowhood Revisited', pp. 323–55. Sharpe also discusses widows' low prospects of remarriage in Colyton, and their place in the labour market. See her 'Literally Spinsters', p. 61.

55 See Richard Wall, 'Women Alone in English Society', *Annales de démographie historique*, 1981, pp. 303–17; Olwen Hufton, 'Women Without Men: Widows and Spinsters in Britain and France in the Eighteenth Century', *Journal of Family History* 9, 1983, pp. 355–76.

56 Osamu Saito, 'Who Worked When: Life-Time Profiles of Labour Force Participation in Cardington and Corfe Castle in the Late Eighteenth and Mid-Nineteenth Centuries', *Local Population Studies*, 1979, pp. 14–29; p. 25.

57 Saito, 'Who Worked When?', p. 23.

58 Sharpe, 'Literally Spinsters', p. 52; William Reddy, *The Rise of Market Culture. The Textile Trade and French Society, 1750–1900*. Cambridge, 1984, chap. 2; Berg, *The Age of Manufactures*, chap. 5.

59 See John Styles, 'Embezzlement, Industry and the Law in England 1500–1800', in Maxine Berg, Pat Hudson, Michael Sonenscher, *Manufacture in Town and Country before the Factory*, Cambridge, 1983, pp. 179–211. Adrian Randall, *Before the Luddites*, shows the extreme to which woollen and worsted spinners operated over a widespread rural area, far from centres of male textile employment.

60 Berg, *Age of Manufactures*, pp. 215, 312.

61 Lindert and Williamson, 'English Workers' Living Standards', pp. 1–25; Hunt, 'Industrialization and Regional Inequality', pp. 935–66.

62 Nicholas Crafts, 'British Industrialization in an International Context', *Journal of Interdisciplinary History* 19, pp. 415–28.

63 Osamu Saito, 'Labour Supply Behaviour of the Poor in the English Industrial Revolution', *Journal of European Economic History* 10, 1981, pp. 633–52, esp. pp. 636, 645–9.

64 Saito, 'Labour Force Participation', p. 646.

65 Alex Gibson and Christopher Smout, *Prices, Food and Wages in Scotland 1550–1780*, Cambridge, forthcoming; Ian Whyte, 'Proto-industrialisation in Scotland', in Pat Hudson, ed., *Regions and Industries*, Cambridge, 1989, pp. 228–52, esp. pp. 242, 247.
66 See Adrian Randall, 'Work, Culture and Resistance to Machinery in the West of England Woollen Industry', in Pat Hudson, *Regions and Industries*, pp. 175–201.
67 For examples, see Berg, 'Women's Work, Mechanisation and the Early Phases of Industrialisation in England', pp. 64–98; Gibson and Smout, *Prices, Food and Wages in Scotland*, chap. 9.
68 Saito, 'Who Worked When', p. 23; also see his 'Labour Supply Behavior', p. 648.

7

Women's labour force participation and the transition to the male-breadwinner family, 1790–1865

SARA HORRELL AND JANE HUMPHRIES

Ivy Pinchbeck argued 65 years ago that the changes in the British economy during the industrial revolution promoted increased dependence on male wages and male wage-earners: a transition which was 'neither welcome nor understood' by the men and women who lived through it.[1] Pinchbeck's verdict has not gone unchallenged. She herself was anxious to shade the picture of declining economic opportunities for women, arguing that although the development of capitalist agriculture originally displaced women workers, by the early decades of the nineteenth century inadequate male wages, the French wars, and fading employment opportunities in domestic industries, followed by the abolition of allowances in aid of wages, combined to promote the appearance of a new class of women day labourers.

Although she recognized the gains in employment for women in the burgeoning textile factories, she did not forget the domestic outwork destroyed by competition with centralized machine methods. She saw a concentration of work (and wages) on some women in certain localities rather than an overall expansion of jobs. Nor did she blithely assume that wages meant independence and were unambiguously beneficial. She lamented the exodus of work from the home to centralized specialized workplaces in that it detached women from the hub of productive life and

We wish to thank the Leverhulme Trust for the generous support which made this work possible, and to thank participants in seminars at the Universities of Michigan and Illinois and Northwestern University, and an anonymous referee for their helpful comments.

relegated them to the rump of economic activities that remained domestic: primarily the administration of consumption and the management of reproduction. But at the same time she argued that this exodus improved domestic circumstances, left working-class women free for the first time actually to create a *home*, and was probably beneficial.

In section I we shall see how other authors have responded to Pinchbeck's arguments. But first we must establish why it is important to study the effects of industrialization on women's work and family lives. Women deserve attention as historic actors whose experiences were not always the same as men's. But an account of women's lives is important not just to provide a more complete understanding of the past but because without it major historical misreadings go unchallenged.

Take the question of what happened to the standard of living of the working class during industrialization: perhaps the most contentious issue in economic history. After more than 50 years of historical research a relatively optimistic consensus has emerged, although the date from which improvement can be established is still contested and probably later than originally thought. But this consensus is based on trends in indices of the real wages of adult males calculated from surviving labour and product market data. The real wage approach implicitly assumes that the same number of people were dependent on the male wage through time, that non-wage inputs into welfare did not decline, and that the earning opportunities of women and children were unaltered. Yet it is in just these areas that industrialization is argued to have brought significant changes.[2] Measuring the impact of industrialization on family living standards merely by changes in the male wage, with no recognition of the importance of these issues, leads to distortion of the complex transition that occurred and neglects vital factors in the determination of family welfare.[3]

To take another example, in the absence of information on the economic activities of women and children, economic historians have used narrow measures of the labour force which in turn distort productivity estimates.[4] A focus limited to the labour input of adult males must overestimate productivity, and if women's and children's labour input varied over the course of the industrial revolution, estimates of productivity growth are likely to be inaccurate.[5] But census estimates of female participation are unavailable prior to 1841 and are suspect thereafter.[6]

This article provides evidence on the economic activity of women and children during the industrial revolution drawn from an innovative dataset of 1,781 household budgets which detail household composition, sources of income in kind or in cash, and expenditures for the years 1787 to 1865. The dataset has been compiled from 59 sources including contemporary social commentators, Parliamentary Papers, local archives, provincial record offices, and working-class autobiographies. Some of the sources are well known and widely quoted; others unpublished and unused.[7] None has been systematically analysed to reveal patterns in women's work and variation in the contribution of women and children to family incomes across sectors and over time during industrialization.

Here we focus on a subset of the sample comprising families which have both a husband and a wife present (1,459 cases), where the husband's/father's earnings are positive and can be identified separately from those of the mother and children, and where the male head is employed in a known occupation (1,161 cases). Thus our data refer to the economic activities of married women whose husband is present and in work, though not necessarily in full work.

Our sample comprises whatever records have survived and been identified, however distributed across time, space, and family type. It is clearly not representative in the sense that average values calculated from it represent population means. To establish historical patterns from such data requires ingenuity. First the observations have to be grouped according to some meaningful principles. Here the putative variation in women's participation and women's and children's contributions to family incomes over time and according to local economic conditions guides the research. The data are sorted according to: (1) the subperiod during which the budget was recorded; and (2) the husband's/father's occupation, taken as a proxy for local economic opportunities. Occupationally specific experiences can then be weighted by the actual importance of the groups at different dates to recover the aggregate trends.

The data are grouped into five uneven subperiods. This periodization represents a compromise between the conventional perception of a watershed in 1815, and our own interest in separating periods of economic recession, namely 1816–20 and 1841–5, from periods of relatively full employment. These subperiods are adequately, if not evenly, covered by the budgets, with the smallest sample in 1841–5 (94 observations).[8]

Our use of husband's/father's occupation as the other main criterion for grouping the budgets may be more controversial. Occupation of the male head of household was taken as the best summary indicator of local economic conditions, and specifically of the job opportunities and types of work available to other family members.[9] It was almost universally recorded for our families, and we consider that it affords a clearer indication of family employment opportunities than an alternative geographical variable such as county of residence.[10] Overwhelming *a priori* evidence that economic conditions in agriculture varied dramatically across major groups of counties prompted the subdivision of those families whose husband/father was an agricultural labourer according to whether he worked in a high- or low-wage county.[11] Although coverage of the broad occupational groups is uneven, there are more than 50 families in each group, with agricultural labourers' families in the low-wage counties constituting the largest sample and tradesmen's families the smallest.

It remains possible that the data sorted by subperiod and male occupation are misleading, if, for example, in one time period the observations for, say, factory families are all drawn from certain districts, while in another subperiod they are drawn from other regions with different experience. Thus it is important to keep track of the original data and any potential regional biases they may contain.[12] The appendix details the geographical coverage of the dataset by time period and male occupational group. Agricultural families are widely dispersed across regions for most time periods. Factory families, not surprisingly, are concentrated in Lancashire and Cheshire, but this is true for all subperiods except 1821–40, when a significant number of families in this group came from Somerset. Outworking families also commonly lived in Lancashire and Cheshire, but are also observed in midland counties. Mining families, although inevitably limited to the mining districts, are spread within these areas and over time. The only obvious potential source of bias is that almost all the budgets for 1816–20 are drawn from Lancashire, although it is not clear either that the Lancashire experience of the postwar dislocations would be significantly unrepresentative, or that this concentration produces a misleading comparison with occupationally specific observations before 1816 or after 1820.

The credibility of the data is reinforced by several additional considerations. First, many of the social commentators involved in collecting the accounts selected their cases with an eye to their representativeness. Secondly, most of our budgets were accompanied by some evidence on expenditures which provide an internal check on the consistency of the income estimates. Finally, the budget estimates of nominal male earnings exhibit reassuring similarities with existing occupational and aggregate series.[13]

In section I we examine the wider literature on women's and children's activities during industrialization and investigate attempts to isolate the competing hypotheses found in varied historical accounts. Next, trends in participation and earnings are identified and discussed as a preliminary to the development of a model of married women's participation behaviour.

I

Orthodox historians have not so much challenged Pinchbeck's views as neglected them. The classic texts simply assumed that the industrial revolution created new job opportunities for women and children, especially in manufacturing.[14] It was left to others to infer that industrialization promoted women's independence and emancipated them from the patriarchy of the pre-capitalist household.[15]

One particular strand in this argument neatly connects the productive deployment of women and children and their expanded contributions to

family income, to the (alleged) ability of the British economy to pull itself up
by its own bootstraps through the expansion of domestic demand. So while
'the small earnings of women and children had made their modest
contribution to the family budget for centuries ... with the industrial
revolution their earnings became central to the domestic economy ... they
made a significantly larger contribution [and] they made it to a significantly
larger number of families'.[16] Through this 'McKendrick effect' women's and
children's increased work and wages becomes a cause as well as a
consequence of the industrial revolution.

More recently, mainstream economic historians have shown greater
awareness of the importance of women's and children's earnings and
activity rates to an evaluation of well being during industrialization. Lindert
and Williamson write that although 'thus far we have taken the orthodox
path by focusing solely on adult male purchasing power. ... Yet questions
about the work and earnings of women and children have always been
lurking in the wings.'[17] They 'add on' some limited quantitative evidence on
women's work and wages, the ambiguity of which seems inconsistent with
their optimistic conclusion that, as far as wages were concerned, working
women may have closed distance on unskilled men from 1750 to 1850:
'gleanings of data on relative weekly earnings ... hint as much'. But they
'cannot be sure that there was any upward trend in the true relative values
of women's work'.[18] Perhaps women simply worked longer hours to
maintain their relative position. Even if relative earnings were constant,
Lindert and Williamson perceive participation to be declining. But again
they are determinedly optimistic, reading this as voluntary, as 'the shadow
price of women's time rose faster than the observed wage rate'.[19]

The view that the industrial revolution increased women's and children's
employment is not always associated with an optimistic perspective on the
standard of living. Pessimists have made much of the negative effects of
women and children's employment in mines and mills during the period of
industrialization.[20] More recently, Berg and Hudson, while not directly
concerned with the standard of living *per se*, have restated the case for
viewing the industrial revolution as a major discontinuity, citing the
employment of women and children as one of its novel features.[21]

Meanwhile a separate but parallel debate on the implications of
industrialization for women's welfare has been rumbling on, both in the
pages of specialist journals and in monographs explicitly focused on gender
issues.[22] Some authors have searched for ways of conceptualizing the links
between changes in the economy and changes in women's work and family
lives. In this context feminist pessimists have argued that in the eighteenth
and nineteenth centuries women's access to resources was unequal. Market,
state, and familial processes of distribution discriminated against them.
Moreover, these processes were not constant in the face of economic change.
Industrialization opened new opportunities but closed others, and, less

guardedly than Pinchbeck, these authors conclude that on balance women lost. This approach dovetails neatly with the influential view that capitalism and patriarchy as dual and imbricated structures 'cause' women's oppression. The most compelling historically specific version of the capitalist patriarchy model identifies the deterioration in women's position with protective labour legislation, the growing influence of chauvinist trade unions, and campaigns for 'a family wage' which are depicted as excluding women from jobs which paid well enough for them to support themselves and their children, and crowded them into badly paid and insecure sectors of the labour market, thereby promoting their dependence on husbands and fathers.[23]

Is it possible to reconcile these seemingly disparate views? One source of compromise is ' *timing*. Perhaps the process of industrialization first increased female opportunities, only then to close them down. Some authors hint at such a scenario.[24] It is also possible that reconciliation can be pursued by distinguishing between proto-industrial activities and factory production. For some authors it is the expansion of the former that was associated with the growth of female employment, while others have focused upon factory production proper.[25] More generally, if outcomes for women were occupationally or perhaps regionally specific, it might help to explain how authors can simultaneously see opportunities both waxing and waning. In addition, occupationally specific stories seem essential to tighten the links between outcomes and the proximate institutional causes cited in the capitalist patriarchy model.

It might be possible to square the claim that industrialization increased women's work with the evidence of a strong female involvement in domestic industry by shifting the emphasis to the terms and conditions of the work. Thus Berg and Hudson write that what was new about women's employment 'in the period of the classic industrial revolution was the extent of its incorporation into rapidly expanding factory and workshop manufacturing and its association with low wages, increased intensification of work, and labour discipline'.[26] Can the empirical evidence help to clarify the arguments?

Unfortunately, empirical evidence is hard to find on any scale and in any detail.[27] Many authors have used nineteenth-century census data to demonstrate declining female participation and increasing employment segregation, although the censuses at best can only help with trends after 1841, in the last lap of the industrial revolution.[28] But even for this period the census enumeration of women's employment is demonstrably inaccurate.[29] In 1841 householders were advised that 'the profession etc of wives, or sons or daughters living with and assisting their parents but not apprenticed or receiving wages need not be inserted' on the census return. In 1851 householders were instructed that 'the occupations of women who are regularly employed from home, or at home, *in any but domestic* duties, [are] to be distinctly recorded'.[30] So householders were not asked to say what work was performed by the members of their households but to specify what was their 'rank, profession or occupation', that is, the definition of participation was based on an occupational designation. Within this framework the extent to which householders and enumerators recorded women's work varied. Checks provided by other local and national evidence such as wage books and oral histories suggest substantial under-reporting of female work in the agricultural sector, in manufacturing, and in certain service occupations.[31]

Frequently enumerators omitted any occupational designation for married women whose work was thus particularly under-reported.[32] Oral histories suggest that part-time work was also systematically under-recorded, again with particularly severe implications for an accurate view of married women's work.[33]

The invisibility of married women's work may well have distorted views of the nineteenth-century labour force; for example the view that factory work was confined to the young and single may be a statistical artefact.[34] At the same time the census probably over-reports domestic servants who frequently bore some blood or marriage relation to other household members, and who are therefore of dubious status.[35] If the census is too late, and should in any case be checked against sources, what evidence can be used?

The alternative is to put together a picture of trends from piecemeal data on employment and participation. The story is complicated by the self-provisioning or handicraft production for direct marketing which occupied many women and children.[36] Somehow estimates of the economic value of these activities have to be factored into the accounts. At this point Pinchbeck's scholarly trawl through the qualitative and quantitative evidence seems masterly. Subsequently progress has stalled. Lindert and Williamson's citation of a few figures on female wage rates stands in sharp contrast to their extensive documentation of men's wage rates over some 18 occupations. More serious attempts to compile series on female earnings contradict Lindert and Williamson's optimism but are themselves occupationally and temporally specific, and stand to be challenged by evidence for other groups of women workers in other times and places.[37]

There is even less certainty about overall trends in opportunities. The census evidence, while widely used to confirm claims of declining trends in the later nineteenth century, can do little to inform us about earlier events. It seems weak to argue that *logically* participation had to be higher in the 1780s than the 1850s because the economy was less developed in the earlier period and could support fewer non-workers.[38]

Creative researchers have mined other data sources to try to get a grip on trends in employment in the pre-census period. Earle has searched depositions of female witnesses before the London church courts in the late seventeenth and early eighteenth centuries for detailed information about women's employment. On this basis he has argued that a very high proportion of the women of the period were wholly or partly dependent on their own earnings; that the structure of occupations was close to that revealed by the 1851 census, as was the degree of gender concentration; and that a high proportion of women's occupations was casual, intermittent, and seasonal.[39]

Snell has used settlement examinations of applicants for poor relief to establish the seasonal distribution of unemployment by gender, and then used this to infer that the division of labour by sex in agricultural work tightened after 1750, bringing with it a declining participation of women within the agricultural workforce.[40] Sharpe has used age at marriage and evidence on female migration to infer the possibilities for female independence afforded by the lacemaking industry in Colyton.[41] But the problem remains that so long as the data cited are regionally and occupationally specific, counter-examples may be forthcoming.

Indeed the problems involved in obtaining empirical evidence have led one recent author to despair of defensible generalizations: 'Histories of women on the grand scale, whether optimistic or pessimistic, are amazingly premature when the available documentation is so sketchy.'[42] But the prospects for less grand histories may not be so bleak. We must work from the detailed studies of particular occupations, and using quantitative data innovatively must push back into the eighteenth century. This article is intended as a contribution to this project.

II

Women's work, and that of married women in particular, was probably just as invisible to the men who gathered the information surveyed here as it was to census enumerators and wages clerks. In describing a family's circumstances our sources were free to record whether or not the wife worked and at what particular occupation. A husband's occupation was considered vital evidence, and was not recorded in only 3 per cent of cases (42 out of the 1,459 husband/wife households in our dataset), whereas for some 567 wives (39 per cent of these cases) either occupation and/or work status is unknown. A further 538 (37 per cent) are explicitly recorded as not working. Defining participation by the designation of an occupation (definition A) gives the first series in table 7.1.

But whether or not our sources were myopic about married women's occupations, they were under some pressure to record the *earnings* of wives and mothers. Their brief was to provide a summary of the economic circumstances of families and this included giving details of expenditure. The omission of women's and children's earnings left household accounts suspiciously in deficit.[43] Sources of income could not be ignored. For some families commentators conflated women's and children's earnings but sometimes it is possible to isolate the earnings of wives/mothers. In the cases where women's and children's earnings are given together it seems unlikely that women's earnings were zero. Non-zero earnings provide a second criterion by which to judge women's membership of the labour force and this definition (B) generates the second series shown in table 7.1.[44]

The occupational definition, as expected, by and large produced lower estimates of participation than the earnings definition. This is especially true for those women who were married to agricultural workers, particularly in low-wage counties. The chronic under-reporting of occupations, while partly ideological, also reflects the intermittent and varied work undertaken and its tendency to be embedded in the family economy.[45] What occupational heading adequately describes the married women who 'supposing her to be . . . industrious' would have spent six weeks hay making, two weeks reaping, two weeks cutting beans, two weeks raking oats and barley, but who would also have earned by her needle and washtub?[46] How should the ubiquitous designation 'assisting' be coded in outworker families?

Not surprisingly, an occupational designation is a less chronic underestimator of the participation of women married to men who had non-agricultural occupations, and so were more likely themselves to have more permanent, full-time, and altogether conspicuous work. In mining and metalworking, for example, although the samples are inevitably small, the A and B definitions give rise to almost identical estimates. Nevertheless, the essentially opportunist and fragmented character of married women's work can be illustrated even within this group: witness the miner's wife who when times were hard in 1842 '[got] a little to make up the rent by making colliers' flannel shirts at 7d. apiece', paid for the black lead and mustard 'by any little job' she could get, obtained salt in exchange for old bones, and took in a lodger![47] Even in the factory districts women often undertook ancillary work which was not subject to mill discipline and organization, for example picking cotton, a hand process that could be done intermittently and at home.[48] Only 49 women with non-zero earnings and a further five with zero earnings reported factory occupations (5 per cent of the sample) though some of the women who earned but had no recorded occupation may also have worked in factories.[49]

The occupational and earnings definitions are also close for women in outworkers' families in the years between 1787 and 1840. But the earnings definition generates dramatically higher estimates of participation in the final periods.

Variation in under-reporting of wives' occupations creates anomalies in cross-sectional comparisons. For example, definition A suggests that women in agricultural families participated in the workforce much less frequently than miners' wives or the wives of outworkers, whereas the earnings

Table 7.1 Summary of trends in married women's participation rates[a]

	High-wage agriculture			Low-wage agriculture			Mining			Factory			Outwork			Trades			Casual			All[b]
	A	B	C	A	B	C	A	B	C	A	B	C	A	B	C	A	B	C	A	B	C	C
1787–1815	23.8	52.4	54.8	33.3	83.8	84.9	40.0	20.0	40.0	26.3	36.8	36.8	45.5	45.5	45.5	62.5	62.5	62.5	0.0	100.0	100.0	65.7
		(42)			(99)			(5)			(19)			(22)			(8)			(1)		(196)
1816–20	31.6	34.2	34.2		n.a.		25.9	27.8	27.8	4.2	4.2	4.2	38.9	38.4	41.9	26.7	30.0	30.0	66.7	66.7	66.7	49.4
		(38)						(54)			(24)			(198)			(30)			(3)		(347)
1821–40	6.7	22.2	22.2	11.8	84.6	84.6	33.3	33.3	33.3	71.4	78.6	85.7	47.9	52.1	54.3	0.0	62.5	62.5	8.3	66.7	66.7	61.7
		(45)			(136)			(6)			(28)			(94)			(8)			(12)		(329)
1841–5	20.0	40.0	40.0	44.4	55.6	55.6	6.3	6.3	9.4	100.0	0.0	100.0	38.6	61.4	72.7	100.0	100.0	100.0	0.0	0.0	0.0	57.5
		(5)			(9)			(32)			(2)			(44)			(1)			(1)		(94)
1846–65	4.6	47.8	47.8	0.0	63.0	63.0	0.0	0.0	0.0	100.0	100.0	100.0	1.8	67.3	69.1	42.9	42.9	42.9		n.a.		45.3
		(46)			(81)			(1)			(5)			(55)			(7)					(195)

Notes: a Participation defined as: A having a recorded occupation; B having non-zero earnings; C having either a recorded occupation or non-zero earnings.
b Aggregated using male employment weights for working-class occupations: see Horrell and Humphries, 'Old questions', n. 40 for the construction of these weights.
Women's participation in low-wage agricultural families in 1816–20 is assumed to be the same as in the previous period. Women's participation in casual occupations in 1846–65 is assumed to be zero as in the previous period. Sample sizes in parentheses.
Source: see text.

definition (*B*) suggests a higher level of participation among the wives of agricultural labourers, although this was probably seasonal and part-time. Note too that the contribution of women in both agricultural and domestic industry families had become almost invisible in accounts of occupations by mid century (capitalism 'in the full flood of industrialism' using 'a principal supply of labour so modestly'[50]) but in both cases the earnings definition suggests a much higher level of involvement. Thus, as other authors have suggested, occupational designations, and therefore the census returns, are likely to underestimate married women's paid work.

The most inclusive definition of participation – by which a woman is counted as active if she has either earnings or an occupation – provides estimates which vary over time by occupation, and within agriculture by region. In all occupations the effects on women's work opportunities of the depression following the Napoleonic wars are evident. While some of the decline may be a consequence of the regional concentration of these observations, some is undoubtedly real. Other authors have noted the severity of this downturn, and the male earnings estimates from the budgets are comparable to alternative occupational series based on wider regional dispersions.[51] The postwar dislocation had a common impact on women's work experience. Subsequently experiences diverged.

Married women's participation does appear to have declined during industrialization for families whose head worked in mining or had a casual occupation. The story is more ambiguous for agricultural labourers' wives. In high-wage agricultural areas women's participation declined, then increased around mid century, consistent with the Pinchbeck hypothesis. In low-wage counties women's participation remained high but showed some decline after 1840.[52] In contrast the participation rates of outworkers' wives increased after the 1816–20 slump: perhaps their contributions became increasingly necessary for family survival as male earnings were squeezed by falling piece rates and competition from machine methods.[53] Women in factory areas also showed steadily increasing participation after the postwar decline. The consequences of industrialization for women's work varied and any overall picture must depend on the weights attached to these individual experiences.[54]

The last column in table 7.1 summarizes the occupationally weighted, aggregate participation series. This shows the sharp decline in participation in the postwar slump, the increase in the 1830s, and further loss of jobs in the 'hungry forties', a trend which continued after mid century.

Overall, then, there is a suggested decline in participation.[55] But these data do not, as yet, tell us anything about causation. Were women leaving the labour force voluntarily as husbands' incomes rose, or were they being driven out by discrimination or structural changes that reduced women's jobs? To help answer some of these questions we turn to the evidence on women's and children's contributions to family income.

III

Table 7.2 summarizes the contribution of men and of women and children together in our sample of families.[56] The patchy increase in the absolute amounts contributed by women and children to low-wage agricultural family incomes represents a fairly narrow range of variation in the percentage contributions. Over the period as a whole, women and children contributed between 18 per cent and 22 per cent of family incomes. There was more variation in the high-wage counties (from 7 per cent to 20 per cent), the relatively high contributions in the earlier years probably reflecting industrial and proto-industrial earnings. The increase in the amounts of income contributed by women and children to agricultural families from 1787–1815 to 1816–20 in the high-wage counties, and from 1787–1815 to 1821–40 in those where low wages prevailed, constitutes some evidence for the 'McKendrick effect' though this was both minor and short lived given the subsequent decline in contributions. The relative contributions of wives and children appear to follow the inverted 'U' shape suggested by some feminist pessimists. The welfare implications of the eventual decline in contributions depend on its causes. The absolute and relative poverty of these families during the years when contributions from women and children were low and falling makes it difficult to see the decline as the result of income effects on the demand for women's and children's leisure.[57]

Miners' and metalworkers' wives and children contributed first more and then less to family incomes: another occupation for which the inverse 'U' shape seems valid. Again any 'McKendrick effect' was transitory and, given the continuous decrease in wives' participation, probably has more to do with trends in children's earnings. The transition for these families to increased dependence on men was perhaps made more abrupt by the Mines Regulation Act of 1842 which generalized the hitherto patchy decline in women's and children's work underground.[58]

Women and children whose husbands and fathers worked in factories contributed a higher share of family income than those in all other occupational categories except outworkers, with some increase during the process of industrialization. But given that few of these women themselves worked in factories, and that the factory districts afforded good employment opportunities for children, the children's contribution was probably paramount.

Contributions of women and children to outworkers' family incomes were persistently high in relative terms, though declining in absolute amounts, illustrating both the adverse secular trends in family incomes and the important role that these earnings played in family survival and the persistence of employment in certain declining occupations. Even here there is a decline in the relative contributions in the post-1845 period.

Table 7.2 Contributions to family income by men, women, and children

	Family income (£)	Sample size	Man's contribution (%)	Woman's and children's contribution (%)	Woman's contribution[a] (%)	Sample size[a]
High-wage agriculture						
1787–1815	25.08	(42)	88.5	10.5	5.2	(39)
1816–20	41.21	(38)	75.8	19.9	3.8	(31)
1821–40	36.68	(45)	87.5	9.2	1.7	(40)
1841–5	34.74	(5)	91.4	7.4	5.0	(5)
1846–65	41.86	(46)	86.1	13.9	0.5	(24)
All time periods	36.19	(176)	85.0	13.0	3.0	(139)
Low-wage agriculture						
1787–1815	23.00	(99)	78.5	18.4	9.6	(99)
1821–40	31.86	(136)	62.6	21.9	11.6	(81)
1841–5	31.29	(9)	77.7	20.4	5.6	(9)
1846–65	37.02	(81)	80.2	19.6	1.9	(35)
All time periods	30.43	(325)	72.3	20.2	8.9	(224)
Mining						
1787–1815	45.37	(5)	74.0	20.1	8.2	(5)
1816–20	53.81	(54)	71.6	26.3	3.9	(54)
1821–40	87.24	(6)	74.0	25.3	3.0	(6)
1841–5	52.56	(32)	86.5	13.4	0.5	(32)
1846–65	78.66	(1)	89.8	0.0	0.0	(1)
All time periods	55.27	(98)	76.9	21.4	2.9	(98)

Factory						
1787–1815	74.77	(19)	67.5	32.7	5.8	(16)
1816–20	67.29	(24)	72.5	25.1	0.7	(24)
1821–40	71.18	(28)	63.3	36.5	9.8	(16)
1841–5	81.90	(2)	60.3	39.7	0.0	(2)
1846–65	93.60	(5)	52.9	47.1	24.3	(1)
All time periods	72.57	(78)	66.4	32.8	4.9	(59)
Outwork						
1787–1815	59.17	(22)	57.4	40.9	5.4	(19)
1816–20	44.19	(198)	62.8	37.0	7.3	(186)
1821–40	43.78	(94)	61.8	35.4	10.5	(78)
1841–5	31.33	(44)	60.7	38.7	11.6	(44)
1846–65	43.15	(55)	73.6	26.4	6.1	(27)
All time periods	43.39	(413)	63.5	35.6	8.3	(354)
Trades						
1787–1815	44.36	(8)	80.0	16.5	3.0	(7)
1816–20	45.74	(30)	80.8	19.2	3.5	(26)
1821–40	47.67	(8)	65.6	23.9	0.0	(3)
1841–5	41.03	(1)	95.1	4.9	n.a.	
1846–65	68.80	(7)	86.7	3.4	3.4	(7)
All time periods	48.72	(54)	79.4	17.2	3.1	(43)

Note: a Observations where women's earnings can be identified separately from those of children.
Source: see text.

The contributions of the wives and children of artisans increased and then decreased in both absolute and relative terms. The pattern is similar to that within agriculture and mining.[59] The occupationally specific trends are compared in the bar charts reproduced as figure 7.1.

With the exception of factory families, women and children do not appear to have increased substantially their relative contributions to the household in most of the occupational groups. If anything, there was a decline, with increasing dependence on male earnings as its mirror image. Moreover, male earnings appear to have increased in relative importance more than the earnings of other family members contracted, as other income declined from the modest levels seen in late eighteenth-century budgets. Insofar as there was a heyday for the democratic sourcing of family incomes it appears to have been in the years after the Napoleonic wars and before 1835, though perhaps later for outworkers.

The aggregate trend may still have been towards increased contributions from women and children if an increasing share of families fell into categories in which male earnings were relatively unimportant. But although the economic restructuring associated with industrialization may have increased the importance of the outworkers' group until the 1830s, its decline thereafter, and the increased importance of artisan and mining families in which women's and children's earnings were less important, suggests that in aggregate the trend in the relative contributions of women and children was probably negative.

Three important conclusions emerge. The first is that accounts of women's and children's contributions to family incomes must be conditional on their occupational and regional identity, which limits 'grand theories' of the causes of women's marginalization. Theories that depict women, whatever their circumstances, as undifferentiated victims of allied economic and ideological forces must give way to detailed analyses of institutional changes at occupational and regional levels.

Second, except in the cases of factory and outworker families, women's and children's contributions were relatively small at the end of the eighteenth century and remained so throughout the period. While few families were entirely dependent on husbands and fathers, for many families male earnings were of crucial importance. This reliance preceded industrialization, with husbands'/fathers' earnings contributing more than three-quarters of family incomes to all groups other than factory workers and outworkers between 1787 and 1815. Industrialization afforded at most a chimera of independence. Only in the case of outworkers did women and children play a persistent and substantial role in the sourcing of income.

Third, the variation of women's and children's contribution over time and across occupations is not consistently related to family income level. Low-wage agricultural families at both the beginning and the end of the period were among the poorest, yet the percentage contributions of wives and

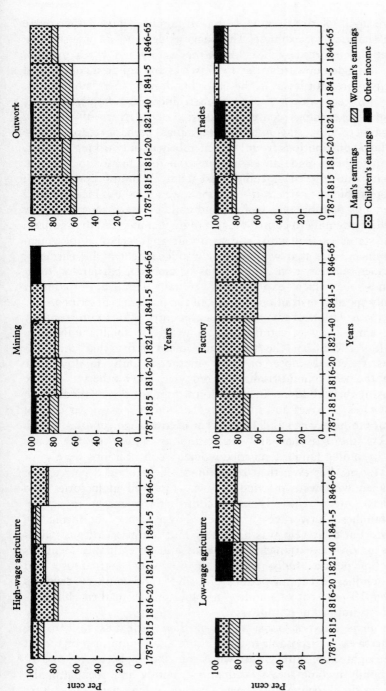

Figure 7.1 Contributions to household income, per cent

Notes: The percentage contributions to total income are taken from table 7.2. Other income is the residual after men's and women's and children's earnings are taken from total income. Women's and children's contributions are separated using the information on women's contributions, leaving children's as a residual. There is no information on the split of women's and children's earnings in the trades category in 1841–5, so the figure shows the whole amount attributed to children.

Source: table 7.2.

children were small relative to much better-off families whose fathers were employed in factories, for example. This suggests demand-side constraints: an interpretation reinforced by the evidence that as total family real incomes in this sector struggled upwards after 1835, wives and children contributed proportionally more, not less. On the other hand, for miners' families the evidence is consistent with a situation where increasing family incomes driven by high male earnings secured a relaxation of the efforts of wives and children. Symmetrically, stagnant male earnings perhaps enforced the persistently high contributions from other members in outworking families. Artisans seem to have made an early transition to a family structure in which women's and children's earnings were relatively unimportant though they were not the highest earners and real male wages did not increase until 1835.[60] It remains possible that women and children were constrained by demand in their attempts to contribute to family income, and that a man's occupational status carried with it ideas about appropriate employment patterns within families that were relatively independent of his earnings. This again rules out universal explanations (capitalism, patriarchy) or at least demands that such explanations contain detailed, proximate, occupationally specific, institutional causes of the outcomes described.

Although the isolation of married women's contributions unfortunately reduces the sample sizes in certain cells to unreliably small numbers, in general, table 7.2 confirms the suspicions voiced above that children's contributions exceeded those of their mothers. Only in low-wage agriculture at the peak of industrialization did wives and mothers match the contributions of their children. In agricultural families the relatively high participation rates of wives and mothers generated at most 5 per cent of family incomes in high-wage and 12 per cent in low-wage counties, which clearly reflects the seasonal and discontinuous nature of the work undertaken. In mining families, married women's contributions were most important early on, but even then constituted only around 8 per cent of income. Women who were married to men employed in factories also appear to have made relatively small contributions except in certain exceptional families. Outworkers' wives added over 11 per cent during 'the hungry forties' but their help was halved by mid century. Artisans' wives were dependent on the earnings of husbands and other family members throughout the period. Only perhaps in low-wage agriculture and outworking families in certain periods did wives' and mothers' earnings make up over 10 per cent of families' incomes and even then children's earnings were as important or more so.[61]

Wives' earnings did not boost those of their husbands to generate significant increases in disposable income. From a fairly uniform picture at the end of the eighteenth century, with wives contributing between 3 and 10 per cent of family income across occupations, untidy and occupationally specific patterns developed: a fairly steady decline in high-wage agriculture and mining; growth and then decline in low-wage agriculture and outwork; perhaps some increase in families whose heads were employed in factories, though the lack of observations in the later periods makes this little more than guesswork; and stability in the archetypically male-breadwinner families of artisans. In almost all the groups the contributions of married women were fading by mid century and had in any case never constituted much more than a taste of independence.

Was the decline in married women's relative contributions simply the result of decreasing participation, or was it the case that even considering only women who worked, their relative earnings were not maintained? A look at those working married women for whom earnings are separately identified suggests that while falling participation was one factor in the decline of women's relative contributions, the latter also fell (as in the case of mining), or rose and then fell (as in all other groups but factory workers) in the all-worker sample (table 7.3).[62] Except for the wives of factory workers, married women who earned in the period 1816–40 added larger percentage shares to incomes than those who worked after 1840. Women's earnings relative to men's followed the same occupationally specific trends.[63]

The variation in relative earnings power over time and across occupations might help to explain the patterns in participation with which we began. While for some occupations women's earnings increased relatively in the second quarter of the nineteenth century, for all occupations they grew at a lower rate than men's (or children's) earnings after 1840. Perhaps it was the inability of married women to hold their relative earnings positions, even if they did work, that fed the declining participation rates and not an exogenous decline in participation rates that drove their falling contributions to family incomes. This tentative suggestion is pursued in the next section which formalizes our search for an explanation of changes in female participation.

IV

Neoclassical economic theory proposes a model of the decision whether or not to work as the outcome of a rational weighing of alternatives, in which the goal is to maximize utility or satisfaction.[64] Individuals, including married women, decide whether or not to participate in paid employment by comparing the value of their time in the market (indexed by the wage rate) with the value of their time in the home ('the reservation wage').[65] The probability of participating is reduced to a function of their own real wage, other real income, including their husbands' earnings (which affect the reservation wage), and a vector of variables to allow for constraints on the participation decision and for heterogeneous tastes. Examples of the former include local employment opportunities, and of the latter, the number and

Table 7.3 Earnings of working married women as percentages of family income and husband's earnings[a]

	1787–1815	1816–1820	1821–1840	1841–1845	1846–1865	All time periods
High-wage agriculture						
% family income	9.2	16.7	13.5	12.5	12.5	11.4
% husband's earnings	11.7	22.3	35.2	16.2	14.3	17.2
Sample size	(22)	(7)	(5)	(2)	(1)	(37)
Low-wage agriculture						
% family income	11.4	n.a.	15.6	10.0	13.4	13.1
% husband's earnings	15.7		27.5	27.6	15.9	20.8
Sample size	(83)		(60)	(5)	(5)	(153)
Mining						
% family income	40.9	13.9	9.1	8.5	n.a.	14.2
% husband's earnings	69.2	26.4	16.7	10.3		26.0
Sample size	(1)	(15)	(2)	(2)		(20)
Factory						
% family income	23.1	17.6	15.6	n.a.	24.3	18.2
% husband's earnings	48.2	21.4	22.6		37.5	29.9
Sample size	(4)	(1)	(10)		(1)	(16)
Outwork						
% family income	14.7	20.9	24.8	18.9	18.3	20.9
% husband's earnings	24.1	41.6	55.3	32.5	23.9	41.1
Sample size	(7)	(65)	(33)	(27)	(9)	(141)
Trades						
% family income	5.2	18.0	n.a.	n.a.	8.0	11.2
% husband's earnings	7.2	24.3			10.9	15.3
Sample size	(4)	(5)			(3)	(12)

Note: a working defined as earnings recorded (participation definition B).
Source: see text.

ages of children and husband's work status conventionally assumed to imply 'a taste' for home production. These variables should then be able to explain all the occupational and temporal differences in women's participation rates, with no role remaining for the influence of ideological and institutional factors. How appropriate is such a model in the context of early industrial labour markets and how easily can it be estimated using historical data?

One problem is that our lack of wage data forces an unconventional recasting of the value of market work on an earnings basis. Can this be defended? The women in our study did not choose their hours conditional on the decision to take a job. By and large, they were offered package deals: harvest work, employment by the piece, so much cotton to pick.[66] Their choices were to exploit these opportunities, fitting the hours around their domestic schedules, or not to earn at all. A second issue is the need to build into the model variable attitudes to married women working and local economic conditions. Occupational dummies serve this purpose. The hypothesis that industrialization had an adverse impact on women's job opportunities can also be tested by the inclusion of time trends. The question is whether these have some explanatory power in addition to the conventional economic arguments.

Another set of problems relates to selection bias. Here the orthodox literature provides some guidance. The participation decision is partly based on the wage the woman could command in the labour market, but information on earnings is available only for those women who actually worked. Non-workers could be omitted from the analysis but this would truncate the sample systematically and introduce bias.[67] We need estimates of the potential earnings for all the women in the sample if we are to investigate the decision not to participate. The usual procedure involves predicting the wages of non-participants from those of participants; the wages of working women are related to characteristics such as education and training, assumed within a human capital model to influence productivity. Not only are the education levels of women in our sample unknown, but we doubt the applicability of the human capital model to historical wage determination. Most early nineteenth-century skills were readily learned; formal education was rare and irrelevant to female jobs; age-earnings profiles were flat.[68] Productivity was more likely to be related to health, and potential earnings to factors exogenous to individual women such as the local employment structure.[69] It is possible to relate the earnings of working wives to variables which reflect local employment opportunities and use this equation to predict the potential earnings of non-participants. Accordingly, women's earnings were related to regional variations in wage rates,[70] to opportunities for agricultural, industrial, or home-working as defined by the male occupational status, to the cost of living,[71] and to time: variables intended to represent the exogenous determinants of earnings (see table 7.4). The regions and available types of

Table 7.4 Probit regression of female participation

Earnings equation		Probit equations on participation[a]	
dependent variable ln (earnings)		predicted earnings without correction	predicted earnings with correction
Constant	0.851 (4.38)[b]	Constant	1.899 (7.14)[b]	-1.873 (-5.10)[b]

Earnings equation		Probit equations on participation[a]	
dependent variable ln (earnings)			**predicted earnings without correction**	**predicted earnings with correction**
Constant	0.851 (4.38)[b]	Constant	1.899 (7.14)[b]	-1.873 (-5.10)[b]
Region:		Predicted female real earnings	-0.049 (-0.69)	1.670 (15.31)[b]
London and Home Counties	-0.603 (-2.05)[c]	Male real earnings	-0.037 (-4.80)[b]	-0.049 (-5.10)[b]
South west	0.110 (0.96)	Real income from parish	-0.023 (-0.83)	-0.071 (-2.16)[b]
Wales	-0.035 (-0.16)	Other family members' real income	-0.023 (-3.93)[b]	-0.031 (-4.42)[b]
Midlands	-0.388 (-2.45)[b]	Child aged under 2	0.689 (5.21)[b]	0.666 (4.33)[b]
Lincolnshire and Yorks	0.155 (0.41)	Number of children	-0.059 (-2.32)[c]	-0.040 (-1.34)
Lancashire and Cheshire	0.163 (1.20)	Time	-0.200 (-9.07)[b]	0.065 (2.16)[c]
Cumberland, Westmorland, S. Scotland	-0.175 (-1.04)	Time^2	0.0057 (8.63)[b]	-0.0034 (-3.59)[b]
Northumberland and Durham	-0.029 (-0.13)			

N. Scotland	0.716
	(1.88)c
Unspecified	−0.365
	(−0.77)
Male occupation:	
Agriculture	−0.285
	(−2.09)c
Factory	0.518
	(2.58)b
Outwork	0.346
	(2.54)b
Time	0.010
	(4.25)b
ln (cost of living)	0.189
	(0.63)
Lambda	0.215
	(1.57)
R²	0.38
Sample size	387

Time³	−0.000044	0.000023
	(−8.29)b	(3.16)b
Mining	−0.089	−1.842
	(−0.44)	(−7.18)b
Factory	0.296	−5.203
	(0.87)	(−11.34)b
Outwork	0.272	−3.713
	(1.34)	(−13.19)b
Trades	−0.038	−1.406
	(−0.15)	(−5.01)b
Casual	0.480	−1.017
	(1.24)	(−2.37)c
Chi-squared	233.2	555.6
Predicted correctly	74.4%	86.2%
Sample size	930	930

Notes: a participation defined as earnings recorded, definition B. t-ratios in parentheses
b indicates significance at 1% level
c indicates significance at 5% level
Source: see text

work had plausible effects and time had a significant positive impact on nominal earnings.[72]

But this is where another kind of sample selection bias can creep in. The women who participated are likely to have had different unmeasured characteristics from those not in work. In contemporary analysis this is interpreted as the effects of training and education which are not captured by the standard measures of these variables. If the correlation between the measured and unmeasured characteristics differs between the two groups a possible bias emerges. It is widely held that unmeasured characteristics which cause a woman to have higher potential earnings will also make it more likely that she participates.[73] Unless this problem is corrected the potential earnings of non-participants will be over-predicted.[74]

Heckman proposes a two-stage method of correcting for this source of bias.[75] The essence of the procedure is to enter an additional term ('lambda') into the wage equation which reflects the positively correlated unmeasured characteristics of those currently employed which enhance their potential earnings. Estimating a probit equation for participation using predicted earnings calculated without the sample selection correction allows the variable capturing the unmeasured differences, lambda, to be created.[76] Lambda is then entered in the earnings equation to correct for the selectivity bias. Although it is not significant in our regression, being in work did have the anticipated positive effect on earnings.[77]

Our interest in correcting for selection bias in earnings is to improve the performance of the probit equation for participation. So although lambda did not prove significant, the theoretical justification for correction is so strong that predicted earnings with the correction were re-entered in the probit and the labour supply model re-estimated (see table 7.4). Note that the correction of the earnings estimates by and large left both the parameters in the participation equation and their significance levels unchanged, the main exception being the women's earnings variable. The coefficient on women's predicted real earnings becomes both positive and significant with the adjustment. This is entirely consistent with the logic underlying the correction procedure.[78]

The probit equation for participation performs well.[79] Perhaps surprisingly, the conventional neoclassical model appears to fit the behaviour of our early industrial wives and mothers. Specifically, women had a positive response to their own real earnings, whereas increased income from other sources reduced the probability of participation.[80] Children had a negative effect on participation but having a child under the age of two increased the probability of the woman working. The positive relationship between the presence of a baby and the probability of participating, so surprising in the context of contemporary studies, documents the historically important life cycle variation in women's work. Women worked during the early years of family formation but dropped out when children were old enough to take their place in the labour market.[81] Finally, the cubic time trend is significant in all three terms. Calculation of turning points showed a maximum in 1797 and a minimum beyond our period in 1871. Controlling for real earnings and income effects, the first half of the nineteenth century was associated with a rapid decline in the labour force participation of married women.

The importance of the trend in explaining women's participation suggests that economic variables, wages and incomes, and household characteristics are not sufficient to capture the changes occurring. Instead, changing institutional and ideological factors played a role and operated to affect adversely women's employment opportunities. The trend follows the predominantly downward path indicated by aggregate participation in table 7.1 and confirms the importance of exogenous factors in the overall picture of women's work during industrialization. But the patterns for the individual occupations are not always the same as those for the whole sample, and the occupational specificity suggests that any search for institutional and ideological obstacles to women's participation be conducted at this level.[82]

Most industrial occupations showed a pattern of dislocation during the Napoleonic wars followed by growing opportunities for women's employment, possibly resulting, as Pinchbeck argued, from the increasingly common practice of putting out work related to factory production and increased industrial employment. The reversal of the trend at mid century may reflect the decline of outwork as well as emerging male-breadwinner ideologies and protective labour legislation. The general trend in agriculture was downwards. Women were losing what employment opportunities they had through the commercialization of agriculture and the decline in outwork activities, as described in the qualitative literature. The high proportion of households still engaged in agriculture largely ameliorates the increased participation of women found in the other occupations, creating a downward trend in the overall pattern of participation.

V

The household budgets illuminate the pattern of married women's labour market activity in the pre-census period. Participation was clearly related in a predictable way to conventional economic and demographic variables, but was also affected by a negative time trend which may substantiate the claims of some pessimistic feminists that there were mounting institutional and ideological obstacles to women working. The decline in participation was neither continuous nor uniform across occupational categories, and this helps to reconcile the disparate hypotheses discussed earlier. In the second quarter of the nineteenth century industrialization was associated with higher relative earnings for some women. These and new job opportunities increased female labour force participation in some occupations above its post-Napoleonic war level. However, this period of increased financial independence for women was short lived; participation rates and relative earnings declined after mid century. There is little support for the argument put forward by Lindert and Williamson that women dropped out of the labour force as the shadow price of domestic work increased relative to wages. The argument that the decline in participation was caused not by supply shifts (changes in the reservation wage) but by changes in demand associated with structural and/or institutional changes still runs. Within the main narrative of women's increasing economic dependence on men, there is room to find pockets of improvement and independence clearly associated with industrial opportunities.[83] Sixty-five years on we find that our evidence largely supports Pinchbeck's views.

Notes

1 Pinchbeck, *Women workers*, p. 122. For a less shaded description of the downgrading effects of economic changes on women's lives see Clark, *Working life*.

2 Humphries, 'Lurking in the wings', p. 37.

3 For a detailed analysis of family incomes during the industrial revolution see Horrell and Humphries, 'Old questions'.

4 In this context note that Deane and Cole's estimates of the pre-1851 labour force and its industrial distribution were based on the adult male labour force figures (available in the censuses from 1831) and the backward projection of the 1851 ratio of adult males to all other employees by industry. While defending this as 'a reasonable assumption', they note that it would give misleading results for industries that were undergoing rapid structural change and 'obscures what seems to have been an important characteristic of the process of industrialisation, namely, the tendency for economic opportunities for child and female employment to increase': Deane and Cole, *British economic growth*, pp. 139–40. This would have the effect of overstating the size of the effective labour force in 1841 and even more so in 1831.

5 E. Higgs, 'Women workers in agriculture' (unpub. conference paper, 1992); Berg and Hudson, 'Rehabilitating', pp. 35–8.

6 E. Higgs, 'Women workers in agriculture' (unpub. conference paper, 1992); Higgs, 'Women, occupations and work'.

7 The data sources and information recorded are described in detail in Horrell and Humphries, 'Old questions', app. I.

8 Alternative periodizations were considered and these led to the same general conclusions.

9 Male rather than female occupations were also used for the pragmatic reason that many women had undefined or multiple occupations.

10 Such a view is consistent with the importance of kinship networks in procuring jobs and with children being increasingly likely to work in the same occupation as their father as industrialisation progressed. See Anderson, *Family structure*; Horrell and Humphries, 'Child labor'.

11 The counties are grouped using information from Hunt, 'Industrialization and regional inequality', pp. 956–66.

12 But note that the regression analysis performed later will control for these potential sources of bias.

13 See Horrell and Humphries, 'Old questions', p. 854 and n. 25.

14 See Deane and Cole, *British economic growth*, pp. 139–40; Deane, *First industrial revolution*, p. 147; Mathias, *First industrial nation*, pp. 175–6.

15 Thus, among the beneficial long-term consequences of the industrial revolution is listed its positive contribution to 'the emancipation of women': see Hartwell, 'Rising standard of living', p. 416. For the importance of this theme in historical sociology, see Thomas, 'Women and capitalism'.
16 McKendrick, 'Home demand', p. 180. See also Mathias, *First industrial nation*, pp. 175–6.
17 Lindert and Williamson, 'English workers' living standards', p. 17.
18 Lindert and Williamson, 'English workers' living standards', p. 17.
19 Lindert and Williamson, 'English workers' living standards', p. 19.
20 Hammond and Hammond, *Town labourer*; Marx, *Capital*.
21 Berg and Hudson, 'Rehabilitating', p. 37.
22 For useful summaries and bibliographies, see Thomas, 'Women and capitalism'; Hudson and Lee, *Women's work*, ch. 1.
23 Hartmann, 'Unhappy marriage'; Barratt, *Women's oppression*; Waltby, *Patriarchy at work*; Benenson, 'Family wage'.
24 Berg and Hudson, 'Rehabilitating', p. 37.
25 Levine, *Reproducing families*; Deane, *First industrial revolution*.
26 Berg and Hudson, 'Rehabilitating', p. 37.
27 Berg and Hudson, 'Rehabilitating', p. 35.
28 Richards, 'Women in the British economy'; Humphries, 'Most free from objection'; Jordan, 'Exclusion of women'; D. C. Betts, 'Women and work: industrial segregation in England and Wales, 1851–1901' (Dept. of Economics, Southern Methodist Univ., working paper, 1991). Furthermore, it is not easy to separate married women's work from the employment of all females in the census data.
29 Higgs, 'Women, occupations, and work'.
30 Higgs, 'Women, occupations, and work', p. 63. Note that the work of women in the family economy was not explicitly included and the directive probably served to restrict the census to work done in the market setting. Moreover, no guidance was given to the treatment of part-time, casual or seasonal work except that to be recorded it had to be 'regular'.
31 E. Higgs, 'Women workers in agriculture' (unpub. conference paper, 1992); Lown, *Women and industrialisation*; Davidoff, 'Separation of home and work'; Walton and McGloin, 'Holiday resorts'; Gerrard, 'Invisible servants'.
32 Lown, *Women and industrialisation*.
33 Roberts, 'Working wives'.
34 Hutchins and Harrison, *Factory legislation*; Branca, 'A new perspective'.
35 Anderson, *Family structure*; Higgs, 'Women, occupations, and work'.
36 Humphries, 'Enclosures', pp. 35–42.
37 See Neale, *Writing marxist history*, p. 117.
38 Richards, 'Women in the British economy', p. 337.
39 Earle, 'Female labour market'.
40 Snell, *Annals*.
41 Sharpe, 'Literally spinsters'.
42 Thomas, 'Women and capitalism', p. 547.
43 Thus in drawing up a comparative statement of the incomes of 48 labourers, one poor law subcommissioner reports his suspicions about one man's accounts: 'refuses to give information of the earnings of his wife who is post-woman, errand woman, and keeps a shop': *S.C. on Poor Law Amendment Act* (P.P. 1837–8, XVIII), pt. III, p. 453.
44 The two definitions can be combined into a broader hybrid definition of participation (C): women are counted in the labour force if they have either an occupational designation or positive earnings. The assumption is that a recorded occupation implied habitual employment even if a specific income was not reported.
45 See, for example, the recent survey by Bythell, 'Women in the workforce', pp. 33–4.
46 *Report from Commissioners on the Poor Law* (P.P. 1834, XXVIII), p. 269.
47 *First Report of Midland Mining Commission* (P.P. 1843, XIII), p. 116.
48 Collier, *Family economy*, p. 17.
49 The budgets do not detail the type of work undertaken by over half of those women with earnings or an occupation recorded, a proportion which remained reasonably

stable throughout. The most important occupation specified was outwork, with less than 10% recording agricultural or casual work. Very few women worked in mining or trades occupations. Around 15% of working married women were recorded as working in factories at the turn of the century and this had declined to 10% by the 1830s. In fact, 60% of women with husbands with factory occupations were themselves working in factories in 1831–50, a higher proportion than the 14% of married women employed in factories in Preston in 1851: see Anderson, *Family structure*, p. 72. In the 1840s, 38% of our women are working; this is considerably higher than the estimate of 7% in Birmingham in 1841: see Barnsby, *Birmingham working people*, p. 195, and again illustrates the downward bias of census estimates.

50 Richards, 'Women in the British Economy', p. 338.

51 Lindert and Williamson, 'English workers' living standards', p. 15, shows the severity of the postwar slump. For comparisons of male earnings from different sources see Horrell and Humphries, 'Old questions', p. 854, tab. 6 and n. 25.

52 Declining opportunities for women in agricultural areas after 1815 are found elsewhere. See Allen, *Enclosure*; Snell, *Annals*.

53 This would be consistent with the evidence of Lyons, 'Family response'.

54 For a qualitative survey, largely supportive of our results, of women's work across several occupations see Bythell, 'Women in the workforce'.

55 The decline of married women's work would imply downward bias in the use of the 1851 census proportions to predict the size of the labour force in earlier periods.

56 The remaining components of household income were poor relief and income in kind, for instance gleaning and coal provided by the employer. Figure 7.1 demonstrates the relative unimportance of this other income beyond 1815 and outside the agricultural sector. Families were heavily dependent on earnings. Poor relief formed much the largest part of other income but this was unimportant for factory, mining, and outwork families and it is only found in 1821–40 for our broadly defined trades families, constituting 7% of total income. The main recipients were agricultural families but poor relief made up less than 1% of total income on average and was virtually non-existent by the final period. The exception was low-wage agriculture in 1821–40 when 8% of family income was from poor relief.

57 For families in the agricultural sector real male earnings were static or falling until the 1840s and real family incomes only began to make minor advances in the 1830s: see S. Horrell and J. Humphries, 'Male earnings estimates from household accounts' (unpub. working paper, 1992).

58 See Humphries, 'Protective legislation'.

59 The numbers in the 'casual' category are too small to permit any general comments although women's and children's earnings were particularly important to these families.

60 Real male earnings and family incomes are given in S. Horrell and J. Humphries, 'Male earnings estimates from household accounts' (unpub. working paper, 1992).

61 To put our findings in perspective: Meyering, using Le Play's French family budgets, found that a peasant's wife in 1861 contributed 20% of family income (not including housework), a weaver's wife at about the same time, some 7% of family income, and the industrious wife of a Republican Guard in Paris in 1881, 15% of family income: Meyering, 'La petite ouvrière'. The figure for Le Play's weaver's wife fits well with our data. The striking difference is the fairly substantial contribution made by the relatively prosperous Parisian. Differences in the expectations of women within bourgeois families in the nineteenth century may help to explain persistent divergences in patterns of female activity between Britain and France. Working married women in Britain in 1984 contributed some 24% of family income (Horrell, 'Working-wife households', p. 53), whereas women in France contributed 34–48% of household income in 1981 (Bouillaguet-Bernard and Gauvin, 'Women's employment', p. 172).

62 The particularly small samples for factory workers' wives for 1816–20 and 1846–65 make it hard to comment on their experience.

63 Table 7.3 relates married women's earnings to those of their husbands. But the fact that a wife worked may well signal that her husband was a relatively poor earner and

that she was a relatively good earner. Therefore the ratio of wife's to husband's earnings will overstate true female relative earnings. The first point is demonstrated by a comparison of male earnings in working-wife families with male earnings in the whole sample. The former invariably fell short of the latter with the gap wider for non-agricultural families and wider over time: evidence suggesting that the usual finding for contemporary studies that, ceteris paribus, the higher a husband's income the lower the likelihood that his wife works can be generalized to historical studies. Put in conventional terms, higher male earnings increase the value of women's time in the home and reduce the probability of their participation in the workforce. The second point is taken up in the final section below.

64 See Becker, 'A theory of the allocation of time'; Mincer, 'Labour force participation of married women'.

65 Major early empirical work on this topic includes Cain, *Married women*; Bowen and Finnegan, *Economics of labor force participation*. Gronau and Heckman have contributed to the development of relevant statistical techniques; see, for example, the collection of papers in Smith, *Female labor supply*.

66 Of our working sample 57% had unclassified occupations; of the remainder 80% did outwork, casual work or (predominantly seasonal) agricultural work.

67 See Heckman, 'Sample selection bias'; Fallon and Verry, *Labour markets*, pp. 64–70 for a less technical explanation.

68 Skill requirements for most workers were no higher than those found for pre-industrial Britain, and very rarely were women found in higher skilled groups. See Tranter, 'Labour supply', pp. 223–4; Rose, 'Social change', p. 265. Only about 50% of women were literate in 1840: Tranter, 'Labour supply', p. 223. In any case, it has been argued that educational qualifications did not increase job opportunities and analysis of wage rates has shown low rates of return to literacy for women. See Deane, *First industrial revolution*, p. 280; Mitch, 'Underinvestment in literacy'. In our sample there are 141 cases where both the woman's earnings and age are known. Controlling for time and occupation, regressions of earnings against age do show age to be a significant, but *negative*, determinant of earnings. Similarly age is found to be a significant determinant of boys' earnings but not of girls'. See Horrell and Humphries, 'Child labor', tab. 6.

69 The significant regional variation in wage rates is shown in Hunt, *Regional wage variations*. Physical health of the labour force is commonly accepted as important in improving productivity. See Tranter, 'Labour supply'.

70 The regions are grouped using information from Hunt, *Regional wage variations*, p. 8.

71 Lindert and Williamson's 'revised best-guess' index until 1850 and the Sauerbeck 'total food' price index subsequently. Lindert and Williamson, 'English workers' real wages', p. 148; Mitchell and Deane, *British historical statistics*, p. 474.

72 Various specifications of the earnings equation were considered. Cubic time trends were not significant so the linear time trend was retained. The presence of a child under two and the number of children may be thought to proxy a woman's age and hence her work experience, but neither of these variables was significant.

73 Smith, *Female labor supply*, for example, makes this argument.

74 And if such biased estimates of earnings are employed in models of labour supply, the responsiveness to own earnings will be underestimated.

75 Heckman, 'Sample selection bias'.

76 Technically 'lambda' is equal to (f/F), the inverse Mill's ratio, where F is the value of the standard normal cumulative distribution function that corresponds to the estimated probability that an individual is in employment. The term f is the value of the standard normal density function that corresponds to F. See Heckman, 'Sample selection bias'.

77 These earnings equation results are virtually the same as those from the initial predicted earnings equation which did not use the sample selection correction parameter.

78 An alternative specification for dealing with the selection bias was tried. An initial probit model of participation was estimated, which excluded predicted own earnings

but included the exogenous variables which are hypothesized as determinants of earnings. Information from this probit was then used to construct an inverse Mill's ratio which was included in a separate earnings equation, the earnings predicted from which were then employed in a second probit equation. The results are virtually identical whichever procedure is used.

79 The earnings definition of participation (B) is used because observations on all working women's earnings are necessary to use the two-stage correction method.

80 A rough interpretation of the associated elasticities can be gained from the proportionality relationship between these coefficients and those of the linear probability model: see Maddala, _Limited-dependent_, p. 23. Evaluated at the means of the regressors, the elasticity of the probability of participation with respect to the woman's real earnings, man's real earnings, and other family income respectively was 2.2, –0.4, and –0.1. These all operate in the expected directions and are within the ranges found in contemporary studies. See, for example, Killingsworth, _Labour supply_; Fallon and Verry, _Labour markets_, p. 50.

81 This effect is found in other historical studies: see Goldin, 'Household and market production'; Rotella, 'Women's labour force participation'; Meyering, 'La petite ouvrière', p. 135. Modern studies would be more likely to interpret the negative relationship between the presence of children and participation in terms of the effects on the shadow price of time in the home.

82 Probit regressions performed for each of the occupational groups separately found time trends with similar patterns to those observed for the occupationally specific participation rates: see table 7.1.

83 A finding which is consistent with the recent evidence for a relative deterioration in the stature of convict women from England during the period of early industrialization: see Nicholas and Oxley, 'Living standards of women'.

References

Allen, R. G., _Enclosure and the yeoman_ (Oxford, 1992).

Anderson, M., _Family structure in nineteenth century Lancashire_ (Cambridge, 1971).

Barnsby, G. J., _Birmingham working people_ (Wolverhampton, 1989).

Barratt, M., _Women's oppression today_ (1980).

Becker, G. S., 'A theory of the allocation of time', _Econ. J._, LXXX (1965), pp. 493–517.

Benenson, H., 'The "family wage" and working women's consciousness in Britain', _Pol. & Soc._, 19 (1991), pp. 71–108.

Berg, M. and Hudson, P., 'Rehabilitating the industrial revolution', _Econ. Hist. Rev._, XLV (1992), pp. 25–50.

Bouillaguet-Bernard, P. and Gauvin, A., 'Women's employment, the state, and the family in France: contradiction of state policy for women's employment', in J. Rubery, ed., _Women and recession_ (1988), pp. 163–90.

Bowen, W. G. and Finnegan, T. A., _The economics of labor force participation_ (Princeton, 1969).

Branca, P., 'A new perspective on women's work: a comparative typology', _J. Soc. Hist._, 9 (1975), pp. 129–53.

Bythell, D., 'Women in the workforce', in P. K. O'Brien and R. Quinault, eds., _The industrial revolution and British society_ (Cambridge, 1993), pp. 31–53.

Cain, G. C., _Married women in the labor force_ (Chicago, 1966).

Clark, A., _Working life of women in the seventeenth century_ (1919).

Collier, F., _The family economy of the working classes in the cotton industry, 1784–1833_ (Manchester, 1964).

Davidoff, L., 'The separation of home and work? Landladies and lodgers in nineteenth and twentieth century England', in S. Burman, ed, _Fit work for women_ (1979), pp. 64–97.

Deane, P., _The first industrial revolution_ (Cambridge, 1967).

Deane, P. and Cole, W. A., _British economic growth, 1688–1959_ (Cambridge, 1962).

Earle, P., 'The female labour market in London in the late seventeenth and early eighteenth centuries', *Econ. Hist. Rev.*, 2nd ser., XLII (1989), pp. 328–54.

Fallon, P. and Verry, D., *The economics of labour markets* (Oxford, 1988).

Gerrard, J., 'Invisible servants: the country house and the local community', *Bull. Inst. Hist. Res.*, LVII (1984), pp. 178–88.

Goldin, C., 'Household and market production of families in a late nineteenth century American city', *Exp. Econ. Hist.*, 16 (1979), pp. 111–31.

Hammond, B. and Hammond, J., *The town labourer* (1917).

Hartmann, H. I., 'The unhappy marriage of marxism and feminism: towards a more progressive union', *Capital & Class*, 8 (1979), pp. 1–33.

Hartwell, R. M., 'The rising standard of living in England, 1800–1850', *Econ. Hist. Rev.*, 2nd ser., XIII (1961), pp. 397–416.

Heckman, J. J., 'Sample selection bias as a specification error', in J. P. Smith, ed., *Female labor supply: theory and estimation* (1980), pp. 206–48.

Higgs, E., 'Domestic service and household production', in A. V. John, ed., *Unequal opportunities: women's employment in England, 1800–1919* (1986), pp. 125–52.

Higgs, E., 'Women, occupations and work in the nineteenth-century censuses', *Hist. Workshop*, 23 (1987), pp. 59–80.

Horrell, S., 'Working-wife households: inside and outside the home' (unpub. Ph.D. thesis, Univ. of Cambridge, 1991).

Horrell, S. and Humphries, J., 'Old questions, new data, and alternative perspectives: families' living standards in the industrial revolution', *J. Econ. Hist.*, LII (1992), pp. 849–90.

Horrell, S. and Humphries, J., '"The exploitation of little children": child labor in the British industrial revolution', *Exp. Econ. Hist.* [32 (1995), pp. 485–516].

Hudson, P. and Lee, W. R., eds., *Women's work in the family in historical perspective* (Manchester, 1990).

Humphries, J., 'Protective legislation, the capitalist state, and working class men: the case of the 1842 Mines Regulation Act', *Fem. Rev.*, 7 (1981), pp. 1–33.

Humphries, J., '"The most free from objection" . . . the sexual division of labour and women's work in nineteenth century England', *J. Econ. Hist.*, XLVII (1987), pp. 929–50.

Humphries, J., 'Enclosures, common rights and women: the proletarianization of families in late eighteenth and early nineteenth century Britain', *J. Econ. Hist.*, L (1990), pp. 17–42.

Humphries, J., '"Lurking in the wings" . . . women in the historiography of the industrial revolution', *Bus. & Econ. Hist.*, 20 (1991), pp. 32–44.

Hunt, E. H., *Regional wage variations in Britain, 1850–1914* (Oxford, 1973).

Hunt, E. H., 'Industrialization and regional inequality: wages in Britain, 1760–1914', *J. Econ. Hist.*, XLVI (1986), pp. 935–66.

Hutchins, B. L. and Harrison, A., *A history of factory legislation* (1903).

Jordan, E., 'The exclusion of women from industry in nineteenth-century Britain', *Comp. Stud. Soc. & Hist.*, 31 (1989), pp. 309–26.

Killingsworth, M., *Labour supply* (Cambridge, 1983).

Levine, D., *Reproducing families* (Cambridge, 1987).

Lindert, P. H. and Williamson, J. G., 'English workers' real wages: a reply to Crafts', *J. Econ. Hist.*, XLV (1985), pp. 145–53.

Lown, J., *Women and industrialisation: gender and work in nineteenth-century England* (Cambridge, 1990).

Lyons, J., 'Family response to economic decline: handloom weavers in early nineteenth century Lancashire', *Res. Econ. Hist.*, 12 (1989), pp. 45–91.

McKendrick, N., 'Home demand and economic growth: a new view of the role of women and children in the industrial revolution', in McKendrick, ed., *Historical perspectives in English thought and society in honour of J. H. Plumb* (1974), pp. 152–210.

Maddala, G. S., *Limited-dependent and qualitative variables in econometrics* (Cambridge, 1983).

Marx, K., *Capital* (New York, 1967).

Mathias, P., *The first industrial nation* (1983).

Meyering, A., 'La petite ouvrière surmenée: family structure, family income and women's work in nineteenth century France', in P. Hudson and W. R. Lee, eds., *Women's work in the family economy in historical perspective* (Manchester, 1990), pp. 76–103.

Mincer, J., 'Labour force participation of married women: a study of labour supply', in A. Amsden, ed., *Women and work* (Harmondsworth, 1980), pp. 41–52.

Mitch, D., 'Underinvestment in literacy? The potential contribution of government involvement in elementary education to economic growth in nineteenth-century England', *J. Econ. Hist.*, XLIV (1984), pp. 557–66.

Mitchell, B. R. and Deane, P., *Abstract of British historical statistics* (Cambridge, 1962).

Neale, R. S., *Writing marxist history* (Oxford, 1985).

Nicholas, S. and Oxley, D., 'The living standards of women during the industrial revolution, 1795–1820', *Econ. Hist. Rev.*, XLVI (1993), pp. 723–49.

Pinchbeck, I., *Women workers in the industrial revolution* (New York, 1969; first pub. 1930).

Richards, E., 'Women in the British economy since about 1700: an interpretation', *Hist.*, 59 (1974), pp. 337–47.

Roberts, E., 'Working wives and their families', in T. Barker and M. Drake, eds., *Population and society in Britain: 1850–1950* (1982), pp. 140–71.

Rose, M. E., 'Social change and the industrial revolution', in R. Floud and D. N. McCloskey, eds., *The economic history of Britain since 1700*, I (Cambridge, 1981), pp. 253–75.

Rotella, E. J., 'Women's labour force participation and the decline of the family economy in the United States', *Exp. Econ. Hist.*, 17 (1980), pp. 95–117.

Sharpe, P., 'Literally spinsters: a new interpretation of local economy and demography in Colyton in the seventeenth and eighteenth centuries', *Econ. Hist. Rev.*, XLIV (1991), pp. 46–65.

Smith, J. P., ed., *Female labor supply: theory and estimation* (1980).

Snell, K., *Annals of the labouring poor: social change and agrarian England, 1660–1900* (Cambridge, 1985).

Thomas, J., 'Women and capitalism: oppression or emancipation?', *Comp. Stud. Soc. & Hist.*, 30 (1988), pp. 534–49.

Tranter, N. L., 'The labour supply 1780–1860', in R. Floud and D. N. McCloskey, eds., *The economic history of Britain since 1700*, I (Cambridge, 1981), pp. 204–26.

Walby, S., *Patriarchy at work* (Cambridge, 1986).

Walton, J. K. and McGloin, P., 'Holiday resorts and their visitors', *Local Historian*, 13 (1979), pp. 323–31.

OFFICIAL PUBLICATIONS

Report from the Commissioners on the Poor Law, Reports of Assistant Commissioners, Appendix A (P.P. 1834, XXVIII).

Report from the Select Committee on the Poor Law Amendment Act and Appendix (P.P. 1837–8, XVIII).

First Report of the Midland Mining Commission (P.P. 1843, XIII).

Appendix

Table A1 Distribution of budgets by county, year, and male occupation

County and occupation	1787–1815	1816–20	1821–40	1841–5	1846–65
Bedfordshire					
Agriculture			117		3
Trades			5		
Casual			10		
Berkshire					
Agriculture	10		1		2
Buckinghamshire					
Agriculture			3		2
Casual			1		
Cambridgeshire					
Agriculture			3		4
Cheshire					
Agriculture	3		7		2
Factory					4
Outwork			1		2
Cornwall					
Agriculture	17				
Mining				4	4
Cumberland					
Agriculture	2		1		2
Mining	2				
Outwork	3				
Derbyshire					
Agriculture	3		1		3
Mining					1
Outwork			1		21
Devon					
Agriculture			3		12
Dorset					
Agriculture	17			1	7
Durham					
Agriculture	7				
Mining	2			1	
Trades	2			3	2
Essex					
Agriculture					2
Gloucestershire					
Agriculture	6		1		
Outwork					
Trades					3
Hampshire					
Agriculture	16			1	
Casual	1				
Hertfordshire					
Agriculture					5
Huntingdonshire					
Agriculture					3
Kent					
Agriculture			6	1	2
Lancashire					
Agriculture	4	38	6		1
Mining	15	50	3	5	
Factory	14	198	5		
Outwork	14	24	65	1	1
Trades	1	30	1		
Casual		3	1		
Leicestershire					
Agriculture	1			1	3
Mining		1		1	
Factory	1				
Outwork				36	
Lincolnshire					
Agriculture			24		2
Middlesex					
Agriculture	1				
Outwork			1		8
Trades			1		5

Table A1 Distribution of budgets by county, year, and male occupation (*continued*)

County and occupation	1787–1815	1816–20	1821–40	1841–5	1846–65
Monmouthshire					
Agriculture	1				
Norfolk					
Agriculture	2		7		2
Northamptonshire					
Agriculture					
Outwork			2		2
Northumberland					
Agriculture			3		2
Mining			1	1	
Nottinghamshire					
Agriculture	10				3
Outwork					8
Oxfordshire					
Agriculture	1				4
Rutland					
Agriculture					3
Shropshire					
Agriculture	2				1
Somerset					
Agriculture	2		1		7
Factory			16		
Outwork			18		
Trades	1				1
Staffordshire					
Agriculture					3
Outwork				2	12
Mining					
Trades					
Suffolk					
Agriculture	1		1	1	3
Surrey					
Agriculture	11				3
Sussex					
Agriculture				1	3
Warwickshire					
Agriculture			4		3
Mining				4	3
Outwork				1	2
Casual					
Westmorland					
Agriculture	8				1
Outwork	4				
Trades	1				
Wiltshire					
Agriculture	1			4	6
Trades	1			1	
Worcestershire					
Agriculture					2
Yorkshire, East Riding					
Agriculture					15
Trades					2
Yorkshire, North Riding					
Agriculture				1	
Yorkshire, West Riding					
Agriculture	6				1
Factory				2	
Outwork				7	
Wales, north					
Agriculture	3				
Wales, south					
Agriculture	3			2	
Mining				12	
Scotland, north					
Agriculture	5				
Outwork			1		
Scotland, south					
Agriculture	2		2		
Mining	1				
Unspecified					
Outwork	1				

AGENCY AND STRATEGY IN WOMEN'S OCCUPATIONS

Commentary

The final section considers women's own instrumentality in the world of work. In the previous section the authors defined the structure of the female labour market with the emphasis on the opportunities and constraints faced by women. However, social history has increasingly been concerned with exploring the agency and strategy of subjugated individuals and groups, be they women, ethnic minorities, the poor, the elderly or children. A reaction against the Marxist-feminist stress on economic change as something which happens *to* women is becoming more important. Women's historians are now as likely to tell the story of women workers as pro-active people who script their own lines in the lives they lead than as downtrodden victims. My own standpoint would be a middle course, which concurs with Sylvia Walby, that 'women's individual agency is found in the myriad ways in which women actively choose options within the constrained opportunities available to them – women act, but not always in the circumstances of their choosing'.[1] These four articles represent different approaches to the subject.

De Vries' analysis goes wider than the English case, but it has particular purchase when considered alongside the picture that we can build up from local case studies. In identifying an 'industrious revolution' preceding the 'industrial revolution' he modernises a rather tired debate about the characteristics of proto-industries and links small-scale local production to consumer demand. The key development in the 'industrious revolution' was a crucial shift in the intensity of female and child labour (an analysis that finds support from Berg in Reading 6), which he associates with a greater desire for the purchase of household goods in the market. Female agency was important in stimulating fashion and fuelling consumer demand. De Vries extends the picture into the contemporary time frame, providing an interesting intersection with Horrell and Humphries on the 'breadwinner–homemaker' household. A different formulation of some of these ideas was made by McKendrick in 1974. He argued that the new fact of women's employment in the eighteenth century kindled consumer demand. Women had less time for production in the home: 'instead of being taught to mend, they were taught to spend'.[2] The working classes, he argued, emulated the elite and thus tastes and fashions trickled down. Other historians, De Vries included, make clear their differences with McKendrick. Women's work was not a novel development during industrialisation and the 'trickle down theory' is open to dispute. Weatherill's study of inventories finds no subculture of female purchasing.[3] Sara Horrell's dataset of budgets, described in Section II, suggests that the expenditure of the working class was not a major boost to industrialisation because they did not spend on the products of the new manufacturing industries, such as textiles and household items, but on traditional goods and services.[4] Maxine Berg finds that the significant new consumption came from urban middling women in Britain's expanding industrial towns. Using probate material from Birmingham and Sheffield, she reasons that 'the bequests show us that women, to a far greater degree than men, noticed their possessions, attached value and emotional significance to them and integrated them into the web of their familial and community relationships'.[5]

Both rural and urban middle-class women lie at the heart of Davidoff and Hall's renowned book, *Family Fortunes*. This excerpt (Reading 9) looks at women's hidden investment in commercial activities in the industrialising period, both in terms of funds and their practical pursuits. Their study is grounded in local sources from Essex and Birmingham. Davidoff and Hall argue that the idea of 'separate spheres' takes on a new potency from the late eighteenth century. In the public sphere, business activities are male-dominated, while in the private sphere home and domesticity form the boundaries of women's world: such gendering of activities is a crucial hallmark of the development of middle-class culture. Maxine Berg has questioned Davidoff and Hall's interpretation of evidence about family trusts.[6] A more comprehensive riposte comes from Amanda Vickery and is reprinted here as Reading 10. This robust and influential critique is at one level a plea for common sense and for not overstating the influence of prescription in real lives. Vickery not only probes the 'separate spheres' formulation but also argues against the narrative of female marginalisation due to capitalism. A great deal of the discussion reviewed in Section II is summed up in Vickery's sentiment that 'Economic change followed many roads and did not arrive at a single destination'. But the appreciation that women's experiences were diverse does not render all explanatory frameworks barren[7]. The value for us as students of this debate is to note the different ways in which a gloss can cast the evidence. One needs to read the whole of *Family Fortunes* to have the full flavour of this, but because sources on women's actual experience which have been written by women themselves are less common and less accessible than the documents on the ideal conduct of women created by men, the interpretation of sources is a weighty matter.

Davidoff, Hall and Vickery are among the historians who have widened the study of women's work beyond the labouring classes to examine the industry of middle-class and elite women. Clearly, work need not take place in the formal labour market and be remunerated to warrant analysis. In the final article reprinted here, Joanna Bourke applies arguments that she had already developed in her study of women's work in late nineteenth-century rural Ireland to England in the same time period.[8] In this forceful polemic, Bourke reacts to what she sees as the ahistorical attribution of motives to women by suggesting that they were unwillingly pushed out of the labour market. Feminist historians have argued that housework subsidises and facilitates male labour in the capitalist market. Bourke's aim is to 'let working-class housewives between 1860 and 1914 speak for themselves'. The danger of this method is that the more reticent and less strategic may not have left their experiences to posterity. A similar analysis of urban housewives is given by Carl Chinn, where a veritable matriarchy rules the backyard and the scrubbed porch of working-class homes.[9] Ellen Ross also provides some sturdy portraits of the mothers of late nineteenth-century east London.[10] In its theoretical basis, Bourke's analysis follows Becker's neo-classical 'New Home Economics', which propounds that women and men allocate their time between paid work, housework and leisure, based on the reward from each. There is a dynamic equilibrium between these sectors so that when wages historically ranged around half of the male rate, it is not surprising that women chose to use their talents at home rather than in the labour market. To return to the quote from Walby at the start of this commentary, however, we can only satisfactorily analyse the choices and opportunities women made by reference to the circumstances and constraints they faced.

Notes

1 I. S. Walby, *Gender Transformations* (London, Routledge, 1997), p. 7.
2 N. McKendrick, 'Home demand and economic growth: a new view of the role of women and children in the Industrial Revolution' in N. McKendrick (ed.), *Historical Perspectives: Studies in English Thought and Society* (London, Europa, 1974), pp. 196–7.
3 L. Weatherill, 'A possession of one's own: women and consumer behaviour in England 1660–1740', *Journal of British Studies*, 25 (1986), pp. 131–56.
4 S. Horrell, 'Home demand and British industrialization', *Journal of Economic History*, 56:3 (1996), pp. 561–97.
5 M. Berg, 'Women's consumption and the industrial classes of eighteenth-century England', *Journal of Social History*, 30:2 (1996), p. 429.
6 M. Berg, 'Women's property and the Industrial Revolution', *Journal of Interdisciplinary History*, 24 (1993), pp. 233–50.
7 Leonore Davidoff reaffirms her belief in the conceptual approach in *Worlds Between: Historical Perspectives on Gender and Class* (Cambridge, Polity, 1995) p. 228.
8 J. Bourke, *Husbandry to Housewifery: Women, Economic Change and Housework in Ireland, 1890–1914* (Oxford, Oxford University Press, 1993). J. Boydston, 'To earn her daily bread': housework and antebellum working class subsistence', *Radical History Review*, 35 (1986), pp. 7–25, provides another interesting perspective on the value of housework.
9 C. Chinn, '*They Worked all their Lives*': Women of the Urban Poor in England 1880–1939 (Manchester, Manchester University Press, 1988).
10 E. Ross, *Love and Toil: Motherhood in Outcast London 1870–1918* (New York, Oxford University Press, 1993).

8

Between purchasing power and the world of goods: understanding the household economy in early modern Europe

JAN DE VRIES

A jibe frequently directed at demographers is that they succeed in turning sex and death into dull subjects. It can now be said of cultural historians that they seek to make the study of commodities fun, liberating the material world of production and consumption from the dead positivist hand of the economic historian. The economist's confining terminology of budget constraints, elasticities of demand, and marginal utility is to be superseded by a symbolic and representational vocabulary whereby commodities reveal fantasies, fetishes, masochistic longings, power urges and internalized oppression. Where the terminology of the economist is designed to remind us of that threadbare cliché 'there is no such thing as a free lunch,' that of the cultural historian invites us to frolic in the pleasure garden of consumption, where the will of the consumer can triumph over scarcity and the will of the historian can triumph over 'the laws of economics.'

Under circumstances such as these it may not be possible to establish a real dialogue among the varied parties interested in the history of consumption. My aim, therefore, is to construct a 'common house,' equipped with a new conceptual framework of the household economy that may someday allow the lion and the lamb to lie together, speaking amicably of demand curves and desire, of tastes and budget constraints.

To the social and cultural historian the economists' great fault, in a word, is the privileging of production: making supply the blade of the supply and demand scissors that does all the cutting. If consumption simply shadows production, its explanatory power must be confined to matters of secondary importance; hence, what Neil McKendrick calls the 'shameful' neglect by economic historians of a consumer revolution.[1] Those attempts by economists to demonstrate demand-driven growth, whether through the growth of foreign markets or through changes in demand patterns based on relative prices, have not stood up well against either empirical studies or theoretical analyses.[2] Joel Mokyr concluded an exhaustive study of the subject with a statement that left little scope for misunderstanding: 'the ... notion that supply and demand were somehow symmetric in the industrialization is unfounded. The determination of "when," "where," and "how fast" are to be sought first and foremost in supply, not demand-related processes.'[3] This did not still the voices advocating an autonomous role for demand so much as shift them from the economic to the cultural sphere: desire, attitude, fashion and emulation furnish the vocabulary for this new discourse.

The argument between economists and social and cultural historians exists quite independently of any particular historical evidence. But it is intensified by the fundamentally different messages conveyed by the two chief types of documentary evidence available for the historical study of consumption. Depending on the sources consulted, the scholar's gaze is cast either over a somber scene of limited purchasing power and painful budget constraints or it surveys an ever-multiplying world of goods, a richly varied and complex material culture.

Two generations of economic historians have labored to chart the long term course of prices and wages and to compare the indexes of real wages.

Taken as a whole, they present a remarkably uniform portrait of the historical course of the purchasing power of labor. The chief findings of such studies, for which the well-known Phelps Brown and Hopkins study of builders' wages over seven centuries is exemplary, are a 'golden age of labor' in the post-Black Death fifteenth century, followed by a disastrous 'long sixteenth century'. By the early seventeenth century the price inflation had so far outstripped the rise of wages as to reduce labor's purchasing power to less than half of its fifteenth-century level. A combination of periodic wage hikes and gently falling prices gradually restored some – but by no means all – of the fifteenth-century real wage. But this recovery was cut short by 1750, when an accelerating inflation swamped further wage increases. Only the restoration of peace after 1815 brought a new era of real wage recovery which, of course, eventually broke through all previous ceilings.

The construction of the real wage indexes, which compare wages and prices, is, however, an exercise fraught with methodological problems. Should we believe their findings? The real wage index is a statistical construction that gives a very precise answer to a very specific question: relative to earlier and/or later periods how much of a specified bundle of goods can be purchased with the daily wage of a particular grade of labor? Under certain conditions, the answer to this question will approximate a valid answer to the broader question that interests us: what happened to the standard of living of the bulk of the population? But the conditions are exacting, and it would be folly to simply take for granted that these are fulfilled. To begin with, the wage index uses a worker's daily wage rate, but it is household earnings, over the course of a full year, that we would prefer to know. Second, wage quotations are most abundant for construction labor and unskilled outdoor labor, leaving the representativeness of such labor for the many other occupations as an open question.

And what about the price index? Historical consumer price indexes almost always do not include all possible consumption items. The prevailing assumption is that food expenditures must have absorbed nearly all of most people's budgets.[4] Thus, the indexes tend to exclude non-consumables, such as housing, taxes and services, and devote little space for all other expenditures other than food, that is, for nearly all the types of purchases that might interest the historian of consumer culture. Finally, usable time series exist for a surprisingly small amount of budget items. The item of consumption must be both widely traded and homogeneous across time and space in order to be taken up in an index. A large number of commodities do not meet this test.

None of the shortcomings of the available price time series and weights used to form the index would be of much concern if all prices moved in harmony with each other. Then the few available prices would be representative of all other prices and neither the absence of commodities nor mis-specification of the weights would alter the final outcome. However, although most commodity prices follow a common long-term inflationary or deflationary trend, each commodity differs in its rate of increase or decrease, and in its short-term variability.[5] When the price of each commodity has its own distinct destiny the weighting of a price index is crucial to the outcome and systematic bias is inherent in the act of constructing a price index. Such a bias grows with the span of time covered by the index. A price index with weights set at an initial date will overstate price increases since no substitutions are allowed, and also because new goods and improvements in the quality of existing goods must be ignored. A price index cannot account for consumers whose *incomes and tastes have not changed* but who alter the mix of goods they buy – buying more of those goods whose prices are falling – in order thereby to maximize the utility they derive from their expenditures in the face of changes in relative prices.

The historian who averts eye contact with wage and price evidence just discussed and fixes his or her gaze on the direct evidence of the world of goods will gain a very different – a decidedly optimistic – picture of the changing standard of living from the sixteenth to the beginning of the nineteenth century. All of the direct sources – physical, visual, literary and archival – encourage us to imaging the gradual and gradually accelerating emergence of a rich and varied consumer culture. But while these sources are evocative, they are also less precise, and they typically suffer from severe restrictions in the range of goods or of consumers that can be observed.

Among direct sources, one stands out for its potential ability to offer evidence on material culture that is systematic and comprehensive, spanning long time periods and available in many Western societies. The probate inventory, a legal document ordinarily drawn up upon the death of an adult leaving heirs, especially minor children, was widely employed throughout western and central Europe and in colonial societies. Although the specific form of the probate inventory and its availability varies from place to place, there are probably hundreds of thousands of such documents yet preserved in ecclesiastical, legal and notarial archives.

Probate inventories list the possessions of the deceased and often their monetary value. When complete, they can illuminate the economic activity of the deceased (describing productive capital, financial assets, livestock and farm implements, etc.), the wealth of the deceased (listing assets and outstanding debts), and the material culture of the deceased, recording the physical possessions found in the house, often room by room.[6]

The detail of the inventories plus the substantial variation in the research strategies of investigators makes a summary of findings all but impossible. Yet, all of the studies I have examined for colonial New England and the Chesapeake, England and the Netherlands consistently reveal two features.[7] With very few exceptions, each generation of decedents from the mid-seventeenth to the late eighteenth century left behind more and better possessions. Even in periods of falling real wages, the pace of material improvement was quickening. However, these growing accumulations of possessions did not come to bulk larger in the total value of estates. Indeed, their relative values fell, and often enough their absolute value as well. The world of goods seems oddly disconnected from the world of wealth.

I have spoken in this essay sometimes of 'material culture' and sometimes of 'consumer demand' and related terms. They certainly should not be used interchangeably. Material culture should refer to that world of goods as it exists, is used and is given meaning by the inhabitants of that world. It is a static concept (no pejorative meaning is intended), one that probate inventories, which give a snapshot of that world at the time of the owner's death, are well suited to address. Consumer demand refers to behavior that changes, augments, replenishes or diminishes the goods accessible to the individual. It is a dynamic concept, and the probate inventory does not address it directly.

Using the (static) probate inventory to address (dynamic) consumer demand involves us in a typical concern of the economist: the stock-flow problem. The less durable the item the less likely it is to leave a residue in the probate inventories. For example, the inventories rarely record such items as newspapers, trinkets, children's toys, and most foodstuffs. New problems arise at the other end of the spectrum, with those goods that are so durable that they function as a store of value. Goods that are chiefly acquired through inheritance obviously say little about current demand, and they may say little about current fashions and tastes. Moreover, they will surely be more important in a period of population stability or decline than in a period of population growth. In a stationary population, the demand for goods that suffer negligible depreciation must be read from the rate of change in the stocks of such goods, not from the size of those stocks.

Thus, a constant stock of consumer durables (as measured in the inventories) does not necessarily imply that the flow of household expenditures on those goods is also constant. Changed depreciation periods (of the sort one might expect when cottons replace woollens and linens, and as glass and pottery replace wooden and pewter tableware) can considerably alter the relationship between stock and flow. This is true whether total wealth increases or not.

Although this result is independent of price changes for the commodities in question, historians have noted that the prices of clothing and many consumer durables fell substantially in the seventeenth and eighteenth centuries. A fall in prices of one half the initial level would then result in a doubling of the quantity of consumer goods represented by a constant level while the speeded depreciation rate would increase the annual expenditure rate needed to maintain the augmented stock of goods. To put the matter differently and, perhaps, more provocatively, if reduced durability and falling prices were the major factors encouraging increased expenditure on consumer goods, both because the lowered prices increased demand and because reduced durability was associated with the more frequent introduction of attractive new fashions, then it is highly likely that probate inventories would show a falling proportion of total value accounted for consumer goods. This helps to account for the seemingly paradoxical findings of so many studies that the diffusion of new goods, the increased quantities of familiar items, the more luxurious character of yet others – all trends now well documented for the late seventeenth and eighteenth centuries – did not express themselves in an enlarged share of total wealth attributable to consumer goods. Indeed, today most people, after a lifetime of frenetic consumerism and prodigious expenditures, die with personal possessions of inconsequential value, hardly enough to pay for a decent burial. In this respect, the probate inventories surely do reveal the rosy dawn of modern consumerism.

The probate inventory is a rich but challenging source for the study of consumer demand. Still, the basic findings of long-term growth in the volume and diversity of consumer possessions appears to be well founded and is reassuringly reinforced by other evidence.

How can this diverse but tangible evidence of growing consumption be reconciled with the somber interpretation of consumer well-being that emerges from the impressively uniform but more highly constructed evidence of prices and wages? There is no significant conflict in the evidence, and no need for reconciliation, if the 'consumer revolution' could be restricted to a small élite, to specific commodities used as substitutes, or to one period, namely the first half of the eighteenth century, when falling prices generate rising real wages to match the growth in consumer demand, as revealed by English probate inventories and the importation of sugar, tea, and tobacco. However, these limitations do not fit the evidence gathered by both sides. Although the lower boundary of the consumer revolution is by no means settled, there can be little doubt that the evidence addresses the consumer behavior of a broad socio-economic band of early modern society. The changes in demand also cover a wide variety of goods that cannot be accounted for simply by substitution of new goods for old. Finally, although most 'consumer revolution' arguments seek to restore demand as a factor in the Industrial Revolution, a post-1750 phenomenon, the same sources that reveal a growth in demand in the first half of the eighteenth century also reveal such growth in much of the seventeenth. In short, growth in consumer demand is a long-term phenomenon that spans periods defined by price and wage trends in the seventeenth and eighteenth centuries.[8]

The industrious revolution

The evidence for a growth in consumer demand is, I believe, compelling, and it cannot be explained away as a phenomenon restricted to a small social group, a few goods, or a brief period of propitious price and wage movements. Nor can it properly be understood with the concept of a 'consumer revolution' defined as the dynamic role of consumers during the British Industrial Revolution. The term 'consumer revolution' should probably be suppressed before frequent repetition secures for it a place in that used car lot of explanatory vehicles reserved for historical concepts that break down directly after purchase by the passing scholar. The emergence of a consumer society was by no means sudden – certainly not confined to the late eighteenth and early nineteenth century – nor was it limited geographically to Britain.

Any effort to explain this phenomenon, and to reconcile it to the real wage data that seem to deny that it could ever have happened, needs to place it in a broader context than industrializing Britain and needs to penetrate, as it were, behind the interplay of supply and demand curves to examine the institutions that helps define the shape and positions of those curves in the first place.

Consumer demand grew, even in the face of contrary real wage trends, because of reallocations of the productive resources of households. A series of household-level decisions altered both the supply of marketed goods and labor and the demand for market-bought products. This complex of changes in household behavior constitutes an 'industrious revolution,' driven by Smithian, or commercial incentives, that preceded and prepared the way for the Industrial Revolution, which was driven by technology and changes in organization. That is, an industrious revolution, with important demand-side features began in advance of the Industrial Revolution, which was basically a supply-side phenomenon.

At the heart of the concept of an industrious revolution is the household. The pre-industrial household was a unit of reproduction and consumption, functions it still retains (the latter chiefly via the redistribution of income among its individual members), as well as a unit of production. Moreover, a large portion of the household's final consumption was supplied internally, by its own production. In any household where auto-consumption plays a significant role, production decisions are integrally related to consumption decisions. Correspondingly, the increased market orientation of such a household cannot be understood simply as a production response to market opportunities; it is also a response to the household's demand for marketed goods, revealed in a higher demand for the money income necessary to acquire such goods.[9] Under these circumstances, the terms on which the household specializes to produce goods for the market and the terms on which its members' labor is offered to the labor market are partially determined by the household's preferences for market-supplied goods and services (versus home-supplied goods and services) and the perceived relative utility of money income versus leisure.[10]

Note how this argument differs from the Keynesian scenario in which rising demand creates employment for idle productive factors. Until a full employment condition is reached, rising demand can be said to 'cause' the growth of production. The industrious revolution argument does not identify idle resources (committed to the market, but unused), it identifies differently deployed resources (not committed to the market) and specifies the conditions under which the household alters its demand patterns and simultaneously alters its offer curves of marketed output and/or labor.

How did this industrious revolution manifest itself in pre-industrial Europe? The earliest steps occurred in those peasant households that could follow the course of specialization by concentrating household labor in marketed food production. Increased allocational efficiency and the static and dynamic gains from internal trade creation accrue to such a household as it reduces the amount of labor devoted to a wide variety of home handicrafts and services and replaces these activities with market-supplied substitutes.[11] The 'Z-goods model' of Hymer and Reznick identifies the formal economic conditions under which a household will be induced to reduce its production of 'Z goods' (non-traded, mainly non-agricultural goods), concentrate productive assets into marketed food production, and substitute purchased manufactures and services (M goods) for the abandoned Z goods.[12] Rising prices for agricultural commodities relative to manufactures obviously encourage this process of resource reallocation, but improvements in the terms of trade for food producers cannot single handedly bring about full specialization. Rising prices for food cause manufactured goods to become relatively cheaper, to be sure, and this encourages the substitution of M for Z in consumption. But the improving terms of trade for the peasant household also imply rising real income, and this could bring about a growing demand for Z goods. I say 'could,' because this income effect depends ultimately on tastes: the perceived superiority of market-supplied goods relative to home-supplied Z goods and leisure. A full redeployment of household labor toward market production is aided by price and technical factors, but it depends on household demand preferences (see Figure 8.1).

The specialization path outlined here was not – could not be – followed everywhere. At a minimum, peasant households needed access to markets and suppliers of incentive goods. Rural households in the maritime regions of the Netherlands achieved substantial market dependence via specialization by the mid-seventeenth century, and many parts of England followed suit in the century after 1650.[13] In northern France, George Grantham has documented a substantial growth in marketed foodstuffs in the century after 1750 wherever farmers had access to market opportunities offered by urbanization. Using detailed village level data, Grantham could find little in the way of technological innovation to account for the growth of agricultural output before the late 1840s. Instead, the growth of

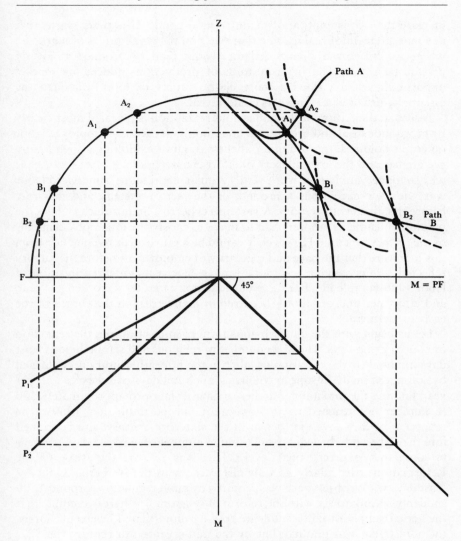

Figure 8.1 Z-goods model

production proceeded 'along a long-run supply curve whose position was established by the beginning of the eighteenth century, if not before.'[14] Farmers worked harder, shifted their crop mix toward marketable products, and used 'underemployed reserves of child and female labor to expand production for home use of the inferior grains and starches, many of which were grown outside normal crop rotations.'[15] The French peasants studied by Grantham did not abandon altogether self-sufficiency in basic foodstuffs, but they reallocated household labor to increase marketed food output and increase their consumption of manufactured goods. Grantham warns that any measurement of real income that relies on the rising prices of marketed wheat as the cost of living deflator would tend to produce an overly pessimistic result. The intensification of production induced by market opportunities had yielded a more elastic supply of foodstuffs than the essentially urban wheat markets could reveal.

A second dimension of the industrious revolution is revealed most clearly by proto-industrial and proletarian households, as the underemployed labor on cottar holdings, the voluntary idleness of labor exhibiting a high leisure preference, and the low intensity of effort characteristic of most labor gave way to longer and harder work. Truly regular, continuous, supervised labor was with few exceptions a product of the factory system, and was rare before the nineteenth century. A vast and evocative literature chronicles the painful adjustments laborers had to make to satisfy the imperious demands of the factory system.[16] However, it would be a grave error to conclude from this literature that the pace and regularity of employment before the factory reflected an unchanging traditionalism. In fact, a major intensification of labor – measurable in labor force participation rates, days worked per year, and effort per unit of labor – occurred in many areas in the course of the early modern era.

Let us begin with the most obvious form of intensification, the reduction of non-working days. The large number of religious and semi-religious feast days honored by the cessation of labor in the fifteenth century is confirmed by sources in many European countries. Such holidays could exceed 50 per year, limiting the maximum number of days of labor to approximately 250 (a number not reached again in western Europe until after 1960). The reduction of free days that began in the sixteenth century, and continued into the eighteenth, brought the maximum number of working days per year to altogether unprecedented levels. This was in part the work of the Reformation, particularly its Calvinist variant. In the Netherlands the 47 feast days whose observance was required by guild regulations around 1500 suddenly shrank to six with the reform of religion. It is hardly credible that the actual supply of labor suddenly rose by more than 15 percent. Surely, the adjustment was gradual; but by the mid-seventeenth century the 307-day maximal work year was definitely in place.

In England a similar process of intensification can be traced. Builders observed some 40 holidays in the late fifteenth century, which an act of Parliament reduced to 27 in 1552. After Cromwell's rule, Restoration governments did nothing to change the Dutch-like practice of observing only a very few holidays around Christmas, Easter and Whitsun. Protestantism was certainly not the only force pushing toward a longer work year, for the number of observed feast days declined in Catholic countries too, albeit not so far. By 1600 the French work year reached the 275–85-day range.[17]

These long-term trends augmented the supply of labor *in theory*; what did so *in practice* was a change in household evaluation of the marginal utility of money income versus leisure time. Peasant and proletarian households alike appear to have decided in favor of income over leisure. This was certainly no universal phenomenon, for special conditions were necessary to bring such decisions about. But, by the mid-eighteenth century, such behavior was sufficiently common to have undermined a basic feature of labor market behavior, the backward bending labor supply curve.

A backward bending labor supply curve (see Figure 8.2) occurs when rising wages, after a certain point, cease to elicit more labor supply and give rise instead to a decline in the amount of labor offered. This behavior is consistent with a desire for a 'target income,' i.e. an income sufficient to secure a 'traditional' or customary standard of living. Income beyond the target level does not possess sufficient utility to justify the necessary reduction of leisure. Consequently, a continued rise of wages, because it permits the target income to be achieved with less labor, causes the supply of labor to decline – to bend backward, as shown in Figure 8.2. Any number of contemporary employers' comments can be found to attest to this behavioral pattern: when real wages were high, 'the labour of the poor is . . . scarce to be had at all (so licentious are they who labour only to eat, or rather to drink).'[18] 'Scarcity' [high food prices], on the other hand,

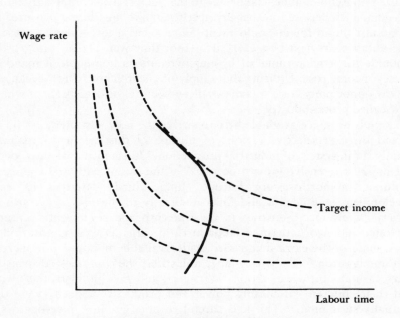

Figure 8.2 The backward bending supply curve

promotes industry . . . [Those] who can subsist on three days' work will be idle and drunken the remainder of the week . . . The poor in the manufacturing counties will never work any more time than is necessary to live and support their weekly debauches.[19]

The same force that could induce peasant households to shift their labor from 'Z goods' – output intended for auto-consumption – to marketed goods served to induce peasant and proletarian households to substitute labor for leisure. In both cases a rise in the utility of money income stands behind the increased offer of marketed goods and labor, and standing behind the augmented utility of income is a growth in the variety of available consumer goods, and a development of consumer tastes that prefers market-supplied goods to their home-produced substitutes. When these conditions are met a key feature of modern consumer society is put in place: the 'target income' behavior gives way to a dynamic materialism where desires are insatiable, where, as Sir James Steuart observed, 'Men are forced to labour now because they are slaves to their own wants,' and where Adam Smith observed that 'workmen . . . when they are liberally paid by the piece, are very apt to overwork themselves.' In Steuart's eyes the new situation was full of promise: 'wants promote industry, industry gives food, food increases numbers.'[20]

The first stages of this process involved securing employment for under-utilized household labor – labor idle in the slack seasons of the agricultural calendar. Such 'leisure time' is very nearly equal to 'involuntary leisure,' the economist's term for unemployment. Since it has a low 'opportunist cost' (the utility of its next best use), such labor time was available in growing amounts for a wide range of by-employments as household demand for money income rose. Utilizing this supply of cheap labor (cheap because of its low opportunity cost) was the challenge before the organizers of what is now called proto-industry.

There is no space available here to survey the now vast literature on the spread through selective regions of Europe of this merchant-organized, mainly rural, system of industrial production.[21] It has medieval antecedents, but its most intensive growth occurred in the seventeenth and eighteenth centuries in northwestern Europe. John Thirsk describes its early development in England, and links it directly to the rise of a consumer society. 'Consumer industries in the sixteenth and seventeenth centuries exploited hitherto underused labor in rural areas as well as absorbing a large share of the extra manpower made available by population increase and immigration.'[22] These consumer industries, she continues, 'dispens[ed] extra cash among wage laborers, cottagers, and small holders, their wives and their children. Purchasing power and productive capacity were thus mutually sustaining.'[23] Thirsk is careful to note, as most investigators of proto-industry must, that 'we cannot speak with certainty of rising *per capita* incomes throughout the population in the seventeenth century.' But, she continues,

> we can point to numerous communities in the kingdom, especially in towns and in the pastoral-industrial areas, where the labouring classes found cash to spare for consumer goods in 1700 that had no place in their budgets in 1550 – brass cooking pots, iron frying pans, earthenware dishes, knitted stockings, even a lace frill for a cap or apron.[24]

The land-poor households whose elastic offer curve of labor fueled these and other consumer industries had their agricultural analogues in those households that offered growing quantities of marketed foodstuffs, and many others, typically with less land, that poured household labor into the production of such labor-intensive and utterly market-oriented crops as tobacco, wine, hops, and madder.[25] All of these variants of intensification gave rise to regional specialization and trade, improving the efficiency of the economy as it increased the market orientation of the households.[26]

By the mid-eighteenth century, before the Industrial Revolution, many socio-economic groups in many regions of Europe had redeployed their household labor and reduced their leisure time to simultaneously increase marketed output and increase money income. The labor of women and children played a prominent role in this process of peasant self-exploitation: the putting-out industries made intensive use of their winter and evening labor while the new, labor-intensive crops typically featured operations – weeding, pruning, plucking, etc. – then deemed well suited to the abilities of women and children.

When placed in this context, the prominent role played by child and female labor in the leading industries of the British Industrial Revolution is hardly surprising; it is only the continuation and, probably, further intensification of an established trend toward greater paid labor force participation, but now beyond the confines of the household in the factory and workshop.

Neil McKendrick, in a useful and vigorously argued article, maintained that a consumer revolution, occurring in the second half of the eighteenth century, and reaching lower than the middle classes to the skilled factory worker and the domestic servant class, 'took much of its impetus to consume from the earnings of women and children.' 'In my view,' he testified, 'the earnings of women and children and the important contribution they made to the family income can play an important part in providing a more satisfactory explanation [for the consumer revolution].'[27] In fact, he later asserts:

> without the addition of female wages and the earnings of children, it is difficult to explain where a sufficiently large surplus of income over

expenditure would have come from, and without a substantial rise in family income it is difficult to see where the increased home demand would come from.[28]

Much of McKendrick's article is devoted to a critique of that vast literature that deplores the participation of women and children in the paid labor force and interprets its incidence during the Industrial Revolution as revelatory of the truly perfidious character of the dark satanic mills. Most of that literature dates from the century after 1850, when both Victorian and reformist opinion held child and female labor to be a proper object of special regulation, and expressed a strong preference for keeping such persons out of the paid labor force altogether.

Viewing the factory labor of women and children from this perspective, McKendrick correctly seeks to supplement the condemnations of the exploitation of women and children with an appreciation of the positive, volitional role played by these workers in the context of the household economy and its consumer aspirations.

However, since McKendrick fails to place the paid labor force participation of women and children in its *pre*-Industrial Revolution context, he gives the erroneous impression that it was something new with the rise of the factories. Without in any way explaining why women and children should now suddenly enter the paid labor force, he attributes to their new, supplementary earnings a major role in explaining a consumer revolution.

But if, as I have argued, an 'industrious revolution' featuring the intensified use of women and children in market-oriented production had been gaining momentum for over a century before 1750, then the new, more conspicuous role of women and children as paid laborers is only the extension into new circumstances of an established trend. It cannot support McKendrick's concept of a consumer revolution because it is but one phase of an older, more broadly based process of increasing the rate of paid labor force participation, and of increasing the intensity of that labor.

This brings us to the third and final dimension of the industrious revolution. Besides the concentration of household labor in marketed production at the expense of auto-consumption (allowing households to capture the static and dynamic gains from trade), and besides the increased paid labor force participation at the expense of leisure (thereby increasing household income faster than the course of individual wage rates can reveal), there appears to have occurred an increase in the pace or intensity of work in the course of the early modern period, especially in Britain. What I mean here is the achievement of higher labor productivity independent of the rise of more or better capital or land. Gregory Clark, in a series of articles, has identified substantial international differences in the productivity of labor in agriculture and in the textile industry during the nineteenth century.[29] These differences remain large even after the effect of capital, training, and natural resources have been taken into account. The performance of British agriculture between 1661 and 1841 offers a particularly striking example: output growth almost kept pace with the rise of population while the number of farm workers grew far less over the nearly two-century interval. Consequently output per worker rose by over 50 percent. Clark found that technical progress could account for but 15 percent of this; the rest he attributed to more labor per worker (i.e. less leisure) and to more intense work.[30] By the early nineteenth century, when comparative evidence is more plentiful, the differences in the rate at which simple manual tasks were performed by farm workers in various counties are enormous: English farm laborers harvested over four times as much grain per day as Polish peasants (or medieval English peasants), even though the tools and techniques used differed but little.[31] As noted above, Grantham found substantial differences in the pace of work within rural France in the 1840s. The proximity to markets had a strong and direct influence on this pattern of labor intensity.[32] With the right incentives, a large amount of extra output could be squeezed out of the pre-industrial technological complex.

The resolution to the contradiction raised by the wage and probate inventory data is at hand. Households desiring to consume more market-distributed goods and services redeployed their productive assets, offering to the market more goods, more labor, and more intensive labor. As a result *annual household money earnings* could grow relative to *individual daily wage rates*, and this could occur independently of technological change or the growth of the capital stock.

The skeptical reader may wonder if the solution to our problem really is at hand. Even if all the outward signs of an industrious revolution are accepted, they could have explanations very different from, even contradictory to, that proffered above.

Price and income effects, independently of any of the changes in tastes that might affect the shape of supply and demand curves, obviously play some role in the processes described above. Just as the rise of post-Black Death real wages influenced the growing number of non-working days, so the sixteenth-century erosion of real wages surely influenced the decline of feast day observance. Relative price changes (particularly the weakness of grain prices relative to manufactures and speciality crops in the century 1650–1750) undoubtedly encouraged the proto-industrialization process, while large and continuing reductions in the prices of tropical imports – such as tea, coffee, and sugar – encouraged their mass consumption independently of any other factors. The analysis presented here does not deny the importance of any of these economic responses, but argues simply that once they are taken into account a large unexplained residual remains.

A second objection focuses on the explanations given for the reduction of leisure and the increased intensity of work. If a large portion of the pre-industrial population lived at the margin of subsistence, the choice to work more and harder may not have existed. Chronic malnutrition would have imposed a ceiling on productive activity that could only be lifted when classic supply-side factors such as are associated with an agricultural revolution began to be felt. The classic statement of this position, by Freudenberger and Cummins, identifies the formerly abundant leisure time as an involuntary period of

> recuperation necessary to sustain [the worker] for the work he was doing, little as that might have been. The short work week before the Industrial Revolution may have been one aspect of an equilibrium situation determined partly by a high prevalence of debilitating disease and by low and unpredictable supplies of food.[33]

Robert Fogel has interpreted recent studies of stature, mortality, and nutrition as consistent with this position. He summarized the provisional findings about caloric intake at the end of the eighteenth century in England and France as follows: in France the bottom 10 percent of the labor force lacked the energy for regular work and the next 10 percent had enough energy for less than three hours of light work daily. 'In England only the bottom 3 percent lacked the energy for day work, 'but the balance of the bottom 20 percent had enough energy for about 6 hours of light work (1.09 hours of heavy work) each day.'[34]

An industrious revolution governed by caloric intake instead of a taste for consumer goods is clearly a very different phenomenon than I have developed in this article: it is governed by the supply of food, and cannot have supported a consumer revolution for the non-essential, non-food goods that we know proliferated in the seventeenth and eighteenth centuries. Conceivably the force of this argument can be deflected by showing that only a small 'lumpenproletariat' faced severe energy constraints, while the rest of the population could make the choices on which the industrious revolution concept depends.[35] My own view is that the estimates of caloric intake are too small, and that a large majority of the northwestern European population did not normally face the dismal prospects outlined by Freudenberger, Cummins and Fogel. Otherwise, this remains an outstanding question in the history of the pre-industrial economy.

It is, in fact, one of a more general class of counter-arguments that have in common an external force coercing household behavior, and specifically fostering market dependence where the household, if left to its own devices, would prefer to avoid it.

The most important of the coercive forces is poverty. As populations grow the available land per household falls, requiring adjustments in household labor allocation to increase the yields on the available land. This long-term process, as described by Boserup, requires a reduction of leisure time and often conforms outwardly to the specialization and labor participation augmenting strategies described above.[36] Moreover, the proto-industry phenomenon is thought by most investigators to be a survival strategy employed by impoverished land-poor households. This had been Mendels' view as he developed the concept of proto-industry in studies of the eighteenth-century Flemish countryside.[37] His vision has been contradicted by the Flemish historian Vanderbroeke, who holds that this industrious society enjoyed a prosperous 'golden age' in the eighteenth century.[38] But the dominant position remains that articulated, for all of Europe, by Medick: 'The adult proto-industrial worker was not able to exist as an individual . . . he had to depend to a growing extent upon the "cooperation" of his entire family.'[39] He then quotes a shoemaker from Northampton who reinforces the point:

No single-handed man can live; he must have a whole family at work, because a single-handed man is so badly paid he can scarce provide the necessaries of life . . . as soon as [the children] are big enough to handle an awl, they are obliged to come downstairs and work.[40]

Moreover, Mendels, Medick, Levine and most other scholars who have developed the concept of proto-industrialization hold that the new earning ability imparted by the spread of rural cottage industry served to increase the size of families – the number of children – rather than the level of consumer demand. Proto-industry, by undermining traditional social controls on demographic behavior, endowed the Industrial Revolution with its labor force, not its consumers.[41]

Taxes were another external force pushing households into greater market involvement. All western European states greatly increased the real tax burden in the seventeenth century, particularly in its second half when falling commodity prices placed great pressure on agricultural households.[42]

What the long-term effects of population growth, proletarianization, and government tax policy could not achieve was more suddenly brought about by the rise of the factory system. By drying up home-based employment possibilities it destroyed any remaining basis for household economic strategies seeking to keep the market at arm's length. By ending the autonomy of the unsupervised worker, it laid the basis for both an extension of the working day and the intensification of work. In short, the supply curves of labor were forcibly shifted to the right by a combination of inexorable demographic and economic processes, social stratification, government policy, and technological change. The 'external constraints' school assumes that the households facing all these forces offered, as Levine put it, 'a deep-rooted resistance to the imperatives of capitalist society . . . [It was an economy] characterized by its "backward-bending supply curve" which means that people worked enough to earn their targeted income and then simply quit.'[43]

Such workers, when forced into the new factories, 'entered a new culture.' As Sidney Pollard put it in a pioneering study of early factory management: 'Men who were non-accumulative, non-acquisitive, accustomed to work for subsistence, not for maximization of income, had to be made obedient to the cash stimulus, and obedient in such a way as to react precisely to the stimuli provided.'[44]

No one can doubt that the external constraints listed above were real, and that they contributed substantially to the greater market orientation and paid labor force participation that is at issue here. In fact, much of what it describes is not inconsistent with the industrious revolution concept. For example, when household labor force participation, or labor intensity, is increased to prevent the loss of an earlier achieving living standard, it might be interpreted as behavior coerced by external forces, but action to defend any particular material standard above a physiological minimum is a social decision, and when repeated as higher levels of well-being are reached, a ratchet effect leads the economy toward an industrious revolution. The immediate moments of decision may have been defensive, but the consequences of those decisions led over time to both labor intensification and higher consumption levels.[45]

At bottom there is but one issue distinguishing the industrious revolution concept from the 'external constraint' arguments reviewed above. It does not involve objective matters, but focuses on motivation: did pre-industrial households respond passively or actively to the threats and opportunities presented by the evolving economic environment? More precisely, did they respond, as Levine suggests, by tenaciously seeking to preserve a traditional regime of limited market involvement and target income, or did they act to realize new tastes and preferences of *their own choosing*? This, of course, is simply a restatement of the moral peasant–rational peasant debate, now extended to the pre-industrial laboring population more generally.[46] Adhering to the industrious revolution concept is the belief that acquisitive, or maximizing behavior, understood in the context of its time, was not alien and 'unnatural,' and, hence, was not imposed in the main by political force on a dispossessed and victimized labor force.

There is no space here to elaborate a defense of this much-debated and politically charged proposition. Suffice it to say that no serious argument for the role of broad-based consumer demand in economic development during the seventeenth through nineteenth centuries can be sustained without it. In its absence one must rely on infinitely persuasive tastemakers, trendsetters and fashion manipulators who succeed in forging lower-class emulation out of whole cloth.[47] The ruling class must not only force recalcitrant workers to become a tractable labor force, it must simultaneously force traditional consumers to desire an appropriate array of goods.

Converting the *ability* to buy novelties and luxuries into a *willingness* to do so, as E. L. Jones puts it, depended on a shift in tastes. Fashion manipulators such as the now-legendary Josiah Wedgwood could do much to give a specific focus to this process. But they could not bring it into being alone, because, as I have argued here, it also took the *willingness* to shift one's tastes to acquire the *ability* to act on that desire.

One final issue remains to be addressed. Throughout this essay I have referred to the household as a producing and consuming unit. The 'household' has made decisions about the composition of its production, the relinquishment of leisure, and the character of its consumer demand. It is high time we directed a flashlight into this hitherto black box. It is, of course, composed of individuals, differentiated by relationship, age, and sex. These individuals did not possess equal power in household decision making, nor did they benefit or suffer equally from those decisions. These intra-family tensions have been most fully explored with respect to intergenerational distributions of household assets and income. Among property-owning households inheritance at once unites the family in maintaining the health of the household economy and has the potential of dividing members over the transmission of assets.[48] Among proletarian households the sparseness of transmissible assets makes its coherence as a productive unit vulnerable at certain stages of the family cycle, particularly by the early departure of children and their default on the obligation to transfer income to elderly parents.[49]

Our chief concern here is not the comparatively well-explored terrain of income and wealth redistributions across time – where the focus is on the relationship between parents and children – but the veritable *terra incognita* of production and consumption distributions across the members of the family: the distribution of labor and leisure as well as the distribution of consumption, plus the decision-making processes that regulated those distributions. Here the least explored relationship is between the sexes, particularly between husbands and wives.

The decisions of immediate concern to the industrious revolution concept are those to supply more labor – where the market-oriented labor of women and children becomes more prominent as their provision of 'Z goods' diminishes – and the decisions that determine how family income is allocated – where the changing composition of consumer demand might reveal shifts in the relative influence of family members.

Who made the decisions for the household? A 'strict patriarchy' model of the household economy posits a single and self-interested source of decision making: the male head of household disposes of the labor of his wife and children and projects his consumer preference onto the household.

An alternative approach is to define the family as a 'realm of altruism': in economic terms, each family member includes the utility of the other members (as defined by that member) in his or her own utility function. Just how the complicated calculus of joint utility maximization is achieved remains unclear – it invites the application of game-theoretic models of considerable complexity – but this economist's definition of 'the family' has the virtue of focusing attention on a process of negotiation among persons with an affective as well as a material stake in a joint enterprise.[50] This negotiation of utility functions could change the relative influence of family members, especially husbands and wifes, without dissolving the essential integrity of the household as an economic unit.

Joan Thirsk alerts us to the possibility of such a shift when she complains that economic historians have paid insignificant attention to the development of English consumer society in the sixteenth and seventeenth centuries. This omission could occur, she argues, because of the criteria of economic importance that 'have been laid down by our menfolk. Starch, needles, pins, cooking pots, kettles, frying pans, lace, soap, vinegar, stockings do not appear on their shopping lists, but they regularly appear on mine. They may ignore them, but could their families manage without them?'[51] Does this inattention of male historians for which Thirsk upbraids them have its parallel in a primarily female origin to the sixteenth- and seventeenth-century consumer demand that buoyed the rural industries chronicled by Thirsk? She does not make this claim explicitly, but McKendrick, addressing the home market during the Industrial Revolution, does. He assumes that the labor of women and children which fueled industrial production provided them with an income that gave them – the women at any rate – a stronger voice as consumers.

> When a man's wages went up in the eighteenth century the first beneficial effects might be expected to occur in the brewing industry, and in the commercialization of sport and leisure . . . gambling, boxing, horse racing and the like. When a woman's wages went up the first commercial effects would be expected in the clothing industries and those industries which provided consumer goods for the home. Her increased earnings released her desire to compete with her social superiors – a desire pent up for centuries or at least restricted to a very occasional excess.[52]

One need not accede to this Andy Capp-like caricature in its entirety (McKendrick here reduces the [im]moral vs. rational peasant debate to a war between the sexes) to appreciate its implications for the industrious revolution concept. The shift from relative self-sufficiency to market-oriented production by all or most household members necessarily involves a reduction of typically female-supplied Z goods and their replacement by commercially produced goods. The role of the wife as a decision maker in consumption was bound to grow, even if her husband was not inclined to frequent bouts of drinking and gambling at the race track. The household strategies that fostered the industrious revolution placed the wife in a strategic position, located, as it were, at the intersection of the household's three functions: reproduction, production, and consumption.[53]

Even when the household was most implicated in the market economy – with many or all family members working for wages outside the home – it did not dissolve into its constituent individual parts, each with his or her own income and demand pattern. The requirements of reproduction, the crucial importance of income redistribution, and the continuing need to provide for intergenerational transfers, gave the proletarian family of the Industrial Revolution a surprising resiliency.[54] The continued importance of the household as a decision-making unit affecting both supply and demand is well illustrated by the tendency, beginning after the mid-nineteenth century, for the long-term processes I have called an industrious revolution to be reversed. Although it takes us beyond the period that chiefly concerns us in this essay, a brief examination of this important phenomenon will help to understand the historical – and contemporary – significance of the industrious revolution.

After the mid-nineteenth century the preference schedule that gave shape to household demand patterns, and simultaneously determined the household's supply of paid labor, shifted in favor of Z goods (home-produced and consumed goods and services). The reverse process in the seventeenth and eighteenth centuries had redirected the labor of family members – mainly wives and children – from home Z goods activities into market-oriented activities. As real earnings rose in the second half of the nineteenth century (the timing varied by social class and country), a new set of Z goods, associated with the health and training of children and the achievement of new standards of domesticity in the home, came to appear superior to the available range of market-provided goods and services. To acquire these Z goods the labor of wives and children was withdrawn from the labor force as the incomes of adult male workers rose. In the context of Figure 8.1 demand patterns now trace out consumption path A rather than path B, characteristic of the industrious revolution.[55] The twinned concepts of breadwinners and homemakers came, for the first time, to define the household economy, as rising adult male wages were used, in effect, to 'buy back' a portion of the household's labor.

The withdrawal of women from field work in agriculture, the suppression of child labor, the regulation of women's labor in factories – all common to the late nineteenth century – are sometimes interpreted as the imposition of a middle-class image of the family onto the working class. Certainly, for families whose breadwinner earned too little to aspire to the new standards, the imposition of compulsory schooling was resisted and the new models of female propriety resented. But the withdrawal of women and children from the paid labor force was too widespread and voluntary to be generally consistent with this 'external constraint' explanation.[56]

Just as the Industrial Revolution had depended on the buoyant home market supported by households that intensified their labor and strengthened their market orientation, so the Victorian and Edwardian household, for want of a better term, depended on the productivity advances that were the fruit of the Industrial Revolution. Household members could now act to secure a set of consumption goals that previously had been beyond reach for most people and which, ironically, were not provided by the market.

The new home-provided goods and services secured 'respectability,' but also lower morbidity and mortality, better nutrition, and higher educational levels. They were directly implicated in the process of investing in human capital, which is to say, these Z goods were crucial to the most basic achievements of modern industrial society.[57] These Z goods had few market-supplied substitutes; but they did have market-produced complements (i.e., goods whose demand rose in conjunction with the rise of these home activities). Home furnishings are perhaps the most obvious complement to this 'cult of domesticity.' Carole Shammas observes that:

> The emergence of a parlour decorated by women and one which they could properly use for the visits of other women and men was, for all but the elite, a post-1800 development, only discarded in the twentieth century, by which time women had invaded the entire dwelling, pushing men into the basement, den, or garage.[58]

This new household behavior pattern had profound consequences for the productive system (which became detached from the home, more capital intensive, and more exclusively oriented to the requirements of full-time male workers),[59] the structure of demand (which focused increasingly on 'family' rather than 'individual' goods: consumer durables, housing, home furnishings),[60] and the goals of reproduction (which, to use a crude expression, focused more on 'quality' – the endowment of human capital in children – and less on 'quantity').[61]

By enumerating these most basic characteristics of the 'breadwinner–homemaker household,' the distinctiveness of household behavior in the industrious revolution – and the interdependence of production, consumption, and reproduction – becomes apparent. Also apparent is the return, in recent decades, of a new version of an industrious revolution, one in which the massive increase in paid labor force participation of women (and children) is associated with the rise of market-provided substitutes for the characteristic homemaker Z goods: food preparation, cleaning, child care, health services, and even (in still limited quantities) reproduction itself. The new industrious revolution, just like its predecessor, pairs a stagnation or decline of individual wages and salaries with a substantial extension of market-oriented activities. In response, the household releases its last labor reserves to the market, on which it comes to depend utterly. In doing so the modern industrious household loses its last practical functions.

Consumer demand becomes more individualized (men, women, and children possessing their own purchasing power), expenditures focus increasingly on less durable, immediate-gratification objects, and the reproduction process (i.e., child raising) relies increasingly on market-supplied services.

The new industrious revolution has important features in common with the old one of the seventeenth and eighteenth centuries, but, if my brief characterization has validity, it also differs in an important way. In both the first industrious revolution and its labor-withholding breadwinner–homemaker household successor the family economy faced the market economy as an autonomous unit, with its own internal functions. Household demand patterns always depended on production and labor allocation decisions internal to the household. In contrast, the new industrious revolution marks the absorption of the remaining substance of the household into the market economy. The last frontier of capitalism is not so much to be found in Third World or other distant markets as it is in the commercialization of the final non-market family labor and production activities.[62]

This excursion into modern times is intended to call attention to the different possible 'modes' of household negotiation with the market economy, and the consequences they can have both for the level of consumer demand and its character. Without wishing to deny the major role that prices and incomes play in determining the position and shape of demand curves in the short run, I have in this essay sought to explore how household preferences could help shape the underlying long-run determinants of both supply and demand. In the seventeenth and eighteenth centuries the industrious household helped lay the groundwork for the Industrial Revolution through demand-led changes in its behavior. It remains to be seen what the current industrious revolution holds in store for us.

Notes

1 Neil McKendrick, 'Introduction,' in Neil McKendrick, John Brewer and J. H. Plumb, eds., *The Birth of a Consumer Society: The Commercialization of Eighteenth-Century England* (Bloomington, Indiana, 1982), p. 5f. The criticism is not new; it was made much earlier, although less stridently, by E. W. Gilboy, 'Demand as a Factor in the Industrial Revolution,' in A. H. Cole, ed., *Facts and Factors in Economic History* (Cambridge, Mass., 1932), pp. 620–39; reprinted in R. M. Hartwell, ed., *The Causes of the Industrial Revolution in England* (London, 1967), pp. 121–38.
2 On the foreign trade argument, see W. A. Cole, 'Factors in Demand,' in Roderick Floud and Donald McCloskey, eds., *The Economic History of Britain Since 1700*, 2 vols. (Cambridge, 1981), vol. 1, pp. 38–9, 43; Donald McCloskey and R. P. Thomas, 'Overseas Trade and Empire, 1700–1860,' in Floud and McCloskey, *Economic*

History of Britain, vol 1, pp. 101–2. On the changes in relative prices, see A. H. John, 'The Course of Agricultural Change, 1660–1760,' in Walter Minchinton, ed., *Essays in Agrarian History* (Newton Abbott, 1968), vol 1, pp. 223–53; John, 'Aspects of Economic Growth in the Eighteenth Century,' in E. M. Carus-Wilson, ed., *Essays in Economic History* (London, 1962), vol II, pp. 360–73; and John, 'Agricultural Productivity and Economic Growth in England,' in E. L. Jones, ed., *Agriculture and Economic Growth in England, 1660–1815* (London, 1967), pp. 172–93. E. L. Jones, 'Agricultural Productivity and Economic Growth in England 1660–1750: agricultural change,' *Journal of Economic History* 25 (1965), 1–18.

More recent work emphasizing the growth of agricultural productivity in the 1650–1750 period includes: N. F. R. Crafts, 'Income Elasticities of Demand and the Release of Labour by Agriculture during the British Industrial Revolution,' *Journal of European Economic History* 9 (1980), 153–68; 'English Economic Growth in the Eighteenth Century: A Reexamination of Deane and Cole's Estimates,' *Economic History Review* 29, second series (1976), 226–35; and *British Economic Growth during the Industrial Revolution* (Oxford, 1985); R. A. C. Allen, 'The Growth of Labour Productivity in Early Modern English Agriculture,' *Explorations in Economic History* 25 (1988), pp. 117–46; and *Enclosure and the Yeoman* (Oxford University Press, 1992); Patrick O'Brien, 'Agriculture and the Home Market for English Industry, 1660–1820,' *English Historical Review* 100 (1985), 773–800.

A notable effort to identify domestic sources of demand after the mid-eighteenth century is: D. E. C. Eversley, 'The Home Market and Economic Growth in England, 1750–1780,' in E. L. Jones and G. Mingay, eds., *Land, Labour and Population in the Industrial Revolution* (London, 1967), pp. 209–52. Recent re-examinations of Eversley's argument have been critical: O'Brien in 'Agriculture and the Home Market,' concludes that

> The slow and faltering development of agriculture [after 1750] did little to extend the home market in manufactures, even if the adverse swing in the terms of trade against industry may have been mitigated to some extent by a recycling of the gains made by landowners and farmers in the form of taxes for central government and as safe investments in the urban economy (p. 785).

Joel Mokyr, 'Demand vs. Supply in the Industrial Revolution,' *Journal of Economic History* 37 (1977), 981–1008; reprinted in Joel Mokyr, *The Economics of the Industrial Revolution* (Totowa, New Jersey, 1985), is similarly negative in his assessment (p. 99).

3 Mokyr, 'Demand vs. Supply,' p. 1006.
4 For an effort to estimate *total* food expenditures see Carole Shammas, 'Food Expenditures and Economic Well-being in Early Modern England,' *Journal of Economic History* 21 (1984), 254–69. Shammas argued convincingly that the percentage of total working-class budgets devoted to food expenditures was substantially lower than the often-assumed 80 percent. Carole Shammas, *The Pre-industrial Consumer in England and America* (Oxford, 1990), pp. 122–33. Studies of Amsterdam orphanage expenditures now being carried out by Anne McCants and myself show that bread expenditures rarely exceeded 20 percent of total food expenditures in the period 1640–1780. Thereafter bread assumed a larger share of the total food budget, but it rarely exceeded 30 percent.
5 See B. H. Slicher van Bath, *Agrarian History of Western Europe, 500–1850* (London: Edward Arnold, 1963), pp. 113–15, 209–10, 223–5; W. Abel, *Agricultural Fluctuations in Europe from the Thirteenth to the Twentieth Centuries* (London: Methuen, Spectrum, 1980), pp. 51–2, 116–23; 187–8, 264–7.
6 Examples of the use of probate inventories for the study of production include: Robert DuPlessis, 'Capital and Finance in the Early Modern Veluwe Paper Industry,' *A. A. G. Bijdragen* 28 (1986), 185–97; Jan de Vries, *The Dutch Rural Economy in the Golden Age, 1500–1700* (New Haven, 1974), pp. 137–53, 215–17; Mark Overton, 'Estimating Crop Yields from Probate Inventories: An Example from East Anglia, 1585–1735,' *Journal of Economic History* 39 (1979), 363–78; Robert C. Allen, 'Inferring Yields from Probate Inventories,' *Journal of Economic History* 48 (1988), 117–25.

On wealth holding see: Alice Hanson Jones, *Wealth of a Nation to be. The American Colonies on the Eve of the Revolution* (New York, 1980); Baudien de Vries, *Electoraat en elite. Sociale structuur en sociale mobiliteit in Amsterdam, 1850–1895* (Amsterdam, 1986).

Among the many works on material culture see: Thera Wijsenbeek-Olthuis, *Achter de gevels van Delft. Bezit en bestaan van rijk en arm in een periode van achteruitgang (1700–1800)* (Hilversum, 1987); A. J. Schuurman, *Materiële cultuur en levensstijl* (Wageningen, A. A. G. Bijdragen no. 30, 1989); J. de Jong, *Een deftig bestaan. Het dagelijks leven van regenten in de 17de en 18de eeuw* (Utrecht, 1987); Lorna Weatherill, *Consumer Behavior and Material Culture, 1660–1760* (London, 1988).

7 See Lois Green Carr and Lorna S. Walsh, 'The Standard of Living in the Colonial Chesapeake,' *The William and Mary Quarterly* 45, third series (1988), 135–59; Gloria L. Main and Jackson T. Main, 'Economic Growth and the Standard of Living in Southern New England, 1640–1774,' *Journal of Economic History* 48 (1988), 27–46; Peter Earle, *The Making of the English Middle Class. Business, Society and Family Life in London, 1660–1730* (Berkeley and Los Angeles, 1989). For Europe, see Daniele Roche, *Le peuple de Paris* (Paris, 1981); Ruth Mohrmann, *Altagswelt im Land Braunschweig, Stadt und landliche Wohnkultur vom 16. bis zum frühen 20. Jahrhundert* (Münster, 1990); and a survey of work in progress: Ad van der Woude and Anton Schuurman, eds., *Probate Inventories. A New Source for the Historical Study of Wealth, Material Culture and Agricultural Development* (Wageningen, A. A. G. Brijdagen no. 23, 1980).

8 This seems to be the message of work by Joan Thirsk, who emphasizes early seventeenth-century rural industry, E. L. Jones, who focuses on rising agricultural productivity and its consequences in the century after 1650, and John and Eversley, who call attention to the rising demand of the first half of the eighteenth century.

9 The basic argument is made in: Jan de Vries, 'Peasant Demand Patterns and Economic Development; Friesland, 1550–1750', in William N. Parker and Eric L. Jones, eds., *European Peasants and their Markets: Essays in Agrarian Economic History* (Princeton: Princeton University Press, 1975), pp. 206–9. Even though I speak of changes in tastes as motivating 'industrious' conduct the concept is, I believe, broadly consistent with the defense of stable preferences in the classic article of George J. Stigler and Gary S. Becker, 'De Gustibus Non Est Disputandum,' *American Economic Review* 67 (1977), 76–90. The point of similarity is the common view that a consumer theory based on the family as 'a passive maximizer of the utility from market purchases' should be replaced by the family as 'an active maximizer also engaged in extensive production and investment activities.' (p. 77). My position is broadly consistent, but not exactly the same: tastes are not inscrutable and capricious, but the process of 'active maximization' creates new situations, to which people respond creatively.

10 Mokyr, 'Demand vs. Supply,' acknowledges this as a valid defense of why 'demand factors mattered.' However he doubts that it could 'account for sustained growth' (p. 985). He is right to hold that shifts in the labor supply curve due to a reduced leisure preference are an exhaustible source of growth. This article seeks to demonstrate that the process of household reorganization had many dimensions. Together, and in combination with resulting efficiency gains, they could sustain growth over a considerable time span.

11 Jan de Vries, *The Dutch Rural Economy in the Golden Age*, pp. 4–17 and Appendix C.

12 Stephen Hymer and Stephen Resnick, 'A Model of an Agrarian Economy with Nonagricultural Activities,' *American Economic Review* 59 (1969), 493–506.

13 De Vries, *Dutch Rural Economy*; Eric L. Jones, 'Agriculture and Economic Growth in England, 1660–1750: Agricultural Change,' *Journal of Economic History* 13 (1965), 1–18. Jones's emphasis on the century after 1650 as the temporal locus of England's agricultural revolution is forcefully confirmed in Ann Kussmaul, *A General View of the Rural Economy of England, 1538–1840* (Cambridge, 1990).

14 George Grantham, 'Agricultural Supply During the Industrial Revolution: French Evidence and European Implications,' *Journal of Economic History* 49 (1989), 44–5.

15 Grantham, 'Agricultural Supply', p. 66.
16 See: Sidney Polland, *The Genesis of Modern Management* (Harmondsworth, 1965); and E. P. Thompson, 'Time Work Discipline and Industrial Capitalism,' *Past and Present* 38 (1967), 59–67.
17 K. G. Persson, 'Consumption, Labour and Leisure in the Late Middle Ages,' in D. Menjot, ed., *Manger et boire au Moyen Age* (Nice, 1984), pp. 219–20; Christopher Dyer, *Standards of Living in the Later Middle Ages* (Cambridge, 1989), pp. 222–3; Leo Noordegraaf, *Hollands welvaren? Levenstandaard in Holland, 1450–1650* (Bergen, the Netherlands, 1985), pp. 57–61; M. A. Beinefeld, *Working Hours in British Industry: An Economic History* (London, 1972), pp. 15–19.
18 'Consideration on taxes' (1764), quoted in Paul Mantoux, *The Industrial Revolution in the Eighteenth Century* (London, 1928; reprinted, New York: Harper and Row, 1961), p. 62.
19 'Consideration on taxes.' A vast body of contemporary commentary on this characteristic is summarized in Edgar Furniss, *The Position of Labour in a System of Nationalism* (New York, 1919), Chapter 6. See also: Peter Mathias, 'Leisure and Wages in Theory and Practice,' in Peter Mathias, *The Transformation of England* (London, 1979), pp. 148–67; D. C. Coleman, 'Labour in the English Economy of the Seventeenth Century,' *Economic History Review* 8, second series (1956), 280–95. Such commentary cannot always be taken as the product of disinterested observation of actual behavior. It also functioned as part of an ideology that defined the 'otherness' and incapacity to self-governance of the working population. In addition, it had the practical benefit, as the 'utility of poverty doctrine,' of justifying low wages. As such, its frequent repetition, growing more insistent in the retelling, is intended to reinforce the ideology rather than add to the cumulative empirical observations. It is ironic that many historians who regard themselves as champions of the common man appropriate this claim. What had served as a *trope* justifying the subordination of the 'dependent classes' because of their lack of self-control and spirit of improvement is used by 'moral economy' advocates as evidence of the pre-capitalist natural innocence of common folk. The misunderstanding of liberal political economists is no less a misunderstanding in the hands of their political opponents.
   Occasionally, historical evidence penetrates this veil of preconception. W. G. Hoskins, in his classic study *The Midland Peasant* (New York, 1965), had to observe that social differentiation was well under way in Wigston Magna long before the village was enclosed and, presumably, subjected to the full onslaught of capitalist farming. 'In a way,' he lamented, 'the peasant community was breeding its own downfall, by producing a class of successful landowners ... whose interests and whole way of thinking gradually became estranged from the peasant system under which their ancestors had lived and prospered in earlier times' (pp. 198–9). Similarly, E. P. Thompson followed convention in blaming the lords and gentry for attacking the customary rights of the English peasantry. But he also acknowledged the spread of individualism among the yeomen as contributing to 'the death of the yeomanry as a class.' E. P. Thompson, 'The Grid of Inheritance: A Comment,' in Jack Goody, Joan Thirsk, and E. P. Thompson, eds., *Family and Inheritance: Rural Society in Western Europe, 1200–1800* (Cambridge, 1978), pp. 329–33.
20 Adam Smith, *An Inquiry into the Nature and Causes of the Wealth of Nations* (1776); Sir James Steuart, *An Inquiry into the Principles of Political Œconomy* (1767; reprinted 1966), p. 67. The gradual shift in elite thought with respect to labor market behavior is discussed in Joyce Appleby, *Economic Thought and Ideology in Seventeenth-Century England* (Princeton, 1978).
21 A 'short course' on this concept might focus on the following: Franklin Mendels, 'Proto-industrialization: The First Phase of the Industrialization Process,' *Journal of Economic History* 32 (1972), 241–62; Mendels, 'Des industries rurales à la proto-industrialisation: historique d'un changement de perspective,' *Annales E.S.C.* 39 (1984), 977–1008; Eric L. Jones, 'The Agricultural Origins of Industry,' *Past and Present* 40 (1968), 58–71; Hans Medick, 'The Proto-industrial Family Economy during the Transition from Peasant Society to Industrial Capitalism,' *Social History* 1 (1976), 291–315; D. C. Coleman, 'Proto-industrialization: A Concept Too Many,'

Economic History Review 36, second series (1983), 435–48; Peter Kriedte, *et al.*, *Industrialization Before Industrialization* (Cambridge, 1981); David Levine, *Family Formation in an Age of Nascent Capitalism* (New York, 1977); Gay L. Gullickson, *Spinners and Weavers of Auffay* (Cambridge, 1986); Maxine Berg, Pat Hudson, and Michael Sonenscher, eds., *Manufacture in Town and Country Before the Factory* (Cambridge, 1983).

22 Joan Thirsk, *Economic Policies and Projects. The Development of a Consumer Society in Early Modern England* (Oxford, 1978), p. 169.

23 Thirsk, *Economic Policies*, p. 174.

24 Thirsk, *Economic Policies*, p. 175.

25 Joan Thirsk, 'New Crops and their Diffusion: Tobacco-growing in Seventeenth Century England,' in C. W. Chalklin and M. A. Havinden, eds., *Urban Growth and Rural Change 1500–1800: Essays in English Regional History in Honour of W. G. Hoskins* (London, 1974), pp. 76–103; H. K. Roessingh, *Inlandse tabak. Expansie en contractie van een handelsgewas in de 17de en 18de eeuw in Nederland* (Wageningen, 1976); Slicher van Bath, *Een samenleving onder spanning; geschiedenis van het platteland in Overijssel* (Assen, 1957).

26 'Proto-industrialization' as defined by Mendels consists not simply of an expansion of market-oriented rural industry, but of an expansion of market-oriented rural industry taking place in regions experiencing simultaneous commercial agricultural development. Thus, households specializing in industrial production were linked, in a complementary regional structure, to households specializing increasingly in food production. Franklin Mendels, 'Les temps de l'industrie et les temps de proto-industrialisation,' *Revue du Nord* 68 (1981), 21–34.

27 Neil McKendrick, 'Home Demand and Economic Growth: a New View of the Role of Women and Children in the Industrial Revolution,' in Neil McKendrick, ed., *Historical Perspectives: Studies in English Thought and Society in Honour of J. H. Plumb* (London: Europa, 1974), p. 172.

28 McKendrick, 'Home Demand', p. 197.

29 Gregory Clark, 'Why Isn't the Whole World Developed? Lessons from the Cotton Mills,' *Journal of Economic History* 47 (1987), 141–73; Clark, 'Productivity Growth without Technological Change in European Agriculture before 1850,' *Journal of Economic History* 47 (1987), 419–32; Clark, 'The Costs of Capital and Medieval Agricultural Technique,' *Explorations in Economic History* 25 (1988), 265–94.

30 Clark, 'Productivity Growth,' p. 432.

31 Clark, 'Productivity Growth,' p. 425.

32 Grantham, 'Agricultural Supply,' p. 70–1.

33 Herman Freudenberger and Gaylord Cummins, 'Health, Work, and Leisure before the Industrial Revolution,' *Explorations in Economic History* 13 (1976), p. 1. See also Herman Freudenberger, 'Das Arbeitsjahr,' in Ingomar Bog, *et al.*, *Wirtschaftliche und Soziale Strukturen im saekularen Wandel* (Hanover, 1974), pp. 307–20.

34 Robert Fogel, 'Second Thoughts on the European Escape from Hunger: Famines, Chronic Malnutrition and Mortality,' in S. R. Osmani, ed., *Nutrition and Poverty* (Oxford: Oxford University Press, forthcoming), p. 41.

35 Fogel appears to suggest this possibility in a footnote, where he identifies the malnourished portion of the labor force as the 'lumpenproletariat' and as 'gens de néant'. Fogel, 'Second Thoughts', p. 51, note 20.

36 Esther Boserup, *The Conditions of Agricultural Growth* (London, 1965). For explication and discussion of Boserup's concepts see: De Vries, *Dutch Rural Economy*, Appendix A, pp. 17–18; Jan de Vries, 'Boserup as Economics and History,' *Peasant Studies Newsletter* 1 (1972), 45–50.

37 Franklin Mendels, 'Agriculture and Peasant Industry in Eighteenth-Century Flanders,' in Parker and Jones, *European Peasants and Their Markets*, pp. 179–204; Mendels, 'Proto-industrialization,' *passim*.

38 Chris Vandenbroeke, *Sociale geschiedenis van het Vlaamse volk* (Beveren, 1982), especially Part III, chapter 1.

39 Medick, 'The Proto-industrial Family,' p. 305.

40 Medick, 'The Proto-industrial Family,' p. 305.

41 Levine, *Family Formation*, p. 9.
42 Key works in a growing literature include: John Brewer, *The Sinews of Power. War, Money and the English State, 1688–1783* (New York, 1989), pp. 88–91; Peter Mathias and Patrick O'Brien, 'Taxation in Britain and France, 1715–1810: A Comparison of the Social and Economic Incidence of Taxes Collected for the Central Governments,' *Journal of European History* 5 (1976), 601–90; James Collins, *The Fiscal Limitations of Absolutism: Direct Taxation in Seventeenth-century France* (Berkeley and Los Angeles, University of California Press); Niels Steensgaard, 'The Seventeenth-century Crisis,' in Geoffrey Parker and Lesley M. Smith, eds., *The General Crisis of the Seventeenth Century* (London, 1978), pp. 26–56.
43 David Levine, *Reproducing Families: The Political Economy of English Population History* (Cambridge, 1987), pp. 19–21, 39.
44 Pollard, *Genesis of Modern Management*, p. 190.
45 This process seems to be what Jones has in mind when he speaks of Europeans having been 'K-strategists' and having experienced a 'ratchet effect' whereby numbers were systematically kept below carrying capacity, and the resulting margin of per capita well-being was used to advance the economy. E. L. Jones, *The European Miracle* (Cambridge: Cambridge University Press, 1981), pp. 3, 20, 56. It can also be related to what Persson called 'break out' from the backward bending labor supply curve. If, referring to Figure 8.2, workers were at the upper left-hand range of the offer curve and experienced a decrease in wage rates, their response might be to preserve the already achieved 'target income' by offering more labor as wages fall. They would 'break out' of the offer curve traced in the figure. If, with a renewed phase of rising wages they did not immediately reduce the supply of labor, they would, by a ratchet effect, achieve yet higher income levels. Persson, 'Consumption, Labour and Leisure,' p. 214.
46 The classic statements of the two positions are found in: James C. Scott, *The Moral Economy of the Peasant* (New Haven, 1976); Samuel L. Popkin, *The Rational Peasant. The Political Economy of Rural Society in Vietnam* (Berkeley and Los Angeles, 1979); Alan Macfarlane, *The Origins of English Individualism* (Cambridge, 1979).
47 On the role of emulation and demand manipulation see: Eric L. Jones, 'The Fashion Manipulators: Consumer Tastes and British Industries, 1660–1800,' in Louis P. Cain and Paul J. Uselding, eds., *Business Enterprise and Economic Change. Essays in Honor of Harold F. Williamson* (Kent, Ohio, 1973), pp. 198–226; Neil McKendrick, 'The Commercialization of Fashion,' in McKendrick, *Birth of Consumer Society*, pp. 34–99. For a critique of these articles, see: Ben Fine and Ellen Leopold, 'Consumerism and the Industrial Revolution,' *Social History* 15 (1990), 151–79.
48 Jack Goody *et al.*, eds., *Family and Inheritance*; Lutz K. Berkner, 'The Stem Family and the Developmental Cycle of the Peasant Household: An Eighteenth Century Austrian Example,' *American Historical Review* 77 (1972), 398–418; Lutz K. Berkner and Franklin F. Mendels, 'Inheritance Systems, Family Structure, and Demographic Patterns in Western Europe (1700–1900),' in Charles Tilly, ed., *Historical Studies of Changing Fertility* (Princeton, 1978).
49 Child default is a theme of Rudolf Braun, *Industrialisierung und Volksleben: Die Veränderungen der Lebensformen in einem landlichen Industriegebiet vor 1800* (Erlenbach-Zurich and Stuttgart, 1960) and Michael Anderson, *Family Structure in Nineteenth-Century Lancashire* (Cambridge, 1971), pp. 131–4. For theoretical formulations of the concept see: Paul David and William A. Sundstrom, 'Old-Age Security Motives, Labor Markets, and Farm Family Fertility in Antebellum America,' *Explorations in Economic History* and 'Did Rising Out-Migration cause Fertility to Decline in Antebellum New England? A Life-Cycle Perspective on Old-Age Security Motives, Child Default, and Farm-Family Fertility,' California Institute of Technology, Social Science Working Paper 610, April, 1986.
50 Paul A. Samuelson, 'Social Indifference Curves,' *Quarterly Journal of Economics* (1956).
51 Thirsk, *Economic Policies and Projects*, pp. 22–3.
52 McKendrick, 'Home Demand,' pp. 199–200. His point is developed further by Maxine Berg, *The Age of Manufactures, 1700–1820* (Oxford, 1986), pp. 169–72.

53 A masterful account of the growing centrality of wives in the household economy as it becomes more market-oriented is found in David Sabean, *Property, Production, and Family in Neckarhausen, 1700–1870* (Cambridge, 1990), especially Chapter 6. On the basis of local court records, Sabean observes: 'As women became producers of products which were exchanged for cash, they began to demand considerable say in the disposal of both the products and the proceeds' (p. 174).

54 Michael Anderson, *Approaches to the History of the Western Family, 1500–1914* (London, 1980), pp. 78–9. See also: Michael Anderson, *Family Structure in Nineteenth Century Lancashire* (Cambridge, 1971).

55 In Figure 8.1 quadrant II shows a production possibilities curve between Z (non-traded nonagricultural goods) and F (food production), quadrant III shows the terms of trade between food and M (manufactures, or nonagricultural goods and services produced outside the household). P_2 represents more favorable terms of trade for the food producer than P_1. Quadrant I shows the consumption possibilities curves that correspond to the relative prices represented by P_1 and P_2. Consumption takes place at the tangency of the consumption possibilities curve and the community indifference curves (dashed curves). The successive tangency points derived by shifting the terms of trade trace out the consumption paths A and B, each reflecting a different set of preferences. The 'industrious revolution' is thought to require a shift from consumption path A to B, as the household devotes more of its resources to the production of the traded good (F), (see quadrant II). As a new set of desirable Z goods (health care, child-training, domestic comfort, etc.) comes within reach, household behavior can be represented by a shift back from consumption path B to A, although the traded good (F) is now more likely to be wage labor.

56 Anderson, *Western Family*, p. 83. This interpretation is, I believe, broadly consistent with the analysis of Joan Scott and Louise Tilly in 'Women's Work and the Family in Nineteenth Century Europe,' *Comparative Studies in Society and History* 17 (1975), 36–64. They speak of the 'continuity of traditional values and behavior' (p. 42) where I invoke the industrious revolution concept; they refer to the 'waning of the family economy' (p. 62) where I speak of the breadwinner–homemaker household, which is, in my view, still very much a family economy, but one with a new emphasis on Z goods.

These claims imply that families pursue 'strategies,' not simply for survival, but for the achievement of goals, which, because we observe them changing, cannot simply be treated as implicit, or 'inculcated predispositions.' For a lively discussion of the family strategy notion see: Leslie Page Moch, Nancy Folbre, Daniel Scott Smith, Laurel L. Cornell, and Louis A. Tilly, 'Family Strategy: A Dialogue,' *Historical Methods* 20 (1987), 113–25. On 'inculcated predispositions' see: Pierre Bourdieu, 'Marriage Strategies as Strategies of Social Reproduction,' in R. Forster and O. Ranum, eds., *Family and Society: Selections from the Annales: Economies, Sociétés, Civilisations* (Baltimore, 1976), pp. 117–44.

57 It is worth emphasizing that while the productivity-raising effects of industrialization that put these new Z goods 'within reach,' they could actually be acquired only through the (re)intensification of a division of labor within the household. A redefinition of gender roles offered major gains from 'increasing returns to investments in sector-specific human capital that raise productivity mainly in either the market or the non-market sphere.' Gary Becker, whose *Treatise on the Family* (second edition, Chicago, 1991, p. 3) is here quoted, treats this process of sphere definition as an outcome dictated by economic incentives to specialization 'even if a husband and wife are intrinsically identical.'

For working-class households desirous of investing in human capital the results of this process (as opposed to its explanation) do not differ in their essentials from the results of Leonore Davidoff and Catherine Hall's study of English middle-class families in the period 1700–1850 (*Family Fortunes* (Chicago, 1987)) where they sought to show how the economic, social, and political aspirations of middle-class men depended crucially on 'networks of familial and female support which underpinned their rise to public prominence.'

58 Shammas, *Pre-industrial Consumer*, p. 187. The central position of women in this
   process is also stressed by Rybczynski:

> Ever since the seventeenth century, when privacy was introduced into the home,
> the role of women in defining comfort has been paramount. The Dutch interior,
> the Rococo salon, the servantless household – all were the result of women's
> invention. One could argue, with only slight exaggeration, that the idea of
> domesticity was principally a feminine idea. So was the idea of efficiency (W.
> Rybczynski, *Home: A Short History of an Idea* (New York, Viking, 1986),
> p. 223).

   In the new industrious revolution phase, this process could be expected to weaken.
   Indeed, the modern tendency for electronic devices to constitute the defining items of
   home furnishing suggests that the historical process sketched by Shammas is now
   being reversed.

59 Altogether consistent is the observation of Maxine Berg, that, beginning in the second
   quarter of the nineteenth century, 'not only did workers' organizations become
   increasingly segmented, but the language of artisan institutions and the perception of
   skill itself became increasingly identified with masculinity.' *The Age of Manufactures*,
   p. 160.

60 A statement that well reflects the spirit of an age in which the new Z goods were held
   up as the highest 'consumer' aspiration of decent folk is made by G. K. Chesterton as
   part of a social critique based on his observation that [in his day] 'the cultured class is
   shrieking to be let out of the decent home, just as the working class is shouting to be
   let into it.' The key to right thinking, Chesterton asserted, was to have a fixed point,
   an ideal, from which to analyze conflicting political claims. He found that fixed point
   'with a little girl's hair.'

> That I know is a good thing at any rate. Whatever else is evil, the pride of a good
> mother in the beauty of her daughter is good. It is one of those adamantine
> tendernesses which are the touchstones of every age and race. If other things are
> against it, those things must go down. . . . With the red hair of one she-urchin in
> the gutter I will set fire to all modern civilization. Because a girl should have long
> hair, she should have clean hair; because she should have clean hair, she should
> not have an unclean home; because she should not have an unclean home, she
> should have a free and leisured mother; because she should have a free mother,
> she should not have an usurious landlord; because there should not be an
> usurious landlord, there should be a redistribution of property; because there
> should be a redistribution of property, there shall be a revolution. That little
> urchin with the gold-red hair, whom I have just watched toddling past my house,
> she shall not be lopped and lamed and altered; her hair shall not be cut short like
> a convict's; no, all the kingdoms of the earth shall be hacked about and mutilated
> to suit her.

   G. K. Chesterton, *What's Wrong With the World* (New York, 1910), as quoted in
   Gilbert Meilaender, 'What Families are For,' *First Things* 6 (1990), p. 34. See also
   Scott and Tilly's 'Women's Work in Nineteenth Century Europe,' where they call
   attention to the fact that 'some socialist newspapers described the ideal society as one
   in which "good socialist wives" would stay at home and care for the health and
   education of "good socialist children" ' (p. 64).

61 On this concept see: Richard A. Easterlin, 'The Economics and Sociology of Fertility:
   A Synthesis,' in Tilly, *Historical Studies of Changing Fertility*, pp. 57–133.

62 This point is prefigured by Joseph Schumpeter's analysis in *Capitalism, Socialism and
   Democracy* (New York, 1942). In chapter XIV, 'Decomposition,' he writes of the
   'disintegration of the bourgeois family.' Although he is chiefly concerned with the
   'upper strata of the bourgeoisie' to which the capitalist order 'entrusts [its] long-run
   interests' he notes that:

> the phenomenon [of decomposition] by now extends, more or less, to all classes.
> . . . It is wholly attributable to the rationalization of everything in life, which we
> have seen is one of the effects of capitalist evolution. . . . The capitalist order rests

on props made of extra-capitalist material [and] derives its energy from extra-capitalist patterns of behavior which at the same time it is bound to destroy (pp. 157–62).

In this context feminism, doing battle against society's last significant extra-capitalist patterns of behavior, may be seen as establishing the conditions for 'the highest stage of capitalism.'

9

'The hidden investment': women and the enterprise

LEONORE DAVIDOFF AND CATHERINE HALL

'tis evident that men can be their own advisers, and their own directors, and know how to work themselves out of difficulties and into business better than women.

Daniel Defoe, Moll Flanders, 1722

Women's identification with the domestic and moral sphere implied that they would only become active economic agents when forced by necessity. As the nineteenth century progressed, it was increasingly assumed that a woman engaged in business was a woman without either an income of her own or a man to support her. She already shared with the men of her class the spiritual stumbling blocks to active pursuit of business. But unlike a man whose family status and self-worth rose through his economic exertions, a woman who did likewise risked opprobrium for herself and possible shame for those around her. Structured inequality made it exceedingly difficult for a woman to support herself on her own, much less take on dependants. But beyond the negative effects on women who openly operated in the market, the construction of domestic ideology and the lure of new patterns of consumption offered attractive alternatives.

At a time when the concept of occupation was becoming the core element in masculine identity, any position for women other than in relation to men was anomalous. In the 1851 census, the Registrar General introduced a new fifth class, exclusively made up of women:

The 5th class comprises large numbers of the population that have hitherto been held to have no occupation; but it requires no argument to prove that the *wife*, the *mother*, the *mistress* of an *English family* – fills offices and discharges duties of no ordinary importance; or that children are or should be occupied in filial or household duties, and in the task of education, either at home or at school.[1]

This conception had been developing over a long period. In the late seventeenth century, for example, trade tokens used by local shopkeepers and small masters carried the initials of the man and woman's first name and the couple's surname, but by the late eighteenth century only the initials of the man were retained.[2] This serves to confirm a contemporary's view (born 1790) that whereas his mother had confidently joined in the family auctioneering business, the increased division of the sexes had seen the withdrawal of women from business life within his own lifetime.[3]

The resulting picture of what middle-class women were actually doing and how they survived is fragmentary. Local records inevitably favour the men's role in both enterprise and market relations. While in both the urban and rural areas women made up just over 50 per cent of the middle-class population, they were only 28 per cent of testators leaving wills and 20 per cent of household heads in the census sample. Information on women's occupations where they were not a household head is so unreliable as to be almost useless, and, by definition, married women were not considered heads of households. In the census sample, 69 per cent of female household heads were widows and 21 per cent single women, and by default the discussion of women's occupations must centre mainly on these groups. For women, marriage was indeed a 'trade' and as economic actors they appear as shadows behind the scenes of the family enterprise.

Alice Clark for the seventeenth and Ivy Pinchbeck for the eighteenth and early nineteenth centuries have outlined the slow shift from women's active participation in commerce, farming and other business pursuits. From their work it is clear that the consolidation of textile production in the market, the first sector to be so organized, had already had a strong impact on women's by-employments such as spinning which had been carried on in even quite prosperous families.[4] The loss of opportunities to earn increased the dominance of marriage as the only survival route for middle-class women as illustrated by the metamorphosis of the term 'spinster', from one who spins to an unmarried woman. By the nineteenth century, the courtesy title, *Mrs* (shortened from mistress), which included single women who had reached middle age, fell into disuse. 'Spinsters' were given this somewhat pejorative label throughout their lives. By the second half of the nineteenth century, a woman's own first name came to be used only when she was single or widowed, while the convention of designating a married woman by both her *husband's* first and surname, prefixed by Mrs, became the common practice and was seen as a form of respect paid to middle-class rather than working-class women.

A number of developments fostered the contradiction between women's perceived and actual relation to the economy. One of the most important was the growth of scale, creating divisions between larger and smaller operations. The 26 per cent of Suffolk farms where only family labour was employed would be a vastly different setting for the farmer's wife and female relatives than for a woman like Jane Ransome Biddell whose husband farmed over 1000 acres, and where numerous servants including a housekeeper were employed, releasing her to take part in the cultural and intellectual life of nearby Ipswich.[5] In manufacturing, the cannibalizing of modest independent workshops by larger, better financed concerns, spelt the doom for many female entrepreneurs. As such enterprises were drawn more heavily into the regional or even national market, the tendency was to specialize, to produce for agents or middle men who would consolidate products. The shift to arable farming, for example, meant that in Essex and Suffolk subsidiary activities like dairying sharply declined, precisely the area of farm work which had been traditionally women's work. Cheese making, which had taken place on almost every farm over a certain size, where the farmer's wife used her own labour augmented by her daughters, nieces, sisters or living-in dairymaids, shifted to centralized production in other parts of the country. By 1843, when the Royal Commission on Women and Children in Agriculture made its investigation, it was announced that the patience, skill and strength needed to produce cheese made this work unsuitable for women.[6] The preferred activities of corn growing and cattle fattening 'give but little trouble to the housewives of the present generations' according to an Essex commentator.[7]

The general trend to supersede craft training and experience was particularly disadvantageous for women, compounded by their exclusion from a more scientific culture. In farming, for example, the introduction of both hand and steam powered machinery, and the use of chemistry for fertilizers increased impediments for women farmers.[8] Larger units of production with more rational work flows implied a larger workforce increasingly made up of day labourers, most of whom no longer had a chance of becoming independent producers, thus destined to remain social inferiors. There was a growing feeling that genteel women, paticularly the young and unmarried, should be removed from contact with such a workforce both by physical separation and psychological barriers. With a predominantly male workforce, it was even more difficult for women to wield authority. This is sharply illustrated by changes in farming practice. For a variety of reasons, since the mid eighteenth century, there had been a gradual displacement of female labour from the fields, except for casual seasonal tasks.[9] The suitability of field work, indeed any outdoor work for women, was almost always discussed in moral terms, thus turning attention from the practical questions of directing labour. According to a Suffolk social commentator,

> Our inquiries have convinced us that it (field labour) is a bad school of morals for girls and that the mixing up with men on whom poverty and ignorance have encrusted coarse and vulgar habits, tends to greatly uncivilise and demoralize women of maturer years; single women whose characters for chastity are blemished, work in the fields, the

topics of conversation and the language that is used amongst the men
and women are described as coarse and filthy.[10]

Such attitudes multiplied the problems already faced by farmer's wives who
no longer acted as house-mistress overseeing the men's domestic life.
Supervision of field work on far-flung acreages meant riding horseback,
often alone, to deal with the labourers. While this may have given added
status and authority to male farmers, thus 'elevated above their work
force',[11] it ran contrary to notions of feminine propriety.

These factors bore particularly heavily on women operating in their own
right. As long as their economic contribution remained within the family
they could continue to be active. It was external relations which raised more
acute difficulties. In addition to dealing with a wage labour force, there were
also clients, bankers, solicitors and agents. These would be men with
increasingly fixed expectations of appropriate feminine behaviour. Many of
these men, while willing to act as protectors and intermediaries for
dependent women, would neither expect nor countenance their independent
economic action.

Within this pattern, certain activities became more closely associated with
one or the other gender. Some of these connections stemmed from previous
male monopolies through the gild system, even where it had faded to a
remnant. The exclusion of women from the ranks of the building trades –
joinery, wheelwrights and smiths – had serious consequences since it was
from these crafts that engineering, surveying and architecture developed.
Other gender typing was of more recent origin. The equation of outdoor
activity with men, and the indoors as the setting for respectable femininity
affected the division of labour in a myriad of ways from farming, as above,
to the expectation that within an enterprise women could do preparation of
products and services of finance as long as these activities were kept out of
sight.

An effort was made to have certain tasks performed by the expected
gender. If a family failed to produce the requisite boy or girl, man or
woman, the wider kinship or friendship network could be tapped to make
up the deficiency. Among the better off, hired labour of the correct age and
sex could be substituted. In lesser establishments, tasks usually assigned to
one gender might have to be undertaken by the other, at least behind closed
doors. This crossing of such a significant boundary, if made visible, could be
taken as a sign of social inferiority when social status was crucial to building
a picture of creditworthiness. The equation of women with domesticity
came to be one of the fixed points of middle-class status. Yet the
development of the market did offer some enticements for women to use
their skills if not their capital. It may, indeed, be argued that the concerted
attack on any display of female *sexual* independence may have much to do
with fears about new opportunities for their *economic* activity.

Women and property

As Ann Whitehead has succinctly argued, property forms indicate relationships between people mediated by the disposition and control of things.[12] The middle class in this period, far from taking the opportunities afforded by the move away from land as the main form of property, continued to build on the principles of patrilineality, and patriarchy. Middle-class women continued to be on 'the margins of ownership' in a manner analogous to the restraints often imposed on working-class women (particularly when married) who had to or wished to sell their labour power with artisan culture.[13] Intense fears surrounded the 'impertinent' independent mill girl who refused the paternalistic discipline of domestic service or even the oversight of the parental home, and who might also, it was felt, refuse to fit the role of respectable working-man's wife. A similar if less often expressed alarm surrounded the idea of middle-class women using their skills or property to establish independent careers. It could, in fact, be argued that much of the concern about women working in mines and fields expressed in the 1840s was a transplanted discussion of deep seated uneasiness about the middle class itself. Although he was proud of his daughter who ran a successful school, a Quaker farmer solemnly warned her that she would never marry if she was known 'only as a School Mistress'.[14]

The relationship of women to property had never been made explicit. While John Locke had directly linked the concept of property ownership to independence, both he and Thomas Hobbes did not clarify how women's control of property and their expected subordination within the family could be reconciled.[15] In legal and practical terms, if anything, women's position had deteriorated from the seventeenth century. As landowners in their own right, women were vastly underrepresented. They made up only 4 per cent of the 404 landlowners in Suffolk at mid century and almost all their land was in small parcels.[16] In the gentry, at least freehold land – real property – had been returned to a woman's control after her husband's death. Middle-class property was, as has been seen, mainly in other forms: leasehold and copyhold land, buildings, investments and effects, which had forgone even this limited right. With the ending of customary rights of dower, a development recognized by law in 1833, marriage virtually turned legal control of a woman's property permanently over to her husband.

The control of women's 'testamentary capacity' extended beyond their male relatives' lifetime. The preponderance of men's over women's wills in the sample (72 per cent men and 28 per cent women) was not only because testators were confined to widows and spinsters by the rules of coverture, but also because many widows were never able to exercise that right. Sometimes the limits are explicitly stated in the wills. Many wives inherited the use of the property only until their children reached majority, while others were allowed its benefit 'as long as she remain my widow and no longer'. A Birmingham artist who died in 1840 left approximately £200 to his wife in the form of a pub and nine houses, but only during her life and even then with conditions. If she were to remarry or to break up the household and stop giving the son a comfortable home, then the young man was to get 7 shillings a week from the property towards his maintenance and no future husband of the widow was to have any rights over the inheritance. At his wife's death the property was to go to his son and his wife's son by a former marriage, the shares carefully spelled out.[17] In an analysis of Colchester wills for the lower sector of the middle class, D'Cruze found a decline of widows given a major control of the property from 42 per cent before 1805 to 27 per cent after that date and those who were left a life interest only almost doubled.[18] Our own sample of wills for both areas shows a 12 per cent increase in men who controlled all aspects of legacies left to widows.

The disabilities which women faced in consolidating property are also indicated by the fact that they more often specified multiple legacies in distributing their own property. One-third of women named more than five legatees but only one-fifth of men, a pattern even more marked in the lower middle class. Furthermore, women tended to leave personal effects and small parcels of money to named individuals, many of them wider kin or friends, a pattern which emphasizes both the dispersion and the personal nature of their property.[19] Finally, a father or uncle had the option in leaving an inheritance to instruct for the breaking of coverture, found in eighteen wills. Whatever a man's motives for this step – concern over keeping property in his line intact for a grandson or to protect his daughter's interests – the fact remained that unless he had made this particular stipulation a woman's inheritance passed to the legal control and use of her husband. In many cases, women undoubtedly used this property, even becoming the moving force in many a commercial undertaking, but the concept of dependence was nevertheless enshrined in such practices.

Patterns of ownership were closely related to patterns of control. It was primarily women who were the beneficiaries of 'passive' property yielding income only: trusts, annuities, subscriptions and insurance. Under the terms of a trust, the needs and wishes of the beneficiary were supposed to be fulfilled but interpretations could vary. Dr Dixon of Witham being called to act as a trustee noted in his diary that 'Miss Cox's present views are of entire indifference to me'.[20] The situation was particularly serious for an Essex woman who wanted to separate from her husband who had already borrowed money against her marriage settlement. Her only other source of income was an uncle's legacy for which her brother was a trustee. She finally managed to wrest control of her own property but only after much struggle.[21] The problem was that trustees were overwhelmingly male kin or friends of the family as we have seen in the sample of wills. In fact one of the most commonly named trustees was a son-in-law, in other words the husband of the woman whose property was in trust.

Even in those cases where women had a direct financial stake in the family enterprise, their legal status prevented them from active partnership. Their investment was often in the form of loans where the maximum they could receive was about 5 per cent in interest rather than sharing in the profits – and the risks – of partnerships.[22] The resulting economic vulnerability was enhanced for special groups of women. Evidence has already been presented concerning the anxiety of professional and salaried men whose incomes ended with their death. This lacuna was noted by the friends of an Essex professional man who had suddenly died leaving a widow with several small children and a capital of only about £50. They set about raising a subscription 'for the purpose of setting up Mrs Martin in some establishment, possibly a school, by which she may be enabled to educate and support her children respectably'. Mrs Martin did not even know of these efforts and was not consulted in any way. Her fate was completely in the hands of male well-wishers. Fortunately for her, the instigator of the subscription emphasized that Mrs Martin had 'conducted herself creditably through this trying time' and thus her proper behaviour was rewarded by male intervention on her behalf.[23]

A separated wife was in an even more unfavourable position. An Essex man who had been accused of a homosexual relationship fled the country to avoid arrest. Despite the fact that she had five young children, his wife was ostracized by her father and brother, who refused to even stand security for payment of her husband's debts. At last a local friend intervened noting with approval that the wife was known as the most active party within the business. His help enabled her to carry on the business, thus keeping both house and income intact. The friend had to intervene again when the husband returned demanding funds from his wife, money which was his by legal right.[24]

The characteristics of women's property reinforced their propensity to turn attention away from economic activity. A clergyman's widow living on the rent from an Essex farm, when pressed to make improvements in the buildings, replied that as she only had the benefit of the income during her lifetime, she should not be expected to bear the costs. Such a realistic assessment of her position partly explains her concern with maintaining a genteel lifestyle. Her sole aim was to extract maximum rent promptly paid from the property and she grumbled at requests for rent abatements in the hard times of the 1820s. Unlike the model ladies of the tracts, she cared little that her tenant had a large family or lacked sufficient capital to farm efficiently. A man might well have taken charge of this situation himself but the widow confessed to being too ignorant in such matters for her opinion to count. She had neither experience, education nor, above all, motivation to expand her property even if she could have been taken seriously in the world of market operations. In fact, she was unable to even stem the decline of prosperity in her little property and had placed herself completely in the hands of a somewhat shady but powerful Colchester attorney.[25]

It is not surprising that women were regarded as poor credit risks given their legal disabilities, dependence on male intervention and good will, and the short-term nature of their business ventures. It was more common for a woman to inherit or raise a lump sum than establish a viable credit chain to support an on-going enterprise. Banks remained wary of lending to women so that their sources of capital and credit continued to be mainly kin and friends well into the period when men were turning to other institutional sources. This general lack of commercial credibility was an important factor in the limited scale of women's business operations.

This is not to say that the *aggregate* of small investments held by women was not an important source of capital in early commercial and industrial development. Quite the contrary; economic historians have begun to recognize that women could make up a substantial proportion of those with financial resources.[26] When an Essex village vestry wanted to build a workhouse school they raised a loan by selling annuities, one-third of which were brought by women.[27] The portfolio of Mrs Henstridge Cobbold (*sic*) from the Ipswich brewing family included bonds in the local canal, rail road and insurance companies as well as the Ipswich Gas Light Company;[28] the last investment was also held by her friend Jane Ransome Biddell whose farmer husband acted as Mrs Cobbold's financial agent.[29] Nor should the above discussion give the impression that some women, at least, did not take an active interest in their own financial affairs: women such as the personal clients of Birmingham's earliest stockbroker, Nathaniel Lea.[30]

Nevertheless women's property, so closely tied to their lifecycle status of daughter, wife and widow, only allowed at most a semi-independence. This limitation was compounded by problems of maintaining their own and their family's status precisely by *not* being openly involved in market activities. Once these overlapping forces are understood, it becomes more understandable why it was so difficult for women to form groups based on mutual interest which also relied on mutual control and manipulation of funds or property. The formation of such groups was a commonplace for middle-class men. Men created and ran societies and organizations grounded on corporate property not only to conduct business but for political, cultural, intellectual and even social life. The bonds forged on the basis of communal control of funds contributed to group loyalties even if only a 'kitty' built up for an annual convivial evening at a local inn. There seem to be no female equivalents to these informal or semi-formal groups. Women could only operate property through kinship networks which, by definition, included both sexes. There is some evidence from the wills and census sample that sisters, and to a lesser extent, aunts and nieces, shared property as well as ways of making a livelihood in all-female households, but this was a mainly unmarried minority. The limitations on women's control of property, then, had not only serious implications for individuals but more generally for the ties of women to each other and the possibility of creating any but the most ephemeral alliances to support their mutual interests.[31]

Women's contribution to the enterprise

In the earlier part of the period when household and enterprise were so intermingled there was only a narrow line between the prohibition on married women acting in a business capacity and their encouragement to pledge their husband's credit as a housekeeper. As the nineteenth century progressed, however, the view hardened that female relatives were and should be dependants. The move to separate family affairs from business was a potent expression of these changes. The same forces which favoured the rise of the private company and ultimately the business corporation, the development of public accountability and more formal financial procedures also shifted the world of women ever further from the power of the active market.

Within this context, it is not surprising that the transformation of honorary positions into salaried posts which has been observed for men is scarcely discernible for women. There was no precedent for female access to a post such as parish clerk, for example, which became secularized in the nineteenth century. The parish clerk had derived from the clerical assistant to the priest, described in an Essex parish as 'a man who is able to make a will or write a letter for anyone in the parish . . . the universal father to give away brides, and the standing god-father to all new born bantlings'.[32] Women had to wait until the late nineteenth-century establishment of bureaucratic positions based on meritocratic principles for which they could prepare themselves and to which they could appeal.

A second consequence of economic dependency has been the overshadowing of women's contribution to the enterprise. Recent sociological studies have had to rediscover the vital part played by wives in small businesses and the support systems they provided for many male occupations, the recognition of women as a 'hidden investment'.[33] But in the nineteenth century female involvement in the enterprise was widespread, not just wives but also daughters, sisters, nieces, mothers, aunts, cousins and occasionally unrelated female 'friends'. First, there is abundant evidence for the direct contribution of women's capital to the family enterprise. The son of an Essex farmer whose brothers had all become farmers was able to combine his self-education with £800 brought by his wife at marriage to start a successful boys' school. When her father died leaving £600 the school was expanded into purpose-built premises.[34] Among the lower middle class, women were constantly used as sources of small sums to start off a business or as credit. In 1831, an Ipswich baker, facing a series of heavy financial demands, borrowed £4 from two of his sisters-in-law to pay off his flour supplier.[35]

This is a story repeated many times over. George Courtauld borrowed lump sums from his sister and a female friend in the early days of the Essex silk mill. When he married, he and his new bride, Ruth Minton, used her marriage portion to live on so that all profits could be re-invested in the mill. She saw this as part of her contribution along with keeping house. She wrote to a friend: 'I am no longer that useless, unconnected being who lived only for herself, a burden to her Friends.' When George later went to America leaving their eldest son, Samuel, in charge, Ruth Courtauld gave up her house which was mortgaged so that Samuel could start free of debt. She went to live with him at the Mill House paying £30 into the household expenses as well as acting as his housekeeper. Samuel acknowledged that this aid in money and kind carried the business through a critical period. In return, his mother gained both a home and livelihood, although at a lower standard. She also felt she had played an active role in the family establishment.[36]

The combination of women contributing resources and gaining a place was common. Dorothy Wordsworth when in her early 20s, lived as a 'mother's help' with her elder brother, a Suffolk vicar. After she had inherited her share of the family property (£1800 invested at 4 per cent), she and her brother William were able to set up housekeeping and later she helped care for William's children.[37] There was a variety of ways in which women made financial contributions to the enterprise. A sister asked no interest on a loan of £150 for the first three years of a manufacturing enterprise as well as keeping house and helping in the business.[38]

The skills and contacts women brought could enrich male careers. In food manufacturing businesses it was the recipe provided by a sister or a wife which became the secret of success.[39] Some women who had been in domestic service had access to employers' good will. A quondam master might stand guarantor or even give a legacy. A Birmingham bookseller's prosperous business was based on the batch of books given to his sister when she left service.[40] Service gave young women wider horizons and specialized skills. An Essex woman, having been an upper servant in a town family, returned to marry a man from a farming family who had descended to being a wage-paid team man. Marriage to this 'remarkable woman' who was able to do dressmaking as well as help run the farm, restored the family to independent farming.[41] Women like these sometimes provided one of the leading elements in commercial success, literacy. A contemporary who admired the wealth and position of an illiterate Birmingham auctioneer noted that:

Providence had given him a help-meet who conducted his correspondence, superintended his books, graced his hospitable board, and otherwise, by the ease and unaffected politeness of her demeanour, and the use of good, sound common sense, had contrived to make his name respected and his acquaintaince deserved by men of all grades and people of all denominations.[42]

It has been recognized that personal contacts played a central role in the functioning of both household and enterprise. Men took a keen interest in these affairs, their letters and diaries are filled with gossip about family and friends and their attendance at social gatherings. Nevertheless, women held a special place in building and maintaining relationships. Sisters, aunts, grandmothers and female cousins were ardent matchmakers. They arranged visits for their offspring and themselves paid long visits to relatives. They gave and received gifts. It was the farmer's wife who provided the Christmas goose to be dispensed to patrons and kin. A mill owner's wife admitted that she wrote letters more often than her husband for 'he considered it more my providence to keep up a correspondence with our distant relatives and friends'.[43] The fact that women more often designated people by name when leaving their small properties at death – a locket to a niece, a petticoat to a sister – emphasizes the importance of personal contacts in their lives.

Women's contribution to the enterprise was centred above all in the creation of its personnel. The marriage of sisters and daughters was a prime source of partners. But beyond this, women bore and raised the next generation of sons and nephews, the future partners and entrepreneurs. This task must, indeed, have consumed much time and energy for mothers and the other women involved, particularly as the physical and moral care of children had become a serious and self-conscious issue. The average of seven plus children born to a family absorbed the married woman's life span from her late 20s (average age at birth of first child was 27.3) to her 40s (average age at birth of last child was 40.6), with birth intervals of fourteen to twenty months.[44] Aunts and older sisters also played a prominent part in raising children. They, like mothers, provided the orderly, disciplined framework which was the basis of the serious Christian household. These women saw moral and religious training as the core of their educational function. They also recognized the importance of understanding the natural world, often seen as an adjunct of the Creator's great design. Even the youngest children were started on the path to habits of self-discipline, fitting for both a commercial and religious future. The daughter of a farmer married to a bank manager looked back in late middle age on the problems of child-rearing. She emphasized the need to arrange the day in a regular pattern of activities with time periods allotted to each. Even for a toddler sitting at a table stringing beads, 'there should be a degree of perfectness and even something approaching to business habits encouraged and expected even in these little amusements to give a worth and interest to them. Perfect play is the anticipation of perfect work'.[45]

In later childhood, boys were encouraged in their exposure to a working environment. An Essex woman ensured that her eldest son was taught the family foundry business from the bottom up, overseeing his instruction by a foreman and applauding his first efforts at casting a plough.[46] For girls, it was more a question of informal apprenticeships in the duties and skills of the household, although at times these overlapped with work for the enterprise. Primarily, however, their efforts were directed to servicing the household and manpower of the enterprise. Women trained not only their own daughters but nieces and other female relatives and friends. In the 1800s, a farming household took in the 15-year-old daughter of a distant relative, also a farmer, whose wife had just died leaving a family of younger children. The girl was taught to run a farmhouse so that she could bake and generally take over the household for her father.[47]

Women played an important role in caring for pupils, shop men, apprentices as well as nephews, nieces and their younger siblings or those of their husbands who might be resident in the household. In addition to providing meals, clean linen and tidy rooms, women were responsible for the moral and emotional development of these young people. An advertisement for an apprentice in a local Birmingham paper assured its readers that the successful applicant would be treated as one of the family.[48] How much provision of either a material or psychological kind was actually given depended on the resources of the family and the personality of the women in charge. Memoirs do indicate, however, that a young aunt, a school-master's wife and others in similar positions could have a strong influence on some boys in their commercial, intellectual or religious development.

Next to wives, daughters and sisters were the most important group in providing these services to households. They took over the care of children left motherless through death in childbirth; they followed their brothers to other towns or villages when they went to set up a new business. In 1822, a corn merchant who had been supporting his mother and seven younger siblings since he was a very young man came to Birmingham, accompanied by his sister as housekeeper. She remained with him in this capacity since his wife died within a year. It was only after his sister's marriage in 1846 that he married again.[49] The organizing and running of these households could reach the proportions of many commercial establishments. A Witham grocer's household included eight children and five male assistants, while establishments of up to a dozen were not unknown.[50] Clergymen who took in pupils or ran small schools regularly catered for from half a dozen to twenty pupils, the average number of resident boys in schools in the two areas being fifteen.[51]

Even unrelated women friends or female relatives not living in the household could play a part in middle-class youths' development. Henry Crabb Robinson, who later became a well-known man of letters in London, was the son of a Bury St Edmunds tanner. His education and general cultural development was taken in hand by Catherine Buck a woman friend of the family, half-a-dozen years his senior. Her own intellectual accomplishments must have been of a high order since she later became the close friend of Dorothy and William Wordsworth and the wife of Thomas Clarkson, philanthropist and anti-slavery advocate. She was instrumental in introducing Crabb Robinson to the London literary world, although she remains unpublished and unknown.[52]

These instances may support the contention that, in a broad sense, women contributed cultural as well as monetary capital to the economic life of the middle class. Both these forms, however, were more indirect than the use of women's labour. Where property and educational resources were more limited, there is abundant evidence that women were working at a wide variety of tasks within the family enterprise. Their general usefulness was recognized in the advice given to young Samuel Courtauld by a business associate of his father: 'if a good wife fell in your way I would take her as an assistant even though she may not be rich in the World's wealth'.[53]

Occasional or even continuous use of wives', daughters' or sisters' labour was easier when living quarters were near or in the working space. As late as 1854, a letter from the wife of an Essex tradesman assumed the combination of household and commercial tasks: 'In settling into my new home and duties here in the business-house, I have earnestly desired to fill my situation rightly, to be enabled to walk before our household in the fear of the Lord.'[54] In some cases, the wife would run a business next door to and often related to that of her husband, thus in the directories are found husband and wife teams of a clockmaker and tea dealer, a grocer and pork butcher. In villages, the wife or daughter/sister of a farmer might use the front room as a small shop. At a more elevated level, James Bissett, who was a Birmingham manufacturer of some standing, enjoyed a hobby of collecting to the point where he turned his house into a commercial museum run by his wife.[55]

Some enterprises were premised on the steady use of female family labour. Schools were jointly run not only because women serviced the boarding pupils, but because they also taught, if only knitting and needlework to the girls. Many salaried positions for men encouraged or even required a female adjunct. Under the terms of an Essex charity, the schoolmaster was paid £32 a year to teach thirty poor boys while his wife, unpaid, was responsible for the forty girls.[56] Retail trade, in particular, enabled women of the household not only to help out but often to be the *de facto* means of providing a livelihood. A Quaker who inherited his uncle's drapery shop 'depended much on his young wife for its effective management'. Her involvement in the shop was recalled by a family story that, when suddenly called away to a customer, she popped the then baby (there were nine children) into an open drawer and forgot where she had put it.[57]

Within the family business there were diverse roles women could play. Emma Gibbins held dinner parties for the partners after meetings of the Digbeth Battery Works conveniently located next door to the house.[58] The wives and daughters of several Witham solicitors regularly witnessed wills, which implies that they may also have copied documents and performed other clerical tasks. An Essex estate agent was proud of his daughter's business ability as she copied all her father's large correspondence.[59] A draper's wife represented her husband at an important funeral – an unusual step for a women – when he was 'all alone in the shop' and could not go.[60] Women might step in when husband, father or brother were ill or absent. They took messages, fended off importunate clients or creditors and ordered supplies. During harvest, if not raking hay or stacking corn, women provided the extra baking and brewing for the field workers. Even the rather flighty 17-year-old whose mid century diary is filled with genteel visiting and hints at attachments with young men, breaks off in June to record that she and her two sisters 'have been working at hay making in the Mill Fields' which prevents her visiting but, 'I don't dislike it half as much as I thought'.[61] Female family labour was called in to cope with specific problems or crises in the enterprise, and many such a success story must have resembled the coach proprietor who built up a business from a small beginning through 'downright industry and systematic application to business in which the female members of the family were called to assist'.[62] The implication is that once a modest level of prosperity had been reached, the female members could withdraw.

The extreme case of women's labour used to make up for the absence of male support was widowhood. The pattern of widows as temporary incumbents of an enterprise discerned in the wills is confirmed from more qualitative sources. Frequently the sequence followed the story of the Woodcock family of High Street, Colchester. William Woodcock had run a watch, clockmaking, goldsmiths and jewellers business. When he became ill, his wife, Ann, added an agency for the East India tea company. He died soon afterwards and she carried on the business with the aid of a journeyman. In 1828, her son married and took over the business which his mother had been holding for him and she retired, now aged 51, to a cottage at the rear of the shop with her three unmarried daughters.[63] It was not unknown for the widows of bankers, merchants and other highly placed families to play a similar part. The widow of Samuel Alexander directed the influential Ipswich bank during the interim before her son took over, while Boulton and Watt of Birmingham continued to deal with the widow of their London banker for many years.[64]

Some young men benefited from this arrangement where their mother (step-mother, aunt) provided an enhanced patrimony by the time they came of age. Maria Savill, the young widow of an Essex builder, despite her responsibility for ten children and two step-children, built up the family business as a spring board for her son to become a successful architect and surveyor and founder of a family firm prominent among Chartered Surveyors for the rest of the century.[65] Nevertheless, the social and business climate made it difficult for a widow to do more than hold her own economically, and many must have either chosen or been forced to settle for small incomes supplemented by traditional women's expedients such as taking in lodgers. Their children would almost certainly lose out in the economic stakes.

Women were expected to move in and out of positions directly supporting the family enterprise. They were accustomed to earning small sums of money in the interstices of household management. Farmer's wives and other female relatives were kept busy smoking, pickling and perserving food as well as daily cooking and baking. Not only did these finishing processes feed the household but 'keeping a good table' was part of their claim to respect in the rural community. It was possible to combine these activities with selling a few goods or services, although records tell us very little about the extent and variety of such income. How much, in fact, did the wife of an Essex farmer benefit from her cow keeping as reported in her husband's diary: 'Total amount for the two Alderney's made in the Year, £50.6.6. My wife took for her hard labour in managing the two cows £5.0.0 and I received £45.6.6 like all other lazy persons for doing nothing.' He also paid his daughter-in-law small sums for rearing puppies for him and his married sister one penny each for ducks she had raised.[66]

Dressmaking, plain sewing and other tasks related to domestic needs would be the most obvious ways of making extra cash, but writing and teaching were also commonly fitted into a household routine. There were more unusual possibilities: Ann Constable, John's eldest sister, bred dogs.[67] Such sidelines provided goods for the household, brought in a little extra cash or in some cases were a pastime for the women of the family. The common factor in many women's activities in households at all levels, however, was that they were seldom paid as individuals. A sister working in her brother's shop, daughters working for their parents, wives with their husbands, seldom had a regular or fixed wage. A woman who had entered a clergyman's household as a religious disciple and unpaid mother's help began to supplement the family income by teaching in the evening, but found that her pupil's parents paid the minister for her services.[68]

As long as the household was able to support its members, the lack of individualized income was not serious. It should be kept in mind that an individual wage did not yet have the symbolic identification with personal worth which it acquired in the twentieth century. But when women were left without support, often also without a home and social place, they might be particularly vulnerable. Often they were left with partial income such as an annuity, too low to support a respectable lifestyle no matter how circumscribed. Such women were forced to move from one relative or friend to another, caring for children, nursing the sick, giving a hand in the shop, acting as companion to an elderly aunt or uncle. The suspicion that even married women might be contributing more than their share to the household establishment and selling short their own interests was seldom voiced. But the wife of a businessman who had retired at 60 with barely enough to maintain a respectable lifestyle and nothing much to occupy his time did have reservations. She had married him to escape the drudgery of school teaching and despite a devout commitment to the values of domesticity she had a sharp eye for women's position. 'The wasted hours of most men would do almost half the work of women', she wrote to a like-minded friend.[69]

In 1809, the *Ipswich Journal* ran an advertisement for a schoolmistress whose most important skills included good manners and correct conduct: 'Any lady of reduced fortune possessing the above accomplishments and being less desirous of a salary than of obtaining an eligible situation, will meet with kind and liberal treatment from the principal of the school.'[70] Such a proposition reveals that women, with some education and culture, were regarded as being able to enhance the reputation or at least give a tone of respectability to an establishment, whether a school or their own household. The appearance and behaviour of the mistress, especially when on display at church or chapel or at public events, proclaimed the reputability of the enterprise as clearly as her bonnets or dresses indicated its spending power. An Essex agent for many large estates noted in his diary how pressure from many landlords favoured Anglican communicants. He also noted that wives were almost always consulted about leases; their sobriety, sense and experience could make a difference as to whether leases would be granted, the terms and renewals.[71]

In their capacity as status bearers for their households, adult women faced a number of contradictory pressures. They were expected to be seen at specified public functions and often had to go from home to pay visits, if not buy household supplies or do errands for the family business. But over the period there was increasing social derogation for women who openly walked or rode horseback except for non-utilitarian recreational or health reasons. In the eighteenth century, a prosperous farmer and brewer's wife thought nothing of riding on horseback the 20 odd miles from her village to the market town to transact her business.[72] But with the growing emphasis on the protection of women, light-wheeled vehicles came to be their acceptable mode of transport, although more expensive to maintain than riding horses. Lack of access to means of mobility and the risks of losing status by being seen in many public places, particularly alone, was a serious disadvantage to a woman doing business.

Such obstacles to physical and social mobility were part of the way status considerations encouraged women to play down selling themselves or their products. Three sisters left in a precarious financial position by the bankruptcy and death of their father, manager for a Suffolk shipping company, turned to writing popular history books. Despite the urging of their guardian and trustee, they often refused payment for their work.[73] For farmers, the various corn, cattle and produce markets were their club where 'gossip of the countryside could be exchanged', particularly information about prices, turnover of farms and new farming practices. Not only were such markets off limits for women with pretensions to gentility, but their adjunct, the public house market day 'ordinary' was hardly a venue for women. By the 1830s, a Suffolk man commented on the notoriety of a female cattle dealer who sat with other dealers at The Swan, drinking and smoking a pipe and locally known as 'The Duchess', by that date considered an eccentric.[74] The change to formal marketing with its male ambience, from the financing by boards of trustees to the convivial dinners held in their spacious halls, was a serious disincentive to women.

The contributions to the enterprise through women's labour were contradicted by their role in displaying rank through the appearance of a non-working lifestyle. This contradiction was related to the more general conflict between achieving a commodious lifestyle and the more religious or cultural emphasis on education and learning, despite protestations that a religious commitment was compatible with a comfortable home life. This latent controversy was often played out by women who were particularly associated with setting the tone of the family lifestyle. Those groups whose claims were solidly based on property – the manufacturers, tradesmen and farmers – were able to build their material 'plant' in a way which was often hard to match for the spokesmen of middle-class values, the clergy. In the countryside, where farmers and clergy formed the backbone of the middle class undiluted by other groups, farmers' female relatives came in for particular criticism for their status pretensions. The wives and daughters of clergymen had seen themselves as leaders of refinement, but nevertheless looked uneasily over their shoulders as wartime prosperity raised the position of their uncultivated neighbours. There was less friction where farmers' families found themselves in areas without resident clergy and playing a leading role against superstition, folk belief and what was viewed as rural ignorance and apathy. Against this they pitted both their intense conversionist religion, commitment to scientific modes of thought and conceptions of respectable behaviour. The less educated or well travelled among the farming group might take an intermediate position on issues such as beliefs in ghosts but on the whole they enthusiastically supported more modern ideals. In the early nineteenth century, a Quaker farmer's wife, recently moved to an extremely remote area in Suffolk and acting as the sole 'lady' of the village, took on such a role when she deliberately exposed her young children to smallpox after having them vaccinated to demonstrate the efficacy of the new frightening procedure to the villagers.[75]

While all groups were deeply committed to the concept of domesticity and women's sphere within it, the explicit statement of these values seems to have been somewhat greater among the households of professional men: army officers, medical men and above all the clergy. It may have been that they were more frequently left without means of support than among those whose livelihood stemmed from more solid property. Their education and background emphasized literacy and, furthermore, their direct contribution to the professional man's earning capacity was more problematic.[76] Mary Ann Hedge, a committed spinster parishioner of the Evangelical William Marsh's church of St Peter's Colchester, wrote books for children, moral tales and novels. In one of these, her heroine was of high degree but her husband had been 'reduced' to acting as land agent to an earl. This female paragon not only does all the household cooking but draws and paints so that when her husband falls ill, she pleads to finish some sketches due for his employer. Mary Ann Hedge's approval is echoed in the husband's acknowledgement that 'the World has admired *as mine* works which were the effort of conjugal affection'.[77] This view effectually conceals the actual economic position of women within the household by presenting the wife's actions in terms of affection and moral duty. Hedge's notion of a wife's role is expressed in language suitable to a scion of a clock manufacturer's family: a wife is to be 'the grand-spring that sets in motion all the machinery of domestic comfort in regular and harmonious motion'.[78] Similar pressures were brought to bear on daughters. For example, the preparation of goods for sale could take place in back premises where the daughter with aspirations to gentility could be shielded from being seen in public but their labour might also be needed to serve customers. The balance between helping out the family enterprise by cheerfully undertaking such duties and an anxiety about maintaining the family's social standing is a constant theme in the literature aimed at young women as we have seen in Jane Taylor's novel, *Display*.

Nowhere were the contradictions and their consequences for individual women more evident than in the attitudes towards widows and their livelihood. Having proved their feminine commitment through marriage, widows were given legal and customary sanctions to enter the market. Indeed, they were often expected to be able to support themselves and their dependent children in a reversal of their acknowledged dependency within marriage, a position sometimes brutally thrust upon them. However, they were not expected to aspire beyond self-support. At a time when the unrestrained pursuit of business by men was still a questionable virtue, it was abhorrent in a woman. The Suffolk poet, George Crabbe, celebrated the wife and mother who died young; her place in the garden, the fireside chair, the church pew were hallowed by reverent memories. She is contrasted with the surviving widow, her head full of accounts, ruling her household with a rod of iron, whose sons long for her death.[79] Few widows had the option of remaining in active business with high incomes. Realistically a widow's chances of operating near that level were remote and above all such ambition ran against the grain of feminine propriety. The bankers, solicitors and agents as well as fellow (*sic*) traders, merchants, farmers or manufacturers with whom she would have to deal would have been men with firm ideas of proper feminine behaviour. For those widows who could, it was easier to retire on to a fixed income. In the 1790s, Matthew Boulton wrote to his partner about the sale of an iron manufactory, reporting that the 'assigned reason for selling is that many of the company are females, who do not find it convenient to carry on such extensive concerns'.[80] By mid century inconvenience had changed to social catastrophe.

Widows faced a range of difficulties. For example, as farming became more rationalized and profit oriented, those landowners who had invested heavily in improvements sought tenants who would be 'intelligent and enterprising',[81] not the received stereotype of a widow. George Eliot, an estate steward's daughter, described a fictional case of the farmer's widow whose husband's dying wish had been for her to carry on the farm. When she goes to plead her case with the landlord she is dismissed in just these terms of an appeal to both the supposed capacities and right conduct of femininity. 'You are about as able to carry on a farm as your best milch cow. You'll be obliged to have some managing man, who will either cheat you out of your money, or wheedle you into marrying him.' The landlord goes on to predict that the farm will run down and she will get in arrears with the rent. She argues back that she knows 'a deal o'farming an' was brought up i' the thick on it' and that her husband's great-aunt managed a farm for twenty years and left legacies to her 'nephys an' nieces. Phsa! a woman six feet high with a squint and sharp elbows, I daresay – a man in petticoats; not a rosy cheeked widow like you'. This widow knows that once all the stock have been sold and debts paid she will have hardly anything to live on. Since this is fiction, the secretly benevolent landlord arranges to have a cottage let to her at low rent with a plot for a cow and some pigs where she will be able to live in suitable retirement.[82]

However, landlords in the real world, while subscribing to a similar view of women's place, were not as helpful or were often unable to be as liberal. John Oxley-Parker, the agent for a large number of landowners in mid Essex in the 1830s, was called in to negotiate the lease of a widow who had kept on a farm after her husband's death. Along with her neighbouring farmers and her brother-in-law, he urged her to give up the attempt. He noted in his diary in connection with this case how important it was for tenants to have both character and capital. The questions he asked himself about a prospective tenant were: 'Was he an energetic farmer? Did he know his job and use his initiative in doing it?' Oxley-Parker finally urged the widow to throw herself on the mercy of the landlord, a member of a wealthy Colchester banking and farming family, but to no avail and she had to leave the farm with no compensation.[83]

For many women, however, a release from the drudgery and anxiety of economic activity was a realistic ambition, not to be dismissed simply as status striving. The prosperous farmer dressed in white buckskin trousers and beaver hat riding over his acres, directing his men, attending market was 'working' but very much in a managerial capacity. So too the farmer's wife aspired to be freed from heavy manual tasks. A farmer's daughter who remembered the work involved in the hot dinners with boiled beef and, at Harvest, special cakes and home brewed beer, was not surprised that 'farmer's wifes were glad when the men boarded themselves and all their wage was paid in money' although it 'snapped some of the ties which bound the servant and master as fellow creatures'.[84]

The majority of women knew that they would have to work within the household if not the enterprise. It was rather the way their contribution was defined which was significant. The evolution of the concept of work in relation to women's activities is suggestive here. Catherine Marsh, Rev. William Marsh's daughter, growing up first in Colchester and then Birmingham as part of an Evangelical household, was held up as a model of feminine behaviour as she helped her father in his ministerial duties. She wrote letters, saw callers and ran the house after her mother's death. Her friend and biographer recalls that Catherine was always busy, always 'working'. She defined this term: 'Fine needlework in young days and when there was a later fashion for crochet bonnets she quickly made 27 for her friends.'[85] 'Berlin wool work' first made its appearance in Colchester in 1796 and was seen as initiating the vogue for amateur needlework and 'useless' crafts, characteristic of nineteenth-century middle-class women's definition of work.[86]

Women, then did not necessarily conceive of themselves as 'working', but they did have a stern conception of duty, the moral imperatives which made them ever ready family aids. They expected and were expected by others to be on call to help family and friends. After his wife's death, the childless shopkeeper, John Perry, made constant calls on the support of his relatives. Among others, his unmarried niece came to stay to help him 'in the department of looking over my linen'.[87] Yet some of the more prescient seemed to have been aware of their vulnerable position. The daughters of a silk merchant tried to educate themselves, partly for enjoyment but also, as one wrote, they had 'early seen how precarious was the tenure of wealth derived from business with its incessant fluctuations'.[88]

The education of women and its effects

Like men, women's first duty was to train themselves for a religious life. But for women this could also be the central aim of education. When Jane Taylor, as editor of a religious youth's magazine, was consulted about a young lady's education she answered: 'The grand end which we ought to propose to ourselves in every intellectual study is *moral* improvement' (her emphasis).[89] Learning was to be used in the service of others. The young sister of a Colchester Independent minister struggled against ill health to 'gain more knowledge to enable me to become an agreeable and suitable companion' to her beloved elder brother.[90] But in addition, since women were regarded as central to the image of family status, their training was directed to that end. The arts, drawing, piano playing, knowledge of French which became the staple, and much derided, fare of female accomplishments, were deliberately paraded as being the opposite of business duties. A tradesman's daughter whose experience had been in teaching young boys tried to obtain a position as a schoolmistress. She could offer a sound grounding in grammar, geography and arithmetic but every advertisement, even for farmer's families in the country required music, French and the various accomplishments of what was called a 'genteel education'.[91] Catherine Hutton recalled in later years that when she was growing up in the Birmingham of the 1770s there was no boarding schools for girls. The day school she went to provided an education limited to spelling and reading from the Bible plus a little needlework.[92]

Given these restricted facilities, what went on in the family was central to girls' development. Some more progressive parents like the members of Birmingham's Lunar Society taught their daughters in the same mode as their sons. One of the society, Erasmus Darwin, published *A Plan for the Conduct of Female Education in Boarding Schools* in 1797, a most enlightened document. Not only did he argue for the importance of girls being educated at school rather than at home, he also wanted science and mathematics in the curriculum.[93] A modest Birmingham manufacturer was ready to sacrifice his dining room furniture for the education of his children, both his sons and daughters.[94] Thus a minority of middle-class girls, especially those from professional families, were exposed to a general liberal education. The aims of that education, however, were specifically non-vocational. Unlike their brothers, such young women were not expected to add vocational training. Even the occasional high standards achieved in painting, music or languages were contained within an amateur framework.[95] In 1805 a girl from a Unitarian Essex family, who had been taught Latin by her father, carefully copied a maxim attributed to Arthur Young into her commonplace book: 'The conversation of men not engaged in trifling pursuits is the best school for the education of women.'[96] Undoubtedly where there was an intellectually inquiring atmosphere in the home and men were committed to the education of their daughters and sisters, young women had a better chance of a broad exposure to a variety of subjects than in the confines of girls' schools. Home education was also preferred since girls' moral and physical development could be more closely supervised and the centrality of the family enhanced.

Most middle-class girls were excluded from the staple fare of the reformed grammar schools as well as the new boys' academies. The original foundation of many grammar schools had been for the respectable poor of both sexes, but had long been appropriated for middle-class boys. Of the 593 adult males in an Essex village at the turn of the century, fifty-six had had a free education at the local grammar school, almost all sons of farmers and tradesmen but also a few 'mechanics'. A handful of these boys, including the two sons of the vicar, took up the annual free place at Christ Church, Cambridge offered through the grammar school.[97] None of these opportunities would have been possible for local girls. Basic Latin and Greek, the ticket for entry into law, medicine and the Anglican clergy, were effectively closed to girls as well as the newer commercial and scientific subjects, although the latter were sometimes offered in a watered down version. Botany, for example, was rewritten for young women with the sexual classification of plants expurgated.[98] Natural history subjects were offered for their moral and religious analogies as much as scientific potential. 'The study of nature leads us to nature's God' wrote Mary Ann Hedge, in a book on the training of girls.[99]

Parents, making a realistic expectation of economic returns from their children's education, invested more heavily for boys. Girls were expected to make do with the teaching of unpaid kin and friends. It was at the margins that these decisions were especially significant, as when a small farmer sent his sons to school but refused to let his daughters go since they needed only to milk, sew, cook and bear children.[100] When girls attended school, their commitment might be less than their brothers. A newly opened seminary for Young Ladies and Gentlemen in Ipswich in 1809 offered reduced prices for 'Young Ladies whose other engagements allow them to attend only half days.'[101] Girls could expect their schooling to last only a year or two or to be interrupted by family demands. The daughter of the manager of a small town gas works was brought back from boarding school to help in the house since no servant was kept.[102] Boys, too, would be recalled to enter the family business, if necessary, but the disjunction between the content and form of their education and their subsequent business life was not as great. Home education could be even more easily set aside if parents or older siblings who were teaching had other demands on their time. The regime of the governess and visiting master was only employed by the wealthiest already committed to a general education for their daughters. For the others, their lessons often had to be fitted in around general household schedules and the distractions of the family business.

Emily Shore was the daughter of a rural clergyman who also boarded half a dozen pupils. A bright child, she was taught Latin and Greek by her father and English and history by her mother. Even at an early age she was teaching her younger siblings. In 1831, at age 13, she wrote a sketch, 'The Interruptions', illustrating the impossibility of reading an extract of history to her mother as the housemaid, cook and nursemaid wanted directions, callers came to the door, a thimble was lost and the younger children wanted attention. Emily Shore's routine included afternoon calls with her mother, visits to the poor and Sunday school teaching, all regarded as equally if not more important than her intellectual development. Undirected, she veered between a passionate, and somewhat guilty love of poetry and a self-imposed heroic programme of reading and rote learning complete with wall charts, a not unusual combination for girls with such tastes. Such an agenda had no aims and no end, either in its own terms or in recognition from external bodies or in leading to an occupation. Often such preoccupations looked odd if not selfish or even immoral. In her mid teens, Emily experienced a breakdown which she interpreted as having 'overtaxed my strength with study' and turned to learning housekeeping which she had previously despised but which now made her feel useful.[103]

Girls from wealthy and cultured homes, such as the Galton and Moilliet banking families of Birmingham, were educated by mothers who themselves were freed from involvement in the enterprise and who had enough help in the household to take their daughters' training seriously. This was supplemented by special teachers coming in for music, languages and dancing plus the odd year at boarding school.[104] In homes with a good library and encouragement to use it, some women in the upper echelons were able to reach high levels of literary and even scholarly achievement. These young women were also likely to be offered at least a limited form of travel within Great Britain if not abroad, a favourite theme in their travels being literary excursions, as, for example, the visit of an Ipswich girl to the setting of Scott's novels.[105] These were the young women who also benefited from long visits to the homes of relatives and friends which widened their horizons. Jane Ransome Biddell, born 1782, was the Quaker daughter of a wealthy Ipswich manufacturer. Both before and after her marriage to an equally wealthy Anglican farmer, through her education and cultural activities she had entry into the upper echelons of the town. She was an admiring friend of local elite families like the Cobbolds, owners of a local brewing firm who themselves had produced a group of clergymen and women who helped to set the tone of Ipswich society. A woman like Jane Ransome Biddell had a housekeeper to aid her management of the household of nine children. She might well have had more time for cultural pursuits than her busy husband who was immersed in the farm and surveying business. She wrote poetry, some of which was published in local newspapers.[106]

Continued self-education was permitted to women like Jane Biddell. It was rather the women in the middle and lower ranks who were culturally most disadvantaged. Their sole avenue of mental cultivation was the Sunday school. There were no facilities beyond the lending libraries which often gave limited access to women. The Mechanics Institutes and Literary and Philosophical Societies which were so important for their male equivalents were usually closed to young women. They might only be admitted to selected public functions or borrow books to read at home; occasionally to use the reading rooms at prescribed times. The Colchester Literary Society only allowed women to use the rooms after 5 p.m. in the later nineteenth century when subscriptions were falling.[107] In most cases, women were excluded from both regular meetings and discussion groups or managing committees. Lower subscriptions and admission fees for women reflect both their secondary status and less ready access to cash. At the Ipswich Mechanics Institute in the 1840s, the novelty of a woman lecturing on women's issues received full press coverage but little local support.[108] The Book Clubs, Debating Societies, and Natural History Field Clubs which were heavily used by apprentices and shopmen were for the most part off limits to young women. Only Quaker and some nonconformist circles encouraged semi-formal outlets for both 'youths and maidens'.

The effect of such a regime on the lives of young women, particularly among those not elevated enough to benefit from a liberal education or lowly enough to take a full part in making a living, was to promote a concept of respectability which began to close off knowledge of the world outside family, friends and co-religionists. Bowdlerized reading matter and lack of experience combined to create a real need for male protection, not least in financial affairs. An exclusive interest in the home, either as the site of a status-enhancing lifestyle or a religious commitment for themselves and their children, reinforced the disinterest in business affairs being put forward in the pescriptive literature. Undoubtedly there were many discrepancies between the aphorisms and ideals copied into girls' commonplace books and the circumstances of their own lives. But to underestimate the effect of such literature would be foolhardy, particularly when it was combined with property forms which reinforced dependence. The preponderance of historical records from men and the shadowy forms of many women's lives makes the interpretation of this problem even more acute. It is almost impossible to know how a woman like Elizabeth Gardener, wife of a brewer and wine merchant in a small Essex town, was regarded or how she saw herself in relation to the family business. The firm was run by her husband from an office in the house next door to the brewery. In the 1840s their income was enough to employ a nurse and two maids to help with the six children, leaving Mrs Gardner free for local philanthropic ventures such as penny readings as well as a social life including friendship with the vicar. She was, however, also intimately connected to the brewery to the point where she was able to take over when her husband died and the business became known as E. Gardner and Son.[109]

Women as teachers

Official sources only allow a detailed knowledge of the occupations of widows and spinsters. By far the largest group of these women, 63 per cent, were listed as 'independent'. Of women in active occupations, the category of professional was most common; undoubtedly mostly school-mistresses either owning their own schools or employed by others. Professionals were followed by trade and then by innkeeping and farming. In part, the occupations of women, as of men, depended on the area. In 1851, female headed households in farming predominated in the villages, for example, while the highest proportion of salaried female heads were found in central Birmingham.[110] In all areas, however, when women were called upon to contribute income or become the sole support of a household, as Mrs Gaskell's little Miss Matty knew, 'teaching was, of course, the first thing that suggested itself'.[111] As the period neared mid century, teaching became the only occupation in which middle-class women could preserve something of their status. By 1851, women made up 64 per cent of the teaching force in Essex and 79 per cent in Birmingham.[112]

A variety of factors attracted women to teaching in addition to its relatively high status. Teaching was seen as an extension of childrearing which was being given special emphasis within serious Christianity. It needed few resources and little training to enter. Changes in the location and methods of instructing the young were making teaching into a more recognized activity, less casual and more formal but not to the point where women were forced out. As with many other activities, to be a schoolmaster or mistress was not necessarily a fixed occupation, although there were moves in that direction. Teaching could be taken up as a by-employment by women running households or engaged in a different family business.[113]

Like other enterprises, too, schools were embedded in the local economy, the commodity of 'education' to be exchanged for other goods and services. An advertisement in a Birmingham paper of 1820 states:

> A genteel school in the vicinity of Birmingham, has now a vacancy for three young ladies as scholars, where their religious and moral education will be strictly attended to. As the Establishment has neither a Miller, Draper, nor Grocer's daughter, the Advertiser would be glad to receive either, as their consumption in each article is very considerable.[114]

Women, as much as men, used religious networks to gain pupils; their membership of a church or chapel would gain them credibility and draw pupils to their school. The close association between religion and teaching meant that when choosing a mistress for a working-class school, religious connections could be the key to a salaried post.

For school proprietors, formal partnerships were not as common as in other business since capital requirements were less. There were arrangements falling between outright ownership of a school and salaried teaching, such as subcontracting to take pupils for a capitation fee. Working partnerships between husband and wife were common, although officially the husband usually owned the school. Elizabeth Fry in her correspondence described William and Hannah Lean's Quaker school in Birmingham as theirs but in the directory it is listed in his name only.[115] Rowland Hill was partner with his father after a long period of serving in the family run boys' school, Hazelwood, in Birmingham. After his father's retirement, new articles of partnership were drawn up between those brothers still involved with the school. Mrs Hill, who had been instrumental in the early days of the foundation, and the two Hill sisters were no longer even included in the business meetings; there was no question of them being legally incorporated in either ownership or management.[116]

One reason for their exclusion was that Hazelwood was a school for older boys. There was no way that young women could take a position of authority in such a setting, even if they had had the necessary classical education. Mary Carpenter who had been educated alongside the boys in her father's academy had also helped with teaching. In 1826 when her father, Lant Carpenter, collapsed with acute depression, an ex-student, James Martineau, was called in to take his place in school and chapel while Mary was sent as governess to a family. In 1829 the boys' school was closed down and Mrs Carpenter, running the domestic side, and Mary doing the teaching, opened a girls' school to support the family. Mary was bored with having to teach a young ladies' curriculum but there was no way she could have maintained the boys' school.[117] By convention, women were confined as both school proprietors and teachers to girls' schools and schools for both sexes under about the age of 7.

A large proportion of the early nineteenth-century educational effort was undoubtedly aimed at the middle class. In the 1840 Birmingham survey, at least one-third of the children between 5 and 15 who were getting some education were at the 'superior schools' and home tuition would raise this figure. Rewards for teachers varied and profits were by no means great except for the largest and therefore almost always, boys' schools. Staff in schools like Birmingham's King Edward's Grammar, where teachers were almost entirely ordained clergymen, had incomes in the £200 to £400 a year range which were then doubled by capitation fees.[118] These positions, in fact, were part of the route to clerical preferment, an option completely closed to women. The income and social standing of the pupils' parents determined the profit, income or status of the teacher. At one end were tiny village schools, such as the one in Suffolk started by the vicar in a former bricklayer's cottage. An ex-farmer and his wife were paid 10 shillings a week plus free housing and the pence they could collect from the children.

The wife was expected to teach the girls and see to the cleaning of the building.[119] Even more lowly, the dame school was usually little more than child-minding for the youngest children, often of working mothers. Nevertheless, occasionally the women who ran such schools were able to give more than basic reading and at least they were able to pick up a little income from such ventures. From the census sample, it would appear that many schoolmistresses were on the fringe of the middle class, particularly in the National or British and Foreign schools. Their male relations included agricultural labourers, small holders, auctioneers, a hostler and a coal carter. Female school teaching undoubtedly reached deeper into the working class than its masculine counterpart. This contributed to the low social standing of a woman in teaching, as Dora Pattison found when, as a vicar's daughter at mid century, she took the schoolmistresses' route to independence.[120]

The differential in salaries for men and women continued down the scale. The Witham National School in 1840 was offering £55 a year for a master and £35 for a mistress.[121] The higher amount paid to men was justified on the grounds that they would have a family to support and would be expected to teach extra, more highly valued subjects such as arithmetic and bookkeeping in the lower grade school and classics in the higher. Men were also more often better qualified. Many men and women in this period owed their own education and recruitment to teaching to the Sunday school movement. But for many women this remained their only experience. No girl would have had access to the university training which permitted a well-known minister to set up a school where fees of £100 a year could be charged.[122]

As a family enterprise, schools for boys and girls differed in their structure as well as aims and curriculum. There was no role for a man in most girls' schools since only the most prestigious and expensive schools provided masters in specialist subjects. Yet an adult female was almost an imperative in boys' and girls' schools alike, preferably a relative: wife, sister, mother, aunt. Her essential tasks were overseeing the domestic side, managing the servants, organizing food and linen, caring for children who were ill and generally supplying a home-like atmosphere. Even a small boarding establishment like the Leans' Birmingham Quaker school, with its six children of the family, added up to seventeen people for meals without the day boys. In 1817, when Hazelwood School had become a substantial establishment, Rowland Hill acknowledged that his mother was 'possessed of courage and spirit, and well adapted to the situation she occupies as manager of a large household'.[123] Girls' schools and the co-educational schools for younger children also used family labour, but it was almost entirely female on both the domestic management and teaching side. Often there was no formal agreement, but younger kin would act as an assistant, although partnerships between sisters, aunt and niece were not unknown.

In the census sample at mid century there were twenty-five schools with women heads and twelve with men. Two-thirds of the women running schools were single, the rest widowed compared to only 15 per cent of men, the remaining 85 per cent being married. However, the 'family atmosphere' felt as desirable for girls was evident in the relative sizes of school households. The average number of boarders in girls' schools was five pupils, compared to fifteen for boys. Taken all together, these schools housed twenty-three adult female relatives and visitors (excluding wives of married schoolmasters), most of whom would be involved in running the school. Of these, ten were sisters of the household head. Futhermore, women were more often found running small, day schools. In 1848, in Colchester, women headed ten day and four boarding schools, while men managed five day but six boarding establishments.[124]

Before the impact of domestic ideology had made women's sphere more synonymous with unpaid labour, there are more examples of married women running schools, especially if the family income was insecure. Mrs Ann Morgan married the Rev. Thomas Morgan, a Baptist minister, in 1803, a year after he had come to Birmingham's Cannon Street chapel where her father had been a deacon. From 1809, her husband's health deteriorated and he resigned in 1811. His stipend had been £100 since Cannon Street was a prosperous church. How was the family now to survive with four young children to support? As one of her sons later wrote, 'Then was the character of the wife and mother tested. On her seemed to be cast the burden of being the chief provider, for a time, for the support of their young family during that crisis of their lives, and she applied herself to undertake the duty.' Mrs Morgan set up a school and in 1813 was able to utilize the money from her marriage settlement, together with 'such other means and help as Mr Morgan could command', to buy a house in Moseley, a village 2 miles from Birmingham, then in countryside. The extra land provided a farming interest for Mr Morgan to the benefit of his health and the family's standard of living. Mrs Morgan managed to educate her own daughters in the school and make enough money to provide for her sons, educating them herself when young, later sending them away to school and further training. By 1820, Mr Morgan recovered sufficiently to take a co-pastorship and, by 1825, the family income was such and the children sufficiently launched for Ann Morgan to retire.[125]

This pattern is characteristic of most schools run by women. Necessity forced women to take on these responsibilities; with prosperity they withdrew. Therefore, there was usually little interest in handing on a school to the next generation. Most girls' schools closed down with changed circumstances of their originators and few records survive. Those that have are the successful and longer lived, the exceptional. Nevertheless, their story may give some insight into one of the few areas where women were able to survive economically on their own and even gain a modicum of independence.

Mary Ann Phipson started her school in Birmingham in the wake of a crisis in the family button business. Up to that time she had suffered from hypochondria and depression and the necessity to open the school was, therefore, acknowledged to have acted as 'the outward call to a vocation for which previously there had been an incipient desire and a personal adaptation'. She started by recruiting four pupils through her contacts with Carrs Lane chapel where her father had acted as deacon to John Angell James, his cousin by marriage. Mary Ann Phipson already had a reputation at the chapel as a responsible Sunday school teacher. At first she despaired of being self-supporting and considered emigrating to Australia. However, slowly the number of pupils grew, sent to her by friends and neighbours.[126] One such neighbour, Thomas Southall, a Quaker chemist, sent his daughters to her school and when Miss Phipson was looking for larger premises in the 1840s he became her landlord.[127] From the beginning her sister Rosalinda helped her, later joined by another sister, Sarah. By 1851, Mary Ann Phipson was living in a large house in a Birmingham suburb with a paid assistant, twenty-three girl pupils aged between 10 and 22, a cook and two housemaids.[128] Throughout their lives, the Phipson sisters had been profoundly influenced by their clerical kinsman and pastor, John Angell James. By 1853, when the school had moved yet again to purpose-built premises in Edgbaston, James himself presided over evening gatherings round the 'domestic circle' encouraged at the school. There he exhorted the girls on their mission and their sphere.[129]

Sarah Bache, too, used a male support group in running her successful Birmingham school for girls. Her father had died young and her mother ran a small school, but Sarah's own education was minimal and she was apprenticed to a mantua maker. She had, however, taught in the New Meeting Sunday school and there came under Priestley's spell. Through this Unitarian connection, she was able to build up her own school which she ran in partnership with her sister until the latter's marriage and then with her half-sister, Phoebe.[130] Later she was joined by a niece whom she herself had educated. Through their membership of the New Meetings and association with the group of men around Priestley, Sarah Bache and Phoebe Penn developed close friendships with three men who were themselves friends, and who helped the young women with their business affairs. One of these was Thomas Hill, also running Hazelwood School. Hill was, in turn, helped by Miss Bache and Miss Penn in 1820 when a fire ravaged Hazelwood's buildings and the girls' school provided stockings for the boys and food for breakfasts. Phoebe Penn's brother-in-law, Lant Carpenter, himself running a school, advised her on advertisements and on the history curriculum, the last a real aid to women with weak academic backgrounds. He lent her money in 1825 when the school moved to a larger house and his wife, Phoebe's sister, was asked to suggest menus for the girls' meals since she had a long experience of feeding a house full of pupils.

Sarah Bache was a competent and intelligent woman who built up a successful school from almost nothing. Unlike many women in this position, she enjoyed her autonomy. She wrote to her sister, Bessy, who came to help her with the domestic side of the school:

> Come then! dear, dear sister; come and share the happiness (for most frequently does happiness inhabit this apartment), of your Sarah, with independent spirits. Let us take our homely but wholesome meal together; enjoying, at once, those two delightful sensations of independence, because we eat the bread we have fairly earned, and of grateful thankfulness to the Being who has put this independence in our power.[131]

Despite her delight in the control of her own life and the freedom this gave her, Sarah Bache was inevitably constrained to educate the girls in her school primarily to be wives and mothers. In 1808 she had consciously resisted making the school more genteel when it had become popular with over sixty pupils and raised fees to discourage further inquiries. 'We do not wish people to think that we shall make it more of a genteel school', she explained to her brother-in-law, 'I shall still continue to be so vulgar as to teach what is useful and not what is fashionable'. The useful programme including reading, needlework, geography and the use of the globes and grammar for 17s. 6d a quarter. Extra was charged for writing and accounts, ancient geography and drawing maps. By 1810, French was introduced and by 1816, when the school moved to its new Edgbaston premises in the elegant house formerly occupied by a banker, the announcement of the opening struck a distinctly fashionable note. Miss Bache and Miss Penn hoped that 'their present plan will enable them to unite with Mental and Moral Culture, a greater Attention to elegant Accomplishments, and that the Salubrity of the Situation be beneficial to their own Health and that of their Pupils'.

Sarah Bache retired and sold the school in 1838 when she was 68. She was unfortunate enough to lose most of her savings two years later when her investments failed. Her former pupils rallied and presented her with £200, proving themselves true 'friends'. In her thanks, she shows how far her attitudes to women had changed since the 1800s. 'I gratefully acknowledge', she told them, 'and most truly enjoy, the pecuniary advantages your purse ... will afford me, but be assured that which constitutes my highest gratification ... is the well grounded hope, that you are rising up faithfully to fulfil "Woman's Mission", by becoming truly Christian Daughters, – wives –, and Mothers'.[132]

The schools of Miss Phipson and Miss Bache were larger and lasted longer than the average concern. A young girl from Birmingham was sent to a more ordinary establishment which offered:

a limited number of young ladies for Board and Education, on the plan which they have successfully adopted for many years, combining the personal comforts of a private family, from the advantages derived from association in study with eligible companions. . . .[133]

Neither Miss Bache nor Miss Phipson had any training in the classics nor, of course, the chance of a clerical career which gave prestige and profit to the larger boys' schools. Only the girls' finishing schools of spa and seaside towns or the Metropolis could charge high fees and their emphasis was almost entirely on social skills and contacts. Keeping these provincial schools on a 'family scale' made the tasks undertaken by the staff seem less like work and more as if the women were carrying on their usual domestic duties.

There was a thin line between being in business and simply catering for and instructing a few extra children. Some of the establishments, indeed, could hardly be called schools – they were simply extensions of a normal household. In this way, such female headed 'educational households' were analogous to those where lodgers were taken to supplement or replace other income sources, a device used mainly by the working class but not unknown higher up the social scale.[134] Taking in lodgers seems to have been a strategy particularly used by female household heads in salaried posts. These households were prominent in central Birmingham in the lower middle-class urban setting, whereas girls' schools flourished in a more suburban context. In the census sample there were six schools run by women in Edgbaston but none in central Birmingham. However, the underlying economic and social motivations were similar.

Women as innkeepers

Servicing lodgers as an extension of women's caring functions was carried out on a larger scale in inns, although the lines between private home, lodging house, public house and inn were sometimes difficult to draw. (Certain categories partly depended on the granting of a liquor licence.) Women were undoubtedly running inns: 6 per cent of female household heads in the census sample. All areas had some public houses and in certain towns along main transport routes, such as Witham in Essex, innkeeping became an important sector of the local economy. Every male innkeeper who made a will in Witham left his business unconditionally to his wife as did most of those in Birmingham, some of these being substantial properties. 71 per cent of the widows of innkeepers were given complete control in contrast to 50 per cent of the whole sample of wills. In 1851 in Witham, Sarah Nunn was still at the Spread Eagle thirteen years after being widowed, while Eleanor Tanner ran the King's Head as a widow from 1847 until her own death in 1853.[135]

These legacies were an important resource for women. In the late eighteenth and early nineteenth centuries, inns and public houses were the centre of several subsidiary activities – the coaching business and provision of short haul vehicles such as the post chaise, being the most important. Innkeepers often doubled as owners of coaches and controlled their own routes since horses had to be stabled and travellers boarded at frequent intervals. Women were able to take advantage of their position within inns to become involved in the transport side. In the 1790s, Deborah Gooding ran the Chelmsford Machine Fly on a lucrative Essex to London route, a journey which often terminated at the Bull, Aldgate.[136] This large City inn was also run by a widow, 'the all powerful Ann Nelson who had found means of making her name known on almost every road out of London'.[137] Although women such as these could find a foothold in the transport business through their management of inns, they faced competition from men who started with capital resources and business experience – men such as Thomas Hedge the younger son of the Colchester clock manufacturing family, who snapped up coaching routes and purchased inns and livery stables to build up a profitable local transport empire.[138]

Other agencies were also based in public houses, which offered a central location and storage facilities as well as a guaranteed clientele. Tools for sale or hire were provided from pub yards and therefore could be managed by women such as the Essex area agent, Mrs Warren dealing in blacksmithing equipment and Mrs Sergeant, a 'machinist' who contracted to rent threshing machines.[139] Women would sometimes run the pub while male relatives farmed or worked in other occupations – a Suffolk publican's husband was a vet, for example. Like the school, the inn or pub was based in the building which housed the family. Much of the brewing was done on the premises and the publican sold his or her own brew in a front room. Even from the outside, a *public* house looked exactly like a *private* house, except for the sign hanging over the door.[140]

However, within this industry changes were also taking place which tended to push women to the margins. In the seventeenth century the slow exclusion of women from beer making had begun, and by the early eighteenth century they had been confined mainly to domestic brewing, this in an industry which was the biggest industrial undertaking at that time. By 1800, more and more public houses were themselves being bought up by breweries turning the publican into a retailer.[141] The usual consequences of the larger-scale, more rationalized, centralized marketing which followed, produced the crop of male managers, clerks and agents, under whose authority many public houses were run.

Internally, the informality of the early pub also changed. The introduction of a counter began to place a 'bar' between the customer and publican. Legislation of the 1830s which created a category of unlicensed beer shops did provide opportunities for women to earn, but at the lowest end of a trade that was increasingly being differentiated by the social rank of its clientele. The Evangelical onslaught on drinking and its association with public disorder, including political disaffection, gave public houses a bad reputation. A farmer who was a churchwarden and right-hand man to the vicar felt rather out of place in the free and easy atmosphere of his local village pub, yet he often went there to attend sales, always held in pubs, for 'as an inhabitant of the district he felt a need to know the values and ownership of lands and houses'.[142] By the 1850s, public drinking places had become specialized and stratified by class, to the point where Brian Harrison has claimed that 'no respectable urban Englishman entered an ordinary public house'.[143] If these reservations held for men, then they were doubly effective in making public houses anathema to genteel or even respectable femininity.

This association proved a serious constraint on women's business activities, and presented a dilemma for the women who owned, managed or worked in public houses. The Woolpack, a Birmingham public house in the 1840s, was regarded by the new owners as having a somewhat objectionable class of customers. The landlord therefore divided the pub into several areas ranging from dining rooms for drovers to a commercial room for businessmen to a smoking room for casual or ordinary visitors and the 'snuggery' behind the bar into which none but a privileged few were allowed to enter. Here the landlady and her daughters also sat. 'The fun occasionally was fast and furious, but no breach of decorum was permitted' and a box was supplied for hospital charity donations levied as 'fines' for bad language.[144]

The most lucrative part of the hostelry trade faded quickly in the 1830s and 1840s with the coming of the railways. Railway building and management were closely associated with engineering, organized on a large scale as private companies and often staffed on military lines, all characteristics uncongenial to women. The heavily male ambience of the railway system has not often been commented on but was a significant factor in the economy of the second quarter of the nineteenth century. Only the less profitable small inns and public houses which continued to supply chaises and other light vehicles for connecting journeys to railways terminals remained allied to transport. A few women did run such businesses, but the livery stables which evolved from these centred on the masculine monopoly of horse culture and women's direct connection with transport was effectively broken by mid century.

On the other hand, the fact that inns and public houses were increasingly rented from breweries and thus could be taken up without much capital meant that women continued on the food, drink and lodging side. Undoubtedly this option remained an important part of the lower middle-class service trades in particular where women were employed as family members. Indeed, women might be deliberately sought as employees in their capacity to provide a home-like atmosphere and control disorderly behaviour. By mid century most of the women independently operating public houses were widows, and only 7 per cent of inns and taverns and 10 per cent of beershops in Ipswich were listed in women's names as opposed to 47 per cent of lodging houses, a smaller scale, less formal alternative.[145] Significantly, the printed census at the same date does, however, list innkeeper's *wives* as a separate category.

Even before the changes which eased women out of the more lucrative parts of the trade, there were limits to what they could make of their position. A landlord might take advantage of the contacts he made in the course of activities as diverse as billeting soldiers, housing itinerant traders, running a post office, swearing in constables, playing host to vestry and other local government meetings, social and political clubs. Freemasons met in public houses and even a chapel was not averse to holding a debate in such a setting. There was nothing to stop a female innkeeper providing any of these services, but their presence on her premises seldom led to other kinds of business activity. A male publican, on the other hand, could evolve into a corn factor or make a more general use of his position. Jonathan Bull, an Essex village publican, worked the small holding surrounding the pub in addition to being an overseer to the Poor Law guardians, helped to raise troops during the war and generally acted as an opinion leader with an interest in any local business going on.[146] He has no known female counterpart.

Women in trade

The largest single occupation of middle-class women earning their livelihood in their own right as well as assisting their male relatives, was in trade. Most of this was at the less capitalized, less formal end of the commercial spectrum with quick turnover and short credit chains. The general shopkeeper, especially in the village, was more often than not a widow taking advantage of the general move to fixed retail distribution.[147] Millinery and dressmaking, catering to an all-female clientele, were the main exceptions to male dominance of the higher reaches of retailing. In Witham, by far the most prominent female establishment was the millinery shop at the socially select end of Newland Street. It was run by two sisters employing six living-in assistants and their mother living on an annuity.[148] Training for the higher branches of these trades required apprenticeships with premiums as high as £50 and starting capital of double that amount.[149] Journeywomen milliners in Colchester earned about 6 shillings a week in 1800, well paid for women's work. In the late eighteenth century, women dominated the retail women's clothing trades: out of nineteen retailers in the town, sixteen were women. Wealthier Colchester milliners travelled to

London during the fashionable spring season to purchase up-to-date stock. Some specialized: Mrs Courtney made muffs, Mary Waynman mended fans, Ann Wilder starched muslin, lawn, gauze and lace. Women like these acted independently, taking apprentices, making out bills in their own name, even when married. For example, Mary Boyle charged the Colchester MP 1 shilling each for twelve favours used in an election campaign. In this period, some remained in business throughout their married life and widowhood and left real estate as well as cash legacies. Yet many milliners, too, withdrew on marriage or other changed circumstances. Even this skilled trade lacked a monopoly; apprenticeship might be an advantage but was by no means compulsory. Rather 'judgement of changing fashions, a genteel manner and a network of local contacts and credit' was more significant.[150]

As with teaching and purveying food, drink and lodging, the range of women offering dressmaking and millinery was wide, and because every girl was taught to sew, there was always the possibility of using unpaid family services. The local records only show a handful of women professionally engaged in these trades in the later part of the period. The daughter of a master baker in Ipswich served an apprenticeship as a dressmaker and went into partnership with her master in the 1830s.[151] The publicity surrounding a fire uncovered a woman running a chemist shop with a living-in apprentice.[152] Two sisters ran the bookselling and publishing business they inherited from their father.[153] There is no indication from either these odd examples or the local directories that any of these enterprises ever expanded to any size or became known for specialized products.

Anxiety about the status of retail trade was particularly acute for women, as is shown by the ambivalence towards the wife of a grocer expressed in a poem by Jane Taylor. Her fictional portrait was based on a real couple who had retired from a grocer's shop to a newly built imposing brick house from which the husband had served as Mayor of Colchester. Here Taylor is ostensibly attacking the prejudices of the 'little gentry of our narrow sphere'.

> The powder'd matron, who for many a year
> Has held her mimic routs and parties here,
> (Exchanging just the counter, scales and till
> For cups of coffee, scandal and quadrille)
> Could boast nor range of thought nor views of life,
> Much more extended than our grocer's wife.

The mayor's wife:

> Her thoughts unused to take a longer flight
> Than from the left hand counter to the right

is portrayed as vulgar, and incapable of refinement, although true religion will make palatable even the ultimate social humiliation of having served behind a counter.[154]

Jane Taylor was acutely aware of the nuances of status between Anglicans and nonconformists as well as within the various noncomformist communities within the town. The connection of retail trade with nonconformity was strong. Twenty-one out of the twenty-four families (88 per cent) who were in trade in the two areas were nonconformists of some variety. Women were more visibly active in retail trade than almost any other family enterprise. They also had a greater part to play in the affairs of the local chapel than in the hierarchically organized Anglican church. It is possible that a combination of these factors contributed to the special concern over the status of women in trade. Whatever the reasons, owning or working in a shop, which might have been the height of ambition for the working-class woman, could represent the depths of degradation from the perspective of the upper middle class.

The marginal place of women in the economy

Women had been active in the early days of manufacturing enterprises when the scale was small and linked to direct sales. Birmingham women in the eighteenth century were known to be manufacturing in workshops, sometimes with male relatives or, as widows, on their own. George Holyoake's father had moved from being an independent bucklemaker to working as a skilled engineer in a foundry. His mother continued the button workshop she had started, before her marriage, the marital home fronting on the shop where she employed several work people. As her son recalled:

> She received the orders; made the purchases of materials; superintended the making of the goods; made out the accounts; and received the money besides taking care of her growing family. There were no 'Rights of Women' thought of in her day, but she was an entirely self-acting, managing mistress. The button business died out while I was young, and from the remarks which came from merchants, I learnt that my mother was the last maker of that kind of button in the town.[155]

Respectable married women did start their own small businesses, for example Mrs Clark who went into the Birmingham fancy trade. However, when her husband prospered through his invention of a machine for winding cotton, she withdrew into domestic exclusion in Ladywood, not necessarily losing caste for her excursion into the business world at this date.[156]

But even without the enticement of domesticity or the possible loss of status entailed in having run a business, women were increasingly hampered by the growth in scale of manufacturing enterprises. They faced the increased problem of maintaining authority over a larger, more distanced workforce, the need to take a more active part in the formal market, the requirement for heavier capital input and for scientific and technical knowledge. As in farming, women in manufacturing and retail families took on a diversity of semi-employments, some of which were directly absorbed in the enterprise such as the jam made for sale by a grocer's wife and daughters. The Mrs John Bright, who acted as agent for Bright's custard powder in an Essex town in 1845, is representative of the woman who acted as agents for a variety of goods and services,[157] as much as the refined spinster who took in convalescent patients and ran a high-class home for the genteel mentally disturbed.[158] Women whose main resource was some education, turned to writing popular books for children, moral tales and tracts and also history, biography and science with titles such as *The Observing Eye* or *What is a Bird* produced by a farmer's daughter.[159] The daughter of a clergyman living on the outlying Essex coast, like her brothers, gained a certain reputation as a composer of hymns. She was not unusual for a considerable proportion of nineteenth-century hymns were written, translated and composed by women (classics such as 'Nearer my God to Thee' and 'All Things Bright and Beautiful' among many others).[160] A Suffolk Independent minister based his successful second career as a choir master on a system of notation invented by a female Sunday school teacher, who, with her sister, had perfected a system of training choirs.[161]

From cases like the above, a pattern emerges of women able to take part in, even to make money from, activities which were seen as primarily part of a family-based avocation, skills which were sometimes used as the basis of a family business. Not without reason did Isaac Taylor call his collective memoir, *The Family Pen*. Within such an enterprise, women were able to establish a niche in the less public part of a field. They etched the engravings and hand tinted the prints, rather than creating the originals. It was more acceptable to them as well as to others to translate than to write under their own names, particularly outside the more acceptable area of children's literature, religious works and fiction. Catherine Winkworth, related by marriage to the Shaen family in Essex, and a friend of Mrs Gaskell and James Martineau, made fairly substantial sums by her translations from the German for which she has gained a lasting reputation. However she was doubtful about the suggestion that she write her own material:

> You can see with half an eye that that would be a very different affair from simply translating a work all ready to hand. The latter would only require a competent knowledge of German and some fluency and taste in English composition, but the former would require *judgement*, literary and historical, and an immense amount of information.[162]

In addition to these subsidiary activities, women contributed to family welfare by acting as part of a team. They entered the salaried positions

available to men, some of these resulting from the growth of state and
voluntary institutions. However, within these posts, women's position
almost invariably reproduced their domestic role. An Essex parish which
had to staff its new workhouse required the governor to 'write a good hand
and be something of an accomptant' as well as supervising the male inmates.
His wife, as governess, in addition to supervising the females, was to attend
the sick and organize lodging, food and clothing. A family enterprise then
emerged as the daughter became a teacher in the girls' school attached to the
workhouse which was subsequently run by an aunt while the son became
master at the boys' school.[163]

With most residential posts, the major difference between a man and a
woman was that the former brought this family with him, often to supply
domestic help, while the latter was mainly in charge of domestic
arrangements for the institution no matter what her subsidiary duties. In
these positions, women were often forbidden to bring dependants. A
Birmingham Unitarian foundation, the Protestant Dissenting Charity
School, advertised in 1836 for a governess who 'must be a single woman or
a widow without a family, and about the middle age'. One applicant was
refused since she wished to bring an adopted child. The spinster who was
appointed later was allowed to have her widowed mother living with her
but only after a meeting of the ladies' committee had considered her long
service and provided that the arrangement in no way interfered with her
duties and there was no financial loss to the school.[164]

The Essex and Colchester Hospital, founded 1820, made a sharp contrast
between the men and women in their employ. The trustees, a committee of
management and physicians (non-stipendiary) were all male and drew up
the conditions of service. The resident apothecary was required to be over
35 years of age and trained to dispense drugs. It was his duty to supervise
the male patients, including leading their prayers morning and evening. He
was provided with board and lodging without restrictions on any family
and a salary of £50 a year. The matron was the only woman at staff level.
She, too, had to be over 35, but was also required to be a spinster or widow
with no dependent children. In addition to supervising and praying with the
female patients, she took charge of household goods, kept accounts of
provisions and overlooked the wards for cleanliness and order as well as
organizing the female nurses and maids. Her rewards in kind were the same
as the apothecary but the salary was £30. The nurses, maids and male
orderlies and groundsmen were 'to be to the Apothecary as their master and
the Matron as their Mistress', thus reproducing a family model with a
sexual division of labour.[165]

In the local records Mary Merryweather was one of the few women in a
salaried white-collar post. She had been imported from London to help in
Courtaulds' mill where she acted as social worker and disciplinarian for the
predominantly female workforce. Her title in the 1851 census is 'Moral

Missionary Amongst Factory Hands' and the fact that she boarded nine factory girls in her home shows how closely her position stressed the feminine type of duty.[166] There are examples of less highly placed women adding to family income and sometimes also receiving housing by acting as a gaoler (although this was forbidden by law in the 1830s), and librarians for small private or voluntary societies which were springing up in provincial towns. The Castle Library in Colchester paid its librarian (who was wife of the town gaoler), 11 gns a year or 4s. 6d a week, not enough to survive on even at the lowest middle-class level.[167] On closer inspection many librarians were more involved in keeping the premises clean, lighting fires and providing refreshment at the meetings of the male subscribers, than dealing with books.

A comparison of the activities of a farmer's wife in the late eighteenth century and one in the 1820s illustrates the shift. Both women were married with children but the woman in the earlier period spent her time helping to manage the farm and work people, travelling extensively on horseback to markets and the provincial town to shop, visit the theatre or consult her lawyer. She speaks of 'doing my brewing' and records drawing bills of credit and the sale of 'my turnips'.[168] The woman of the later period is caught up in renovations in the farmhouse, including new kitchen equipment and adding a parlour. Her world is confined to church going, social visits, a little church related philanthropy and family affairs, subjects which the earlier diary certainly does not overlook but which form only a part of its interests.[169]

The same forces which relegated women's economic activity to these shadowy areas, have affected the historical sources. When family status could be tarnished by acknowledging that its womenfolk worked for an income, it is likely that much went unrecorded. Women's marginalization increased as the economy itself became defined as part of the public domain. A sample from the directories for Birmingham, for example, does not list a single female merchant after 1800, yet as late as the 1830s evidence from only a sample of wills produces a bone, timber and marble merchant who left instructions for their wives to take over the business. The pattern is well defined by the field of medicine. Much eighteenth- and early nineteenth-century health care, particularly in the countryside, was still in the hands of women who gathered and grew the herbs which were the basis of most remedies. With enclosure of common lands, sources of supplies were cut back. At the same time, male apothecaries began to make drugs, while the increasing manufacture and sale of commercial cosmetics tended to be run by men. Professional medicine with its specialized training and scientific rationale was closed to women, both in its earlier form based on a knowledge of the classics and the later development of experimental method. But women were not excluded from health *care*. On the contrary, middle-class wives and mothers were seen to have an important, if sharply circumscribed, role as responsible for the fitness of their family through the provision of a healthy home and diet, and careful home nursing in illness. The Birmingham doctor, Pye Henry Chevasse, made this division of labour explicit in his popular books, *Advice to Wives on the Management of Themselves during the Period of Pregnancy, Labour and Suckling* and *Advice to Mothers on the Management of Offspring*; works which increased both his purse and his reputation, locally and nationally.[170]

Some women continued to practise herbal medicine at least for their poorer neighbours, but middle-class taste was turning to the more expensive and prestigious male doctors favoured by the women in both local studies. The struggle over medical territory was particularly centred around childbirth and childcare. The Suffolk poet, George Crabbe, himself trained as a doctor, portrayed the change in the fate of the village midwife, originally recipient of respect from both rich and poor until a young farmer married a townswoman who called in a doctor for her confinement.

> Fame (now his friend) fear, novelty and whim,
> And fashion, sent the varying sex to him. . . .

The doctor gained the custom of the rich, leaving the poor to the midwife:

> 'Nay', said the Doctor, 'dare you trust your wives,
> The joy, the pride, the solace of your lives,
> To one who acts and knows no reason why,
> But trusts, poor hag! to luck for an ally?–
> Who, on experience, can her claims advance,
> And own the powers of accident and chance?
> A whining dame, who prays in danger's view,
> (A proof she knows not what beside to do;)
> What's her experience? In the time that's gone,
> Blundering she wrought, and still she blunders on:–
> And what is Nature? One who acts in aid
> Of gossips half asleep, and half afraid.
> With such allies I scorn my fame to blend,
> Skill is my luck and courage is my friend;
> No slave to Nature, 'tis my chief delight
> To win my way and act in her despite:–'[171]

Women, men and occupational identity

Medicine is a striking instance of the general way men's occupations have been shaped by the structure of sexual inequality. This point is often overlooked by studies which concentrate only on women's work, and ignored in general studies of work which usually focus on men without explicitly saying so. It is instructive to look at a range of activities from the local records which encompass both masculine and feminine experience especially in the earlier stages of a person's career. It should also be remembered that young men, too, were at times constrained into positions which were uncongenial to their tastes. Such a young man had to be reconciled to his duty by being reminded of his 'natural' destiny. If he proved restive, these expectations would be made explicit in the sermons he heard, in the moral tales he read and most effectively by his loving relatives and friends. Young Samuel Courtauld was not too eager to join his father in the silk mill for he longed to play the violin and at one point toyed with the idea of entering the Unitarian ministry. His mother wrote to him in 1809: 'Consider, dear boy, that the comfort of your old mother and young brothers and sisters may yet depend on your care and industry. I assume this Idea will act as a sufficient stimulus. . . .'[172] It did, and Samuel threw himself into mill management with some enthusiasm.

Middle-class men were expected to be active economically, they had access to patronage, education, training, contacts, experience and legal forms which enhanced these expectations in varying degrees.[173] In the expanding opportunities of the early nineteenth century, some men were able to build careers on previous training and skills. A young man who had been apprenticed to a miller found little difficulty in being taken on to the management of an engineering business, having picked up relevant skills while acting as a millwright.[174] Others started in the related crafts of carpenter and wheelwright. From such a base, virtually a male monopoly, large-scale building operations were mounted where sons or grandsons in several local families became surveyors, estate agents or architects.[175] Through their building interests, these men were also in a position to acquire property and become a powerful presence in the local community, sealing their arrival by marriage into high status families.[176]

One reason why women found it so difficult to operate in these areas was the prohibition on manual skills (outside the domestic) which was so closely tied to their feminine status. The 'common-sense' attention to tools and materials which created an area of mutual interest for many men, from skilled artisans to highly educated scientists, had no female counterpart. Nowhere was this more evident than in the subject of horse culture, a rapidly expanding field. In the eighteenth century, the care and use of horses was steeped in tradition, often allied to the knowledge of 'cunning men' and 'wise women' and it remained so in some isolated rural areas.[177] But with the development of new stock breeding and more valuable animals, the trade of 'farrier' came to be a masculine specialism which in the second quarter of the nineteenth century was evolving into veterinary science.[178] In a small village on the Essex/Cambridge border, a family of labourers who began to specialize as horsemen produced one member who, through informal training and knowledge, set up as a veterinary surgeon. His sons became, respectively, a doctor and a professor of physiology at Cambridge.[179] Occupations connected to the sea provided another sphere of opportunities for middle-class men. Women occasionally were found as merchants or managing wharfing facilities. However, they could never move back and forth between these functions and going to sea themselves, either as a ship's officer, or to carve out a career in the Royal Navy (more open to talent than the Army at this period).

The occupations so far surveyed were based on activities traditionally closed to women. But there were areas from which women had not been excluded. Middle-class girls were positively encouraged to draw and paint and, where resources permitted, were given training in developing their artistic talents. Some reached high standards, even exhibiting locally and nationally. Like their brothers, some of the more accomplished had been trained in the studios and workshops of their fathers. Unlike their brothers, however, what these women could not do, except in the most unusual circumstances, was to become professional artists with a commercial reputation in their own right.[180] High art implied a free floating individualism which ran counter to the modesty and willingness to divert energies to others, demands which were so central to femininity.

The opportunity to turn a knack for drawing into a livelihood was more important for the ordinary young person. In a town like Birmingham, designing for the metal trades might be combined with teaching, as with a man who set up a flourishing Drawing Academy, later run by his son.[181] A Suffolk artisan's son was making £200 a year by mapmaking and surveying at the height of his practice.[182] Birmingham and the market towns of Essex and Suffolk boasted several painters making a living producing portraits and decorative art for a middle-class clientele. A Colchester engraver of 'humble parentage' who had been apprenticed to a local printer, left his provincial origins and pursued his career in the metropolis, where he used his rural background to specialize in landscapes.[183] Many women did engraving, colouring and illustrating but they did so as part of a family. An artistic talent might set them to teaching the neighbourhood daughters or be an aid in obtaining more regular school teaching. However, many must have remained like the young Quaker woman who helped run the house at the farm and brewery of her parents and who did her flower painting on silk by getting up before the household was awake. Her brother became a professional artist.[184]

Middle-class men and women both had become keenly interested in gardening as well as the more theoretical branches of horticulture and botany. Humphrey Repton, who lived most of his life in Essex, had been apprenticed to a wool merchant but had a passion for botanical studies. As a young man he made a deliberate decision to turn this into a profession, using the term *landscape gardening* and passing on the speciality to his son.[185] Opportunities for such professional work were increasing with the creation of scientific bodies and specialist gardens.[186] Commercial nurseries were also an expanding sector for men with more practical gardening experience and several seed firms such as Thompson and Morgan of Ipswich which were founded in this period have survived into the twentieth century. While undoubtedly many women were vital to the development of a family horticultural business, as a group they had lost their previous prerogative of the farmer and cottager's wife supplying seeds and propagating plants. Women's interests in both gardening and botany was rather guided into a hobby or to act as a healthful 'restorative'.

The lack of opportunity to exchange scientific and practical information, as well as the absence of public recognition for their work, was a special stumbling block for women with interests in botanical subjects as well as horticulture and gardening. Most botanical societies did not admit women, at least not to full membership. The papers they had written might be read out for them by a male member, but women remained isolated from the informal support so vital to building a professional image and expertise.[187] The young men who gathered to search for and study specimen plants and animals in the Natural History Field Clubs were often apothecaries' apprentices or shop men, some of whom later turned their hobby into employment. By the 1840s, the class composition of these associations covered a wide range from artisans to upper middle-class men, but no women were admitted to these clubs.[188] A few women from the local areas wrote and published on botany, natural history and horticulture, often for a juvenile audience. It was clearly more acceptable to express these interests in print from the confines of their own homes.

The experience of a set of twins from a wealthy Suffolk timber merchant's family well illustrates the differing expectations for young men and women. In his late teens, Samuel Scott entered the family business as junior to his uncle. His twin sister, Charlotte, after her education as a young lady was complete, returned to live at home where she developed an interest in botany. When she was about 19, her uncle, head of the family as well as her guardian, indulgently noted that Charlotte's botanical collection and greenhouse occupations 'seem at this time to occupy her greatest share of attention'. Two years later, Samuel had become established as a partner in the business with the prospect of eventually taking charge, while Charlotte's interests had become centred in a mysterious illness, a nervous complaint which gained her uncle's deep concern but which fixed her firmly in a career as an invalid and her botanical interests dwindled.[189] Not all middle-class women with such talents became invalids, of course. Charlotte Scott may have been especially disadvantaged by living in a remote village. Nevertheless, the trivializing of a genuine enthusiasm seems to have been at least as common as the flowering of upper middle-class women in the guise of recognized amateurs of distinction.

It is difficult to judge how women like Charlotte Scott reacted to their situation. Despite the blandness of the sources, there are hints that conflicts over resources within the family were not unknown, particularly between brothers and sisters. It has been seen how both Archibald Kenrick in Birmingham and Samuel Courtauld in Essex as young men starting out in business demanded a lion's share of the family property for their ventures in opposition to their mothers who specifically wished to protect their daughters' interests. The female family members had a difficult case to sustain, for as Samuel somewhat ingenuously explained: 'It is proposed that this money should be actively employed for the more immediate advantage of one individual [himself] but in a general view of the family collectively.' Although he admitted that the property would be 'somewhat endangered' if invested in the mill, like young Kenrick, he won his point since his sisters had in mind to open a school which would only have served for their own short-term support. As soon as the mill was solvent, Samuel gave his sister Sophia a larger allowance so that she could give up going out as a governess and be spared 'all the mortifications' of that position.[190]

When family resources were stretched, it was expected that sisters would assist in educating brothers, if necessary to earn income to enable them to train and to generally underwrite the young men's economic ventures. A widow would often run a school with her daughters in order to give her sons a rudimentary education and have the means for their further training. As one brother later wrote to his sister: 'How you girls toiled that we boys might be well prepared for later life; for which I am ever grateful to you.'[191] The expectation was that when the young man had reached his goal, he would support the mother, aunt or sister who had thus invested in his future. However, this did not invariably follow and some men felt uneasy about admitting that they had been dependent on a woman's work to support them. There exist a few bitter denunciations by sisters who gave support – financial, emotional and in doing all household tasks – only to later find that the brother despised them as ungenteel when he had reached his professional or commercial goal.[192] Others had to stand by and watch a brother lose the common patrimony through mismanagement or personal failure. The notion of female influence must have had an ironic flavour for the wife of a failed shopkeeper whose constant moves of living quarters along with the shop had made her ill with anxiety. Her husband feared losing her: 'so tenderly loved, despite little differences in worldly affairs' when she tried, '*I am sure* to be my good Counsellor.'[193]

The restrictions on middle-class women were made up of a combination of forces, including subtle associations of places, activities and images which strongly defined femininity and masculinity. The association of men with the dynamic engine of the industrial age, manufacture, was particularly vivid and, for a variety of reasons already discussed, women's part in a manufacturing enterprise was usually limited. A woman manufacturer in her own right was regarded as an anomaly. The unmarried farmer's daughter who successfully ran a brick and tile kiln on a commercial scale was 6 feet 3 inches tall and had waived all claims to a customary feminine identity; she appears as an oddity in the family chronicle.[194] From childhood play with drawings, tools and bits of machinery indulged in by a boy, the association of masculinity with production persisted. Even where a girl showed an aptitude in that direction it was difficult to sustain. A Birmingham iron master who had made his fortune by improving an iron puddling process, had an eldest daughter with a gift for practical invention. According to a memoir by her son, she turned this to solving household problems. Having noted the wastefulness of the open fire place, from her own templates she cut a piece of iron and mounted it on bricks so reducing draughts and saving coal. As her son commented, 'she anticipated the slow combustion grate'.[195] What he did not add was that she did not turn this invention into a mass produced product which might have made another fortune.

Practical mechanical skills, the heart of the Birmingham metal industry, were clearly outside the rubric of the feminine sphere. But for women the canons of scientific thought were also limited to private affairs and, ultimately, to non-utilitarian ends. The solid education and training in science and rational thought which was given to the daughters of men in groups such as Birmingham's Lunar Society, could be used only within the confines of the household or in female philanthropic ventures. Two grandsons of Lunar Society members were the cousins, Francis Galton and Charles Darwin who both carried the tradition of ordering and classifying their world into their scientific work and through which they gained world-wide recognition in the later nineteenth century. One of Francis Galton's aunts had been raised in a similar atmosphere but lived out a quiet domesticated existence in Birmingham. She applied a systematic world view closer to home. She is recorded as possessing:

> a triple inkstand with three coloured inks, triple penwipers and pens; every conceivable apparatus for writing; printed envelopes for her various banks and business correspondents; printed questions for her grooms, 'Has the mare had her corn' etc; a dozen or more cash boxes, elaborately arranged to receive in square labelled compartments each kind of coin from each type of her property. The apparatus for the instruction and relief of the poor – tracts, ounces of tea and sugar, worsted stockings, bundles for mothers' aid etc. etc. were arranged in separate indexed presses, with records of all transactions relating thereto. The crockery ware of the store-room and housekeepers' room was all lettered and all metal articles, pans and pots were duly labelled, as were the garden tools, and there were corresponding labels on the pegs on which they were hung. As many as 100 painted labels have been counted in a flower bed of hers of 12 square feet.[196]

How did women survive?

In both rural and urban areas and over the whole period, women made up between 5 and 15 per cent of the economically active population listed in the directories. However, by mid century the range of their activities had noticeably narrowed. In the 1790s their occupation included gaoler, whitesmith, plumber, butcher, farmer, seedsman (*sic*), tailor, saddler. Even in the first decades of the new century, male curtain ring, pipe, gun and varnish manufacturers specifically instructed in their wills that their wives should carry on the business. By the 1850s, dressmaking, millinery and teaching were by far the main occupational groupings listed for middle-class women.[197]

The result was a predictable massive overcrowding, and low wages symbolized by the fate of the governess in both fact and fiction. The presence of unpaid family female labour primed with just these skills and waiting in the wings to take over if income did not run to paying for professional services was a constant threat to any attempt at monopoly which women in these occupational groups could muster. In that most egalitarian group, the Quakers, the women of the 1780s and 1790s had run shops and schools and roamed the countryside as lay ministers, but by the next generation they were transmuted into respectable domesticity. Lucy Greenwood, born in the 1820s, had a mother active in the Quaker ministry who aided the wholesale/retail business that laid the foundations of her son's successful business career. Lucy, however, took no part in such activities but spent her life voluntarily organizing and running the Halstead Industrial School for girls. She never married and lived on the school premises, where for over thirty years she was as absorbed in its daily life as any owner of a proprietary school, but far from making a living from her work, she spent her patrimony lavishly in its service.[198]

By mid century, whenever family finances would permit, the energy, organizational skill and sense of commitment which middle-class women had put into economic activity were deflected into domestic affairs. They managed a set of servants or themselves undertook domestic tasks and organization which set a standard of personal services unknown before (or since). Occasionally women were able to turn these formidable skills and energy into publicly recognized philanthropy using organizing techniques and business routines picked up from their close association with the family business and various male relatives and friends. The scale of charity affairs, like bazaars organized and run by women, gives a glimpse of this hidden world. As their chronicler, Prochaska, has written, 'philanthropic enterprise was, in a sense, *laissez-faire* capitalism turned in on itself'.[199]

From this study, the appropriate question to be asked may not be what occupations were held by middle-class women in this period, but rather how were these women surviving? The brief answer must be: as part of a family or household enterprise, whether working entirely on the domestic side, contributing behind the scenes, engaged in part-time paid work, living on and contributing investment income or more likely a combination of any of these options. Even a crude indicator like the 1851 census shows 109 daughters over age 30 living with parents compared to fifty-eight sons in the local areas. The census sample from both areas contained 296 widows, 200 or 68 per cent who were household heads. Of the remaining widows who were not in a position to head a household, 55 per cent were living either as mothers or mothers-in-law, that is with adult children. Just under a half of these dependent widows were in the homes of married men. Another 21 per cent were living with other widows who headed the household, an example of female kin and friends pooling resources.

The women who were in occupations needing little capital and much energy included a high proportion of younger widows. 43 per cent of female household heads in trade were widows in the 25–55 age range. Of those in professional occupations (overwhelmingly teaching) almost all were in the same group and 60 per cent of these were widowed. Older widows predominated in occupations requiring some property; they were the majority in farming and innkeeping. Many of these widows would be holding the inn or farm for a son to take over. However, by far the largest group of female household heads in the census sample was of 'independent' means. Edgbaston was peppered with households such as number 16 Hagley Road where Sarah Green, age 75, lived on the rental of house properties and provided a home for four middle aged children, a sister and an unmarried nephew, all without occupations and in receipt of rents and annuities. At number 18 on the same road, were two spinster sisters in their late 60s, existing on a combination of landed property and investments. With a house at a rateable value of £23 a year and two female servants, they were comfortably off, but by no means had the resources to move in the highest Edgbaston circles.[200]

Two-thirds of female household heads living on 'independent means' were widows, but they were considerably older – 67 per cent were over 55 (and one-quarter actually over 70). This pattern was even more marked for upper middle-class women of independent means and, in any case, the upper middle class made up 83 per cent of all independent female household heads. In Edgbaston, virtually all the upper middle-class female household heads were over 40, as were almost all in the town centres of Essex and Suffolk. This contrasts with the position in central Birmingham where a large group of female household heads were in trade at a modest level, 25 per cent, and another 15 per cent were innkeepers mostly in the younger age band.

From the local studies it is evident that women's decision to enter the market depended on their control over family property. As the discussion has emphasized, the form of property – whether in land, building, investments, skill or individual income – was an important element. Professional men made up only 5 per cent and salaried men only 1 per cent of those even making a will, although they were 20 per cent and 13 per cent respectively of the middle class in the census sample.[201] The widows or orphaned daughters of these men, who had access to enough house room, could replace income by taking pupils, lodgers or boarders. Another expedient was to let the home, with or without shop premises, and live at a more modest level using the rent as income, a course easier to follow if the house was owned but quite possible under sub-leasing.

These strategies confirm that the major identity of most middle-class women was undoubtedly familial rather than occupational, whatever *tasks* they were actually doing. Of the women over the age of 25 in the census sample who were not households heads, two-thirds were wives living with their husbands, and the other one-third were female relatives. Of these, the largest single group, as may be expected, was unmarried daughters followed by sisters. Prescriptive literature about the desirability of sisters being companions to their brothers who would support them is confirmed by numerous cases in the local records.

From the census sample, it appears that men took on the support of sisters-in-law and mothers-in-law in addition to adult daughters and their own sisters, while female headed households were more likely to contain mothers, aunts and nieces as well as sisters and daughters. In many of these cases, women contributed both labour and income, whatever the expected direction of support might have been. Helping with housekeeping and childcare or sick nursing was the preferred existence for a single woman or widow and might bring some of the authority and privileges of being mistress of a household. Many of the numerous female visitors found in middle-class households on census night could well have been acting in such a capacity for friends; a quarter of all widows who were not themselves household heads were listed as visitors. However, women's position in these households was vulnerable. Not only were they exposed to the same vicissitudes as men within the family enterprise, they were also ultimately dependent on the capacity and good will of relatives and friends, not to speak of the emotional and psychological dependency they might have built up over the years. A minority of women seem to have spread the risks by combining resources with other women. The chances of an adult unmarried woman living as a relative in a household headed by a woman were almost double what would have been expected if adult female relatives had been randomly distributed among all households in the census sample.[202]

For a middle-class woman of the early nineteenth century, gentility was coming to be defined by a special form of femininity which ran directly counter to acting as a visibly independent economic agent. Despite the fact that women could hold property, their marital status always pre-empted their economic personality. The ramifications of this fact for their social and economic position were profound. It can be argued that nineteenth-century middle-class women represent a classic case of Parkin's distinction between property as active capital and property as possession, in this case enforced by coverture. Absence of property as capital has been seen as the most powerful element in 'social closure', that is exclusion from control over one's own life chances.[203] This conception lay at the heart of women's sexual and political dependency, a situation recognized by early feminists whose first aim was reform of married women's property. While material circumstances differed widely, all strata within the middle class operated within the same legal and customary framework. The forms of property and inheritance they practised were not significantly different. The reading material offered, the sermons preached and, most of all, their own experiences, offered few alternatives to the conventional view of female respectability with all its contradictory consequences. Many of these contradictions flowed directly from the dominant upper middle-class conception. Mrs Ellis expressed this view with chilling finality:

> gentlemen may employ their hours of business in almost any degrading occupation and, if they but have the means of supporting a respectable establishment at home, may be gentlemen still; while, if a lady but touch any article, no matter how delicate, in the way of trade, she loses caste, and ceases to be a lady.[204]

Notes

ABBREVIATIONS

Newspapers
ABG   *Aris's Birmingham Gazette*
BC   *Birmingham Chronicle*
IJ   *Ipswich Journal*

Location of sources
BRL   Birmingham Reference Library
BUL   Birmingham University Library
ERO   Essex Record Office, Chelmsford, Essex
FHL   Friends House Library, London
IRO   Ipswich Record Office, Suffolk
PRO   Public Record Office, London

Archives
DQB   Unpublished Dictionary of Quaker Biography held at Friends House Library, London and Haverford College, Philadelphia, Pennsylvania
DNB   *Dictionary of National Biography*

London is the place of publication unless otherwise stated. Citation is given in full the first time it is used in each chapter.

1 Census of Great Britain, 1851; *Population Tables*, part 2, vol. 1 (1854).
2 Will Smith, archivist Greater London Council, personal communication.
3 M. P. Medlicott, *No Hero, I Confess: a Nineteenth Century Autobiography* (1969).
4 A. Clark, *Working Life of Women in the Seventeenth Century*, 3rd edn (1982). I. Pinchbeck, *Women Workers and the Industrial Revolution 1750–1850*, 2nd edn (1981).
5 G. E. Evans, *The Horse in the Furrow* (1960); 'Account Book of Mrs Mann, Arthur Biddell, Housekeeper 1814–1917', IRO HA2; Jane Ransome Biddell, Unpublished commonplace book, IRO HA2/D/1 and 2.
6 Quoted in E. W. Martin, *The Secret People: English Village Life after 1750* (1954), p. 243.
7 J. Player, *Sketches of Saffron Walden and its Vicinity* (Saffron Walden, 1845), p. 57.
8 For a fuller discussion of this point see: L. Davidoff, 'The role of gender in "the First Industrial Nation": agriculture in England 1780–1850', in R. Crompton and M. Mann (eds.), *Gender and Stratification* (Oxford, 1986).
9 There is some debate about the origins and timing of the phasing out of women's field labour in the Eastern counties. The point here, however, is that the subject at the time was discussed mainly on moral grounds. K. D. Snell, 'Agricultural seasonal unemployment, the standard of living and women's work in the South and East, 1690–1860', *Economic History Review*, 34 no. 3 (1981)
10 J. Glyde, *Suffolk in the 19th Century: Physical, Social, Moral, Religious and Industrial* (c. 1855), p. 367.
11 J. Obelkevich, *Religion and Rural Society: South Lindsey 1825–1875* (Oxford, 1976), p. 50.
12 A. Whitehead, 'Kinship and property; women and men: some generalizations', in R. Hirschon (ed.), *Women and Property; Women as Property* (1983).
13 The marriage settlement which included 'restraint on anticipation' (that is to discourage fortune hunters), shows clearly how both the notion of dependency and expectation that capital would follow daughters out of the kinship line were built into gentry and upper middle-class institutions. T. Murphy, 'Female shadow, male substance: women and property law in 19th century England', unpublished paper, by permission of the author.
14 W. Beck, *Family Fragments Respecting the Ancestry, Acquaintance and Marriage of Richard Low Beck and Rachel Lucas* (Gloucester, 1897), p. 8.
15 J. B. Elshtain, *Public Man, Private Woman: Women in Social and Political Thought* (Princeton, 1981).
16 J. Glyde, *Suffolk*, p. 324.
17 Birmingham Wills.
18 S. D'Cruze, 'The society now surrounding us: Colchester and its middling sort, 1780–1800', unpublished M. A. Thesis, University of Essex (1985), p. 56. In the sample of wills there was a reversal of this trend post-1830 when more widows, once again, were left to their own discretion.
19 A pattern strikingly illustrated in the wills of Isaac and Ann M. Taylor. Ann left voluminous directions for disposal of her books, clothes and trinkets to named children and grandchildren, including leaving her wedding ring, earrings and mother's hair to Jemima which 'I recommend to her particular care', PRO Prob. 11/1773 and 1764. This male/female pattern of legacies is confirmed in S. D'Cruze, and for the US in S. Lebsock, *The Free Women of Petersburg: Status and Culture in a Southern Town 1784–1860* (New York, 1984).
20 H. Dixon, 'Unpublished diary' (26 November 1845), by permission of Dr Denholm.
21 J. Oxley-Parker, *The Oxley-Parker Papers: From the Letters and Diaries of an Essex Family of Land Agents in the 19th Century* (Colchester, 1964).
22 There were legal debates on the status of widows in relation to husbands' partnerships. See J. Collyer, *A Practical Treatise on the Law of Partnership* (1840), p. 26.
23 Letter to R. Arkwright (5 May 1828), ERO D/DAr. C7/9.
24 J. Harriott, *Struggles Through Life Exemplified*, 2 vols. (1807), vol. 1, p. 329.
25 C. Shrimpton, 'The landed society and the farming community of Essex in the late

18th and early 19th centuries', unpublished Ph.D thesis, University of Cambridge (1966), p. 233.

26 C. Chalklin, *The Provincial Towns of Georgian England: A Study of the Building Process 1740–1820* (1974), p. 242; J. Field, 'Bourgeois Portsmouth: social relations in a Victorian dockyard town 1815–1875', unpublished Ph.D. thesis, University of Warwick (1979), p. 132.

27 J. E. Oxley, *Barking Vestry Minutes and other Parish Documents* (Colchester, 1955).

28 Mrs Henstridge Cobbold, 'Inventory of house and estate, 1849', IRO HA2/A2/886.

29 Philip Hills, personal communication.

30 Nathaniel Lea, 'Unpublished memorandum book, 1837–8', by permission of Mr I. C. Lea.

31 Therefore the importance of 'love and friendship' as a location for women's consciousness but also its limitations. See Caroll Smith Rosenberg, 'The female world of love and ritual: relations between women in nineteenth century America', *Signs*, 1 no. 1 (autumn 1975).

32 J. Oxley, p. 30.

33 R. Scase and R. Goffee, *The Real World of the Small Business Owner* (1980), p. 94. See also J. Finch, *Married to the Job: Wives' Incorporation in Men's Work* (1983).

34 M. Karr and M. Humphreys, *Out on a Limb: An Outline History of a Branch of the Stokes Family, 1645–1976* (Ongar, Essex, 1976), p. 39.

35 Jeremiah Howgego, 'Unpublished diary, 1829–1832', by permission of V. Sheldrake.

36 S. L. Courtauld, *The Huguenot Family of Courtauld*, 3 vols. (1957), vol 2, p. 13.

37 E. De Selincourt, *Dorothy Wordworth: A Biography* (Oxford, 1933), p. 183.

38 T. A. B. Corley, *Quaker Enterprise in Biscuits: Huntley and Palmers of Reading: 1822–1972* (1972).

39 Corley, *Quaker Enterprise*.

40 W. Hutton, *The Life of William Hutton, Stationer of Birmingham and the History of his Family* (1816).

41 A. E. Fairhead, *The Fairhead Series 1–10* (n.d.), ERO, p. 3.

42 T. Cross, *The Autobiography of a Stage-Coachman*, 2 vols. (1861), vol. 2, p. 162.

43 L. Maw, *A Tribute to the Memory of Thomas Maw: by his widow* (1850), p. 20.

44 Based on eighty-three cases from both areas.

45 M. Bayly, *The Life and Letters of Mrs Sewell* (1889), p. 104.

46 J. Wentworth Day, 'A Victorian family's inventive genius', *Country Life* (2 May 1963), p. 962.

47 M. Bayly, p. 36; a pattern confirmed in George Eliot's *Adam Bede* where the farmer's wife, Mrs Poyser, has taken Hetty Sorrel, her husband's niece, to train in dairying and also given a home to her own orphaned niece, Dinah, in return for household help.

48 ABG (4 January 1830).

49 Birmingham File, see Joseph Sturge.

50 Census of 1851: Witham.

51 Census of 1851: whole sample.

52 E. J. Morley, *The Life and Times of Henry Crabb Robinson* (1935); Wordsworth's daughter Catherine was named for Catherine Buck. She was the daughter of a wealthy Bury St Edmund's brewer, see R. G. Wilson, *Greene King: A Business and Family History* (1983).

53 S. L. Courtauld, vol. 2, p. 27.

54 E. J. Robson, *A Memoir of Elizabeth Robson, late of Saffron Walden* (1860), p. 37.

55 J. Bisset, 'Reminiscences of James Bisset', Leamington Public Library, CR 1563/247.

56 Walker's Charity in Fyfield Essex, *Charity Commission Reports*, vol. XVIII (1833).

57 W. Beck, p. 2.

58 E. Gibbins, *Records of the Gibbins Family also a few reminiscences of Emma J. Gibbins and letters and papers relating to the Bevington family* (Birmingham, 1911), appendix I.

59 J. Oxley-Parker, p. 128.

60 J. Perry, 'Unpublished diary 1829–1832', FHL, Box T (August 1838).

61 Mary Alice Parker, 'Unpublished diary 1867', by permission of William Lister.
62 T. Cross, vol. 1, p. 113.
63 B. Mason, *Clock and Watchmaking in Colchester* (1969).
64 Essex and Suffolk File; Birmingham File. An interesting fictional mid century account of a woman taking over the family bank is Mrs Oliphant's *Hester*, first published 1883 (1984).
65 J. A. Watson, *Savills: A Family and a Firm 1652–1977* (1977).
66 Robert Bretnall, 'Unpublished diary 1846', ERO D/DBs F38.
67 R. B. Beckett, *John Constable's Correspondence: the Family at East Bergholt 1807–1837* (1962).
68 M. Smith, *The Autobiography of Mary Smith, Schoolmistress and Nonconformist* (Carlisle, 1892).
69 M. Bayly, p. 166.
70 IJ (24 June 1809).
71 J. Oxley-Parker.
72 Mary Hardy, *Diary* (Norfolk Record Society, 1968).
73 J. M. Strickland, *Life of Agnes Strickland* (1887).
74 J. Glyde, 'The autobiography of a Suffolk farm labourer', in *Suffolk Mercury* (1894), p. 74.
75 M. Bayly, p. 33.
76 *The Lady Magazine*, published from 1770 to 1830 (price 6d), debated women's use of their property as a prominent theme. Information from E. Copeland, Pomona College, California.
77 M. A. Hedge, *Life or Fashion and Feeling: A Novel* (1822), p. 75.
78 M. A. Hedge, p. 62.
79 G. Crabbe, 'The Parish Register', *Poems* (Cambridge, 1905).
80 S. Pollard, *The Genesis of Modern Management* (1965), p. 146.
81 E. L. Jones, *Agricultural and Economic Growth in England, 1650–1815* (1967).
82 George Eliot, 'Mr Gilfil's love story', in *Scenes from Clerical Life*, 2 vols. (Edinburgh, 1856), vol. 1, p. 158.
83 J. Oxley-Parker, p. 107.
84 M. Bayly, p. 31.
85 The only money Catherine Marsh ever earned was for readings of handwriting to raise money for charity. L. E. O'Rorke (ed.), *The Life and Friendships of Catherine Marsh* (1917), p. 25.
86 A. T. Gilbert, *Autobiography and other Memorials of Mrs Gilbert*, 2 vols. (1874), vol. I, p. 108.
87 J. Perry (December 1838).
88 M. J. Shaen, *Memorials of Two Sisters: Susanna and Catherine Winkworth* (1908), p. 13.
89 QQ in *Youth's Magazine or Evangelical Miscellany* (1820), p. 370 (pseudonym for Jane Taylor).
90 E. L. Edmunds, *The Life and Memorials of the Late W.R. Baker* (1865), p. 4.
91 M. Smith, p. 169.
92 Mrs C. Hutton Beale, *Reminiscences of a Gentlewoman of the Last Century* (Birmingham, 1891).
93 Elizabeth A. Wheler, 'Memorials of my life', 2 vols., by permission of Mr J. L. Moilliet; E. Darwin, *A Plan for the Conduct of Female Education in Boarding Schools* (1797); M. McNeil, 'A contextual study of Erasmus Darwin', unpublished Ph.D. thesis, University of Cambridge (1979).
94 Phipson Children, *A Tribute to a Father's Memory* (Birmingham, 1864).
95 In this emphasis we would differ from the conclusions drawn by M. J. Peterson, 'No angel in the house: the Victorian myth and the Paget women', *American Historical Review* (June 1984).
96 Rebecca Solly Shaen, 'Unpublished commonplace book', John Johnson Collection, Bodleian Library, Oxford, Ms 18 and 19.
97 F. H. Erith, *Ardleigh in 1796: Its Farms, Families and Local Government* (East Bergholt, Essex, 1978).

 98 A. Shteir, ' "The Fair Daughters of Albion" and the popularization of British botany', Paper delivered at the British Society for the History of Science (March 1982), p. 8.
 99 M. A. Hedge, *Affections Gift to a Beloved God-child* (Colchester, 1819), p. 22.
100 J. Obelkevich, p. 53.
101 IJ (24 June 1809).
102 A. Watkins, *Extracts from the Memoranda and Letters of Ann Watkins* (Ipswich, 1888), p. 3.
103 E. Shore, *Journal of Emily Shore* (1891), pp. 220, 352.
104 E. A. Wheler; Amelia Moilliet, 'Memoranda', both by permission of J. L. Moilliet.
105 Harriet Walker, 'Journal of a tour made in the spring of 1837', IRO HD/236/3/5.
106 Suffolk File; A. Smart and S. B. Attfield, *Constable and His Country* (1976).
107 A. F. J. Brown, 'Voluntary public libraries', in W. R. Powell (ed), *A History of the County of Essex* (bibliography) (1959). However, a water colour of the village reading room at Writtle shows a woman and three children seated at a table. Corder collection, ERO T/B 228.
108 Quoted in J. Glyde, *The Moral, Social and Religious Condition of Ipswich in the Middle of the 19th Century* (1971), p. 173.
109 Hilda Sebastian, 'A brewing family in Essex', typescript prepared for Coggeshall Women's Institute (n.d.), by permission of the author.
110 Census of 1851: whole sample.
111 E. Gaskell, *Cranford* (1980), p. 130.
112 Census of 1851.
113 M. Reeves, *Sheep Bell and Ploughshare: the Story of Two Village Families* (1980).
114 ABG (10 July 1820).
115 W. Lean, 'Scholars at his school', compiled by J. H. Lloyd, BRL 662590; Birmingham Directories File.
116 R. and G. B. Hill, *The Life of Sir Rowland Hill and the History of Penny Postage*, 2 vols. (1880); F. Hill, *An Autobiography of Fifty Years of Reform* (1893); D. Gorham, 'Victorian reform as a family business: the Hill Family', in A. S. Wohl (ed.), *The Victorian Family, Structure and Stress* (1978).
117 J. Manton, *Mary Carpenter and the Children of the Streets* (1976).
118 Birmingham Statistical Society, 'Report on the state of Education in Birmingham', *Journal of the Historical Society of London*, 3 (1840); King Edward VI School, Birmingham, Governors Order Book, 1832–41, 1842–50, by permission of Mr Walkington, Secretary to the Governors.
119 R. Fletcher, *The Biography of a Victorian Village: Richard Cobbold's Account of Wortham, Suffolk* (1977).
120 J. Manton, *Sister Dora: The Life of Dorothy Pattison* (1971), p. 137.
121 M. L. Smith, 'Witham schools' (Witham, n.d.), p. 6.
122 J. Manton, *Mary Carpenter*.
123 R. and G. B. Hill, vol. 1, p 142.
124 Essex Directories File.
125 A. E. Morgan, *Kith and Kin* (Birmingham, 1896), p. 9.
126 E. T. Phipson, *A Memorial of Mary Anne Phipson* (Birmingham, 1877), Phipson Children.
127 I. Southall, W. Ransom and M. Evans (eds.), *Memorials of the Families of Shorthouse and Robinson and Others Connected with Them* (Birmingham, 1902).
128 Census of 1851: Birmingham.
129 E. T. Phipson.
130 Phoebe Penn's sister had married the Bristol school proprietor Lant Carpenter, father of Mary Carpenter.
131 A. W. Matthews, *Life of Sarah Bache* (1900), p. 20.
132 Matthews, pp. 71, 92.
133 E. A. Wheler, vol. I, p. 56.
134 L. Davidoff, 'The separation of home and work? Landladies and lodgers in 19th and early 20th century England', in S. Burman (ed.), *Fit Work for Women* (1979).
135 Witham File.
136 J. E. Tuffs, *Essex Coaching Days* (Letchworth, n.d.).

137 T. Cross, vol. 2, p. 206.
138 B. Mason.
139 J. Booker, *Essex and the Industrial Revolution* (Chelmsford, 1974), p. 32.
140 M. Girouard, *Victorian Pubs* (1975), p. 28 (our italics).
141 P. Mathias, *The Brewing Industry in England 1700–1830* (Cambridge, 1959).
142 G. Sturt, *A Farmer's Life with a Memoir of the Farmer's Sister* (Firle, Sussex, 1979), p. 26.
143 B. Harrison, *Drink and the Victorians: The Temperance Question in England 1815–1872* (1971), p. 46.
144 E. Edwards, *The Old Taverns of Birmingham* (Birmingham, 1879), p. 82.
145 W. White, *Directory of Ipswich* (1844).
146 F. H. Erith.
147 J. A. Chartres, 'Country tradesmen', in G. E. Mingay (ed.), *The Victorian Countryside*, 2 vols., vol. 2, p. 308.
148 Census of 1851: Witham.
149 D. Alexander, *Retailing in England During the Industrial Revolution* (1970).
150 S. D'Cruze, '"... To Acquaint the Ladies": women proprietors in the female clothing trades, Colchester c. 1750–1800', unpublished paper (1985), by permission of the author, pp. 2, 3, see *The Local Historian*, 17 no. 3 (1986).
151 J. Howgego, p. 28.
152 G. Torrey, *Chelmsford Through the Ages* (Ipswich, 1977), p. 59.
153 John Pudney, unpublished diary of an Essex farmer 1757–1823, ERO T/P 116/62.
154 J. Taylor, 'Prejudice', in *Essays in Rhyme on Morals and Manners* (1816), p. 6.
155 G. J. Holyoake, *Sixty Years of an Agitator's Life* (1900), p. 10.
156 W. H. Ryland (ed.), *Reminiscences of Thomas Henry Ryland* (Birmingham, 1904).
157 W. White, *History Gazetteer and Directory of the County of Essex* (Sheffield, 1848).
158 R. Fletcher.
159 For example, Bernard Barton's sister, Maria Hack, published books for children such as *The Discovery and Manufacture of Glass: Lenses and Mirrors*. All her books were published by Harvey and Darton, the children's book publishers who gave Ann and Jane Taylor their start.
160 Marianne Nunn, *Dictionary of National Biography*; C. Porteous, 'Singing the praises of women', The *Guardian* (22 December 1982).
161 J. S. Curwen, *Memorials of John Curwen: with a Chapter on his home life by his daughter* (1882).
162 M. J. Shaen, p. 39 (her italics). Note George Eliot began her literary career by doing translations.
163 J. Oxley, p. 222.
164 'Minute Book of the Committee of the Protestant Dissenting Charity School, 12 vols. (1761–1922), 1836–47, BRL 471911.
165 J. Penfold, 'Early history of the Essex County Hospital', unpublished manuscript by permission of the author (1980), p. 13.
166 J. Lown, 'Gender and class during industrialization: a study of the Halstead silk industry in Essex, 1825–1900', unpublished Ph.D. thesis, University of Essex (1984).
167 Colchester Castle Club records.
168 M. Hardy.
169 Anon, unpublished diary of a farmer's wife on the Warwick/Leicester border (1823), BUL, Heslop Collection, Ms 10/iii/15, 1823.
170 Birmingham File.
171 G. Crabbe, p. 215.
172 D. C. Coleman, *Courtaulds: An Economic and Social History*, 2 vols. (Oxford, 1969), vol. 1, p. 126.
173 This point is forcefully argued in J. Newton, 'Pride and Prejudice: power, fantasy and subversion in Jane Austen', *Feminist Studies*, 4 no. 1 (February 1978).
174 For example Dillwyn Sims, apprenticed to a miller in Ipswich before joining Ransomes, the agricultural engineering firm. DQB.
175 The Hayward family of Colchester, personal communication, Paul Thompson; the Beadel Family of Witham, Witham File; for the Savills of Chigwell see J. A. Watson.

176 At the artisan level note the male usurpation of funeral arrangements through joinery and the making of coffins over women's traditional function of laying out the dead.

177 For Suffolk see G. E. Evans, *The Horse in the Furrow* (1960); Hannah More's barbed portrait of the 'strong minded' Miss Sparkes in *Coelebs in Search of a Wife* highlights her unfeminine interest in the stables. See Chapter 3. [*Family Fortunes* (1987)].

178 J. D. Sykes, 'Agriculture and science', in G. E. Mingay (ed.), *The Victorian Countryside*, 2 vols. (1980), vol. 1.

179 A. Richards and J. Robin, *Some Elmdon Families* (Cambridge, 1975).

180 We are grateful to Deborah Cherry for allowing us to read her unpublished manuscript, 'Women artists'; R. Parker and G. Pollock, *Old Mistresses: Women Art and Ideology* (1981).

181 S. Lines, *A Few Incidents in the Life of Samuel Lines, Senior* (Birmingham, 1858).

182 J. Blatchly, *Isaac Johnson 1754–1835* (Suffolk Record Office, 1979), p. 9.

183 Samuel Williams; DNB. He illustrated an edition of Jeffrey Taylor's, *The Farm*.

184 W. Beck.

185 D. Stroud, *Humphrey Repton 1752–1818* (1962).

186 William Jackson Hooker was the first director of Kew Gardens. He, his son and son-in-law were eventually knighted for their contributions to horticulture. His daughter, wife of the latter, illustrated the journal edited by the Hooker family. N. Scourse, *The Victorians and their Flowers* (1983). See also John Claudius Loudon's enterprise, Chapter 3 [*Family Fortunes*].

187 D. Allen, 'The women members of the Botanical Society of London; 1836–1856', *The British Journal for the History of Science*, **13** no. 45 (1980), p. 247.

188 D. Allen, *The Naturalist in Britain: A Social History* (Harmondsworth, 1978), p. 167.

189 E. Mann, *An Englishman at Home and Abroad 1792–1828* (1930), p. 201.

190 S. L. Courtauld, vol. 1, p. 44; D. C. Coleman, vol. 2, p. 469.

191 J. Manton, *Mary Carpenter*, p. 39.

192 See N. Stock, *Miss Weeton's Journal of a Governess*, 2 vols. (Newton Abbot, 1969), vol. 1, p. 23.

193 J. Perry (August 1838) (his italics).

194 H. Sebastian, personal communication.

195 R. D. Best, *Brass Chandelier: A Biography of R. H. Best of Birmingham* (1940), p. 25.

196 K. Pearson, *The Life, Letters and Labours of Francis Galton*, 3 vols. (Cambridge, 1914), vol 1, p. 124.

197 Birmingham File; Essex and Suffolk File.

198 Halstead and District Local History Society Newsletter, **3** no. 10 (December 1979).

199 F. Prochaska, *Women and Philanthropy in 19th Century England* (Oxford, 1980), p. 106.

200 Census of 1851 – Edgbaston; Ratebook for Edgbaston.

201 It should be kept in mind that the wills sample starts in 1780 when there were fewer professional and salaried posts than in 1851, the date of the census. But the point still stands.

202 59 per cent of adult female relatives lived with male household heads and 41 per cent in households with a woman head, compared to the 80 per cent male and 20 per cent female household heads in the whole sample. Sisters living with salaried single males made up a fifth of all adult sisters living with their unmarried brothers. Salaried men tended to be younger and less well off than other occupations. Census sample – whole. For an important discussion of spinsters in nineteenth-century Britain see M. Anderson, 'The social position of spinsters in mid-Victorian Britain', *Journal of Family History*, **9** no. 4 (1984).

203 F. Parkin, 'Social closure as exclusion', in *Marxism and Class Theory: a Bourgeois Critique* (1979), p. 53. On the more general meaning of gender and hereditary practices see, C. Delphy and D. Leonard, 'Class analysis, gender analysis and the family', in R. Crompton and M. Mann (eds.), *Gender and Stratification* (1986).

204 Mrs S. Stickney Ellis, *The Women of England: Their Social Duties and Domestic Habits* (1839), p. 463.

10

Golden age to separate spheres? A review of the categories and chronology of English women's history

AMANDA VICKERY

I

'Public and private', 'separate spheres', and 'domesticity' are key words and phrases of academic feminism. The dialectical polarity between home and world is an ancient trope of western writing; the notion that women were uniquely fashioned for the private realm is at least as old as Aristotle. But the systematic use of 'separate spheres' as *the* organizing concept in the history of middle-class women is of more recent vintage. Formative for American feminist historians in the 1960s and 1970s was the idea that gender oppression, the experience of sisterhood and a feminist consciousness have a natural, evolving relationship. Resulting studies undertook a quasi-marxist search for this developing consciousness. Nineteenth-century advice books, women's magazines, evangelical sermons and social criticism provided chapter and verse on the bonds of womanhood at their most elaborate, although such literature was prescriptive rather than descriptive in any simple sense. Thus a particularly crippling ideology of virtuous femininity was identified as newly-constructed in the early to mid-nineteenth century. What Barbara Welter dubbed the 'cult of true womanhood' prescribed the attributes of the proper American female between 1820 and 1860. She was to be pious, pure, submissive and domesticated, for the true woman turned her home into a haven for all that was civilized and spiritual in a materialistic world.[1] The assumption that capitalist man needed a hostage in the home was endorsed by subsequent historians who linked the cult of true womanhood to

The arguments herein were first raised at a workshop on consumption and culture at the Clark Library, UCLA in May 1991. A version was also presented to the Social History Seminar, King's College, Cambridge and the Eighteenth-Century Seminar, Institute of Historical Research, London University. I would like to thank the organizers and participants at all events for many useful comments. For additional criticisms, references and suggestions, I am grateful to Sophie Badham, Kelly Boyd, Leonore Davidoff, David Feldman, Anne Goldgar, Margaret Hunt, Joanna Innes, Ludmilla Jordanova, Lawrence Klein, Jon Lawrence, Susan Lippitt, Peter Mandler, Alastair Reid, Lyndal Roper, John Styles, Stella Tillyard, Naomi Tadmor, Tim Wales and Keith Wrightson. I am particularly indebted to Penelope Corfield and Pat Thane for their critical interest and moral support.

a shrinkage of political, professional and business opportunities for women in the years 1800–1840.[2] In this way, the glorification of domestic womanhood became associated with the deterioration of women's public power, which was itself presented as a function of industrialization. Consequently, the early nineteenth century assumed its present status as one of the key, constitutive periods in the history of gender.

With the publication of Nancy Cott's influential study of early industrial New England, the history of woman's sphere became even more closely fused to a narrative of economic change. Cott related the formation of separate gender spheres: the private sphere of female domesticity and the public sphere of male work, association and politics to the emergence of modern industrial work patterns between 1780 and 1835 and, by implication, to the dominance of the middle class and its ideals.[3] But it was not until the appearance in 1981 of Mary Ryan's study of the family in Oneida County, New York, between 1790 and 1865, that a story of class making was brought to the narrative forefront. Ryan's central hypothesis was the notion that 'early in the nineteenth century the American middle class moulded its distinctive identity around domestic values and family practices'.[4] Ultimately, therefore, the cult of true domestic womanhood was presented as both a consequence of the rise of the middle class, and a vital component in the reproduction of middle-class collective identity.[5]

In the meantime, the analysis of manuscripts written by middle-class women themselves prompted a more sophisticated understanding of the cult of domesticity. Instances were found of American women using notions of domestic virtue for their own purposes, particularly in the attempt to justify their efforts at moral reformation both within the family and outside the home.[6] Furthermore, it was argued that in accepting the conventional message as to their domestic mission, women saw themselves increasingly as a group with a special destiny and their consciousness of sisterhood was thereby heightened. In other words, the bonds of 'womanhood bound women together even as it bound them down'.[7] However, life in a separate sphere was not in all senses impoverished, for it was in the private sphere that historians such as Carroll Smith-Rosenberg discovered and celebrated a rich women's culture of sisterly cooperation and emotional intimacy.

> Women's sphere had an essential integrity and dignity that grew out of women's shared experiences and mutual affection ... Most eighteenth and nineteenth-century women lived within a world bounded by home, church, and the institution of visiting – that endless trooping of women to each others' homes for social purposes. It was a world inhabited by children and by other women. Women helped each other with domestic chores and in times of sickness, sorrow, or trouble.[8]

Implicit in Carroll Smith-Rosenberg's account, and explicit in that of Nancy Cott is the theory that the private sphere nurtured a sense of gender-group solidarity which was ultimately expressed in mid-Victorian feminism, a sisterhood which foreshadowed the culture and ideals of the 1970s women's movement.[9] Thus, by now it should be apparent that these various chapters in the history of women can be incorporated into a long positive story, making sense of a swathe of time from the establishment of the first textile mill to the 19th Amendment to the Constitution, and beyond. For many, the foregoing elements fused together to create the most powerful and satisfying narrative in modern American women's history. As Nancy Hewitt regretfully concluded in 1985, despite the fact that Barbara Welter, Nancy Cott and Carroll Smith-Rosenberg all regarded their work 'as speculative and carefully noted parameters of time, region and class, the true woman/separate spheres/woman's culture triad became the most widely used framework for interpreting women's past in the United States'.[10]

Although the foundation of the separate spheres framework was established through a particular reading of didactic and complaint literature, ensuing primary research was rarely designed to test the reliability of significance of this sort of evidence. Many women's historians neglected to ask the questions posed by early modern family historians: did the sermonizers have any personal experience of marriage? Did men and women actually conform to prescribed models of authority? Did prescriptive literature contain more than one ideological message? Did women deploy the rhetoric of submission selectively, with irony, or quite cynically? And to quote Keith Wrightson, did 'theoretical adherence to the doctrine of male authority and *public* female subordination' mask 'the *private* existence of a strong complementary and companionate ethos'.[11] Those modernists who reminded us that 'the attitudes of ordinary people are quite capable of resisting efforts to reshape or alter them' had little impact on the development of the field.[12] Instead, research confidently built on the sands of prescription. The old sources predetermined the questions asked of the new. The process is here illuminated by Nancy Cott describing the evolution of the historical characterization of the 'woman's sphere' from domestic cage, to ambivalent arena of both constraint and opportunity, to the safe haven of a loving female subculture:

> The three interpretations primarily derived from three different kind of sources; the first from published didactic literature about woman's place and the home, the second from the published writings of women authors, and the third from the private documents of non-famous women. It is worth pointing out that the more historians have relied on women's personal documents the more positively they have evaluated woman's sphere.[13]

However different these successive interpretations might seem, the conceptual importance of a constraining 'women's sphere' is constant. Rather than conclude from positive female testimony that women were not necessarily imprisoned in a rigidly defined private sphere, the dominant interpretation simply sees the private sphere in a better light. Moreover, the assumption prevails that it is helpful and appropriate to examine culture and society in terms of intrinsically male and female spheres.

And indeed the dichotomy between the home and the world continued to structure the bulk of work on nineteenth-century American women until the mid to late 1980s. Recently, however, crucial criticisms of the American historiography have been offered by Linda Kerber, leading her to ask 'why speak of worlds, realms, spheres at all?' and American research now in progress seems more sceptical in its approach.[14] Yet this interpretive tradition was by no means restricted to American women's history, having predetermined the way historians have conceptualized the experience of middle-class women in England.[15] And as British historians were slower to elaborate this conceptual framework, so now they are slower to abandon it.

Of course, elements of the interpretation were hardly new in British historiography. After all, in popular understanding 'Victorian' has long served as a general synonym for oppressive domesticity and repressive prudery. But more specifically, as early as the 1940s and 1950s cultural historians such as Walter Houghton, Maurice Quinlan and Muriel Jaeger had seen the assertion of a new model of femininity as a central component in the rise of Victorianism – a shift in standards and behaviour which Quinlan and Jaeger saw in process from the closing decades of the eighteenth century.[16] Using the same sources (the sanctimonious novels and sermons of Evangelicals like Hannah More, Mrs Sherwood and Mrs Trimmer, the didactic manuals of Sarah Stickney Ellis and her ilk, and the sentimental or chivalric fantasies of Coventry Patmore, John Ruskin, Alfred Lord Tennyson, and so on), a younger generation of women's historians told essentially the same story but with greater rhetorical flourish, arguing that a new ideology of ultra-femininity and domesticity had triumphed by the mid-Victorian period. The first studies painted a highly-charged picture of the typical woman of the nineteenth-century middle class. A near prisoner in the home, Mrs Average led a sheltered life drained of economic purpose and public responsibility. As her physicality was cramped by custom, corset and crinoline, she was often a delicate creature who was, at best, conspicuously in need of masculine protection and, at worst, prey to invalidism. And yet she abjured self-indulgence, being ever-attentive and subservient to the needs of her family. Only in her matronly virtue and radiant Christianity did she exercise a mild authority over her immediate circle. She was immured in the private sphere and would not escape till feminism released her.[17]

Thereafter, the rise of the ideology of domesticity was linked, as in the American case, to the emergence of middle-class cultural identity. It was separate gender spheres which allegedly put the middle in the middle class.

Definitions of masculinity and femininity played an important part in marking out the middle class, separating it off from other classes and creating strong links between disparate groups within that class – Nonconformists and Anglicans, radicals and conservatives, the richer bourgeoisie and the petite bourgeoisie. The separation between the sexes was marked out at every level within the society in manufacturing, the retail trades and the professions, in public life of all kinds, in the churches, in the press and in the home. The separation of spheres was one of the fundamental organizing characteristics of middle-class society in late eighteenth and early nineteenth-century England.[18]

Of course, as organizing characteristics go, class had long been seen as central to the history of nineteenth-century England. In adding gender to the picture of class society, historians of women confirmed a vision of the past shared by most social historians in England in the 1960s and 1970s. And indeed class was to remain a more powerful category in English women's history than in its American counterpart, and as a result the notion of a universal sisterhood which triumphantly bridged the gulf between mistress and servant, prosperous philanthropist and poor recipient never took a firm hold in English historiography.

Less pronounced in the English literature than in the American was the argument that life in a confined sphere could be emotionally enriching for early Victorian women, although there is some work on the support networks and intense friendships of late Victorian rebels.[19] However, the argument that women in prosperous families were robbed of economic and political function and incarcerated in a separate private sphere in the early years of the century came to serve as useful prelude to accounts of feminist assault on public institutions in the later period. Implicit and sometimes explicit in such accounts was the assumption that the private sphere operated was a pressure cooker generating pent-up frustrations which eventually exploded as mass female politics.[20] Revealingly, the first significant history of the English women's movement, written by the activist Ray Strachey in 1928, had opening chapters entitled: 'The prison house of home, 1792–1837', 'The stirring of discontent, 1837–1850', 'The widening circle, 1837–1850' and 'The demand formulated, 1850–1857'.[21]

As Ray Strachey's subtitles suggest, support for the argument that feminism was a reaction to a new regime of domestic incarceration was found in the protests of the late Victorian and Edwardian feminists themselves. Many of them called from the soap-box for a female invasion of the male public sphere and used metaphors of confinement, restriction, stunting and belittlement to convey the frustrations of their girlhoods.[22] The literary children of the Victorians, such as Vera Brittain and Virginia Woolf, who penned graphic portraits of stuffy parental mores, have also lent useful support to the familiar account of nineteenth-century woman languishing or raging within an upholstered cage. Of course, in their efforts to debunk the reputation of the preceding generation, female critics were not alone. Convinced that they had thrown off the fetters of the nineteenth century (a conviction that became even more pronounced after the Great War), several early twentieth-century rebels turned a scathing eye on their parents' shortcomings, and thus it is to the likes of Lytton Strachey, Samuel Butler, Edmund Gosse and so on that we owe the enduring caricature of the hidebound and home-loving Victorians.[23]

Buttressed therefore by three types of evidence – didactic literature, contemporary feminist debate and post-Victorian denunciations – the separate spheres framework has come to constitute one of the fundamental organizing categories, if not *the* organizing category of modern British women's history. Moreover, through the medium of women's studies, the orthodoxy has been communicated to adjacent disciplines, where 'public and private', 'separate spheres', and 'domesticity' are rapidly becoming unquestioned key words.[24]

Of course, interpretations have developed over time. Proponents of the British separate spheres framework have revised many of their early generalizations. Sceptics have debated particular aspects of the framework, with varying degrees of effectiveness. Most are now at pains to present women as sentient, capable beings rather than as passive victims, emphasizing the ways in which women shaped their own lives within a male-dominated culture. The Angel-in-the-House model of Victorian ladyhood has proved most vulnerable to criticism. Using household manuals aimed at the lower middle-class wife managing on about £200 a year, Patricia Branca contested the representativeness of the pure and passive stereotype. Only prosperous upper middle-class ladies, she argued, idly received callers and supervised staff with cool aplomb. The vast majority of middle-class housewives coped with heavy housework and quarrelsome servants, while simultaneously struggling with the nervous art of creative accounting.[25] Meanwhile, using the manuscripts of the wealthy, professional Paget family, Jeanne Peterson disputed the usefulness of the model for even the privileged few.

> According to the received wisdom, Victorian ladies cared for nothing but homes and families, their education was 'decorative adornment' and they submitted to fathers and husbands. Three generations of Paget women do not conform to this. Their education was more than decorative, their relationship to money less distant than we thought, their physical lives more vigorous, expansive and sensual than either scholars today or some Victorians have led us to believe.[26]

The breathless inadequacy model of bourgeois femininity has also been questioned in studies of intrepid emigrants, formidable travellers and driven philanthropists. Feeble females would simply not have been capable of the courageous enterprise and conscientious administration that recent work reveals.[27] In fact, as Pat Thane has astutely argued, it is actually rather difficult to reconcile the 'strong sense of social responsibility, purpose and commitment to hard work with which Victorians of both sexes and all classes were socialised' with the conventional story of *increasing* female passivity.[28]

In fact, where historians have researched the activities of particular individuals and groups, rather than the contemporary social theories which allegedly hobbled them, Victorian women emerge as no less spirited, capable, and, most importantly, diverse a crew as women in any other century.[29] Not that diversity should surprise us. Early modern family historians have long stressed the unique role of character and circumstance in shaping a women's freedom of manoeuvre in marriage. Assuredly, stern patriarchs sometimes married biddable girls,[30] but by the same token strong women sometimes married weak men. Martin Pugh, for example, in an analysis of four elite Victorian marriages, the Duke and Duchess of Marlborough, Lord and Lady Londonderry, the Earl and Countess of Jersey, and Lord and Lady Knightley, observes: 'each of these husband and wife teams included a partner who tended to be home-loving, unambitious and easily exhausted by the stress of public life; in every case it was the male'.[31] As women in the past have varied in strong-mindedness and the ability to exert influence, so brains, force of character and a lofty indifference to persuasion have not been equally distributed amongst the male population – a fact which novelists have noted even if historians have not:

> The theory of man and wife – that special theory in accordance with which the wife is to bend herself in loving submission before her husband – is very beautiful; and would be good altogether if it could only be arranged that the husband should be the stronger and greater of the two. The theory is based upon the hypothesis and the hypothesis sometimes fails of confirmation.[32]

The endless permutations in matrimonial power relations that can result from the accidents of circumstances and character have led some scholars to argue for the unpredictable variety of private experience, in any given period, whatever the dominant ideology.[33] But even if we reject such extreme particularism, the history of ideas tells us that in every era alternative 'ideologies' are usually on offer. Another look at Victorian sexual debate, for instance, reveals it may not have been so universally 'Victorian' as we have been led to believe.[34] Wherever angelic uniformity was to be found, it was not in Victorian sitting rooms, despite the dreams of certain poets, wistful housewives, and ladies' advice books.

Most historians now concede that few women actually lived up to the fantasies of Ruskin and Patmore, but still differ as to how seriously the

Victorians took their didactic medicine. Martha Vicinus, for instance, reflects that if 'nineteenth-century women were not always the passive, submissive and pure creatures of popular idealizations . . . neither were they completely free from this stereotype'.[35] However, much recent scholarship has refused to see the domestic ideal as a force which, in and of itself, severely limited a woman's freedom of manoeuvre. Most vehement in this vein is Jeanne Peterson, who concludes that the ideal of the domesticated Madonna was simply an irrelevance in upper middle-class households. The imposition of such a constraining behavioural model, she suspects, would have made rebellious New Women of an entire generation. 'Instead the freedom, the adaptability, the choices inherent in genteel family life laid the basis for a profound conservatism.'[36] In parallel, Martin Pugh's study of aristocratic women and conservative politics signals the important possibility that ladies paid only lip-service to formal subservience in order to spare their husband's flimsy egos or perhaps the censure of posterity. Certainly, the memoirs of many late Victorian female politicians seem contrived to convey a suitably unthreatening picture of satisfied maternity and genteel leisure, so much so that they sometimes contain no reference whatsoever to a customary gruelling work-load of canvassing, committees and public speaking which can be substantiated from other sources.[37] Similarly, a thorough conversance with conservative assessments of woman's proper place (worried over in her diary) failed to keep Lady Charlotte Guest from translating the *Mabinogion* from medieval Welsh and managing the Dowlais iron works after her husband's death, while simultaneously mothering her ten children.[38] Of course, these particular examples are culled from the records of the socially exalted, who were better placed than most to flout convention or indulge exciting hobbies if they chose. Nevertheless their experiences still serve to remind us of the elementary, but crucial, point that women, like men, were eminently capable of professing one thing and performing quite another. Just because a volume of domestic advice sat on a woman's desk, it does not follow that she took its strictures to heart, or whatever her intentions managed to live her life according to its precepts.

Nevertheless, faith in the constitutive power of domestic precepts still lingers in the explanation of the achievements of mid-Victorian heroines. The heroic narrative assumes that a model of domestic femininity was *actively imposed* on women, who experienced feelings of entrapment of such strength that they were led fiercely to resist their containment, resulting in a glorious escape from the private sphere. To be sure, extraordinary women like Florence Nightingale have left passionate writings which ask us to see public heroism as an inevitable reaction to a previous period of mind-numbing cloistration. However, while Nightingale felt her early career aspirations cruelly thwarted, she herself had been taught Latin and Greek by her father, and was expected to engage in a ceaseless round of good works and charitable visiting in young adulthood.[39] Although Nightingale undoubtedly lacked scope for her great ambitions, she was hardly locked in the parlour with nothing but advice books for nourishment.

The power of domestic ideology as a catalyst is an implicit argument in Jane Rendall's thoughtful micro-study of female aspirations and activity amongst the fortunate. As young women in the 1840s and 50s, Bessie Parkes and Barbara Leigh Smith both resented and complained of their limited horizons.[40] By extension, Rendall implies that their subsequent formidable careers as managers, campaigners, essayists, travellers and energetic participants in radical and bohemian London society should be seen as a reaction to this stultifying containment, rather than evidence that domestic prescripts had limited purchase in certain circles. Interestingly, however, both Parkes and Leigh Smith, like many of their confederates in the Victorian women's movement, hailed from radical political backgrounds. Of course, the importance of the radical inheritance has long been acknowledged (and not least by Rendall),[41] yet few have reflected on the possibility that equal rights feminism was less a reflex response to a newly imposed model of stifling passivity, than the fruition of a political tradition.[42] Privileged women saw social and political freedoms newly won by their fathers and brothers, while their own rights as citizens languished. Liberal feminists borrowed the rhetoric of unjust exclusion and applied it to their own case. But a feminist consciousness of educational disadvantage, virtually non-existent career structure, and exclusion from the major institutions of state is not, in itself, proof that the majority of women in comfortable households had no engagement with the world outside their front door. Nor, when exploring the question of causation and chronology, need a flowering of female politics be read as evidence that the preceding years had witnessed the social internment of middle-class women.

In consequence of recent work both theoretical and empirical, doubts now circulate within women's history about the conceptual usefulness of the separate spheres framework. As Jane Lewis remarked in 1986: 'while such a separation of spheres appears to fit the recent historical experience of western women well, anthropologists have found, first that the dichotomy conflates too easily with public/private and reproduction/production to be a useful conceptual tool and second that it has more descriptive than analytical power'.[43] But despite the dissenting voices, the questions, focus and chronology of the separate spheres framework still holds an uneasy sway. At conferences and seminars, participants raise queries and criticisms, while defendants of 'separate spheres' acknowledge the weaknesses of many aspects of the framework, yet still 'separate spheres' is believed to be of central importance in the history of nineteenth-century women and remains the model taught to students. To add to the confusion, the vocabulary of separate spheres also overlaps with that deployed by political historians to rather different ends; specifically, in the argument that the eighteenth century saw the creation, through the market in print, of a public sphere of politics, in contrast to the previously closed political world of Westminster and the royal court.[44] A major study by Leonore Davidoff and Catherine Hall has tried to take account of recent doubt and debate, but still asserts the historical significance of the ideology of separate spheres.[45] As a result, *Family fortunes: men and women of the English middle class* offers the most complex use of separate spheres as an organizing concept to date. Indeed, many see the book as the last word on the subject. Unquestionably, therefore, a landmark of English women's history, *Family fortunes* is an appropriate focus of detailed critical attention.

The explicit aim of *Family fortunes* is to insert an awareness of the constitutive role of gender into the main agenda of social and historical analysis.[46] This is achieved by bringing the analysis of gender relations to bear on the question of mid-Victorian class formation. To this end, *Family fortunes* offers an account of the economic, associational, religious and domestic lives of middle-class families in Birmingham, Essex and Suffolk, between the years 1780 and 1850. And indeed the study impresses as a massively detailed and richly elaborated account of gender relations in a certain religious and institutional milieu. It offers much invaluable illumination of the complexities which lie beneath the stereotypes: the hidden investment of female knowledge, labour and capital in apparently male-only enterprises; the varying organization of the different churches and religious associations which offered women a place, albeit circum-scribed; the role of wider kin in the life of the supposedly intensely nuclear bourgeois family; and the contradictory nature of middle-class taste and aspiration – even in the papers of the pious families studied, the scandalous Lord Byron was cited almost as often as the unexceptional William Cowper and Hannah More. If anything, however, the richness and singularity of the picture Davidoff and Hall reconstruct refuses the general structure they seek to impose. The picture still stands although the claims they make for it, in my opinion, do not. In brief, they argue that gender played a crucial role in the structuring of an emergent, provincial, middle-class culture, for it was the ideology of domesticity and separate gender spheres which gave distinctive form to middle-class identity. Yet this claim rests upon a series of problematic assumptions which must be explored if women's historians are truly to assess the usefulness of the modified separate spheres framework and to build on the research of Davidoff and Hall in creative ways.

First and foremost, *Family fortunes* rests on the conviction that a class society emerged between 1780 and 1850. For many historians of women, E. P. Thompson's inspirational masterpiece *The making of the English working class* celebrated the making of a class with the women left out. *Family fortunes*, by contrast, presents the making of the middle class with women and the family emphatically in the spotlight. Without reference to the ever-growing literature on the culture and consequence of the early modern middling sort, Davidoff and Hall assert that the provincial middle class took shape in the late eighteenth and early nineteenth centuries. Set apart from aristocracy and gentry by virtue of Evangelized religion, a domestic value-system and non-landed wealth, the middle classes experienced a 'growing desire for independence from the clientage of landed wealth and power' which culminated in the political incorporation of the First Reform Act. Despite internal differences in income and outlook, the nineteenth-century middle class were bound together by a distinctive culture: moderate, rational and commercial, but above all moral and domesticated. These cultural values stood in marked contrast to the lavish and licentious mores of the aristocracy and gentry, although eventually the middle-class world view would become 'the triumphant common sense of the Victorian age'.[47]

This account, however, begs many questions. The last decade has witnessed a massive rethinking of Marxian categories and narratives, particularly in the context of early nineteenth-century England.[48] Yet despite all the recent scholarship, both theoretical and empirical, the old theories about class making remain fundamental to *Family fortunes*, and surprisingly are not open to debate. Their picture of a mid-Victorian bourgeois triumph does not account for new research and novel interpretations. Nineteenth-century historians have re-emphasized the resilience of landed power in government, economy and society, the strength of vertical allegiances up and down the social structure as a whole, and the internal divisions among the commercial classes themselves.[49] Meanwhile seventeenth- and eighteenth-century historians might ask what was so novel about men of middling wealth enjoying both political power in urban institutions and a sense of moral purpose from a cosy home life?[50] And indeed *exactly* how and why the transition from a 'middling sort' to the archetypal 'middle class' is made between 1688 and 1850 has not yet been elucidated.[51]

Although concerned to assert the distinctiveness of middle-class culture, Davidoff and Hall's research was not designed to test the extent to which the posited 'middle-class values' were shared by provincial gentry or, for that matter, by urban artisans. An untested assumption throughout is the vitality of an oppositional culture of commerce versus land. Thus the pious, domesticated burgher is contrasted to the profligate, indiscreet aristocrat. While some aristocrats may have conformed to the melodramatic stereotype, recent scholarship tends to stress the canny commercialism and social restraint of noble land-owners. But, in any case, the vast majority of untitled landed gentlemen were far from fast, loose and raffish. The peerage were few and exceptional (only 267 families in 1800[52]), while the gentry were legion and cautious. Despite their enormous numbers, the role of the lesser gentry in the epic battle of commercial versus gentle mores is virtually never mentioned. By implication, the gentry can be subsumed into one camp or the other: either they represented the lesser echelons of aristocracy, somehow sharing the world view of noble families with one hundred times their income, or they should be seen as rural *rentier* bourgeois.[53] In fact, it remains to be seen whether the mid-Victorian gentry differed so markedly in life-style and outlook from wealthier merchants, manufacturers and professionals. Perhaps they shared a common, polite, provincial world far removed from aristocratic licence and the London court. But to be sure, the notion of a cultural chasm yawning between an emergent 'middle class' and a regressive 'aristocracy' is extremely unhelpful in the context of rural, provincial society between 1750 and 1825, however embryonic these formations are supposed to be before Victoria.

The possible complexities of genteel society in the provinces emerge in my own micro-study of north-east Lancashire between 1750 and 1825.[54] By reading the papers of commercial families in conjunction with, instead of in isolation from, gentry collections, an altogether neglected aspect of the pyramid of local society is revealed. In social and administrative terms, this part of Lancashire was dominated by landed gentry, professional and commercial families – a local elite who exhibited considerable cohesion. The menfolk of these families served together on local turnpike commissions and were listed side by side on the commissions of the peace for Lancashire and Yorkshire. They employed between five and eight servants, and most of their households were sufficiently unassuming to escape the tax on male servants levied in 1777. In addition to their shared role in administration, landed gentlemen, professional gentlemen and gentlemen merchants stood shoulder to shoulder on the grouse moor and river bank. They combined for hearty, exclusively male meals, notably pre-expeditionary breakfasts and formal dinners at local inns. Meanwhile, their wives exchanged information on child-bearing and child-rearing, servants, prices, fashions, recipes and remedies. Whole families encountered each other at dinner parties and ate off similar mahogany dining tables – most of these purchased from the same craftsmen, Gillows of Lancaster. Intellectual sympathy across the elite was pronounced. Establishment prejudice, both Whig and Tory, and unenthusiastic Anglicanism is everywhere apparent. Nevertheless, polite dissenters, such as the gay Quakers of Lancaster, could be absorbed into the elite, since the most significant religious fault-line in the county ran between Protestants and Catholics, not between Anglicans and dissenters. Possessed of the same intellectual and material culture, these families all enjoyed the equipment of gentility. Of course this local elite did not exist in a vacuum. Gentry and professionals were sometimes linked by blood and friendship to the supreme county families; many commercial and gentry families had relatives struggling in lesser trades. All of these factors led to minute discrimination within the local elite itself – by their associations were they known – but snobbery was not a powerful enough solvent to separate into distinct landed, professional and commercial fractions families who had so much else in common. Nor did snobbery lead the old landed families to associate themselves with the values of the fashionable aristocracy. They read of the scandalous activities of London-based lords and ladies with an appalled and untiring fascination, but strongly defined themselves against such outrageous self-indulgence.

But was this social cohesion peculiar to north-east Lancashire? After all, the parish of Whalley is not England. Different social relations may have prevailed in areas without a large lesser gentry presence, a long history of manufacturing, or with a different religious history. Yet because fewer historians have concerned themselves with the lesser gentry, the case studies which would settle the issue are scarce. This is not to suggest, on the other hand, that north-east Lancashire was aberrational. Far from it. Equivalent studies of eighteenth-century Leeds, Bury St Edmunds and Norfolk have also emphasized the extent of cultural homogeneity.[55] Moreover, my own recent work on genteel correspondence in Yorkshire, Cumbria and Northumberland has tended to confirm the Lancashire picture of an inclusive local elite throughout the period 1750–1825. However, all this is not to assert that prosperous provincial families were utterly unaffected by the course of economic change – a cohesive local elite may not have survived intact into the mid-Victorian period[56] – but it is to demonstrate that local studies can reveal both the social integration of families involved in very different economic activities, and that assumptions about appropriate behaviour for men and women were shared across land and trade. Ultimately, therefore, if the lesser gentry practised virtually the same domestic life and sexual division of labour as merchants and manufacturers, it is hard to see how definitions of masculinity and femininity could have made the archetypal middle class.

In the assertion that modern class and gender relations were made in the period from 1780 to 1850, Davidoff and Hall call into play vintage assumptions about the impact of economic change. The period from 1780 to 1850 is a conventional choice for nineteenth-century historians and in characterizing these 70 years as formative, Davidoff and Hall are not unusual. They do not aim to examine the late eighteenth century in any detail; in fact their close focus is saved for the period 1820–50. Again the eighteenth century is the sketchy before-picture, the primeval sludge out of which modern, industrial society emerges. There seems to be a consensus in the literature about nineteenth-century society that 1780 is a key social and economic moment. Implicitly this derives from an old idea of a late eighteenth-century industrial 'take-off'[57] which enabled historians to cite the industrial revolution as the *deux ex machina* accounting for most social developments.[58] But in the light of a revised economic history which has variously stressed the vigour of seventeenth-century and early eighteenth-century international commerce and domestic manufacturing, and/or down-played the socio-economic contrast between 1750 and 1850 in England as a whole,[59] it is surprising that social historians should continue to present, with relatively little qualification, an apocalyptic industrial revolution, 1780–1850, as the midwife of modernity. After all, seventeeth- and early eighteenth-century wealth creation was sufficiently impressive for there to be plenty of commercial families supporting non-earning wives, prospering long before Hannah More and William Wilberforce took up their campaigns. Similarly, the ideas and institutions which allegedly defined both economic man and a manly economy – accounting, banking, an investment market, a complex retail network and so on – were also well established before 1780.[60]

If the economic changes of the period 1780 to 1850 were not as dramatic as *Family fortunes* implies, it cannot be said that the same years were unmomentous in terms of politics. Davidoff and Hall stress the role of the shock-waves of the French revolution and the campaigning zeal of the Evangelicals in creating a new moral climate in English social and political life discernible from the 1790s. In the turbulent decades ahead, it is argued, the image of pure womanhood unsullied by public cares was to offer the English middle class a vision of harmony and security in an uncertain world. What should we make of this version of events? Firstly, it is clear that texts extolling domestic virtue and a clear separation of the realms of men and women circulated long before 1789, so it cannot be the case that political fears begat this particular theory of social organization.[61] Secondly, while no-one would deny that Evangelicalism was a crucial force in nineteenth-century society, the extent to which Evangelicalism was an exclusively middle-class project is unclear: the Clapham sect themselves hailed from lesser gentry, while the appeal of Methodism was obviously felt far down the social hierarchy. Thirdly, it would be mistaken to see Evangelical enthusiasm thriving in every middle-class home, just because the history of the tepid, the backsliding and the utterly indifferent nineteenth-century households remains to be written. And, fourthly, the extent to which shifts in public morality actually stripped women of important powers and freedoms is also obscure. Of course, it is beyond question that the Victorians were different from the mid-Georgians in their public reactions to sex. Moreover, many early nineteenth-century commentators believed that manners and mores had undergone a transformation in their lifetime. Witness Emily, Duchess of Leinster musing in retrospect in 1804 on the explicit writing style of Mary Wortley Montagu:

Lady Mary's are certainly not hints, but very plain speaking, and I am apt to think that want of delicacy was very much the fashion in those days [i.e. 1720–40]. It was going off in my times [i.e. 1750–65], but I still remember it was retained by all those women who were [regarded?] *wits* among the old ones, and there was always a fan held up to the face when their jokes were repeated before any young people by those middle age. Lady Townsend went on with it for many years when quite out of fashion, but she was singular.[62]

Similarly, looking back on his youth in 1827, Sir Walter Scott reflected that elite men no longer dared 'to insult decency in the public manner then tolerated' although he was undecided as to whether a profound transformation of values had occurred or merely a change in outward appearances: 'we are not now, perhaps, more moral in our conduct than men of fifty years ago, but modern vice pays a tax to appearances, and is contented to wear a mask of decorum'.[63] Assuredly, the behaviour of both women *and* men became more constrained in certain public contexts. Yet does the onset of prudishness necessarily signal the haemorrhage of important freedoms for women? That so many of us have presumed it does, *ipso facto*, is perhaps more of a testimony to the continuing strength of the 1960s belief that sexual adventure and social liberation are synonymous, than the result of research on the early nineteenth century. Still, Evangelical fervour *may* have resulted in the discrediting of certain public arenas within which privileged woman had once been active, like the theatre auditorium, the assembly room and the pleasure garden, although research on this issue is in its infancy. Nevertheless, if Evangelized religion took from some women's public lives with one hand, it undoubtedly gave with the other in the burgeoning of religious associations, moral campaigns and organized charity. Certainly, this was Wilberforce's rather self-serving conclusion:

> There is no class of persons whose condition has been more improved in my experience than that of unmarried women. Formerly there seemed to be nothing useful in which they could naturally be busy, but now they may always find an object in attending the poor.[64]

Moreover, Linda Colley has recently argued that the conservative backlash of the 1790s offered opportunities for *greater* female participation in a new public life of loyalist parades, petitions and patriotic subscriptions. Viewed from this angle, in fact, reactionary politics offered these 'angels of the state' a higher public profile, not an upholstered private cage.[65]

And this brings us back to the vexed question of separate spheres. Taking account of feminist revisionism, Davidoff and Hall recognize that the prescriptions of sermons and conduct books can never offer a perfect design for living. (In fact, Davidoff herself suggested in an important essay in 1977 that the ideal system laid out in sermons and manuals was belied by the complexity of lived experience.[66]) Davidoff and Hall argue that the spheres could never be truly separate and that it was impossible for Victorians to live as if that separation was absolute. Nevertheless, they still assert that the ideology of separate spheres had a powerful hold on the imagination of the

Victorian bourgeoisie and that negotiating this ideology was a central middle-class concern. It was the middle-class belief in appropriate spheres which shaped the formal organization (if not the day-to-day running) of their emergent institutions. Their argument for the ideological significance of 'separate spheres' rests upon the existence of a large body of nineteenth-century texts extolling the strict separation of the public and private, and the fact that religious institutions tended to segregate the formal activities of men and women. But does this juxtaposition offer sufficient proof that the Victorians exerted themselves to live up to the rhetoric of separate spheres? Davidoff and Hall do not offer evidence from personal manuscripts of a constant dialogue between precept and practice. Instead, they detail the attempts of churchmen of all denominations to ensure a proper division of labour between the sexes: women were allotted subsidiary roles, directed to single-sex committees and for the most part expected to content themselves dispensing liquid and emotional refreshment.[67] However, this raises a crucial question – is the maintenance of a sexual division of labour within institutions *the same thing as* the separation of public and private spheres? If we decide it is, then we must conclude that the drive to create separate spheres is universal, transcending class and time, for throughout history and across cultures there are virtually no institutions which have not differentiated between men and women when it comes to dispensing power and prestige. Of course, if the segregation of men and women within church organization can be shown to be a novel development, then it might be read as another manifestation of the forces that spawned the separate spheres literature, thereby confirming the status of 'separate spheres' as a powerful ideology. And in this vein, Davidoff and Hall assume: 'as so often, increased formality led to the increasing marginalization of women'.[68] Yet, few eighteenth-century historians would claim that women enjoyed an institutional heyday in their period. If anything, the early nineteenth-century growth of female committee work and the like looks like an expansion of the female role, not a diminution. Indeed, one might go further and argue that the stress on the proper female sphere in Victorian discourse signalled a growing concern that more women were seen to be active *outside* the home rather than proof that they were so confined. The broadcasting of the language of separate spheres might in fact be a conservative response to an unprecedented *expansion* in the opportunities, ambitions and experience of late Georgian and Victorian women.

In questioning the ideological power of the separate spheres rhetoric in the making of the middle class, or the confinement of women, this essay does not argue that the vocabulary of public and private spheres had no currency in nineteenth-century society. Linda Colley's female patriots used the rhetoric of separate spheres to legitimize their actions. 'Posing as the pure-minded Women of Britain was, in practice, a way of insisting on the right to public spirit.'[69] Equally, philanthropists deployed this rhetoric to justify their non-domestic activities. That they should call on the language of true womanly duty is hardly surprising. After all, even St Paul conceded that good works became good women. Moreover, sentimentalists like Ruskin handed rhetorical success on a plate when they mused: 'a woman has a personal work or duty, relating to her own home, and a public work and duty which is also the expansion of that' and 'wherever a true wife comes, [home] is always around her'.[70] In arguing that organized charity represented an altogether natural extension of female domestic duties, a form of 'social housekeeping', activists defeated the opposition with its own weapons. Demonstrably, also, the language of separate spheres was deployed in the late Victorian controversy about women's citizenship. Numerous campaigners stated categorically that they wanted access to the public sphere, by which they clearly meant the universities, the professions, local and central government. Gissing's fictional New Woman called for 'an armed movement, an invasion by women of the spheres which men have always forbidden us to enter' and categorically rejected 'that view of us set forth in such charming language by Mr Ruskin'.[71] As the reference to John Ruskin suggests, feminist speeches were tactically contrived to argue with those who contended that women ought to return to their traditional responsibilities and stay out of institutional life.[72] Feminist polemic was designed to convert and galvanize an audience; it did not pretend to be a nuanced account of women's everyday lives and informal powers. Of course, to stress the debating role of feminist rhetoric is to labour the blindingly obvious, but the proselytizing function is worth remembering, before we assume firstly that the well-reproduced speeches offer a simple description of the daily reality of life in domestic prison, and secondly that what campaigners meant by the public and the private coincidences with what those words mean to historians.

It should be emphasized that none of this is to argue that Victorian women had a fine time of it. It is beyond question that they laboured under great disadvantages: legal, institutional, customary, biological and so on. Nor should one suppose that all was happiness and harmony in the middle-class family. Clearly, if a husband was deaf to persuasion, resolved to push his prerogatives to the utmost, then marriage could mean miserable servitude for his unlucky wife. But it is to say that the metaphor of separate spheres fails to capture the texture of female subordination and the complex interplay of emotion and power in family life, and that the role of an ideology of separate spheres in the making of the English middle class, 1780–1850, has not been convincingly demonstrated. It is also to suggest that our preoccupation with the ideology of separate spheres may have blinded us to the other languages in play in the Victorian period. As a sociological study of a particular set of gender relations at a particular historical moment, *Family fortunes* has much to offer to the next generation of women's historians, but the overarching historical narrative it seeks to tell should be discussed and debated, not given the unwarranted status of holy writ.

II

The unquestioned belief that the transition to industrial modernity robbed women of freedom, status and authentic function underlies most modern women's history. One can hardly pick up a text on women's lives in the nineteenth century which is not founded on the conviction that things ain't what they used to be. But were the work opportunities and public liberties enjoyed by propertied women before the factory so much greater than those of the Victorian period? Much of the literature on early modern women's work and social lives would have us believe so. The second major account of change in the history of middle-class women rests on a tale of female marginalization resulting from early modern capitalism. Like so many theories in social and economic history, the intellectual origins of this story lie in the nineteenth century. Socialist writers, particularly Friedrich Engels and the first generation of female professionals, were preoccupied with the idea that women were infinitely better off before the coming of commerce. The overthrow of capitalist society, Engels confidently predicted, would see a return to the traditional equality of the sexes. Political democracy would not crumble if women were admitted as full citizens, implied the first female historians, since reforming legislation would simply restore the status *quo ante*.[73] In so arguing, however, these pioneer thinkers engendered a compelling vision of a pre-capitalist utopia, a golden age, for women, which shapes the writing of history to this day. At the same time, they sketched a social, cultural and economic transformation so abstract that it could be applied to almost any region or historical period.

And indeed it has. Countless historians follow Engels by presenting women as valued and productive on page one of their study, but then ultimately devalued and redundant by the conclusion, usually 50 years later. Take two classics of English economic history: Alice Clark's *Working life of women in the seventeenth century* (1919) and Ivy Pinchbeck's *Women workers and the Industrial Revolution* (1930). These historians held differing views on the quality of industrial life and the implications of female exclusion from it. Nevertheless, both saw the declining role of the woman worker and the associated rise of the male breadwinner as a consequence of capitalism in various guises, although for Alice Clark the *key* period of loss was the late seventeenth century, while for Pinchbeck the crucial decades fell between 1790 and 1840. Despite the chronological inconsistencies, however, Clark and Pinchbeck share many assumptions about the character and consequences of economic change which have been assimilated to a generalized narrative.

According to customary wisdom, sometime between 1600 and 1800 a wholesome 'family economy' wherein men, women and children shared tasks and status gave way to an exploitative wage economy which elevated the male breadwinner and marginalized his dependants. The commercialization of agriculture and the enclosure movement strangled the informal livelihood contrived by many labouring families on the land. The housewife lost her ability to contribute through husbandry, while female workers who had previously worked shoulder to shoulder with their menfolk were suddenly marginalized in sporadic, demeaning and low-paid agricultural occupations. Meanwhile, the mechanization of industrial processes took manufacturing out of the early modern home and into the modern factory, separating for ever after the home and workplace.[74]

Thus, in brief, the orthodox version. However, there is now a growing chorus of heretical voices. In 1983, Olwen Hufton questioned the validity of the decline and fall model of women's work in early modern Europe, since it rests on the dubious assumption of a lost egalitarian Eden, which has proved an elusive to empirical research. The more research that is done, concluded Hufton, the more the vision of the *bon vieux temps* recedes into an even more distant past. In parallel, Judith Bennett argued in 1988 that if women's work was 'low-skilled, low-status and low-paying' in the nineteenth century then it always had been. Thus the basic continuities in women's work between 1200 and 1900 must render inadequate the conventional explanation of female subordination in terms of capitalism and industrialization.[75] Along with general criticisms of the master narrative, the last few years have also seen the publication of case studies which undermine particular aspects of the story for early modern England. Unfortunately for our purposes, most of this work concentrates on the experience of labouring women. However, it is useful briefly to summarize some of the new findings here as they have important implications for the discussion of the wealthier women that follows.

The saga of the good old days and their sorry demise has been problematized by new work on agriculture, rural manufacturing and urban labour. When it comes to women's work in agriculture, the universal narrative fails to capture the different histories of sheep-corn and wood-pasture farming, the contrast between the well-studied south-east and the under-researched north-west, and the different experiences of families with a skilled and unskilled head.[76] Moreover, even for the corn belt, the notion of a sudden metamorphosis of the sturdy independent small-holder into the landless proletarian is belied by the long, drawn-out history of enclosure. After all, there had been waged day labour on the land since at least the sixteenth century. And, most significantly, there is little convincing evidence that men and women's agricultural work had ever been interchangeable. Certainly, one of the few substantial case studies, a recent examination of Norfolk farming in the late sixteenth century, convincingly demonstrates that men and women's work was clearly differentiated in terms of tasks, status and remuneration. Unless old, feeble or simple, men rarely did jobs like weeding or picking over corn, 'any more than women built houses, hewed timber, ploughed, harrowed, threshed, carted hay and corn, dug ditches or cut hedges'.[77] But if early modern agriculture was no bed of roses for women, was rural industry any better? While it is undoubtedly the case that women experienced substantial losses in this sector due to the mechanization of handspinning in the late eighteenth century, it is not clear that women's non-agricultural paid labour was especially rewarding before the factory. The received picture of a self-sufficient, non-alienating family enterprise is not supported by the available case studies. In fact, production by the family as a unit was far from being the norm. For example, for the vast majority of the worsted handspinners of Yorkshire and the lacemakers of Devon, their work was not a complement to their husband's trade, but an entirely separate form of waged employment.[78] Emphatically, waged work was no invention of nineteenth-century industrialists, nor was work before the factory as household-centred and as communitarian as has been suggested. But even where men and women did work alongside each other on a shared project, in the classic proto-industrial family, for example, a sexual division of labour usually prevailed. Furthermore it is not clear that a woman's industrial work was any more agreeable when directed by a husband, rather than a formal employer, or that her obvious contribution to the family's manufacturing output necessarily translated into higher status. Indeed the belief that a heavy workload automatically translates into power and prestige is a curious one for women's historians to espouse.[79]

Yet even if the history of the textile industry *could* be made to fit the conventional chronology of economic decline, an all-inclusive chronology for women's labour should not be derived from textiles alone. Firstly, women had a different experience in other rural industries. In metalwares and the smaller domestic industries mechanization only reinforced a pre-established division of labour, and women's labour remained paramount throughout the nineteenth century.[80] Secondly, whatever the change over time in women's work roles in the countryside, there was virtually none in the city. Peter Earle's recent comparison of female employment in London in 1700 and in 1851 reveals that domestic service, charring, laundry, nursing, and the making and mending of clothes were the most common occupations in both periods. While participation rates declined, the general structure of the female labour market remained the same. There was no systematic reduction in the range of employments available to labouring women over the period.[81] So while the end of the eighteenth century was distinctive in the history of women's work insofar as this period witnessed the grievous loss of remunerative employment in one important sector of the economy, the domestic manufacture of textiles, the decline of handspinning is not sufficient in itself to support a theory of absolute and comprehensive decline for every working woman in everything from economic power and legal independence to public assertiveness and sexual respect.[82]

It is against this background of scepticism about a history which blindly insists that women's status had deteriorated from a past golden age that we should assess the parallel arguments about wealthier women. Here the central tragic theme is the much-lamented metamorphosis of the seventeenth-century business woman or diligent housekeeper into the nineteenth-century parasite. In the sixteenth and early seventeenth centuries, so Alice Clark famously argued, the wives of craftsmen and manufacturers made a substantial contribution to the family enterprise since the home and workplace were usually one. Women at all social levels were true partners to their husbands, they demonstrated a capacity for business and their engagement in commercial life aroused no comment. It was usual for gentlewomen to be active in household and estate management, public affairs and even government. But as the century wore on the rapid increase of wealth permitted the wives of prosperous men to withdraw from all forms of productive activity. In parallel, the spread of 'capitalistic organization' ensured that manufacturing became concentrated on central premises. Once production left the home, the wife was divorced from her husband's trade and lost the informal opportunity to learn his skills. Creative housekeeping fell into decay. In contrast to their hardy and resourceful Elizabethan grandmothers, the moneyed ladies of the Restoration were distinguished only by their 'devotion to idle graces'.[83]

This resonant tale of a female descent into indolence and luxury has been frequently reiterated.[84] Moreover, it is tacit in most accounts that the female liberation from manual labour is *ipso facto* disempowering. Lawrence Stone, for instance, leaves us in no doubt about the frivolousness and futility of a woman's life once she had vacated the dairy and laid down the distaff.

> Wives of the middle and upper classes increasingly became idle drones. They turned household management over to stewards, reduced their reproductive responsibilities by contraceptive measures, and passed their time in such occupations as novel reading, theatre going, card playing and formal visits. ... The custom of turning wives into ladies 'languishing in listlessness' as ornamental status objects spread downwards through the social scale.[85]

Some have built on the tale of woman's divorce from useful labour to assert that the 'new domestic woman' was the inevitable bride of the new economic man.

> [With the] eighteenth-century glorification of 'Man' came a radical narrowing of women's participation in and contribution to productive and social life, and a drastic diminution of women's stature. It was not

merely a relative decline. Pre-capitalist woman was not simply relatively eclipsed by the great leap forward of the male achiever; she suffered rather an absolute setback.[86]

Echoing nineteenth-century preoccupations, scholars of English literature have tried to chart the construction of domesticated femininity, although there is a certain confusion as to whether the new domestic woman was the epitome of bourgeois personality, or was an ornament shared by the middling ranks and the landed. But whatever her social background, it is agreed that the sweet domesticate was created 'in and by print'. Kathryn Shevelow's study of early eighteenth-century periodicals leads her to conclude that 'during the eighteenth century, as upper and middle-class Englishwomen increasingly began to participate in the public realm of print culture, the representational practices of that print culture were steadily enclosing them within the private sphere of the home'.[87] But for all the stress on the constitutive power of language in the emergence of homely virtue, most of the literary studies take on trust the prior existence of an entirely new breed of bored, housebound, cultural consumers created at a particular historical moment by capitalism.[88] Therefore, whether informed by Foucault, Lacan or Greenblatt, recent feminist literary criticism still depends ultimately on a narrative of social and economic change which has barely changed since 1919.

So on what basis did Alice Clark found her original argument? In fact, her evidence for change over time was remarkably slight. She used diaries, letters and depositions to establish the courage and capability of ladies in the late sixteenth century and early to mid-seventeenth century, but to demonstrate that 'their contact with affairs became less habitual as the century wore away' she relied on a different order of source material.[89] She cited unflattering comparisons of the inadequate English lady with her sober Dutch counterpart, Mary Astell's sorrowful criticisms of the 'Ladies of Quality', the stock characters of Restoration drama, and the fact that Samuel Pepys was surprised and pleased to hear a friend's wife talk like a merchant. (In addition to such commentary, she cited the declining number of women who were named as sole executrix of their husband's will as proof of a withering of female ability. However, whether it is possible to detect a single pattern of testamentary practice over the centuries and to attribute any change in practice to a growing perception of feminine inconsequence remains a very open question.[90]) But it is undeniably the case that the late seventeenth century saw a steady increase in texts grumbling about unemployed womanhood, a muttering which grew to a clamour from the 1690s. A new character graced the pages of plays, commentaries and complaint literature – the London woman who scorned productive labour for the sake of consumerism and pleasure. Most critical and subsequently most quoted was Daniel Defoe: 'As ladies now manage', he remarked, they 'scorn to be seen in the compting house, much less behind the counter; despise the knowledge of their husband's business, and act as if they were ashamed of being tradesmen's wives, and never intended to be tradesman's widows.' Instead she will 'sit above in the parlour, receive visits, drink tea and entertain her neighbours, or take a coach and go abroad'.[91] However, the redundant woman of the Augustan period, languishing on her sofa, may not have been as novel a creature as the indictments suggest. Perhaps it was her flamboyant habits that were new and public, rather than her actual lack of occupation. It could even be argued that such criticism was merely another symptom of the general moral panic in the late seventeenth century about the decline of spartan virtue and the rise of luxurious corruption, rather than evidence of any new social group or practice. After all, in their fears about the vicious consequences of wealth, writers fell back upon stereotypical images of devouring, unreasonable womanhood, images that were as old as Eve herself – something which suggests we might better view such accusations as testimony to the persistence of *male* anxieties, rather than a simple guide to *female* behaviour.[92] And, of course, scholars of print might suggest that the rising tide of complaint and conduct literature owes far more to the relaxation of censorship after the failure to renew the licensing act in 1695 than it does to the outbreak of a new disease called female parasitism.

But if this flowering of public discussion was not necessarily a simple reaction to the mass female abandonment of active enterprise, was it subsequently responsible for the creation of an entirely new model of feminine behaviour? Did the *grand peur* about female ostentation and publicity lead to the inscription of a new pattern of virtuous, domesticated womanhood? To be sure, many scholars have detected a growing emphasis on women's innate moral superiority and a declining preoccupation with uncontrollable female sexuality in Augustan literature. Backed by an impressive survey of courtesy literature written between 1670 and 1750, Fenela Childs argues that cloying idealization set in from 1700, although she stresses the obvious but important point that visions of female nature had for centuries oscillated between impossibly pure and irredeemably depraved.[93] Similarly, Marlene Legates suggests that we should not overestimate the novelty of eighteenth-century view of women. She argues that chastity and obedience were ancient pre-requisites of the ideal woman, that a belief in woman as redeemer was as old as courtly love, that positive views of marriage had coexisted with explicit misogyny in classical and humanist thought, and that even the sentimental themes of love, marriage and virtue under siege had a long pedigree. Legates concludes that the eighteenth century saw not so much a dramatic break with past assumptions about the good woman, as a compelling dramatization of her traditional predicament.[94] Evidently, eighteenth-century literature contained much that nineteenth-century historians might identify as 'domestic ideology', yet these themes were far from revolutionary. Moreover, periodicals, novels, sermons and conduct books undoubtedly contained many other ideological messages besides and were probably subject to multiple and/or selective readings. Indeed, as this essay has frequently implied, we should not presume without evidence that women (or men) mindlessly absorbed a particular didactic lesson like so many pieces of blotting paper.[95]

In any case, research on the seventeenth and early eighteenth-century economy raises doubts about the conviction that female enterprise decayed substantially between 1700 and 1850. Firstly, it is clear that the explanatory power given to the notion of the separation of the home and workplace is unwarranted. Of course, if industrial change had involved a simple linear transition from family workshop to factory this process could have had a devastating impact across the board. But as D. C. Coleman remarked in another context, there were many key early modern enterprises which simply could not be performed in a cottage by husband, wife and children. In mining, shipbuilding, iron smelting, pottery firing, glass blowing, paper making, soap boiling, fulling wool and so on, the place of work was of necessity divorced from bed and board from the very inception of the industry. Moreover, the factory was far from being the normal unit of production in the mid-nineteenth century.[96] Economic change followed many roads and did not arrive at a single destination. And, secondly, when we consider those businesses that women pursued in their own right, continuity is more apparent than change. Peter Earle's study of late seventeenth-century London reveals women *already* clustered in the so-called feminine trades: petty retail, food and drink, and textiles. (In fact, women's businesses in York were concentrated in petty retail, food and drink, and textiles *as far back as the fifteenth century*.[97]) Widows had long been unwilling to pursue their late husband's business if it was an uncongenial trade. They tended either to remarry a journeyman or sell up. Moreover, single women were prominent in the London rental and investment market, as they were in rural money lending, suggesting that the economic choices of wealthier women were already biassed against active, risky business.[98] It was probably considerably easier for an heiress to operate as a landlady, money lender, *rentier*, or investor than to run a male business in a male world. Indeed, it could be argued that a female withdrawal from active enterprise was essentially a function of increasing wealth. Therefore *any* study of an expanding business, be it in fourteenth-century York, seventeenth-century London, or nineteenth-century Birmingham, would be likely to show a reduction over three generations in the formal participation of female members of the owning family. In determining the incidence of female withdrawal from business over the long term, what may be crucial is not the growth of capitalism as such, but increases in the number of businesses generating sufficient wealth to allow such withdrawal. What we need are careful comparisons across time and space of the role of women in enterprises of a similar scale. Yet even at this early stage of research, it is already clear that many centres of commerce and manufacturing had boasted a select population of non-earning ladies long before the flowering of literature advocating domestic womanhood – a fact which must be taken on board when making large statements about causation and chronology in the lives of wealthier women.

However, if women in commercial, professional and gentry families did not formally share an income generation, this did not mean that they made no informal contribution or that they performed no work of their own. My own late eighteenth-century evidence demonstrates the extent to which the complexities of women's work are obscured by a literature which defines labour solely in terms of market-oriented production. Among the wealthy, both mercantile and landed, women's work was essentially organizational and administrative. Letter writing was a key component of female business. Their letters sustained relations with the cousinhood, garnered 'friends' or sponsors for their children, gathered information about business and apprenticeship opportunities for them, kept a finger on the pulse of the local labour market for servants, helped provision the household and were the means by which many of its choicest artifacts were acquired.[99] But these ladies did more than wield the pen, they were interventionist house-managers not hothouse blooms. Rare was the employer who could boast of reliable servants capable of assuming responsibility for the smooth running of the household. Maids were unlikely to acquire the requisite expertise since they moved on so frequently. Merchant's wife Elizabeth Shackleton of Alkincoats, saw 29 maids pass through her household in a single year, 1772. Fourteen of these women were theoretically employed on a permanent basis, yet ten of them worked for less than 30 days. Judging by available diaries and account books. Mrs Shackleton was not unusually plagued by transient personnel. At this social level, few women were at liberty to languish on their couches due to the pressing responsibilities of management. Elite women might not have spun cloth or made butter, but neither did their husbands plough fields, dig ditches, or carry cloth on their backs to the local piece hall. Ladies, like gentlemen, had a working knowledge of the processes under their supervision, but instructed their inferiors to carry out the necessary manual labour.[100]

Of course, such women's lives were also structured by their maternal responsibilities, although they always described their mothering role in terms of natural fulfilment and inescapable duty, never in terms of work. Nevertheless in rural Lancashire and Yorkshire, motherhood knocked out 10–15 years of women's social lives. During this period, the number of letters written to friends declined markedly, matrons tended to stay closer to home than they had as girls, and as a result their public profile was often lowered until they re-emerged post menopause in the role of chaperon. The sheer pressures of pregnancy, nursing and mothering infants limited a wealthy woman's freedom of manoeuvre in my period, as doubtless it had done for centuries. So could we describe these women as 'domestic women'? Certainly, a celebration of the pleasures of home life emerges from eighteenth-century letters. But there is no proof that the fostering of cosy sentimentality constrained these women any more than they were already by the sheer practicalities of maternity.[101]

Consider the letters a Charterhouse schoolmaster wrote to his landed cousin in the 1760s and 70s. Reverend William Ramsden waxed poetical when he contemplated his robust wife and first born, writing:

> From the arm of my wife's easy chair, a situation I wo'd not change with the king of Prussia: no, nor (with a man a million more times to be envyd) with George the 3rd king of Britain: my good woman at the same time with glee in her eye contemplating her little boy who also in his turn seems as happy as this world can make him only with his leather bottle. Pardon this gossip Madam but the air of a nursery is infecting.[102]

And he was never more at peace with the world than when anticipating the arrival of the family meal: 'Here comes supper (Dinr I should say) smelts at top, 'sparagus at bottom, a smiling wife, who'd be a king?'[103] His wife, Bessy Ramsden, was also well versed in the language of cosy intimacy and artless pleasure. 'Tomorrow three weeks we break up again for a month. Deary is looking for some snug country box to carry me and my lambkins to grass.'[104] Yet, she herself was no stay-at-home; at every available opportunity she swept out to visit, play cards, gossip and shop, and to attend public trials, pleasure gardens, assemblies and the theatre. Almost invariably, she set out alone, or in the company of other ladies, leaving her schoolmaster behind to guard the domestic hearth. Witness three typical reports:

> The baggage . . . is frolicked away to the play (May, 1769).

> I say no more of Madam, than that she has been *gambling* out every night this week, leaving her good man at home to dry nurse (December, 1770).

> My Duchess in her heart is a rake; this evening she is out making bridal visits about St James Square (December, 1773).[105]

A successful housewife and an incurable street-wife, Bessy Ramsden saw no inconsistency in enjoying sentimental domesticity at one time of day and independent socializing at another. All of which serves to remind us that although the language of domesticity implied privacy, it was not necessarily synonymous with female seclusion and confinement. A typical day in the life of Bessy Ramsden, incorporating as it did work, domesticity, idleness and pleasure also raises problems for the historiography of women's work, which has insisted on seeing labour and leisure as two consecutive stages in the evolution of bourgeois women.[106] Finally, this testimony from the 1760s and 1770s should remind us that self-conscious domesticity was neither the invention nor the sole property of Evangelical businessmen.

The wives of the merchants and manufacturers I have studied were definitely not idle, but it cannot be said that they enjoyed extensive commercial opportunities which their Victorian equivalents subsequently lost. Nor should the eighteenth century be seen as a golden age of female public life. And this point takes us back to my earlier discussion of separate spheres. In no century before the twentieth did women enjoy the public powers which nineteenth-century feminists sought – the full rights of citizenship. Public life for the gentlemen I have studied invariably incorporated some form of office, but there was no formal place for their wives in the machinery of local administration. Customarily, a wealthy woman wielded power as a mother, kinswoman, housekeeper, consumer, hostess and arbiter of polite sociability. If all this adds up to a separation of the public sphere of male power and the private sphere of female influence, then this separation was an ancient phenomenon which certainly predated the misogyny of the 1690s, Evangelicalism, the French revolution and the factory.

The public/private dichotomy may, therefore, serve as a loose description of a very long-standing difference between the lives of women and men. What is extremely difficult to sustain, however, is the argument that sometime between 1650 and 1850 the public/private distinction was constituted or radically reconstituted in a way that transformed relations between the sexes. The shortcomings of the public/private dichotomy as an analytical framework are many, but most obviously there is little unanimity among historians as to what public and private should be held to mean in this context. Current interpretations of 'the public' vary enormously. In a historian's hands, a public role can mean access to anything from politics, public office, formal employment, opinion, print, clubs, assembly, company, the neighbourhood, the streets, or simply the world outside the front door. However, we should take care to discover whether our interpretation of public and private marries with that of historical actors themselves. Take again the excellently documented experience of Elizabeth Shackleton of Alkincoats. She resorted often to the 'publick papers', perpetuated her dead husband's 'publick spirit' by selling his famous rabies medicine at an affordable price, witnessed her second husband's 'publick humiliation' in the house of a tenant, and saw her own kitchen become 'very publick' with a stream of unexpected visitors. Doubtless, the likes of Mrs Shackleton figured in that 'publick' addressed by both the *Ladies Magazine* and the *Leeds Intelligencer*.[107] Most of her labour took place within the house, yet from her medicine room she traded with men throughout the north, and from her writing desk wrote business letters to a national network.

Evidently, her public and private cannot be mapped on to the physical home and the external world. The 'publick' for Elizabeth Shackleton was inextricably bound up with company, opinion and information. She had access to all of these. For the aforementioned Bessy Ramsden, going out 'in publick' in the 1760s and 1770s meant a visit to the theatre, the assembly, the pleasure garden or a trial. Another wife of a London professional, the diarist Anna Larpent, listed all 'the publick places and private entertainments' she visited and enjoyed between 1773 and 1787. Public places listed in 1773 included the play, the opera, Richmond assembly and Ranelagh – all venues which could be penetrated for the price of a ticket and where visitors could see and be seen. Private entertainments were exclusive gatherings entered by invitation only.[108] So while women such as Elizabeth Shackleton, Bessy Ramsden and Anna Larpent were obviously severely disabled when it came to institutional power, they did not lack access to the public sphere, *as they understood it*. It seems likely that eighteenth-century conceptions of publicity were different from those of nineteenth-century feminists and twentieth-century historians. All of which underlines the deficiencies in our knowledge of the distinctions between public and private in language, never mind as social practice.

III

This, then, is the contradictory inheritance of seventeenth- and nineteenth-century women's history. In essence, the rise of the new domestic woman (whether in her seventeenth- or nineteenth-century guise), the separation of the spheres, and the construction of the public and private are all different ways of characterizing what is essentially the same phenomenon: the marginalization of middle-class women. Like the insidious rise of capitalism, the collapse of community, the nascent consumer society and the ever-emerging middle class, it can be found in almost any century we care to look. When confonted with the numerous precedents, nineteenth-century historians of this phenomenon may claim that early modern developments represent only the *germ* of what was to come on a grand scale for the Victorian middle class. But the obvious problems of periodization which result cannot be brushed aside with the explanatory catch-all of 'uneven development'. The problem is exemplified if we try to reconcile Susan Amussen's work on early modern Norfolk and Leonore Davidoff's on nineteenth-century Suffolk.[109] Are we to believe that women were driven out of a public sphere of production and power in one district in the seventeenth century, while just over the county border the same development was delayed by well over a hundred years? Surely uneven development of this magnitude would have raised some contemporary comment, or at the very least female migration.

As a conceptual device, separate spheres has also proved inadequate. The economic chronologies upon which the accounts of women's exclusion from work and their incarceration in domesticity depend are deeply flawed. At a very general level, eighteenth- and early nineteenth-century women were associated with home and children, while men controlled public institutions, but then this rough division could be applied to almost any century or any culture[110] – a fact which robs the distinction of analytical purchase. If, *loosely speaking*, there have always been separate spheres of gender power, and perhaps there still are, then 'separate spheres' cannot be used to explain social and political developments in a particular century, least of all to account for Victorian class formation.

To conclude, this paper suggests that the orthodox categories of both seventeenth-century and nineteenth-century women's history must be jettisoned if a defensible chronology is to be constructed. Of course, such a renunciation carries a cost. A belief in the wholesale transformation wrought by capitalism on the economic role of women has provided early modern women's history with an alluring big picture. Without that faith, we must accept a less heroic and more provisional chronology. Nevertheless, the notion of separate spheres in particular has done modern women's history a great service. With this conceptual framework women's history is moved beyond a Whiggish celebration of the rise of feminism, or a virtuous rediscovery of those previously hidden from history. In asserting the instrumental role of the ideology of separate spheres in modern class formation, historians asserted the wider historical significance of gender. Thereby the interpretation offered powerful justification for the study of women when the field was embattled. Yet strategic concerns do not in themselves justify the deployment of an artificial and unwieldly conceptual vocabulary. In the attempt to map the breadth and boundaries of female experience, new categories and concepts must be generated, and this must be done with more sensitivity to women's own manuscripts.

The burden of this piece has not been to argue that the discourses of femininity and masculinity, space and authority, found in printed literature are not important. Yet their power to shape female language and behaviour needs to be demonstrated not taken as read.[111] Otherwise virtually any printed text we come across can be deemed to have ideological potency regardless of the form of the publication, its popularity with the readers, or the currency of the ideas contained within it. In short, 'intertextuality' must be researched, not simply asserted in the abstract. Case studies are needed of the economic roles, social lives, institutional opportunities and personal preoccupations of women from the seventeeth to the nineteenth centuries. In parallel, we need a long span, but integrated, history of the full range of debates about women's proper role covering the same period. (For too long it has been assumed that domestic ideology hogged the discursive stage unchallenged.) All this needs to be undertaken with especial sensitivity to changes in the range of language and categories employed. Only then will we establish with any precision the extent to which women accepted, negotiated, contested or simply ignored, the much quoted precepts of proper female behaviour in past time. Only then will we establish whether the rhetoric of domesticity and private spheres contributed to female containment, or instead was simply a defensive and impotent reaction to public freedoms already won.

Notes

1 B. Welter, 'The cult of true womanhood, 1820–60', *American Quarterly*, XVIII (1966), 151–74.
2 See especially G. Lerner, 'The lady and the mill girl: changes in the status of women in the age of Jackson', *Midcontinent American Studies Journal*, X (1969), 5–15.
3 N. F. Cott, *The bonds of womanhood: woman's sphere in New England, 1780–1835* (New Haven, 1977), 19–100.
4 M. Ryan, *Cradle of the middle class: the family in Oneida County, New York, 1790–1865* (Cambridge, 1981), 15.
5 Ryan, *Cradle of the middle class*, 239.
6 In this vein, consider D. Scott Smith, 'Family limitation, sexual control and domestic feminism in Victorian America', in M. Hartman and L. Banner (eds), *Clio's consciousness raised: new perspectives on the history of women* (New York, 1974), 119–36; and N. F. Cott, 'Passionlessness: an interpretation of Victorian sexual ideology', *Signs*, 4 (1978), 219–36.
7 For the quotation, see Cott, *Bonds*, 1. But consider also 100 & 197.
8 C. Smith-Rosenberg, 'The female world of love and ritual: relations between women in nineteenth-century America', *Signs*, I (1975), 1–29. For the quotation, see 9–10.
9 Read Cott, *Bonds*, 160–206.
10 N. A. Hewitt, 'Beyond the search for sisterhood: American women's history in the 1980s', *Social History*, X (1985), 301. Hewitt's extensive bibliography is testimony to the remarkably wide currency of these concepts and categories and the extent of uncritical acceptance and repetition. Her analysis of the development of the field is astute and convincing. Consequently, it is all the more surprising that Hewitt herself takes it as read that the interpretation fits the experience of most wealthy, white women, while rejecting this framework for the study of black and non-bourgeois women. The orthodox picture of bourgeois shackles is necessary to Hewitt's conception of working-class resistance. Working women refused to be taken in by domestic ideology as peddled by middle-class women.
11 K. Wrightson, *English Society 1580–1680* (1982), 92. See also V. Larminie, 'Marriage and the family: the example of the seventeenth-century Newdigates', *Midland History*, IX (1984), 1–22, and A. Wall, 'Elizabethan precept and feminine practice: The Thynne family of Longleat', in *History*, LXXV (1990), 23–38.
12 C. N. Degler, 'What ought to be and what was: women's sexuality in the nineteenth century', *American Historical Review*, LXXIX (1974), 1490. Another widely cited, but apparently unheeded, article has stressed the possible difference between what a woman was told to do, what she thought she was doing and what she actually did: J. Mechling, 'Advice to historians on advice to mothers', *Journal of Social History*, IX (fall, 1979), 44–63.
13 Cott, *Bonds*, 197.
14 L. Kerber, 'Separate Sphere, female worlds, woman's place: the rhetoric of women's history', *Journal of American History*, LXXV (1988), 9–39. The implications for future research were raised by L. Kerber, N. Cott, R. Gross, L. Hunt, C. Smith-Rosenburg, C. M. Stansell, 'Forum. Beyond roles, beyond spheres, thinking about gender in the early republic', *William and Mary Quarterly* XLVI (1989), 565–85. The burden of Kerber's argument is that we should regard 'separate spheres'

primarily as a rhetorical device, which people called upon to express power relations for which they had no other words. However she thinks we should not regard 'separate spheres' as a satisfactory explanatory framework, since it obscures a great deal more than it illumines and its continued use prevents us from moving on to more satisfying analyses. 'To continue to use the language of separate spheres is to deny the reciprocity between gender and society and to impose a static model on dynamic relationships' (37–9). My argument endorses Kerber's at certain key points, although Kerber is primarily concerned with language and discursive strategies, while I have a greater interest in social and economic history and want to retain a focus on female behaviour. Obviously, my piece also differs from hers in its focus on England and in its preoccupation with chronologies of change from 1700–1900.

15 The argument has its analogue for working-class women in the debates around the rise of the male breadwinner and the family wage. However for reasons of space this material has not been discussed. A summary of the debate can be found in E. Roberts, *Women's work, 1840–1940* (Basingstoke, 1988).

16 W. E. Houghton, *The Victorian frame of mind, 1830–1870* (New Haven, 1957), 341–93; Muriel Jaeger, *Before Victoria: changing standards and behaviour, 1787–1837* (London, 1956), 113–130; Maurice Quinlan, *Victorian prelude: A history of English manners 1700–1830* (New York, 1941), 139–59.

17 The classic work on vulnerable and cloistered femininity is M. Vicinus (ed.) *Suffer and be still: women in the Victorian age* (Bloomington, Indiana, 1972). The socialization of trainee domesticates is the theme of D. Gorham, *The Victorian girl and the feminine ideal* (Bloomington, Indiana, 1983) and F. Hunt (ed.), *Lessons for life: the schooling of girls and women, 1850–1950* (Oxford, 1987). On the inhibition of female sexuality and physical activity, read E. Trudgill, *Madonnas and magdalens: the origins and development of Victorian sexual attitudes* (1976), 65–78, L. Duffin, 'The conspicuous consumptive: woman as invalid', in S. Delamont and L. Duffin (eds.), *The nineteenth-century woman: her cultural and physical world* (1978), 26–56, and H. E. Roberts, 'The exquisite slave: the role of clothes in the making of the Victorian woman', *Signs* II (1977), 554–69. On the rigid demarcation of public and private physical space, see A. Clark, *Women's silence, men's violence: sexual assault in England, 1770–1845* (1987).

18 C. Hall, 'Gender divisions and class formation in the Birmingham middle class, 1780–1850', in R. Samuel (ed.), *People's history and socialist theory* (1981), 174. See also C. Hall, 'The early formation of Victorian domestic ideology', in S. Burman (ed.), *Fit work for women* (1977), 15–32. These and other notable articles have been republished in C. Hall (ed.), *White, male and middle class: explorations in feminism and history* (Oxford, 1992). Together these articles constitute one of the most undiluted statements on capitalism, class formation and female marginalization hitherto published.

19 See M. Vicinus, 'One life to stand beside me: emotional conflicts in first generation college women in England', *Feminist Studies*, VIII (1982), 603–8, and M. Vicinus, 'Distance and desire: English boarding school friendships', *Signs*, IX (1984), 600–22.

20 M. Vicinus, *Independent women: work and community for single women, 1850–1920* (1985), 3; M. Shanley, *Feminism, marriage and the law in Victorian England* (1989), 6–7; J. Horowitz, *Strong-minded women: and other lost voices from nineteenth-century England* (Harmondsworth, 1984), 5.

21 R. Strachey, *The cause: a short history of the women's movement in Great Britain* (1978).

22 For a brief, but suggestive, discussion of the vocabulary of feminist autobiography, see C. Dyhouse, *Feminism and the family in England, 1880–1939* (Oxford, 1989), 14–16.

23 The problems such portraits present to historians are glimpsed in a telling comparison by Carol Dyhouse. She observes that Bera Brittain's retrospective autobiography written in 1933 attributes much more pent-up frustration to her younger self growing up in Edwardian Buxton than was ever expressed in the diary written at the time, which in fact conveys 'an image of a thoughtful but very

exuberant young girl, much involved in dancing parties and pretty clothes': C. Dyhouse, 'Mothers and daughters in the middle-class home, c. 1870–1914', in J. Lewis (ed.), *Labour and love: women's experiences of home and family, 1850–1940* (Oxford, 1986), 42. For a cautionary note about over-reliance on those writings shaped by the fashion for looking back in anger, see J. Tosh, 'Domesticity and manliness in the Victorian middle-class', in M. Roper and J. Tosh (eds.), *Manful assertions: masculinities in Britain since 1800* (1991), 60–1.

24 Particularly striking in this vein is work of the so-called 'new' art historians. On the nineteenth-century ideology of domesticity, read D. Cherry, 'Picturing the private sphere', *Feminist Art News*, V (1982), 5–11, L. Nead, *Myths of sexuality: representations of women in Victorian Britain* (Oxford, 1988), especially 12–47, and R. Parker, *The subversive stitch: embroidery and the making of the feminine* (1984). For a wholesale acceptance of the separate spheres framework, consider J. Wolff, 'The culture of separate spheres: the role of culture in nineteenth-century public and private life', in J. Wolff, and J. Seed (eds.), *The culture of capital: art, power and the nineteenth-century middle class* (Manchester, 1988), 117–34.

25 See P. Branca, 'Image and reality: the myth of the idle Victorian woman', in Hartman and Banner (eds.), *Clio's consciousness raised*, 179–91 and P. Branca, *Silent sisterhood: middle-class women and the Victorian home* (1975).

26 M. J. Peterson, 'No angels in the house: the Victorian myth and the Paget women', *American Historical Review*, LXXXIX (1984), 693.

27 The earnest enterprise and managerial skill of which Victorian women were capable is amply demonstrated by F. K. Prochaska, *Women and philanthropy in nineteenth-century England* (Oxford, 1980); A. Summers, 'A home from home: women's philanthropic work in the nineteenth century', in S. Burman (ed.), *Fit work for women* (1977), 33–63. Ladies who displayed gumption, if not 'political correctness', are the subject of D. Birkett, *Spinsters abroad: Victorian lady explorers* (Oxford, 1989) and A. J. Hammerton, *Emigrant gentlewomen* (1979).

28 P. Thane, 'Late Victorian women', in T. R. Gourvish and A. O'Day (eds.), *Later Victorian Britain, 1867–1900* (Basingstoke, 1988), 175–208.

29 See P. Jalland, *Women, marriage and politics, 1860–1914* (Oxford, 1986); B. Caine, *Destined to be wives: the sisters of Beatrice Webb* (Oxford, 1988); M. J. Peterson, *Family, love and work in the lives of Victorian gentlewomen* (Bloomington, Indiana, 1989). And despite the authors' assumptions, the following contain copious evidence of female diversity. P. Rose, *Parallel lives: five Victorian marriages* (New York, 1983), and Horowitz, *Strong-minded women*.

30 Tosh, 'Domesticity and manliness', 50–1.

31 M. Pugh, *The Tories and the people, 1880–1935* (Oxford, 1985), 48. He concludes that 'the stereotyped view of men who go boldly out into the world and women who love to stay at home disintegrates upon close examination of several late Victorian marriages'.

32 A. Trollope, *The Belton estate* (1865; Oxford, 1991), 132.

33 This conclusion is expressed most forcibly by Larminie, 'Marriage and the family', 18.

34 Consider, F. B. Smith, 'Sexuality in Britain, 1800–1900: some suggested revisions', in M. Vicinus, (ed.), *A widening sphere: changing roles of Victorian women* (Bloomington, Indiana, 1977), 182–98.

35 M. Vicinus, 'Introduction', in *A widening sphere*, xix.

36 Peterson, 'No angels', 708.

37 Pugh, *Tories and the people*, 47.

38 See R. Guest and A. John, *Lady Charlotte: a biography of the nineteenth century* (1989). This study reproduces some of the very few instances I have ever seen of a woman actually *debating* with herself over domestic duty. Charlotte Guest sometimes claimed to be 'quite careless of all but matters of domestic solicitude' or recorded that 'to remain in quiet and undisturbed pursuance of my duties is now my only wish' (33). However, as the authors shrewdly point out, these pious statements 'almost invariably followed a particularly active period of literary or business activity and were at the same time one way of adjusting to the fact that she was

about to produce yet another child'. Perhaps, therefore, it will be focused studies like this which will help us get the measure of the interaction of conventional lip-service and 'unconventional' behaviour in the future.

39 See Florence Nightingale, *Cassandra*, republished in Ray Strachey, *The cause*.

40 J. Rendall, 'Friendship and politics: Barbara Leigh Smith Bodichon (1827–91) and Bessie Rayner Parkes (1829–1925)', in S. Mendus and J. Rendall (eds.), *Sexuality and subordination: interdisciplinary studies of gender in the nineteenth century* (1989), 136–70. See also the response by Rendall and Mendus to Peterson's 'No angels', 131–5.

41 The importance of the radical political heritage in the world view of Parkes and Leigh Smith is elaborated in J. Rendall, 'A moral engine? Feminism, liberalism and the English woman's journal', in J. Rendall (ed.), *Equal or different: women's politics, 1800–1914* (Oxford, 1987), 112–38. The argument that radical reform constituted the cradle of mid-Victorian liberal feminism is made most forcibly by B. Harrison, 'A genealogy of reform in modern Britain', in C. Bolt and S. Drescher (eds.), *Anti-slavery, religion and reform: essays in honour of Roger Anstey* (Connecticut, 1980). But the contribution of a radical family background is also raised by O. Banks, *Becoming a feminist: the social origins of the first wave of feminism* (1986), 33, and discussed with some sensitivity in P. Levine, *Feminist lives in Victorian England: private roles and public commitment* (Oxford, 1990), 15–41.

42 In a similar vein, Sally Alexander has reflected that 'the emergence of mass female politics is often attributed to the effects of the industrial revolution and the ideological hegemony of the bourgeoisie. The former by separating work and home, the latter by instilling ideas of domesticity among the working classes, allocated women to the private and public domains respectively. But we come closer to the terrain of feminist grievance and capture a decisive moment in its political temporality if we examine the forms of working class politics themselves in the 1830s and 40s, and their language of demand and aspiration.' See S. Alexander, 'Women, class and sexual differences in the 1830s and 40s: some reflections on the writing of a feminist history', *History Workshop Journal*, XVIII (1984), 130.

43 J. Lewis, 'Reconstructing women's experience', in Lewis (ed.), *Labour and love*, 20. However, in raising the question, Lewis does suggest that 'separate spheres' offers a fair description of the results for culture of industrial modernity.

44 The *locus classicus* is J. Brewer, *Party, ideology and popular politics at the accession of George III* (Cambridge, 1976). For more on the theory of the public sphere of politics, see J. Habermas, 'The public sphere', *New German Critique*, 3 (1974), 45–55 and G. Eley, 'Rethinking the political: social history and political culture in eighteenth and nineteenth-century Britain', *Archiv für Sozialgeschichte*, XXI (1981), 427–57. For an enlightening review of the burgeoning literature, see D. Goodman, 'Public sphere and private life: toward a synthesis of current historiographical approaches to the old regime', *History and Theory*, XXXI (1992), 1–20.

45 L. Davidoff and C. Hall, *Family fortunes: men and women of the English middle class, 1780–1850* (1987).

46 Davidoff and Hall, *Family fortunes*, 29.

47 Davidoff and Hall, *Family fortunes*, 28.

48 The modern historical vision of class making through the interaction of radical politics and economic transformation was minted by E. P. Thompson, *The making of the English working class* (1963), and held sway for almost 20 years. However, many historians have been doubtful about the relationship between the sociology of class and the language of politics; a scepticism which has been particularly pronounced since the publication of G. Stedman Jones, 'Rethinking chartism' in Stedman Jones, *Languages of class: studies in English working class history, 1832–1982* (Cambridge, 1983), 90–178. Attempts to defend the conventional class project include N. Kirk, 'In defence of class: a critique of recent writing on the nineteenth-century English working class', *International Review of Social History*, XXXII (1987), 2–47 and R. Gray, 'The languages of factory reform in Britain, c. 1803–60', in P. Joyce (ed.), *The historical meanings of work* (Cambridge, 1987), 143–79.

49 For a readable synthesis of recent scholarship, consult F. M. L. Thompson, *The rise of respectable society: a social history of Britain, 1830–1900* (1988).
50 A wealth of data on the early modern middling sort is in P. Earle, *The making of the English middle class: business, society and family life in London, 1660–1730* (1989). On the domestic preoccupations and associational lives of commercial families before 1800, see especially M. Hunt, 'English urban families in trade, 1660–1800: the social relations of early modern capitalism' (unpublished Ph.D. thesis, New York University, 1986). While Hunt's thesis was conceived within the framework bequeathed by nineteenth-century historians – an emergent middle class is linked to a novel separation of the public and private spheres, *c.* 1660–1800 – Hunt marshalls much evidence which undermines the claim that nineteenth-century middle-class culture was the result of Evangelicalism, the French revolution and the factory. Moreover, Hunt has since modified her earlier view of increasing female marginalization over the eighteenth century: see Hunt, 'Women and trade in eighteenth-century England' (unpublished conference paper, Eighth Berkshire Conference on the History of Women, June 1990). Despite the authors' assumptions about separating spheres, further useful information on commercial families before Victoria can be found in S. D'Cruze, 'The middling sort in provincial England: politics and social relations in Colchester, 1730–1800' (unpublished Ph.D. thesis, University of Essex, 1990) and J. Smail, 'From the middling to the middle: class formation in Halifax, Yorkshire in the century before the industrial revolution' (unpublished D.Phil., Stanford University, 1988).
51 Davidoff and Hall drew heavily on the then unpublished work of R. J. Morris. This has since appeared as R. J. Morris, *Class, sect and party: the making of the British middle class, Leeds 1820–50* (Manchester, 1990), which stresses the role of voluntary associations, while underestimating their significance in the seventeenth and eighteenth centuries.
52 J. Cannon, *Aristocratic century: the peerage of eighteenth-century England* (Cambridge, 1984), 15.
53 In ignoring the gentry, Davidoff and Hall are not alone. One of the only historians to address the ambivalent position of the gentry is E. P. Thompson on the 'agrarian bourgeoisie', see Thompson 'Eighteenth-century English society: class struggle without class?', *Social History*, III (1978), 162.
54 A. J. Vickery, 'Women of the local elite in Lancashire, 1750–1825' (unpublished Ph.D. thesis, University of London, 1991).
55 R. G. Wilson, 'Towards an economic history of country house building in the eighteenth century' (unpublished seminar paper, Eighteenth Century Seminar, Institute of Historical Research, London University, October 1988); R. G. Wilson, *Gentleman merchants: the merchant community in Leeds, 1700–1830* (Manchester, 1971), 194–237; J. Fiske (ed.). *The Oakes diaries: business, politics and the family in Bury St Edmunds, 1778–1800* (Woodbridge, 1990), 191–200.
56 Perhaps manufacturers became progressively frozen out of land-based polite society. Indeed, it is Wilson's contention that while the Yorkshire elite could easily absorb greater merchants in the eighteenth century, it drew the line at manufacturers in the nineteenth. Certainly, a literary distinction between genteel merchants and vulgar manufacturers had popular currency throughout the period. The commentator and cleric Josiah Tucker, for example, distinguished in 1757 between 'farmers, freeholders, tradesmen and manufacturers in middling life and . . . wholesale dealers, merchants and all persons of landed estates . . . in genteel life', Tucker, *Instructions for travellers* (1757), 26. Meanwhile, novelists sympathetic to trade made heroes of merchants at the expense of new manufacturers: J. Raven, 'English popular literature and the image of business, 1760–90' (unpublished Ph.D. thesis, Cambridge University, 1985). See especially the case study of Mrs Gomershull of Leeds, 281–317. Nevertheless, the experience of the Preston Cotton manufacturers John and Samuel Horrocks, whose children married into clerical and Domesday families, suggests the continued inclusiveness of Lancashire high society in the 1810s and 1820s, a feature which has been remarked by other studies of the county: P. Joyce, *Work, society and politics: the culture of the factory in later Victorian England* (1980), 1–50.

57 W. W. Rostow, 'The take-off into self-sustained growth', *Economic Journal*, LXVI (1956), 25–48.

58 A prime example is H. Perkin, *The origin of modern English society, 1780–1880* (1969).

59 Read M. Fores, 'The myth of a British industrial revolution', *History*, LXVI (1981), 181–98 and D. Cannadine, 'The present and the past in the English industrial revolution, 1880–1980', *Past and Present*, CIII (1985), 131–72. Recently, however, there has been an attempt to resurrect the idea of economic transformation: see M. Berg and P. Hudson, 'Rehabilitating the industrial revolution', *Economic History Review*, 2nd ser., XLV (1992), 24–50.

60 For Davidoff and Hall's account of the construction of the independent economic man, see *Family fortunes*, 198–271. A swift introduction to some of the structures and processes of the early modern economy, can be gained via P. G. M. Dickson, *The financial revolution in England: a study in the development of public credit* (1967); L. Pressnel, *English country banking in the industrial revolution* (1956); H. and L. Mui, *Shops and shopkeeping in eighteenth-century England* (19898); J. A. Chartres, *Internal trade in England, 1500–1700* (1971); and M. Hunt, 'Time-management, writing and accounting in the eighteenth-century English trading family: a bourgeois enlightenment', in *Business and Economic History*, 2nd ser., XVIII (1989), 150–9.

61 For example, Dod and Cleaver's *Household government* (1614) made it clear that while a husband was to 'Travel, seek a living ... get money and provisions ... deal with many men ... dispatch all things outdoor', a wife's duties were to 'keep the house ... talk with few ... boast of silence ... be a saver ... oversee and give order within'. (I am indebted to Susan Lippit for this reference.) The notion of women as guardian of the family's heart and virtue was also well-established. In 1697, Mary Astell cited the mother's crucial influence over men in childhood as reason enough to support any scheme to improve female education: M. Astell, *A serious proposal to the ladies, for the advancement of their true and greatest interest by a lover of her sex* (1697), 97. Addison, Steele and many other writers of courtesy literature glamorized the pure domestic woman in the early decades of the eighteenth century. At mid-century Thomas Marriott praised women for their superior purity, their crucial role as mothers and their smiling guardianship of the sanctuary of the home. Women's virtue, he asserted, was vital to the preservation of the state and the British race. This exemplary virtue justified female efforts to reform society's morals: T. Marriott, *Female conduct, being an essay on the art of pleasing practised by the fair sex* (1759).

62 British Library, HHMS (1804), letter from Emily Duchess of Leinster to Hon. Caroline Fox. (I am indebted to Stella Tillyard for this reference.)

63 Quoted in Quinlan, *Victorian prelude*, 255. For further instances see 254–80.

64 Quoted in Jaeger, *Before Victoria*, 37.

65 L. Colley, *Britons: forging the nation, 1707–1837* (1992), 237–81.

66 Davidoff, 'The separation of home and work? Landladies and lodgers in the nineteenth and twentieth centuries', in Burman (ed.), *Fit work*, 64–97. This study serves as a reminder 'that there is no natural or fixed separation between a private and public sphere' (93).

67 Davidoff and Hall, *Family fortunes*, 107–48.

68 Davidoff and Hall, *Family fortunes*, 119.

69 Colley, *Britons*, 281.

70 J. Ruskin, 'Of Queen's Gardens', in *Sesame and lilies* (1907), 71, 60.

71 G. Gissing, *The odd women* (1893; 1980), 135.

72 Consider the contemporary arguments related in J. Lewis (ed.), *Before the vote was won: arguments for and against women's suffrage* (1987) and B. Harrison, *Separate spheres: the opposition to women's suffrage in Britain* (1978).

73 See F. Engels, *Origin of the family, private property and the state* (1972), *passim*, and the introduction by M. Chaytor and J. Lewis to the first Routledge edition of A. Clark, *Working life of women in the seventeenth century* (1982), ix–xliii.

74 For a summary of orthodox views on this topic, see B. Hill, *Women, work and sexual politics in the eighteenth century* (Oxford, 1990), 24–68. The saga of decline

and fall in the corn belt has been most recently articulated by K. Snell, *Annals of the labouring poor: social change and agrarian England, 1660–1900* (New York, 1978), especially in K. Snell, 'Agricultural seasonal unemployment, the standard of living, and women's work in the South and East, 1690–1860', *Economic History Review*, 2nd ser., XXXIV (1981), 407–37. Consider also M. Roberts, 'Sickles and scythes: women's work and men's work at harvest time', *History Workshop Journal*, VII (1979), 3–28. The authority on the impact of new technology on women's industrial work remains Pinchbeck, *Women workers*, 111–239.

75 O. Hufton, 'Women in history: early modern Europe', *Past and Present*, CI (1983), 126; J. Bennett, 'History that stands still: women's work in the European past', *Feminist Studies*, XIV (1988), 269–83. Others have since followed suit in discussion pieces and reviews. See J. Rendall, 'Women's history beyond the cage', *History*, LXXV (1990), 63–72; A. J. Vickery, 'The neglected century: writing the history of eighteenth-century women', *Gender and history*, III (1991), 211–19; P. Thane, 'The history of the gender division of labour in Britain: reflections on "herstory" in accounting: the first eighty years', *Accounting, Organizations and Society*, XVII (1992), 299–312; K. Honeyman and J. Goodman, 'Women's work, gender conflict and labour markets in Europe, 1500–1900', *Economic History Review*, XLIV (1991), 608–28.

76 The different economic experiences of families headed by specialist and non-specialist rural labourers is suggested by the excellent A. Hassell Smith, 'Labourers in late sixteenth-century England: a case study from north Norfolk, parts one and two', *Continuity and Change*, IV (1989), 11–52, 367–94. Much less work has been done on pastoral regions, which is ironic since these were traditional areas of high female employment. Nevertheless, even at this stage of research it seems unlikely that female predominance in the dairy was seriously threatened until the rise of big commercial dairies in the later nineteenth century. See D. Valenze, 'The art of women and the business of men: women's work and the dairy industry *c.* 1740–1840', *Past and Present*, CXXX (1991), 142–69. In addition, research on agricultural work also has a profound bias towards the south and east. Yet it is clear that the north and west had a very different history. Roughly speaking, this part of the country was more often characterized by a rugged terrain, higher rainfall, poorer soils, coal deposits, successful proto-industry and later the classic factories, and startling urban growth. A chronology for women's work based on enclosure, the decline of handicraft manufacturing, and the exacerbation of rural poverty therefore seems most unhelpful.

77 Hassell Smith, 'Labourers', 377. See also J. Bennett, *Women in the medieval English countryside: gender and household in Brigstock before the plague* (Oxford, 1987).

78 The vast majority of the worsted handspinners of Yorkshire and the lacemakers of Devon were not married to men in textile-related trades. For the Devon findings, see P. Sharpe, 'Literally spinsters: a new interpretation of local economy and demography in Colyton in the seventeenth and eighteenth centuries', *Economic History Review*, 2nd ser., XXXXIV (1991), 46–65. The Yorkshire findings are those of John Styles based on an examination of Yorkshire convictions for the false reeling of worsted, see WYRO QE 15/1-13 (1777–1781), QE 15/39 (1795) and QE 15/40 (1797). For the vast majority of married spinners who were convicted, husbands' occupations are also given. From this information it was calculated that well over two-thirds of convicted wives were married to men outside the textile trades. Since there is no reason to believe that convicts were not broadly representative of worsted spinners as a whole, this data must cast doubt on the automatic assumption of widespread family production units before the factory (personal communication).

79 Cautions against reading hard work as a simple index of power and status are in J. M. Faragher, 'History from the inside out: writing the history of women in rural America', *American Quarterly*, XXXIII (1981), 548, and J. Bennett, 'Medieval women, modern women: across the great divide', in D. Aers, *Culture and history, 1350–1600: essays on English communities, identities and writing* (1992), 169.

80 M. Berg, 'Women's work, mechanisation and the early phases of industrialisation in England', in P. Joyce (ed.), *The Historical Meanings of Work* (Cambridge, 1987), 69–76, 76–88.

81 P. Earle, 'The female labour market in London in the late seventeenth and early eighteenth centuries', *Economic History Review*, 2nd ser., XLII (1989), 328–52.

82 Nor should the particular marginalizations of the late eighteenth century be seen as a unique cataclysm, *the* moment when capitalism tossed labouring women aside. Rather, there were several moments in the last millennium when women were drawn into the formal economy in enormous numbers only to be dispensed with when demographic conditions or technological innovations rendered their contribution less vital. A fluctuating pattern of mass female engagement in different areas of the formal economy is suggested by the work of Shelaigh Ogilvie on early modern Germany and Jeremy Goldberg on later medieval England: S. C. Ogilvie, 'Women and proto-industrialisation in a corporate society: Wurtenberg woollen weaving, 1590–1760', in P. Hudson and W. R. Lee (eds.), *Women's work and the family economy in historical perspective* (Manchester, 1990), 6–103, and J. Goldberg, ' "For fairer or laither": marriage and economic opportunity for women in later medieval Yorkshire' (unpublished seminar paper, Women's History Seminar, Institute of Historical Research, London University, November, 1991).

83 See Clark, 'Working life', 14, 41, 296. Interestingly, Clark included the aristocracy and *nouveau riche* businessmen in her category of 'capitalists' since the two groups approximated to each other in manners, see 14–41.

84 Consider S. Amussen, *An ordered society: gender and class in early modern England* (Oxford, 1988), 187; C. Hall, 'The history of the housewife', in Hall, *White, male and middle class*, 43–71; M. George, *Women in the first capitalist society: experiences in seventeenth-century England* (Brighton, 1988), 1–10; Hill, *Women, work and sexual politics*, 49–52, 78–80, 126–9, 245–9. On 'the restriction of women's professional and business activities at the end of the eighteenth century', see Pinchbeck, *Women's work*, 303–5. And on the ambition of the wealthier farmer's wife to achieve 'gentility' by having 'nothing to do', see 33–40.

85 L. Stone, *The family, sex and marriage in England, 1500–1800* (1977), 396.

86 M. George, 'From goodwife to mistress: the transformation of the female in bourgeois culture', *Science and Society*, XXXVII (1973), 6.

87 K. Shevelow, *Women and print culture: the construction of femininity in the early periodical* (1989), 5 and 1.

88 N. Armstrong, 'The rise of the domestic woman', in Armstrong, *Desire and domestic fiction: a political history of the novel* (Oxford, 1987), 59–95; V. Jones (ed.), *Women in the eighteenth century: constructions of femininity* (1990), 10–11; R. Ballaster, M. Beetham, E. Frazer and S. Hebron, 'Eighteenth-century women's magazines', in Ballaster, Beetham, Frazer and Hebron, *Women's worlds: ideology, femininity and the women's magazine* (Basingstoke, 1991), 43–74; Shevelow, *Women and print culture*, 53–7.

89 Clark, 'Working life'.

90 On English traditions, consult Amy Erickson, 'Common law versus common practice: the use of marriage settlements in early modern England', *Economic History Review*, 2nd ser., XLIII (1990), 21–39. For a thoughtful analysis of the different considerations which could be at work when a male testator drew up a will, read Gloria Main, 'Widows in rural Massachusetts on the eve of the revolution', in R. Hoffman and P. J. Albert (eds.), *Women in the age of American revolution* (Charlottesville, Virginia, 1989), 67–90.

91 D. Defoe, *The complete English tradesman* (1726), 348. On the 'displeasing spectacle of idle womanhood', see also P. Earle, *The world of Defoe* (1976), 244–5, and George, 'Good wife to mistress', 157–9. Much useful material is in F. Nussbaum, *The brink of all we hate: satires on women, 1660–1750* (Lexington, Kentucky, 1984).

92 For an introduction to the debate on luxury, see J. Sekora, *Luxury: the concept in western thought, Eden to Smollett* (Baltimore, 1977).

93 F. Childs, 'Prescriptions for manners in English courtesy literature, 1690–1760, and

their social implications' (unpublished D.Phil. thesis, Oxford University, 1984), 285–7. Margaret Hunt also argues that interest in women's moral influence was increasing over the eighteenth century: M. Hunt, thesis, 240–55, but sees in this the triumph of Puritan-bourgeois expectations.

94 M. Legates, 'The cult of womanhood in eighteenth-century thought', *Eighteenth-Century Studies*, I (1976), 21–39.

95 A salutary development in this context is the attempt to recover the history of the reader herself. Two essays which contest the conventional image of the leisured reader passively ingesting eighteenth-century texts in private are N. Tadmor, 'Household reading and eighteenth-century novels', and J. Brewer, 'Anna Larpent: representing the reader', both in J. Raven, N. Tadmor and H. Small (eds.), *The practice and representation of reading in Britain: essays in history and literature* (Cambridge, 1996).

96 D. C. Coleman, 'Proto-industrialization: a concept too many', *Economic History Review*, 2nd ser., XXXVI (1983), 435–48. See also R. Samuel, 'Workshop of the world: steam power and hand technology in mid-Victorian Britain', *History Workshop Journal*, III (1977), 6–72.

97 See Earle, 'Female labour market' and Goldberg, 'Marriage and economic opportunity'. Earle, however, assumes that there was a time when women were numerous in masculine trades. He also takes the 'no smoke without fire' attitude to the plethora of pamphlets complaining about wealthy, unemployed womanhood. Dubious circumstantial evidence is found in the growth of the silk industry; but a woman need not be idle all day to wear a silk dress all evening.

98 On the generation of income, see P. Earle, *The making of the English middle class: business, society and family life in London, 1660–1730* (1989), 158–74, and B. A. Holderness, 'Credit in a rural community, 1660–1800', *Midland History*, III (1975), 94–115. The difficulties faced by active businesswomen are richly elaborated in Hunt, 'Women in trade'.

99 Vickery, thesis, 175–219. In fact, the female contribution is remarkably similar to those female activities described by Davidoff and Hall as the 'hidden investment' in nineteenth-century enterprises: *Family fortunes*, 272–320.

100 On women's work as housekeepers and consumers, see Vickery, thesis, 175–219, and Vickery, 'Women and the world of goods: a Lancashire consumer and her possessions, 1751–81', in J. Brewer and R. Porter (eds.), *Consumption and the world of goods: consumption and society in the seventeenth and eighteenth centuries* (1993).

101 See Vickery, thesis, 131–74, 278–331.

102 Lancashire Record Office, DDB/72/175 (26.2.1763), W. Ramsden, Charterhouse to E. Parker, Alkincoats. For a gloss on this letter and others like it, see Vickery, thesis, 110–13, 172–3.

103 LRO, DDB/72/236 (1770), B. Ramsden, Charterhouse to E. Shackleton, Alkincoats.

104 LRO, DDB/72/75 (30.7.n.y.), B. Ramsden, Charterhouse to E. Shackleton, Alkincoats.

105 LRO, DDB/72/224, 242, 265 (1769–73), W. Ramsden, Charterhouse to E. Shackleton, Alkincoats.

106 Witness a summary of the woman's day in an exalted professional family, from the pen of a London diarist: Huntington Library, HM 31201, Diary of Anna Margaretta Larpent, vol. 1, 1790–5, unfoliated. See entry for 1 January 1790: 'In the course of this day I read about two hours ... I spent about an hour in the morning in household arrangements and family accounts. About two more in teaching my two boys ... I walked for an hour. In the evening I worked part of a neck cloth for Mr Larpent, and play'd two rubbers at whist. I saw no company today.' HL, HM 31201, vol. 1, 1790–5, entry for 13 January 1790: 'I pray'd morning and evening. I heard Seymour read for about an hour in Voltaire's *Histoire de Pierre Le Grand*. I was employed an hour in settling ye weeks bills; and busy the rest of the morning in looking over my linen and clothes, selecting the bad, giving some to mend & c. I walked out for an hour – the evening I worked at the chair; & play'd a rubber at whist. I saw no company.' (I am grateful to John Brewer who first drew my attention to the existence of this source.)

107 Jasper Goodwill, *The ladies magazine or universal entertainer* (London, 1750), Number 1 for Saturday 18 November 1749, vol. 1, preface.

108 Huntington Library, HM 31207, Methodized Journal of Anna Margaretta Larpent, unfoliated. See entries for 1773.

109 Here I am indebted to Tim Wales, who first pointed out this discrepancy to me.

110 See M. Z. Rosaldo, 'The use and abuse of anthropology: reflections on feminism and cross-cultural understanding', *Signs*, V (1980), 389–417; and Kerber, 'Rhetoric of women's history', 18–19.

111 It goes without saying that we can only try to access the 'realities' of women's lives through texts. No-one would deny that a manuscript diary, deposition, account book or will is as 'constructed' a document as is a published conduct book or novel. Nevertheless, in my opinion, it is crucial for women's historians to retain a sense of the important differences between texts; not least because some are more useful than others for particular projects. For instance, an unpublished account book kept by a woman in eighteenth-century Lancashire surely tells us more about the language, preoccupations and activities of Lancashire women than does a published diatribe written by a male author living in London. Indeed it is particularly vital for feminists to cast their nets wider than the over-used didactic sources if they are to approach a history of women's lives, not simply to reproduce a catalogue of male anxieties. Ideally, a historian would use as many different sources as possible, for it is often in the discrepancies between different accounts that interesting conclusions are drawn. Of course, some scholars informed by the new literary criticism may read this statement as proof of my naive belief in a phantom of 'real' history living in the Lancashire Record Office, yet even those who assert that nothing exists outside language usually have non-linguistic phenomena and convenient supporting 'facts' lurking in their footnotes – most popular in my experience being capitalism, the Industrial Revolution, the consumer society, international trade, the rising middle class, the companionate marriage, rural poverty and ruling-class hegemony.

11

Housewifery in working-class England 1860–1914

JOANNA BOURKE

In 1939 Frank Steel looked back into his youth and remembered the following discussion:

> 'Listen, Dad!' I recollect saying once, 'didn't you say this woman on the money – the one with the helmet – is Britannia? What is she doing?'
>
> 'Why', said father, 'she's ruling the waves, of course . . .'
>
> 'But, Dad!', I persisted, 'it isn't a ruler she's holding; it's a toasting fork! . . .'
>
> 'Oh, ah, yes!', said Dad, after considering the matter a moment, 'this must be one of the days when she rests from ruling, and stays home making toast'.[1]

This exchange took place between a small boy and his father in a working-class area of London in the 1870s, at a time when increasing numbers of married working-class women were redefining themselves primarily as housewives – with paid employment as a second, and less desirable, option. In Steel's story, Mother England 'rests from ruling' to make toast. Is this what working-class women at the end of the nineteenth century were doing when they began to concentrate their labour in the domestic sphere? The speakers in the reminiscences are a boy and a man. What were married working-class women thinking and speaking?

We all know that there are serious problems in attempting to quantify the movement of married women in and out of the paid labour force. Census statistics are inadequate and most certainly understate the number of women who were employed.[2] However, whether we base our conclusions on census statistics or on other sources, most historians agree that the access of married women of all classes to paid employment was increasingly restricted.[3] In 1911, 90 per cent of wives were not engaged in paid employment, compared with only one-quarter in 1851.[4] With the collapse of the home-employment system, and the development and expansion of industrial, commercial and factory systems outside the home, working-class married women were hardest hit. Although most such women continued to spend some time engaged in paid employment (usually at the lower echelons of the market and frequently on a part-time or casual basis), they increasingly came to define themselves primarily as housewives.[5] Furthermore many seemed pleased to do so.

Today we seem less pleased with their choice. Working-class women are portrayed as creatures buffeted about by a nebulous, oppressive ideology or by dominating fathers, brothers and husbands. Historians speak of the 'growing exclusion [of women] from waged labour outside the home' as though some economic demon was forcing them into the domestic sphere.[6] Heidi Hartmann and Michèle Barrett stress the role of trade unions in pushing women into the home; Judy Lown and Ellen Jordan blame employers.[7] Sally Alexander, Sonya O. Rose, Cynthia Cockburn and Sylvia Walby believe that the important factor was the joining together of the interests of capitalists and male workers.[8] Whatever explanation is adopted, this movement of women into the unpaid domestic sphere is generally assumed to be one of the great oppressive changes in history.[9] Ann Oakley contends that the role of the housewife in the nineteenth century was a demeaning one, consisting of monotonous, fragmented work which brought no financial remuneration, let alone any recognition.[10] June Purvis argues that the lives of working-class women in the nineteenth century were characterized by 'daily misery, poverty, and exploitation'.[11] Peter N. Stearns writes:

One thing is certain: if British workingmen had added some middle-class notions about women to their own culture, working-class women were not able to join their wealthier sisters in complaint. Long deprived, they were demoralized further by the changes in their lives at the end of the Victorian era. Though no longer traditionally resigned, they were far from possessing the ability to protest as women.[12]

Working-class housewives were 'manipulated consumers' who practised 'self-denial' for the sake of their families.[13] They were overworked and exploited by either patriarchy or capital (or both). Rebellion for the housewife, according to Wally Seccombe, was 'objectively untenable and subjectively unthinkable'.[14]

In addition to being portrayed as oppressed, the value of their domestic work is discounted. Although the struggle to 'make ends meet' is frequently acknowledged, it is portrayed as a rather pointless one producing little of intrinsic value.[15] Working-class housewives are criticized for failing to join the socialist or feminist fight when things were bad, or for uniting with their 'idle' middle-class sisters when things were good.[16] Thus argues Rosemary Collins:

> Middle-class women were now [by the middle of the nineteenth century] economically idle – their main role was to organize homes displaying their husband's wealth. Working-class women continued to be economically active ... Towards the end of the Victorian period, working-class women began to withdraw from industrial life into the home, where they tried to emulate the domestic lifestyles of the wealthy.[17]

In other words, they too became 'economically idle'. Like Hannah Mitchell's husband, historians need to acknowledge that 'meals do not come up through the tablecloth, but have to be planned, bought, and cooked'.[18] How, indeed, did working-class women understand domesticity?

The chief aim of this article is to let working-class housewives between 1860 and 1914 speak for themselves. My interest is in social agency, or seeing housewives not simply as determined, but also as determining their own history. In the words of Jean Comaroff, we need to see working-class housewives as human beings who 'in their everyday production of goods and meanings, acquiesce yet protest, reproduce yet seek to transform their predicament'.[19] There are three parts to my argument.

First, if full-time housewifery entailed a reduction in the power of the individual woman, why did so many working-class women from the end of the nineteenth century wholeheartedly embrace this new identity? What is striking is the fact that many women thought that housewifery was a good – even the *best* – option. The intensification of the two spheres of labour was acceptable to women in this period because it was seen as a better and less risky way of increasing their power over their own lives and the lives of their families.[20] This is not to argue that the search for a better life was what *motivated* women moving into full-time housewifery; rather that it was not *against* their interests to make the move. There was a price to pay for the movement; but the benefits were perceived as being cheap at the price.

Secondly, there were serious risks involved in devoting one's time to unwaged housework. The family is a confrontational unit; husbands may beat up wives; women may get a smaller share of the household goods. By not earning a wage, women were more vulnerable to the power of wage-earners within the home. Housewives tackled these risks directly. As the nineteenth century drew to a close, working-class housewives attempted to consolidate their power within the home. They did this by adopting and adapting a language of domesticity and by domestic education. Married women in working-class homes attempted to recreate the world in their own image. Their actions involved a consciousness of themselves as a group with shared values and special needs. The actions of these housewives to improve their status from within the domestic spheres have been ignored or belittled by historians for a number of reasons. To begin with, there was no revolutionary change. Then, their actions do not coincide with the class-based analyses many historians find congenial. Furthermore historians do not generally share the values of the housewives they are studying, and they have trouble taking these values seriously. We need to ask what is the meaning of housework to housewives; they did not disparage it as we do.

Thirdly, these quiet, individualist and educational attempts to create a powerful, comfortable space for women-as-housewives were not un-ambiguously successful. Married working-class women forced to earn a wage because of the collapse of household finances entered the employment market from a worse position. Many husbands continued to act in oppressive, domineering ways. Working-class housewives maintained their neighbourhood-based consciousness of their group as a group and actively resisted male power over them. Strategies for asserting one's power within the household ranged from passive methods of subversion to physical violence. Whatever the strategy employed, the site of conflict was the home: the kitchen, the bedroom. Domestic production is intimate; it is not surprising that housewives should want to protest in personal, individualized ways. This said, the striking feature about the resistance of housewives was the degree to which the conflict was arranged around a set of values shared by women-as-housewives and either opposed or ignored by men-as-'breadwinners'. Resistance requires expression in language and symbols. Analogies with statecraft provided the language; capitalism the symbols.

I

By the end of the nineteenth century, many working-class women had come to view full-time housewifery as an ideal, and one which was increasingly attainable.[21] Most working-class married women did not want paid employment. While it is true that alternatives to housework were often unattractive and that working for an exacting mistress or a grumpy overlord may not confer a good deal of self-esteem on any worker, women were not moved to toil within the home as a result of reading a stirring tract on blissful domesticity. There were advantages and disadvantages in both unwaged domestic labour and paid employment; and many women decided that paid employment was worse.

Working-class women gave many reasons for their reluctance to enter the employment market. Employment doubled their workload.[22] Mrs Hook, the wife of a carter in Sanderstead (Surrey) in the 1860s, explained, 'It never answers for a woman to go out to work; if you earn 1s. you lose 1s. 6d. I used to go to work, and then had to sit up at nights to wash'.[23] Furthermore employment could be more expensive than not being employed. Besides paying for wear and tear on clothing and shoes,[24] child-care costs had to be considered. Mrs Cawthorn, wife of a labourer in Epworth (Lincolnshire), argued:

> I don't think wives ought to go out at all. When a wife goes out they can't put their victuals to the best. Then there's the clothes. I've been out many a day when I should have saved money by staying at home, what with paying 2d. and 4d. for my babies to be taken care of.[25]

The 'free' child-care provided by older children was often unacceptable. The fear that one's child would be injured through carelessness or ignorance was prevalent, and this fear grew with increased investment in children. Mrs Hoskins's husband was a labourer in Michel Troy (Monmouthshire). In 1867 he was in bad health and some weeks earned less than 2s. To her dismay, she was often forced to undertake labouring jobs:

> When I go out I am obliged to leave the children to take care of themselves; one is only a few months old, and none are old enough to take any real care of the others. I lock them into the kitchen, and they play about. Must leave a bit of fire because of the supper, but it is dangerous, and I am always afraid they may come to some harm. Still we are so poor, must go out to work.[26]

A female agricultural labourer and mother of thirteen children in Studley (Wiltshire) had similar worries:

> I think it a much better thing for mothers to be at home with their children, they are much better taken care of, and other things go on better. I have always left my children to themselves, and God be praised! nothing has ever happened to them, though I have thought it dangerous. I have many a time come home, and have thought it was a mercy to find nothing has happened to them.[27]

When all the costs of wives and mothers working for money were calculated, it was frequently decided that female labour lowered the household's standard of living.[28] Poor women in a number of different counties repeated the saying, 'Between the woman that works and the woman that doesn't there is only 6*d*. to choose at the year's end, and she that stays at home has it'.[29]

Furthermore by the end of the nineteenth century changes in the structure of wages enabled more women to move into the domestic sphere. A wage sufficient to provide basic food and housing needs was necessary if the household was to be supported by only one wage-earner. As one female labourer said in response to criticisms about women's work in the fields: 'if the farmer paid the men properly, the women could stop at home'.[30] Between 1870 and 1900 this was the case. Historians differ as to when real wages started to increase, and the magnitude of the increase, but agree that a significant change occurred between 1850 and 1900. The received wisdom is that working-class wages rose by 55 to 70 per cent in these years.[31] This rise in the real wages of working-class men gave married women an opportunity to move out of employment themselves and invest their time in managing the extra income and improving domestic production.[32] In other words, rising wages led to an increased demand for female labour within the home. It was no longer possible for a working-class household to maintain acceptable levels of domestic production and consumption without the full-time investment of the housewife's labour in the home, converting income into consumable goods.[33] Economists talking about the increased living standards of working-class households at the end of the nineteenth century focus on the 'benefit in terms of extra consumption'[34] without acknowledging that consumption needs cannot be met without labour. When total household earnings reached a certain level (probably between 21s. and 30s.), the productivity of female labour in the domestic market surpassed the productivity of women in the employment market.[35]

In addition, the relative productivity of domestic labour was influenced by changes concerning children. Of course we have to take note of the fact that women traditionally worked in the textile industry but, in other forms of employment, it began to make better sense to have an unwaged adult woman taking care of young children rather than depending on older children. This shift occurred for three reasons, broadly corresponding to three time periods. First, although women replaced child workers in some industries (such as the pottery industry) from the 1840s, in agricultural work, general labouring employment and many factories, children replaced women. Substitution of child labour for adult women's labour occurred between the 1840s and the 1860s, when the gap between what an adult woman could earn and what children could earn narrowed. Thus in 1867 Mrs James Green, wife of an agricultural labourer in Pinchbeck

(Lincolnshire), sent her young children to work in the fields. She explained that, if her children did not work, she would have to and, if she took employment, the household would have to buy bread instead of baking it themselves:

> I've heard tell they want to stop the children [i.e., from working]. I wish they'd tell us how we're to live, when a man's wages won't keep us in bread. They should just see the poor folk's baker's bill, them that talk so . . . I only go a few odd days; my place is at home. I've 6 children and women with a family are better there.[36]

The Royal Commissions on the labour of children and women in agriculture in 1843 and 1867–8 were concerned precisely with the problem of women retiring from the fields and being replaced by children. Those giving evidence, the commissioners, medical officers, school boards and poor law authorities struggled with the contradictory desire to restrict the employment of children in the fields while approving of the withdrawal of women from those same fields.[37] Pressure also came to be placed on poor parents to send their children to school. The success, or lack of success, of this legislative pressure is debated by historians. However, by the turn of the century a large proportion of working-class children were attending school regularly. Thus older children were less available to look after younger siblings or other children.[38] In addition, from the last decade of the nineteenth century, changes in financial management, diet and cleaning made the labour of housework more complex, reducing the effectiveness of child labour in the home – of this more later.

The decision of working-class women to invest more time in domestic production was not only based on assessing the negative features of paid employment. Housework exerted a separate positive 'pull' on female labour. Housework was seen as the best option because it promised to improve the living standards of themselves and their families. The increased prosperity of working-class households from the 1860s was created not only by higher wages, but also by improved housewifery. Households containing employed women lacked 'domestic or material comfort', compared with those containing full-time housewives.[39] The productivity of household members earning a wage improved with proper domestic labour. In a report on Northumberland, it was noted that unmarried girls worked in the fields, but married women devoted most of their time to housework. The success of this division of labour bore testimony to the 'beneficial results of an active outdoor life when combined with good feeding at home' and was preferred to a situation where married women also worked in the fields without the backup provided by domestic labour.[40] Mrs Jeremiah Pratt was the wife of a labourer in Sprowston (Norfolk). In 1868 she took up labouring work, but doubted whether there was 'any real gain' in her wages because 'if a woman can stay at home and cook a bit of warm victuals, there would be more stay in it for a man than cold bread'.[41] It was through improvements in health and nutrition resulting from changes in housewifery that productivity and general well-being were enhanced.[42]

But housewives were not only interested in the strength and vitality of their 'breadwinners'. Improved living standards were linked with the improved status of women. David Vincent argued that it was the prosperity of the labouring poor in the second half of the nineteenth century which facilitated the emergence of more 'humane' forms of family life.[43] Both Nancy Tomes and Peter N. Stearns concluded that the increased standard of living among working-class families was primarily responsible for the decline in marital violence from the late nineteenth century.[44] In the words of the M.P. for East Norfolk, Clare Sewell Read, in 1867: 'much of the happiness of the poor man depends on the preparation of his food. His capacity for labour, his health, and consequently his comfort and good temper, are mainly dependent upon it'.[45]

There were other practical gains from housewifery. Domestic labour was vital for the management of money. This was especially important in households with children, since periods of high expenditure coincided with periods of lowest family income.[46] The mother could raise family living standards not by bringing in an additional wage, but by manufacturing rather than buying necessary goods. Domestic manufacture was inefficient, but practical. Frequently the calculations were marginal. Thus, a poor Yorkshire woman (a 'respectable citizen') would patronize four different shops to buy four pounds of apples – being served one pound in each shop in order to get the benefit of the 'draw' of the scales four times. In aggregate this might mean an extra apple.[47] According to economists like Gary Becker and Jacob Mincer, time costs money.[48] But people need not be profit maximizers. Indeed the strategy of the working-class housewife was closer to that of the peasant; that of 'working the system to their minimum disadvantage'.[49] To such a way of calculating, time was the one free commodity.

The housewife gained status by her management of scarce resources.[50] The movement into full-time housewifery enabled the special needs and tastes of the individuals within the household to be catered for – and it was the housewife who created this collective identity. The great symbol was the parlour where the relationship between the housewife and her family, as well as the relationship between the family and the wider community, were symbolized and structured in subtle yet distinctive ways. The parlour was a symbolic space. In working-class England, it came to represent the housewife's power and control over her family. The parlour was a confirmation of the housewife's pre-eminent role in the management of resources, and symbolized her success as the domestic manager.[51]

By investing time in the household, housewives experienced the pride and sense of well-being that comes from creating beautiful things. Cooking a variety of dishes was important.[52] One of the pleasures spoken about by women moving into full-time housewifery was the joy of spending more time nurturing children. Mrs Mary Cole, wife of a shepherd in Ingoldisthorpe (Norfolk), had fourteen children. Believing that her children would have 'suffered' if she had taken a paid job, she spent her time looking after them, rather than trying to boost her husband's low wages. Child-rearing was her chief pleasure (or so she told the commissioners):

> They were her happy days when she used to hear their innocent prattle when they used to come home from school. [She] Remembers the time when flour was 3s. 6d. a stone, and she had nine children at home, and nothing coming in but her husband's wages, which were then 'heined' (raised) to 12s. a week. They were hard times, surely, but by the blessing of God she struggled through, and never had a penny from the parish.[53]

The point that not all pleasures have a money price was not always understood by middle-class commentators on working-class life. In 1895 one landowner in Norfolk showed a lack of appreciation of domestic beauty when he complained:

> If you build a cottage with a good living room, and a kitchen containing a copper, oven, etc. they insist on living in the kitchen, and shutting up the front room as a 'drawing room' to be entered probably only once a week. You put in patent ventilators and they promptly shut them up. They block up the windows of the sitting-room with a blind curtain, and flowers.[54]

Although my main argument is that domestic arranging and rearranging had a function in creating a human environment which was both pleasurable to 'make' and pleasurable to 'consume', there was some economic purpose to actions intended to keep up a good 'front' in the eyes of the neighbours. Maintaining acceptable standards of beauty and order were crucial to achieving good credit levels with the local shopkeeper, the pawnbroker and the neighbours.

All this domestic work took a great deal of time, energy and skill. Furthermore, relative to the other members of the household, the housewife did not get her 'fair share' of leisure. In one sense, *her* work facilitated *their* leisure. It was the housewife who was doing the work necessary for leisure; she made the comfortable kitchen in which the family could talk; she packed the cold lunch for the trip to the seaside; she budgeted for the special fête.[55] Yet the full-time housewife reaped more of the benefits of increased leisure in comparison with women working a double shift in the factory and the home.

II

There were risks associated with the move into full-time housewifery. It increased the housewife's insecurity by making her more dependent on someone else's wage. The exclusive receipt by men of money wages led to many abuses, including the skimming of wages before they reached the communal purse and the unequal distribution of resources such as food and clothing within the household.[56] Ann Hodder, wife of a labourer in Halberton (Devonshire) who earned only 9s. a week, and the mother of five children under the age of eleven years, said 'I get a bit of meat, perhaps 2 lbs. of mutton, once a week for my husband; the children and I usually live on tea, bread and treacle'.[57] However, the problem of unequal distribution was not one intrinsic to the status of full-time housewife. Women engaged in paid employment were also provided with less food and clothing.[58] The security or independence that a woman achieved by bringing in her own wage was dubious. Wages may increase female power, widen their number of choices and provide access to status outside the family, but in practice the extent to which this actually did occur was variable.

It is incorrect to assume a simple linear relationship between power and housework. Many historical and sociological studies of women treat task allocation as the indicator of power, rather than as a process requiring study. Thus the person who performs housework is – for that reason – automatically assumed to be the least powerful person.[59] This type of reasoning ignores the complex nature of power. Power is a relationship. It may be the ability to compel a person to submit to your will, but it may also be the ability to limit the scope of another person's decision-making to those issues which the power-wielding person finds non-threatening. In this way power is the ability to preclude action, to forestall debate. Power is control over one's environment and over one's time; it is also the ability to ensure that other people do not question your authority within a specific sphere. Power is control as much as ownership. Owning an independent wage may provide a woman with certain rights *vis-à-vis* other wage-earners in the household, even though these other wage-earners (if men) were liable to be better paid. In exchange for giving up these rights, the housewife raised her standard of living and chiselled out an independent space in which her level of control was significant. The trade-off was worthwhile if the 'breadwinner' could be made dependent on the housewife. Attempts by housewives to *widen* the distinction between the two kinds of labour were aimed at reducing their own powerlessness.

One of the main ways in which the spheres of labour could be widened was by broadening the range and quality of domestic tasks through education in cookery, laundry-work and general housewifery. Classes in domestic education were organized by private organizations, local authorities and education authorities from the 1880s. Although these classes affected working-class women and girls, the most significant courses were those established in elementary schools. Financial constraints on the implementation of a cookery syllabus in elementary schools were significantly reduced by the Education Code of 1882. This code recognized cooking as a subject of instruction and allowed a grant of 4s. for every girl who attended a minimum number of lessons. Cookery was not the only subject offered to girls; they could also attend classes in laundry-work, household sewing, dressmaking, hygiene and combined domestic subjects. The type of domestic education given to girls in elementary schools was further advanced in 1911, when a separate grant was established for 'Housewifery' as distinct from the grant for 'Combined Domestic Subjects' which required premises where cooking, laundry-work and housework could be taught concurrently. This new grant provided a basic and broad education in cookery, laundry-work and housewifery in a shorter period of time. It was intended to meet the requirements of working-class girls unlikely to remain in school long enough to take the complete course in 'Housewifery'. In 1883 seven thousand girls earned the cooking grant. Within a dozen years this had jumped to over 146,000 girls annually. By 1911 nearly every schoolgirl in England was attending domestic education classes.[60]

Recent work by Dena Attar, Anna Davin, Carol Dyhouse, June Purvis and Annmarie Turnbull all portray education in housework as part of an attempt by the middle classes to disseminate a particular form of domestic ideology among working-class girls. Domestic education was intended to ensure that women (and especially working-class women) knew their 'place' in society.[61] Also, these writers claim, domestic classes endeavoured to teach young girls desirable traits such as docility. To leave the analysis at that point is insufficient, however. Working-class girls and women proved eager to attend the classes.[62] Girls frequently stayed at school for an extra year in order to get training in housewifery.[63] They would walk long distances to attend, and teachers were besieged with applications to admit older girls and women.[64] When given a choice, parents would send their daughters to schools which taught domestic education, as opposed to less well-provided schools.[65] Teachers discovered that the threat of removing a child from cookery classes was effective in enforcing good behaviour.[66] Girls were less liable to 'skip' cookery classes.[67] Scholars who missed out on domestic education at school 'lamented' their bad fortune and joined evening classes.[68] The passive acceptance of a middle-class ideology of domesticity does not explain the popularity of domestic education. Rather, working-class girls and women attending the classes were actively seeking to redefine their status as women *within* the household.

More women accepted that the status of women as housewives had to be improved than accepted that their status as employees needed tackling. For housewives, the importance of education in the home was seen as necessary and obvious.[69] It was needed in order to dispel the idea that housework was 'natural' and therefore simple.[70] The taint of 'servitude' and 'domestic service' had to be removed from housework.[71] Working-class homes were also suffering from a shortage of cheap domestic helps to share household tasks. Increasingly the head-housewife had to do the most menial tasks herself. These tasks had to be reformed and redefined. Housework required skill.[72] Housework was not all 'dirty' work; it could be the work of 'queens' and 'ladies'.[73] The classes were popular because they provided an opportunity for girls and women to improve their status within the home by reducing the 'menial' elements of housework and emphasizing the more specialized and skilled forms of domestic labour.

Improving the quality of goods and services produced by the housewife seemed to be the key to raising the status of women. The requirements of housewifery had increased dramatically. In part the concentration of domestic education classes in working-class areas was a function of changes in consumption within these districts. Housing improvements raised standards of cleaning.[74] Dietary diversification was a notable feature of working-class life from the 1850s, but especially from the 1880s.[75] As diet diversified, so did the degree of specialized knowledge required by housewives. Food variety had higher time costs in terms of preparation and management. Simple domestic technologies, such as gas cookers, a range of cutlery, pots and bowls, simple washing and mangling machines, and cooling facilities, were encouraged in the domestic classes, in part because machinery conferred higher status on the domestic labourer. Working-class housewives did not use these so-called 'labour-saving' devices to improve their efficiency; rather, they used them to raise their standards of domestic work which, in the long run, increased rather than decreased their labour.[76]

Furthermore education in housework was an exclusion tactic. Housework became more specialized and skilled, progressively excluding male members of the family and enhancing the bargaining power of women. The exclusion of men was not only based on biological or psychological differences between men and women. It was an exclusion based also on the need of women to ensure their underlying eminence within the household. Thus, while none of the mainstream domestic classes included men, classes in cookery established for men working on ships and boats caused no comment.[77] Men were able to learn domestic skills, but only in contexts which did not threaten the predominance of women within the home. This can also be seen in the opposition of some working-class mothers to school meals. In the words of Anna Martin in 1911:

[these] women have a vague dread of being superseded and dethroned. Each of them knows perfectly well that the strength of her position in the home lies in the physical dependence of her husband and children upon her, and she is suspicious of anything that would tend to undermine this.[78]

It is not surprising to hear that housewives often resisted male intervention in the domestic sphere on the grounds that it disrupted their routine, resulted in the lowering of standards and encroached on their power-base.[79] If men were to be allowed to do housework, they were made responsible for the more menial aspects, such as scrubbing boots, dirty cleaning, carting water and sweeping.[80] Significantly, these jobs were also the responsibility of children.[81]

Of course the position of head-housewife was not only threatened by the male members of the household. Women have resisted sharing or subdividing power with other women as well. The failure of co-operative kitchens is well documented. Some daughters were not allowed to do housework because the mother was 'jealous[ly] clinging to power, in every department of the house'.[82] Sheehan described an old woman, unable to perform domestic labour and forced to allow another woman to do it, with the words: 'one could see how the sense of her dethronement and subjection was telling on the old woman',[83] Daughters were not thanked if they attempted to usurp the power of the kitchen-kingdom. In 1909 an Irish journalist, Robert Lynd, related the following story about the relationship between a daughter who had attended a domestic education course and her mother:

> A farmer's daughter in the south, having returned home with her training in cookery, was permitted amid some excitement to prove her gifts in getting ready the midday dinner. She prepared a magnificent steak pudding, the like of which had never been seen in the house before ... 'We must always let Mary do the cooking after this!' [the father] cried ... the woman of the house, hearing this, suddenly lifted up her voice and wept. 'Oh!' she lamented, wringing her hands. 'After me cooking and slaving for you for twenty years! And now to have my own daughter put against me!' And she finished with a flood of tears ... no one ever dared to propose Mary as family cook again.[84]

Who produced *what* was important.

III

Attempts by women to improve their status by education were not an absolute success. Working-class housewives maintained consciousness of their group identity and actively resisted male power over them. This resistance was carried out within a system of shared values. A husband was a 'good' man if he let the housewife do her work without interference.[85] He was a 'bad' man if he attempted to oversee or intervene in the home. When this happened, the housewife was liable to express resentment and resistance. This is not to deny that the housewife was less powerful than her husband. Clearly the housewife had relatively less power to coerce and, when it came to the crunch, the husband's superior physical strength and financial bargaining power gave him a considerable advantage. However, the bullied housewife may not have felt ill-treated or oppressed. For her, there was an important distinction between legitimate and illegitimate uses of power.

Subversion is at the centre of all oppressive structures. In 1974 E. P. Thompson wrote: 'The same man who touches his forelock to the squire by day – and who goes down in history as an example of deference – may kill his sheep, snare his pheasant or poison his dogs at night'.[86] A woman may express contradictory opinions about her husband and family depending on the audience, the issue being discussed and the immediate circumstances. One moment she may be heard approving; the next, denying. To one person she may express resentment; to another, merely a desire to see things slightly modified. Occasionally (though not rarely) she uses violence to fight for what she considers to be her rights. Furthermore subversion and resistance were part of the accepted reality of marital relations and were explicitly promoted in female-dominated media. Thus, women's magazines published articles entitled 'Strategy with Husbands', 'The Kingdom of the Home and How to Rule It' and 'Are Men Inferior?'[87]

Housewives sometimes physically fought men who did not appreciate the subtle balance between the rights of husbands to a degree of symbolic authority and the rights of wives to rule the household. In the words of one poor London woman in 1906, 'I chastise my husband like a child'.[88] Violence was most frequently adopted by women in response to a man's attempt to assert his will aggressively. Women would fight back when beaten up by husbands.[89] Thus, in 1908, when the district nurse, M. Loane, expressed dismay on hearing that a certain husband hit his wife, a working-class neighbour explained: 'She isn't a bit afraid o' he. If he do give her a good smack, she do give he another'; on which Loane commented: 'I gathered that this was the usual custom in the neighbourhood if husbands so far forgot themselves, which was rather rare'.[90] Sometimes violence was only used after a wife's patience in 'talking him down' was used up. Then she might 'go berserk and clump the old man for all she was worth'. She would threaten to 'brain him'; a threat which always worked since no one doubted that she would do it.[91] Husbands were liable to find heavy bass mats, irons, trays of toffee, brooms, loaves of bread, boxes of buttons, shovels, sheep's heads and whatever else was at hand thrown at them, if they arrived home late ('more foolish than when they went out') or drunk or were unappreciative of the wife's efforts in the home.[92] A girl in the East End resented the fact that her husband took his time coming to bed ('He seemed to forget he had a wife with a lovely little fanny just waiting for him'), so she threw a book at him.[93] More dangerously, knives could be waved in front of stubborn husbands.[94]

Less aggressive, but still daring, ways of resisting included lying about money or stealing from husbands. A correspondent in the *Pawnbrokers' Gazette* mentioned a wife who stole her husband's wooden leg while he slept. She pawned his leg, saying 'now he'll have to stop at home until he shells out'.[95] A domestic servant in London at the turn of the century justified the fact that she lied to her husband about how much profit she had made from a certain bargain with the words, 'Now, if I do say I'll do a thing, I do do it, and everyone that do know me will tell you the same. Now me husband, he's not straight. If anyone do act fair with me, I do do the same with them'. Or, in the words of another poor woman, 'If anyone tries to do me, I does them'.[96] In other words, certain forms of 'stealing' were legitimate, because wives have a right to the income earned by household members, and they have a right to be treated fairly and honestly.

Language could also be used in a confrontational manner. A noisy argument might help a housewife get her own way within the household.[97] A man could be rebuked for being a few minutes late for dinner, 'after me slavin' away all mornin'".[98] The use of swearing is another example. When Jasper's mother was angry with her husband, she would call him all the 'miserable old gits' she could remember and these words would 'start a real bust-up'.[99] Men – and husbands in particular – considered swearing as a deliberately provocative action. Nancy Tomes's analysis of wife-beating shows that swearing was generally mentioned by wife-beaters as the 'final straw'.[100]

These forms of open insubordination were, however, often dangerous and counter-productive. It is not surprising, therefore, to discover that the most common forms of resistance for housewives were non-confrontational: manipulation, slander and disdainful silence. At this level the housewife was relatively 'safe'. In the words of Edward B. Harper, in the context of lifelong indentured servants in India:

> Even though the master could retaliate by refusing to give his servant the extra fringe benefits, he was still obliged to maintain him at a subsistence level if he did not want to lose his investment completely. This method of passive resistance, provided it was not expressed as open defiance, was nearly unbeatable.[101]

Withdrawal and silence were powerful (and frequently used) weapons.[102] A husband could be locked out of his home.[103] Equally unlucky husbands might find themselves sleeping alone in bed every night, if they refused to obey their wives.[104] Husbands who dared to have an affair with another woman might be banished from the bed altogether.[105] Grumpy husbands – even those dying of TB – could simply be left until their manners improved.[106] Silence was used by Kathleen Behan's sister-in law in her struggles for power:

That was a ceremony in every house, when the man handed over the wages each week. My brother Peadar had a God Almighty row with his wife once. When he came in, he didn't *hand* her the wages, but put them on the mantelpiece. She wouldn't have that. Quite right too – it was degrading, as if she were some kind of lodging-house keeper, not the woman of the house. So she wouldn't take the money off the mantelpiece, but waited for him to put it into her hand. They both sat there for a time, staring at this money and at each other, and in the end, without a word, my brother took the money off the mantelpiece himself and took it down to the pub. That was it for the rest of the week for them.[107]

Just because this gesture was not successful – indeed was counter-productive – should not lead us to ignore her protest and the reasons for it.

Much conflict, however, centred not around the allocation of resources, but what E. P. Thompson has called the 'contest for symbolic authority'.[108] A favourite form of subverting the power of the 'head of the household' was through unflattering or insulting references about him behind his back.[109] Gossip and 'slagging-off' could impose heavy penalties on a man by ruining his reputation within the community or household. A husband who persisted in getting drunk, neglected his wife, or failed to show proper respect for the kitchen or parlour, was treated as 'less than dust' by neighbouring wives.[110] Irrespective of the ranking of the husband in the 'wider' world, within the household and neighbourhood women allocated social prestige and reputation.

Many women found the most effective way was to use her domestic skills to soften or persuade. Super-sweetness could win many battles.[111] If sweetness failed, she could punish her husband by refusing to perform domestic labour. His meal could be burnt or fed to the dog if he came home late or drunk.[112] A plate of hash could be tipped over his head.[113] We hear of housewives going 'on strike'.[114] The refusal of a wife to cook a meal, apparently trivial, could be an important mechanism by which to enforce decision-making. It is no coincidence that a large number of popular tales focus on the wife refusing to continue performing domestic labour because she is insufficiently appreciated – and exchanging the tasks with her husband. In these stories *his* work is found to be replaceable, while he (predictably) makes a mess in the home.[115]

Central to these non-confrontational ways of exerting power was the use of symbolic language. To be successful, it was wise for the housewife to wrap her words in the cloak of symbolic deference. Again, such techniques were promoted by women's magazines in general. In an article of 1890 in *The Housewife*, entitled 'Strategy with Husbands', an anonymous writer gave advice to housewives living in homes where the 'master' considered that he 'knows best about all domestic matters' and intervened in domestic affairs in an 'irascible, overbearing and obstinate' manner:

> By a constant series of little deceptions the tyrant is led to believe that his measures are carried out, whereas, in point of fact, they are quite properly ignored. I do not say that the wife is blameless, but I say that the fault lies first with the husband, whose tiresome tyranny forces his wife into subterfuges for the sake of the general good.[116]

When Richard Church's mother had succeeded in dominating her husband, she would 'contrive to restore his dignity and set him up again as the head of the house who could do no wrong and whose word was law'.[117] Hannah Mitchell's mother followed this strategy:

> Even my mother, who quite definitely ruled the roost in our home, paid lip service to the idea of the dominant male. She always spoke of my father as 'The Master', and when the dealers came to buy cattle, she always left the room while they bargained, as if leaving him to decide, although in reality she and my father had previously agreed the price to be asked.[118]

Different forms of address were adopted if a husband needed to be persuaded – forms such as 'my dear', 'love', 'darling' and so on.[119] Housewives may use appropriate linguistic forms of deference to get their own way, but this should not be taken to mean that they believe in the superiority of the 'master'. To his face, they may cajole; behind his back they may sneer. In working-class Salford at the turn of the century, Robert Roberts's mother responded to a visitor's question 'An' is the master at home now?' with 'I haven't one . . . but my husband's out'.[120] To get a man to do the housework while the housewife is ill, they might beg for his 'help' and praise his 'goodness', while knowing behind his back that it was his duty. To make a husband stop beating his wife, neighbouring wives could use the language of chivalry, but that does not mean that they believed in male superiority.[121] Significantly, when all other protests had gone unnoticed by the 'male head', a woman most commonly resorted to arguments based on an ideology of women's weakness. For instance, Richard Church's mother publicly rebuked her husband for making them cycle too far in the cold:

> One of these scenes when Mother broke her usual policy of government by seeming acquiescence, and staged an open revolt . . . She referred to the disabilities of the female body and particularly of mothers of children, she pointed out the singular delicacy of her own children and enumerated several reasons for it, all connected with Father's heredity, personal stupidity and callousness. She called upon God to witness the universal unfairness between the sexes, with women as the eternal victim and slave.

He was duly snubbed.[122]

These 'risk-averse' forms of resisting made sense given the dilemma of working-class women lacking good employment opportunities, subject to pregnancy and facing restricted sexual outlets outside marriage. Indirect subversion was appropriate: it did not require the co-operation of other people; advance planning was unnecessary; formal networks did not have to be brought into play (but if things went wrong, informal networks could be relied upon); it avoided direct confrontation and, most important, it did not hold the *family* up to public ridicule. It is this sort of non-confrontational power that causes working-class autobiographers simultaneously to assert the dominance of the mother, while denying that the mother was actually dominant. For example, one such autobiographer wrote:

> It will have been noticed by now how every other object on the screen of memory fades back when my mother appears there. It was so in life, for she was dominant wherever she might be. I can't explain why, for she was never assertive.[123]

We should not dismiss small acts of resistance as somehow less 'political' than mass movements of resistance.[124] Risk-averse protests were not lower forms of resistance; they were the *preferred* response to oppression. For the housewife, the personal (sometimes anonymous) character of her resistance was not only an integral part of her position within society and the family, but also an integral part of the very value system she was defending. Her goals were not to overthrow the family, but to protect it from the threats posed by 'breadwinners', not to drive away her husband, but to consolidate her role as housewife. It was no less radical for all that.

IV

This article has been concerned with the sexual division of labour and power. Arguing that housewifery was considered by many working-class women to be a worthwhile option is not to glorify the domestic sphere. Clearly housework in this period was not easy. In the words of a wife of an agricultural labourer in Sussex in 1867: 'Farm labour isn't so hard as the washtub'.[125] Furthermore this article has looked only at working-class women. Different things were happening to other groups of women. Clearly the ability of a working-class housewife to make the most of her domestic power depended on factors such as the chief wage-earner's income and the stability of that income. Crucial to her status within the household and within the community of housewives were her age, health and number of children. Geographical location also exerted an independent force: women living in housing estates may have found it easier to create a 'space' separate from the masculine world of employment; women living in crowded accommodation in London lacked the symbolic power of the parlour; women in small towns possessed advantages not shared by their sisters in the cities. Although ignored in this article, these geographical aspects are clearly crucial. However, although the concept of neighbourhood identities was uppermost in the minds of women who lived in such areas, their situation was not radically different in other parts of England.

There was much to gain from full-time housewifery. Many married women never reaped the benefits; many had to compete from a disadvantageous position in both waged and domestic worlds. But whatever their position, they actively resisted what they defined as unlawful power over them. Working-class housewives in the period spanning the late nineteenth century and the First World War described their work as meaningful and felt justified in protesting when they considered their menfolk were being unjust. Housework was not 'invisible' work. It was very visible – especially to other housewives, who competed with each other and punished (through social ostracism and gossip) those who were seen as lowering standards. They worked to increase their power within the household in this period by focusing on the irreplaceability and indispensability of their skills and resources. The home was not known by many housewives as a place of confinement. Rather, for many, it was a neighbourhood power-base, but a power-base none the less.

Notes

1 Frank Steel, *Ditcher's Row: A Tale of the Older Charity* (London, 1939), p. 42.
2 For the best discussion of the problems of under-enumeration in the censuses, see the debate between F. L. Jones, 'Is It True What They Said about Women? The Census 1801–1911 and Women in the Economy' (unpubd paper, Dept Sociology, Australian National Univ., Canberra, 1983), and Desley Deacon, 'Political Arithmetic? Women and the Census, 1861–1891' (unpubd paper, Dept Sociology, Australian National Univ., Canberra, 1982). See also Edward Higgs, 'Domestic Servants and Households in Victorian England', *Social History*, viii (1982), pp. 201–10; June Purvis, *Hard Lessons* (Oxford, 1989); Elizabeth Roberts, *Women's Work, 1840–1940* (London, 1988), pp. 18–20.
3 Sally Alexander 'Women's Work in Nineteenth-Century London: A Study of the Years 1820–50', in Juliet Mitchell and Ann Oakley (eds.), *The Rights and Wrongs of Women* (Harmondsworth, 1976), pp. 59–111; Michael Anderson, *Family Structure in Nineteenth Century Lancashire* (Cambridge, 1971); John Benson, 'Work', in John Benson (ed.), *The Working Class in England, 1875–1914* (London, 1985), pp. 63–88; Charles Booth, 'Occupations of the People of the UK, 1801–1881', *Jl Roy. Statistical Soc.*, xlix (1886), p. 322; Clara C. Collet, 'The Collection and Utilization of Official Statistics Bearing on the Extent and Effects of Industrial Employment on Women', *Jl Roy. Statistical Soc.*, lxi (1898), p. 229; Clara C. Collet, *Women in Industry* (London, [1900]); Eric Hobsbawm, *Worlds of Work* (London, 1984), pp. 93–4; Margaret Hewitt, *Wives and Mothers in Victorian Industry* (London, 1958); Lee Holcombe, *Wives and Property; Reform of the Married Women's Property in Nineteenth-Century England* (Oxford, 1983); Ellen Jordan, 'The Exclusion of Women from Industry in Nineteenth-Century Britain', *Comparative Studies in Society and Hist.*, xxxi (1989), pp. 273–96; Jane Lewis,

Women in England, 1870–1950 (Brighton, 1984); Eric Richards, 'Women in the British Economy since about 1700: An Interpretation', *History*, lix (1974), pp. 337–57; Louise A. Tilly and Joan W. Scott, *Women, Work and Family* (New York, 1987), pp. 149–56.

4 Wally Seccombe, 'Patriarchy Stabilized: The Construction of the Male Breadwinner Wage Norm in Nineteenth Century Britain', *Social History*, xi (1986), pp. 53–76; Alexander, 'Women's Work in Nineteenth-Century London'; Hewitt, *Wives and Mothers in Victorian Industry*; Bridget Hill, *Women, Work and Sexual Politics in Eighteenth-Century England* (Oxford, 1989); E. A. Hunt, *British Labour History, 1815–1914* (London, 1981), pp. 17–25; Purvis, *Hard Lessons*, pp. 27–8, 40–6.

5 The concepts of 'housework' and 'housewives' are complex. What constitutes 'work'? What are the boundaries of the 'house'? Many 'housewives' are not married. For a discussion of these problems, as well as a more detailed analysis of the theoretical aspects of my argument, see my *Husbandry to Housewifery: Women, Economic Change and Housework in Ireland, 1890–1914* (Oxford, 1993). See also Brian Harrison, 'Class and Gender in Modern British Labour History', *Past and Present*, no. 124 (Aug. 1989), pp. 121–58. An excellent article pointing out the extent to which working-class women earned money at home through taking in lodgers or boarders, casual cleaning and child-minding, and taking in washing is Leonore Davidoff, 'The Separation of Home and Work? Landladies and Lodgers in Nineteenth and Twentieth Century England', in Sandra Burman (ed.), *Fit Work for Women* (London, 1979), pp. 64–97.

6 Lydia Morris, *The Workings of the Household: A US–UK Comparison* (Cambridge, 1990), p. 16. See also Rosemary Collins, ' "Horses for Courses": Ideology and the Division of Domestic Labour', in Paul Close and Rosemary Collins (eds.), *Family and Economy in Modern Society* (London, 1985), p. 66; Ross Davies, *Women and Work* (London, 1975), p. 39.

7 Michèle Barrett, *Women's Oppression Today* (London, 1980); Heidi Hartmann, 'The Historical Roots of Occupational Segregation: Capitalism, Patriarchy, and Job Segregation by Sex', *Signs*, i, no. 3, pt 2 (Spring 1976), pp. 137–69; Jordan, 'Exclusion of Women from Industry in Nineteenth-Century Britain', pp. 273–96; Judy Lown, 'Not So Much a Factory, More a Form of Patriarchy: Gender and Class during Industrialization', in Eva Gamarnikow *et al.* (eds.), *Gender, Class and Work* (London, 1983), pp. 28–45.

8 Alexander, 'Women's Work in Nineteenth-Century London'; Cynthia Cockburn, *Brothers: Male Dominance and Technological Change* (London, 1983); Sonya O. Rose, 'Gender Antagonism and Class Conflict: Exclusionary Strategies of Male Trade Unionists in Nineteenth Century Britain', *Social History*, xiii (1988), pp. 191–208; Sonya O. Rose, ' "Gender at Work": Sex, Class and Industrial Capitalism', *History Workshop Jl*, xxi (1986), pp. 113–31; Sylvia Walby, *Patriarchy at Work: Patriarchal and Capitalist Relations in Employment* (London, 1986).

9 August Bebel, *Women in the Past, Present and Future* (London, 1885); Margaret Benston, 'The Political Economy of Women's Liberation', *Monthly Rev.*, xxi, no. 4 (1969); Mariarosa dalla Costa, *The Power of Women and the Subversion of the Community* (Bristol, 1972); Christine Delphy, *Close to Home: A Materialist Analysis of Women's Oppression* (London, 1984); F. Engels, *The Origin of the Family, Private Property and the State*, ed. Eleanor B. Leacock (New York, 1972); Beatrice Ferneyhough, 'On the Confinement of Women to Housework as an Exclusion from Social Production', *Polit. Affairs*, liii (1974), pp. 50–5; Shulamith Firestone, *The Dialectic of Sex: The Case for Feminist Revolution* (London, 1972); Lewis, *Women in England*; Juliet Mitchell, 'Women: The Longest Revolution', *New Left Rev.*, no. 40 (1966), pp. 11–37.

10 See Ann Oakley, *Women's Work: The Housewife, Past and Present* (New York, 1974). For other (less carefully researched) arguments, see H. Z. Lopato, *Occupation Housewife* (New York, 1971).

11 Purvis, *Hard Lessons*, p. 46.

12 Peter N. Stearns, 'Working-Class Women', in Martha Vinicus (ed.), *Suffer and Be Still* (London, 1972), p. 120.

13 Terry Fee, 'Domestic Labor: An Analysis of Housework and Its Relation to the Production Process', *Rev. Radical Polit. Economics*, viii (Spring 1976), p. 8; Wally Seccombe, 'The Housewife and Her Labour under Capitalism', *New Left Rev.*, no. 83 (1974), p. 19.

14 Seccombe, 'Housewife and Her Labour under Capitalism', p. 21.

15 The best works on women's role in budgeting are Paul Johnson, *Saving and Spending: The Working-Class Economy in Britain 1870–1939* (Oxford, 1985), and Melanie Tebbutt, *Making Ends Meet: Pawnbroking and Working-Class Credit* (London, 1983).

16 For the most elaborate arguments along these lines, see Seccombe, 'Housewife and Her Labour under Capitalism', pp. 21–3; Dalla Costa, *Power of Women and the Subversion of the Community*.

17 Collins, 'Horses for Courses', p. 66.

18 Hannah Mitchell, *The Hard Way Up: The Autobiography of Hannah Mitchell, Suffragette and Rebel*, ed. Geoffrey Mitchell (London, 1968), p. 113.

19 Jean Comaroff, *Body of Power, Spirit of Resistance: The Culture and History of a South African People* (Chicago, 1985), p. 1.

20 For a similar argument based on research in Pakistan, see Hanna Papanek, 'Purdah in Pakistan: Seclusion and Modern Occupations for Women', *Jl Marriage and the Family*, xxxiii (1971), pp. 517–30; Hanna Papanek, 'Purdah: Separate Worlds and Symbolic Shelter', *Comparative Studies in Society and Hist.*, xv (1973), pp. 289–325. For a comparative argument in an American context, see Kathryn Kish Sklar, *Catharine Beecher: A Study in American Domesticity* (New Haven, 1973); Johnny Faragher and Christine Stansell, 'Women and Their Families on the Overland Trail, 1842–1867', *Feminist Studies*, ii (1975), pp. 150–66.

21 Jane Rendall, *Women in an Industrializing Society: England, 1750–1880* (Oxford, 1990), p. 85.

22 The working-class women inteviewed by Elizabeth Roberts made this point: 'Women who worked full-time were certainly not regarded as emancipated by their contemporaries, rather as drudges. Women whose husband earned sufficient money to clothe, feed and house the family preferred to have a reduced work load rather than extra income': Elizabeth Roberts, *A Woman's Place: An Oral History of Working-Class Women, 1890–1940* (Oxford, 1984).

23 *Commission on the Employment of Children, Young Persons, and Women in Agriculture (1867): Appendix Part II to Second Report, Evidence from the Assistant Commissioners*, Parliamentary Papers (hereafter P.P.), 1868–9 (4202-I), xiii, p. 293. See also p. 296, evidence from the son of an agricultural labourer in Biddleston, Wiltshire; Mrs Mary Bayly, *Home Rule: An Old Mother's Letter to Parents* (London, 1886), p. 38.

24 See *Commission on the Employment of Children, Young Persons and Women in Agriculture (1867): Appendix Part II to the First Report, Evidence from the Assistant Commissioners*, P.P., 1867–8 (4068-I), xvii, p. 430, letter from Mr J. Beasley of Chapel Brampton, Northamptonshire; *Appendix Part II to Second Report*, p. 294, comment by Mrs Austin, wife of a labourer in Harbury, Warwickshire.

25 *Commission on the Employment of Children, Appendix Part II to the First Report*, p. 296. See also *Appendix Part II to Second Report*, p. 296, comment by Mrs Lush, wife of a labourer in Berwick St John, Wiltshire; *Appendix Part II to the First Report*, p. 275, comment by the unnamed wife of a farm-servant at Aycliffe, Darlington, Co. Durham.

26 *Commission on the Employment of Children, Young Persons, and Women in Agriculture (1867): Third Report of the Commissioners with Appendix, Part I and Part II*, P.P., 1867–8 (C. 70), xiii, p. 143.

27 *Reports of Special Assistant Poor Law Commissioners on the Employment of Women and Children in Agriculture*, P.P., 1843 (510), xii, p. 68.

28 *Commission on the Employment of Children, Young Persons, and Women in Agriculture (1867): Appendix Part II to the First Report*, p. 176, evidence by Revd W. T. Beckett, rector of Ingoldisthorpe, Docking Union, Norfolk, and diocesan inspector of schools in the deanery of Heacham.

29 Lincolnshire: *Appendix Part II to the First Report*, p. 301; Berkshire: *Commission on the Employment of Children, Young Persons, and Women in Agriculture (1867): First Report of the Commissioners, with Appendix, Part I*, P.P., 1867–8 (4068), xvii, Appendix, p. 17: in this case, it is 4d. a year difference. For very similar statements, see *Appendix Part II to the First Report*, pp. 441–2, comments by John Jervis, a labourer from Islip, Northamptonshire, and James Marriott, a labourer from Stanwick, Northamptonshire; *Appendix Part II to Second Report*, pp. 136, 292–3, 295, comments by Mrs Finnimore (wife of a labourer in Broadclyst, Devon), William Muggleton (gardener in Byfleet, Surrey), Mrs Hook (wife of a carter in Sanderstead, Surrey), and two labourers named John Topp and William Olden from Ashton Gifford, Wilts.; *Reports of Special Assistant Poor Law Commissioners on the Employment of Women and Children in Agriculture*, pp. 67–8, evidence from Mrs Sumbler, wife of a labourer near Calne, Wilts.

30 *Royal Commission on Labour: The Agricultural Labourer, Vol. I, England, Part III, Reports by Mr. Arthur Wilson Fox (Assistant Commissioner), upon Certain Selected Districts in the Counties of Cumberland, Lancashire, Norfolk, Northumberland and Suffolk, with Summary Report Prefixed*, P.P., 1893–4 (C. 6894-III), xxxv, p. 97, labourer from Swaffham, Norfolk. This is a common theme in *Commission on the Employment of Children, Young Persons, and Women in Agriculture (1867): Appendix Part II to the First Report*.

31 Geoffrey Best, *Mid-Victorian Britain, 1851–1875* (London, 1971); A. L. Bowley, *Wages and Income in the United Kingdom since 1860* (Cambridge, 1937), pp. 30, 122; S. G. Checkland, *The Rise of Industrial Society in England, 1815–1885* (London, 1964); G. D. H. Cole, *A Short History of the British Working-Class Movement, 1789–1847* (London, 1948), p. 140; Eric Hopkins, 'Small Town Aristocrats of Labour and Their Standard of Living, 1840–1914', *Econ. Hist. Rev.*, 2nd ser., xxviii (1975), pp. 222–42; Hunt, *British Labour History*, pp. 73–6; H. Perkin, *The Origins of Modern English Society, 1780–1880* (London, 1969). Charles Feinstein has questioned the sharpness of the change in real wages in 'A New Look at the Cost of Living, 1870–1914', in James Foreman-Peck (ed.), *New Perspectives on the Late Victorian Economy: Essays in Quantitative Economic History, 1860–1914* (Cambridge, 1991), pp. 151–79.

32 This is also argued by William Ashworth, *An Economic History of England, 1870–1939* (London, 1960), p. 192.

33 For an interesting discussion of this point, see *Royal Commission on Labour: The Agricultural Labourer, Vol. V, Part I, General Report by Mr. William C. Little (Senior Assistant Agricultural Commissioner)*, P.P., 1893–4 (C. 6894–XXV), xxxvii, pt 2, p. 55.

34 Christopher Bliss, 'The Labour Market: Theory and Experience', in Michael Beenstock (ed.), *Modelling the Labour Market* (London, 1988), pp. 3–4.

35 For justification for choosing the 21s. to 30s. level as the threshold, see D. J. Oddy, 'Working-Class Diets in Late Nineteenth-Century Britain', *Econ. Hist. Rev.*, 2nd ser., xxiii (1970), pp. 314–23; B. Seebohm Rowntree, *Poverty: A Study of Town Life* (London, 1901).

36 Her children were eating meat pie and suet pudding for dinner when she was interviewed: *Commission on the Employment of Children, Young Persons, and Women in Agriculture (1867): Appendix Part II to the First Report*, p. 309.

37 For an explicit statement, see *Commission on the Employment of Children, Young Persons and Women in Agriculture (1867): Appendix Part II to the First Report*, p. 30, Weston-Longville, Norfolk.

38 *Royal Commission on Labour: The Agricultural Labourer, Vol. I, England, Part III, Reports by Mr. Arthur Wilson Fox (Assistant Commissioner)*, p. 153. For a discussion of the extension of education for working-class children, see Brian Simon, *Studies in the History of Education, 1780–1870* (London, 1960).

39 See *Royal Commission on Labour: The Agricultural Labourer, Vol. I, England, Part III, Reports by Mr. Arthur Wilson Fox (Assistant Commissioner)*, p. 86, letter from Dr H. G. Foster, medical officer of health for Wayland and Swaffham; *Vol. V, Part I, General Report by Mr. William C. Little (Senior Assistant Agricultural*

Commissioner), p. 55, comment for Glendale Union, Northumberland. For a historical treatment, see the discussion by Roberts, in *A Woman's Place*, of standards of housekeeping in those areas employing large numbers of married women (for instance, in Blackburn, Burnley, the City of London and Hinkley).

40 *Royal Commission on Labour: The Agricultural Labourer, Vol. V, Part I, General Report by Mr. William C. Little (Senior Assistant Agricultural Commissioner)*, p. 55, Glendale Union, Northumberland.

41 *Commission on the Employment of Children, Young Persons, and Women in Agriculture (1867): Appendix Part II to the First Report*, p. 195.

42 Christopher Bliss and Nicholas Stern, 'Productivity, Wages and Nutrition: Part I – The Theory', *Jl Development Economics*, v (1978), pp. 331–62; H. Leiberstein, *Economic Backwardness and Economic Growth* (New York, 1957); Joseph E. Stiglitz, 'The Efficiency Wage Hypothesis, Surplus Labour and the Distribution of Income in LDCs', *Oxford Econ. Papers*, xxviii (1976), pp. 185–207; John Strauss, 'Does Better Nutrition Raise Farm Productivity?', *Jl Polit. Economy*, civ (1986), pp. 297–320.

43 David Vincent, 'Love and Death and the Nineteenth Century Working Class', *Social History*, v (1980), p. 247.

44 Nancy Tomes, 'A "Torrent of Abuse". Crimes of Violence between Working-Class Men and Women in London, 1840–1875', *Jl Social Hist.*, xi (1978), pp. 328–45; Stearns, 'Working-Class Women', pp. 100–20.

45 *Norfolk News*, 9 Nov. 1867, p. 3.

46 Paul Johnson, 'Credit and Thrift and the British Working Class, 1870–1939', in Jay Winter (ed.), *The Working Class in Modern British History: Essays in Honour of Henry Pelling* (Cambridge, 1983), p. 148. For the role of women in making those things which could more cheaply have been bought, had money been available, see Ben Turner, *About Myself, 1863–1930* (London, 1930), pp. 19–20, talking about his mother in a Yorkshire working-class family in the 1860s and 1870s.

47 John Sykes, *Slawit in the 'Sixties: Reminiscences of the Moral, Social and Industrial Life of Slaithwaite District, in and about the Year 1860* (London, 1926), p. 85.

48 For two examples, see Gary Becker, *A Treatise on the Family* (Cambridge, Mass., 1981), and Jacob Mincer, 'Labor Force Participation of Married Women', *Aspects of Labor Economics* (New York, 1975), pp. 63–97.

49 Eric J. Hobsbawm, 'Peasants and Politics', *Jl Peasant Studies*, i (1973), pp. 3–22.

50 Grace Foakes, *My Part of the River* (London, 1974), pp. 69–70.

51 Arthur Barton, *The Penny World: A Boyhood Recalled* (London, 1969), p. 173; John Benson, *The Working Class in Britain, 1850–1939* (London, 1989), pp. 102–3; M. J. Daunton, *House and Home in the Victorian City: Working-Class Housing, 1850–1914* (London, 1983), pp. 282–3; Harrison, 'Class and Gender in Modern British Labour History', p. 129; Walter Southgate, *That's the Way It Was: A Working Class Autobiography, 1890–1950* (London, 1982), p. 67.

52 Neville Cardus, *Autobiography* (London, 1955), p. 24; *Reports of Special Assistant Poor Law Commissioners on the Employment of Women and Children in Agriculture*, p. 90.

53 *Commission on the Employment of Children, Young Persons, and Women in Agriculture (1867): Appendix Part II to First Report*, p. 198.

54 *Royal Commission on Agriculture, England: Report by Mr. Henry Rew (Assistant Commissioner) on the County of Norfolk*, P.P., 1895 (C. 7915), xvii, p. 45.

55 Charles H. Welch, *An Autobiography* (Banstead, 1960), pp. 38–9.

56 Jane Humphries, 'Protective Legislation, the Capitalist State and Working Class Men: The Case of the 1842 Mines Regulations Act', *Feminist Rev.*, vii (1981), pp. 1–33; Laura Oren, 'The Welfare of Women in Laboring Families: England, 1860–1950', in Mary Hartman and Lois Banner (eds.), *Clio's Consciousness Raised: New Perspectives on the History of Women* (New York, 1974), pp. 226–44; Seccombe, 'Patriarchy Stabilized', pp. 53–76. For an amusing example, see Jack Lawson, *A Man's Life* (London, 1932), p. 74.

57 *Commission on the Employment of Children, Young Persons, and Women in Agriculture (1867): Appendix Part II to Second Report*, p. 142. For other accounts

see Mary Chamberlain, *Fenwomen: A Portrait of Women in an English Village* (London, 1975), p. 36; Bob Copper, *Early to Rise: A Sussex Boyhood* (London, 1976), pp. 11, 222; *Maternity: Letters from Working Women*, ed. Margaret Llewelyn Davies (London, 1989; first pubd 1915), p. 151; Rose Gamble, *Chelsea Child* (Bath, 1980), pp. 8–9; Josephine Gibney, *Joe McGarrigle's Daughter* (Kineton, 1977), p. 20; Helen Forrester, *By the Waters of Liverpool* (London, 1981), p. 107; Harrison, 'Class and Gender in Modern British Labour History', p. 125; Lawson, *A Man's Life*, p. 74; M. Loane, *Simple Sanitation: The Practical Application of Laws of Health to Small Dwellings* (London, 1905), p. 63; T. Oliver, 'Diet of Toil', *Lancet*, 29 June 1895, pp. 1629–35; D. Noel Paton, J. Crawford Dunlop and E. Inglis, *A Study of the Diet of the Labouring Classes in Edinburgh* (Edinburgh, 1902), p. 17; Robert Roberts, *A Ragged Schooling: Growing Up in the Classic Slum* (Manchester, 1976), p. 76; Joseph Toole, *Fighting through Life* (London, 1935), pp. 61–2; Robert Tressell, *The Ragged Trousered Philanthropists* (London, 1914), p. 44.

58 Michael Anderson, *Family Structure in Nineteenth Century Lancashire* (Cambridge, 1971); Neil McKendrick, 'Home Demand and Economic Growth: A New View of the Role of Women and Children in the Industrial Revolution', in Neil McKendrick (ed.), *Historical Perspectives: Studies in English Thought and Society in Honour of J. H. Plumb* (London, 1974), pp. 152–210; Oren, 'Welfare of Women in Laboring Families'; J. W. Scott and L. A. Tilly, 'Women's Work and Family in Nineteenth-Century Europe', *Comparative Studies in Society and Hist.*, xvii (1975), pp. 36–64.

59 For examples, see J. A. Ericksen, W. L. Yancey and E. P. Ericksen, 'The Division of Family Roles', *Jl Marriage and the Family*, xlvi (1979), pp. 301–13; Abigail J. Stewart and David G. Winter, 'The Nature and Causes of Female Suppression', *Signs*, ii (1976–7), pp. 531–53; Sharlene Hesse-Biber and John Williamson, 'Resource Theory and Power in Families: Life Cycle Considerations', *Family Process*, xxiii (1984), pp. 261–78; Robert O. Blood and Donald M. Wolfe, *Husbands and Wives: The Dynamics of Married Living* (Glencoe, Ill., 1960); Peter M. Blau, *Exchange and Power in Social Life* (New York, 1964).

60 For further discussion of domestic classes, see my ' "The Health Caravan": Domestic Education and Female Labor in Rural Ireland, 1890–1914', *Eire-Ireland*, xxiv (1989), pp. 21–38. See also *Board of Education: General Report on the Teaching of Domestic Subjects to Public Elementary School Children in England and Wales, by the Chief Woman Inspector of the Board of Education* (London, 1912), p. 38; Fanny L. Calder, 'The Training of Teachers in Cookery', *Jl Education*, 1 Dec. 1894, p. 712. Calder was the Hon. Secretary of the National Union for the Technical Education of Women in Domestic Science and the Hon. Secretary of the Liverpool Training School of Cookery and Technical College for Women: *Board of Education: Special Report on the Teaching of Cookery to Public Elementary School Children in England and Wales, by the Chief Woman Inspector of the Board of Education* (London, 1907), p. i.

61 Dena Attar, *Wasting Girls' Time: The History and Politics of Home Economics* (London, 1990); Anna Davin, ' "Mind That You Do as You Are Told": Reading Books for Board School Children, 1870–1902', *Feminist Rev.*, iii (1979), pp. 89–98; Carol Dyhouse, 'Good Wives and Little Mothers: Social Anxieties and the Schoolgirl's Curriculum, 1890–1920', *Oxford Rev. Education*, iii (1977), pp. 21–35; Carol Dyhouse, 'Towards a "Feminine" Curriculum for English Schoolgirls: The Demands of Ideology, 1870–1963', *Women's Studies Internat. Quart.*, i (1978), pp. 291–311; June Purvis, 'Domestic Subjects since 1870', in Ivor Goodson (ed.), *Social Histories of the Secondary Curriculum: Subjects for Study* (London, 1985), pp. 145–76; Annmarie Turnbull, 'Learning Her Womanly Work: The Elementary School Curriculum, 1870–1914', in Felicity Hunt (ed.), *Lessons for Life: The Schooling of Girls and Women, 1850–1950* (Oxford, 1987), pp. 83–100.

62 See the reports in Public Record Office, London (hereafter P.R.O.), ED. 77/8, 96/198, 164/3.

63 *Board of Education: Report of the Consultative Committee on Practical Work in Secondary Schools*, P.P., 1913 (Cd. 6849), xx, p. 302, evidence by Miss S. A. Burstall, headmistress of Manchester High School, on 9 December 1909; Miss

Rowland, 'Wales (with Monmouthshire): Domestic Subjects in Public Elementary Schools Annual Report 1911–1912', P.R.O., ED. 92/10.

64 *Board of Education: General Report on the Teaching of Domestic Subjects*, pp. 10, 32, 36; Rowland, 'Wales (with Monmouthshire): Domestic Subjects'.

65 *Report of the Committee of Council on Education (England and Wales), with Appendix, 1883–84*, P.P., 1884 (C. 4091-I), xxiv, p. 387; *Report of the Committee of Council on Education (England and Wales), with Appendix, 1897–98*, P.P., 1898 (C. 8987), xxii, p. 296.

66 *Report of the Committee of Council on Education (England and Wales), with Appendix, 1885–86*, P.P., 1886 (C. 4849-I), xxiv, p. 284.

67 *Report of the Committee of Council on Education (England and Wales), with Appendix, 1892–93*, P.P., 1893–4 (C. 7089-I), xxvi, p. 87.

68 *General Report for the Year 1894, by Revd C. H. Parez, One of Her Majesty's Chief Inspectors on the Schools in the North Central Division of England*, P.P., 1895 (C. 7814-II), xxviii, p. 22.

69 Horace Plunkett, 'Agricultural Education for Women in Great Britain, Ireland and the Colonies', in The Countess of Warwick (ed.), *Progress in Women's Education in the British Empire: Being the Report of the Education Section, Victorian Era Exhibition, 1897* (London, 1898), p. 124.

70 Lilian K. Buckpitt, 'For the Sake of the Child', *Child*, ii (1912), p. 893.

71 Flora Klickmann, *The Mistress of the Little House: What She Should Know and What She Should Do When She Has an Untrained Servant* (London, 1912), provides a lively discussion of this issue. See also *Board of Education: General Report on the Teaching of Domestic Subjects*, pp. 15–16; Sophia H. E. Landmaid, *A Woman's Work and How to Lighten It* (London, 1904), p. 11.

72 *Board of Education: Interim Memorandum on the Teaching of Housecraft in Girls' Secondary Schools* (London, 1911), pp. 35–6; Cameron, 'How To Train Housewives', p. 107; Mary Harrison, *Simple Lessons in Cookery: For the Use of Teachers of Elementary and Technical Classes* (London, 1898), pp. vii–viii.

73 Norman Nicholson, *Wednesday Early Closing* (London, 1975), pp. 77–8.

74 Hunt, *British Labour History*, pp. 90–9.

75 For a review of the literature, see Hunt, *British Labour History*, pp. 85–7. See also T. E. Kebbell, *The Agricultural Labourer: A Short Summary of His Position* (London, 1893); A. Wilson Fox, 'Agricultural Wages in England and Wales during the Last Fifty Years', *Jl Roy. Statistical Soc.*, lxvi (1903), p. 295.

76 For a contemporary discussion, see Klickmann, *Mistress of the Little House*, p. 1. For further historical analysis, see Clarence D. Long, *The Labor Force under Changing Income and Employment* (Princeton, 1958); Ruth Schwartz Cowan, *More Work for Mother: The Ironies of Household Technology from the Open Hearth to the Microwave* (New York, 1983); Ruth Schwartz Cowan, 'The "Industrial Revolution" in the Home: Household Technology and Social Change in the 20th Century', *Technology and Culture*, xvii (1976), pp. 1–23; Ruth Schwartz Cowan, 'A Case Study of Technology and Social Change: The Washing Machine and the Working Wife', in Hartmann and Banner (eds.), *Clio's Consciousness Raised*, pp. 245–53; Hunt, *British Labour History*, p. 94.

77 P.R.O., H.O. 45/9839/1310432, letters between the Shipmasters' Society and the Commission of Council on Education, April 1891; ED. 164/3, Committee of Management of the National Training School for Cookery, 16 Feb. 1904, pp. 205–7; ED. 164/4, Committee of Management of the National Training School for Cookery, 4 April 1911, unpaginated; Rowland, 'Wales (with Monmouthshire): Domestic Subjects'; Alexander Quinlan and N. E. Mann, *Cookery for Seaman* (Liverpool, 1894).

78 Anna Martin, *The Married Working Woman: A Study* (London, 1911), p. 30.

79 For a heated discussion between a farm wife and a lecturer on farming who dared to 'pass the threshold of the female domain' in one of his lectures, see Henry Tanner, *Jack's Education, or How He Learnt Farming* (London, 1879), pp. 9–10. See also Richard Church, *Over the Bridge: An Essay in Autobiography* (London, 1955), p. 210; Margaret Powell, *My Children and I* (London, 1977), pp. 45–6. For a modern discussion, see Morris, *Workings of the Household*, p. 101.

80 Frederick C. Wigby, *Just a Country Boy* (Wymondham, 1976), p. 4; Loane, *Simple Sanitation*, pp. 13, 18; Bessie Harvey, 'Youthful Memories of My Life in a Suffolk Village', *Suffolk Rev.*, ii (Sept. 1960), p. 73; Ernest Egerton Wood, *Is This Theosophy?* (London, 1936), p. 48.

81 Lawson, *A Man's Life*, pp. 50–1; Church, *Over the Bridge*, p. 123; Turner, *About Myself*, pp. 38–9; Sir Reader Bullard, *The Camels Must Go: An Autobiography* (London, 1961), p. 27; Wil Jon Edwards, *From the Valley I Came* (London, 1956); Welch, *Autobiography*, p. 36; Harry Pollitt, *Serving My Time: An Apprenticeship to Politics* (London, 1940), p. 19.

82 Lucy H. M. Soulsby, *Home Rule, or Daughters To-Day* (Oxford, 1894), p. 14.

83 P. A. Sheehan, *Glenanaar* (New York, 1905), pp. 161–3.

84 Robert Lynd, *Home Life in Ireland* (London, 1909), pp. 22–3.

85 For a superb chapter on domestic violence, see Carl Chinn, *They Worked All Their Lives: Women of the Urban Poor in England, 1880–1939* (Manchester, 1988), pp. 155–66.

86 E. P. Thompson, 'Patrician Society, Plebeian Culture', *Jl Social Hist.*, vii (1973–4), pp. 382–405.

87 *Housewife*, v (1890), pp. 217–18, 443, 535–6, 679–80, 757.

88 M. Loane, *The Queen's Poor: Life as They Find It in Town and Country* (London, 1906), p. 1 (the first sentence in the book). See also the story told by Celia Davies about her father at the turn of the century in *Clean Clothes on Sunday* (Lavenham, 1974), p. 17.

89 Pat O'Mara, *The Autobiography of a Liverpool Irish Slummy* (London, 1932); 'Tiger' O'Reilly, *The Tiger of the Legion* (London, 1936), p. 26; Maurice Levinson, *The Trouble with Yesterday* (London, 1946), p. 50.

90 M. Loane, *From Their Point of View* (London, 1908), pp. 120–1.

91 Albert S. Jasper, *A Hoxton Childhood* (London, 1969), pp. 17–18. See also Lawson, *A Man's Life*, p. 20; George Edwards, *From Crow-Scaring to Westminster: An Autobiography* (London, 1922), p. 26; *Commission on the Employment of Children, Young Persons, and Women in Agriculture (1867): Appendix Part II to the First Report*, p. 199, Robert Webb of Ingoldisthorpe, farm labourer.

92 Molly Weir, *Best Foot Forward* (Bath, 1979), p. 39; O'Reilly, *Tiger of the Legion*, p. 26; Vera Alsop, 'A Woman's Part', in Durham 'Strong Words' Collective (eds.), *But the World Goes on the Same: Changing Times in Durham Pit Mines* (Whitley Bay, 1979), p. 71; Loane, *Queen's Poor*, p. 1; Ted Willlis, *Whatever Happened to Tom Mix? The Story of One of My Lives* (London, 1970), p. 92; Jasper, *Hoxton Childhood*, p. 33; Elizabeth Ring, *Up the Cockneys!* (London, 1975), p. 103; George Hitchin, *Pit-Yacker* (London, 1962), p. 11.

93 Ring, *Up the Cockneys!*, p. 135.

94 Willis, *Whatever Happened to Tom Mix?*, pp. 102–3; Bim Andrews, 'Making Do', in *Destiny Obscure: Autobiographies of Childhood, Education and Family from the 1820s to the 1920s*, ed. John Burnett (Harmondsworth, 1982), p. 127.

95 Cited in Tebbutt, *Making Ends Meet*, p. 60. For other examples of stealing from husbands, see Nancy Sharman, *Nothing to Steal: The Story of a Southampton Childhood* (London, 1977), p. 15; Bessie Wallis, 'Yesterday', in *Destiny Obscure*, ed. Burnett, p. 309; A. B. Rogers, *Four Acres and a Donkey* (London, 1979), p. 33. For an example with a tragic outcome, see Tomes, 'Torrent of Abuse', p. 332.

96 Both quotations are from Loane, *From Their Point of View*, p. 95. In the words of an old Rottingdean song (cited in Copper, *Early to Rise*, p. 222):

> When father came home at night and drunk we used him rob,
> And after the course of a week or two we save up seven bob.
> One day my mother did say, Come along with me, my boy,
> We will go to Moses and Sons for a suit of corduroy.
> Right tiddy fol lol fol lol fol lol right tiddy fol lol fal lay.

97 Delderfield's mother 'treasured her defiance' and relished arguing with her husband most days of her life: R. F. Delderfield, *Bird's Eye View* (London, 1954), p. 3.

98 Edward Ezard, *Battersea Boy* (London, 1979), p. 24; Peter Fletcher, *The Long Sunday* (London, 1958), p. 81.

99 Jasper, *Hoxton Childhood*, p. 33.

100 Tomes, 'Torrent of Abuse', pp. 328–45. For a good discussion of the symbolic importance of swearing in working-class culture, see Bernice Martin, *A Sociology of Contemporary Cultural Change* (Oxford, 1981), pp. 67–8.

101 Edward B. Harper, 'Social Consequences of an Unsuccessful Low Caste Movement', in James Silverberg (ed.), *Social Mobility in the Caste System in India: An Interdisciplinary Symposium* (The Hague, 1968), pp. 48–9.

102 Jim Hooley, *A Hillgate Childhood: Myself When Young* (Stockport, 1981), n.p. [p. 29]; Jasper, *Hoxton Childhood*, pp. 112–13; James Allan Bullock, *Bowers Row: Recollections of a Mining Village* (East Ardsley, 1976), p. 55.

103 George Henry Hewins, *The Dillen: Memoirs of a Man of Stratford-upon-Avon* (London, 1981), p. 64.

104 Winifred Brown, *Under Six Planets* (London, 1955), pp. 36–7.

105 Mollie Harris, *A Kind of Magic* (Oxford, 1985), p. 135.

106 Alice Linton, *Not Expecting Miracles* (London, 1982), pp. 53–4.

107 Kathleen Behan, *Mother of All the Behans: The Autobiography of Kathleen Behan* (London, 1985 repr.), p. 80.

108 E. P. Thompson, 'Eighteenth-Century English Society: Class Struggle without Class?', *Social History*, iii (1978), pp. 158–9.

109 For examples, see Fletcher, *Long Sunday*, p. 20; Dorothy Scannell, *Mother Knows Best: An East End Childhood* (Bath, 1974), pp. 5–6.

110 Elizabeth Roberts provides many examples in 'Learning and Living – Socialization Outside School', *Oral History*, iii, no. 2 (1975), p. 22.

111 Lawson, *A Man's Life*, p. 144.

112 Roberts, *Ragged Schooling*, p. 76; Fletcher, *Long Sunday*, p. 20.

113 Roberts, *Ragged Schooling*, p. 76.

114 *Maternity*, ed. Llewelyn Davies, p. 50.

115 For example, see Wanda Gag, *Gone is Gone, or The Story of a Man Who Wanted to Do Housework* (London, 1936; repr. 1975).

116 'Strategy with Husbands', *Housewife*, v (1890), p. 443.

117 Church, *Over the Bridge*, pp. 110–11.

118 Mitchell, *Hard Way Up*, p. 114.

119 Fletcher, *Long Sunday*, p. 61. For an interesting use of language to assert one's power in the household, see Anon., *'They Might Have Been Together Till the Last': An Essay on Marriage, and the Position of Women in England* (London, 1885), p. 27, where a young village woman in the 1880s, saying her marriage vows in church, twice substituted the word 'opey' for 'obey' in the service – only when the vicar ('in sympathy with the rights of husbands') asked the bride for a third time to repeat the words 'to obey', did she pronounce it correctly.

120 Roberts, *Ragged Schooling*, p. 61.

121 Tomes, 'Torrent of Abuse'.

122 She had tried to protest by silence at first: Church, *Over the Bridge*, p. 116.

123 Church, *Over the Bridge*, p. 61. For a similar statement, see Allan Jobson, *The Creeping Hours of Time* (London, 1977), p. 15.

124 For an excellent justification for calling these acts of resistance, see James C. Scott, *Weapons of the Weak: Everyday Forms of Peasant Resistance* (New Haven, 1985).

125 *Commission on the Employment of Children, Young Persons, and Women in Agriculture (1867): First Report of the Commissioners, with Appendix, Part I*, Appendix, p. 17. *Ibid., Appendix Part II to the First Report*, p. 136, the Revd Hugh J. Hare, curate-in-charge of Docking Union, Norfolk, noted that several women in his parish were 'early ruptured', but this was due to carrying water, not from working in the fields.

Further reading

A comprehensive bibliography is provided by the references to each individual Reading in this book. This final section aims to highlight recent and additional major printed sources for the history of women's work.

Bibliographies

Bell, P. (ed.), *Victorian Women: An Index to Biographies and Memoirs* (Edinburgh, Bell, 1989). In three volumes from the late eighteenth century.

Frey, L., M. Frey and J. Schreider, *Women in Western European History* (Westport, Conn., Greenwood Press, 1984). Supplements have followed.

Hannam, J., A. Hughes and P. Stafford (eds.), *British Women's History: A Bibliographical Guide* (Manchester, Manchester University Press, 1996).

International Labour Office, *Bibliography on Women Workers (1861–1965)* (Geneva, 1970).

Kanner, B., *Women in English Social History 1800–1914: A Guide to Research in Three Volumes* (New York and London, Garland, 1987).

Printed primary sources and collections of documents

Black, C. (ed.), *Married Women's Work* (London, 1915; Virago, 1983). Clementina Black's report for the Women's Industrial Council 1909–10.

Hamilton, S. (ed.), *Criminals, Idiots, Women and Minors: Nineteenth-Century Writing By Women on Women* (Peterborough, Ontario, 1995).

Hill, B., *Eighteenth-Century Women: An Anthology* (London, Routledge, 1984).

Hollis, P., *Women in Public: The Women's Movement 1850–1900* (London, Allen and Unwin, 1979).

Jalland, P. and J. Hooper (eds.), *Women from Birth to Death: The Female Life Cycle in Britain 1830–1914* (Atlantic Highlands, N.J., Humanities Press International, 1986).

Llewelyn Davies, M., *Maternity: Letters from Working Women* (London, 1915; Virago, 1978). Autobiographical letters about childbirth and motherhood.

Llewelyn Davies, M., *Life As We Have Known It* (London, 1931; Virago, 1977). Letters by ordinary women who were members of the Women's Co-operative Guild.

Theoretical works

Allen, J., *Evidence and Silence: Feminism and the Limits of History* in C. Pateman and E. Gross (eds.), *Feminist Challenges: Social and Political Theory* (Sydney, Allen and Unwin, 1986).

Bennett, J., 'Feminism and history', *Gender and History*, 1 (1989).

Bock, G., 'Challenging dichotomies in women's history', in K. Offen and R. R. Pierson (eds.), *Writing Women's History: International Perspectives* (London, Macmillan, 1991).

Fox-Genovese, E., 'Placing women's history in history', *New Left Review*, 133 (1982).

Hartmann, H. I., 'Capitalism, patriarchy and job segregation by sex', *Signs*, 1 (1979).

Kelly, J., 'The social relation of the sexes: methodological implications of women's history', *Signs*, 1 (1976). Reprinted in J. Kelly (ed.), *Women, History and Theory* (Chicago, Chicago University Press, 1984), ch. 1.

Riley, D., '*Am I that Name? Feminism and the Category of "Women" in History*' (London, Macmillan, 1988).

Recent textbooks and useful survey articles

Anderson, B. S. and J. P. Zinsser, *A History of their Own*, vol. 2 (New York, Harper and Row, 1988; Harmondsworth, Penguin, 1990).

Branca, P., 'A new perspective on women's work: a comparative typology', *Journal of Social History* 9 (1975).

Davis, N. Z., 'Women's history in transition: the European case', *Feminist Studies*, 3 (1976). Also reprinted in J. W. Scott (ed.) *Feminism and History* (Oxford, Oxford University Press, 1996).

Fletcher, A., *Gender, Sex and Subordination in England 1500–1800* (New Haven and London, Yale University Press, 1995).

Frader, L. and S. O. Rose (eds.), *Gender and Class in Modern Europe* (Ithaca, Cornell University Press, 1996).

Fraisse, G. and M. Perrot, *A History of Women in the West: Emerging Feminism from Revolution to World War*, Vol IV (Belknap, Cambridge, Mass., 1993).

Hufton, O., *The Prospect before Her: A History of Women in Western Europe* (London, HarperCollins, 1995).

Hufton, O. and J. W. Scott, 'Survey articles: women in history', in *Past and Present*, 101 (1983).

Humphries, J., 'From work to dependence? Women's experience of industrialisation in Britain', *Refresh*, 21 (1995).

Purvis, J., *Women's History: Britain 1850–1945* (London, UCL Press, 1995).

Simonton, D., *A History of European Women's Work, 1700 to the Present* (London, Routledge, 1998).

Thane, P., 'Women and work in Britain *c*. 1870 to World War One', in P. Matthias and J. A. Davis (eds.), *Enterprise and Labour* (Oxford, Blackwell, 1996).

Wiesner, M. E., *Women and Gender in Early Modern Europe* (Cambridge, Cambridge University Press, 1993).

Case studies: recent English studies and international comparisons

Baron, A. (ed.), *Work Engendered: Towards a New History of American Labor* (Ithaca, Cornell University Press, 1991).

Coffin, J. G., *The Politics of Women's Work: The Paris Garment Trades, 1750–1915* (Princeton, Princeton University Press, 1996).

Davin, A., *Growing up Poor: Home, School and Street in London 1870–1914* (London, Rivers Oram Press, 1996).

Davis, N. Z., *Women on the Margins: Three Seventeenth-Century Lives* (Belknap, Cambridge, Mass., 1995).

Dublin, T., *Transforming Women's Work: New England Lives in the Industrial Revolution* (Ithaca, Cornell University Press, 1994).

de Groot, G. and M. Schrover (eds.), *Women Workers and Technological Change in Europe in the Nineteenth and Twentieth Centuries* (London, Taylor and Francis, 1995).

Gullickson, G. L., *Spinners and Weavers of Auffay: Rural Industry and the Sexual Division of Labour in a French Village 1750–1850* (Cambridge, Cambridge University Press, 1986).

Haftner, D. (ed.), *European Women and Preindustrial Craft* (Bloomington and Indianapolis, Indiana University Press, 1995).

Henderson, J. and R. Wall, *Poor Women and Children in the European Past* (London, Routledge, 1994).

Matthei, J. A., *An Economic History of Women in America* (New York, Schocken Books; Brighton, Harvester Press, 1982).

Roberts, E., *A Woman's Place: An Oral History of Working-Class Women 1890–1940* (Oxford, Blackwell, 1984; reprinted 1995).

Szreter, S., *Fertility, Class and Gender in Britain 1860–1940* (Cambridge, Cambridge University Press, 1996).

Vicinus, M., *Independent Women: Work and Community for Single Women 1850–1920* (London, Virago, 1985).

Wiesner, M. E., *Gender, Church and State in Early Modern Germany* (London, Longman, 1997). Reprints three of Wiesner's essays on early modern men's and women's work and gives further detail on early modern European case studies in her bibliographical essay.

Wiesner, M. E., *Working Women in Renaissance Germany* (New Brunswick, N.J., Rutgers University Press, 1986).

Index